Essential
Psychopathology

BY THE SAME AUTHOR

Rational Hospital Psychiatry
by Jerrold S. Maxmen, Gary J. Tucker,
Michael LeBow

The Post-Physician Era:
Medicine in the 21st Century

A Good Night's Sleep:
A Step-By-Step Program for Overcoming
Insomnia and Other Sleep Problems

The New Psychiatry:
How Modern Psychiatrists Think About Their
Patients, Theories, Diagnoses, Drugs,
Psychotherapies, Power, Training, Families
and Private Lives

A NORTON PROFESSIONAL BOOK

Essential
Psychopathology

Jerrold S. Maxmen, M.D.

W · W · NORTON & COMPANY · *NEW YORK* · *LONDON*

Quotations in the text are used with the permission of the authors and publishers of the following:
Diagnostic and Statistical Manual of Mental Disorders (Third Edition). American Psychiatric Association, © 1980.
Diagnostic and Statistical Manual of Mental Disorders (Second Edition). American Psychiatric Association, © 1968.
Othmer, E. & DeSouza, C. A screening test for somatization disorder (hysteria), *American Journal of Psychiatry*, 142, 1146–1149. © 1985, American Psychiatric Association.
Maxmen, J. S. *The New Psychiatry.* New York: William Morrow, 1985.
Messer, H. D. The homosexual as physician. In R. D. Green (Ed.), *Human Sexuality: A Health Practitioner's Text* (2nd ed.). Baltimore: Williams & Wilkins, 1979.
Sederer, L. I. Depression. In L. I. Sederer (Ed.), *Inpatient Psychiatry: Diagnosis and Treatment.* (Second Edition) Baltimore: Williams & Wilkins, 1986.
Horowitz, M. J. Disasters and psychological responses to stress. *Psychiatric Annals, 15*, 161–167, 1985.

Published simultaneously in Canada by Penguin Books Canada Ltd, 2801 John Street, Markham, Ontario L3R 1B4

Printed in the United States of America

Library of Congress Cataloging-in-Publication Data

Maxmen, Jerrold S.
  Essential psychopathology.

  "A Norton professional book"—P. facing t.p.
  Bibliography: p.
  Includes index.
  1. Psychology, Pathological. 2. Mental illness—
Diagnosis. I. Title. [DNLM: 1. Mental Disorders—
diagnosis. 2. Psychopathology. WM 131 M464e]
RC454.M3 1986   616.89'075   86-12420

ISBN 0-393-70029-1

W. W. Norton & Company, Inc. 500 Fifth Avenue, New York, N.Y. 10110

W. W. Norton & Company, Ltd., 37 Great Russell Street, London WC1B 3NU

  2 3 4 5 6 7 8 9 0

To Robert

Contents

Preface

UNTIL RECENTLY, psychiatric diagnosis was ridiculed by social critics and downplayed by most professionals: At best, diagnoses were meaningless categories; at worst, denigrating labels. In the past few years, however, psychiatric diagnosis has become the acknowledged cornerstone for *all* clinical practice. During the 1970s, major developments in psychiatric epidemiology, psychotherapy, and pharmacotherapy spurred the development of something psychiatry never had: a clinically useful nosology. (A "nosology" is a system for naming and classifying diseases.) In July 1980, the American Psychiatric Association published this nosology as the third edition of the *Diagnostic and Statistical Manual of Mental Disorders*, or *DSM-III*.

This volume is the greatest advance in psychiatric diagnosis in the past 70 years. Instead of merely tinkering with old categories or adding nosological blubber, *DMS-III* introduced major conceptual and practical shifts and, for the first time, favored scientific evidence over theoretical speculation as a basis for diagnosis. *DSM-III*'s respect for rigorous scientific thought has spread to all aspects of clinical practice. Psychotherapy, once a strictly intuitive affair, is now researched by the same standards used in other sciences. Since *DSM-III*, meetings of the various mental health professions have undergone a mind-boggling transformation: Participants now ask such once ill-mannered questions as: "Where's the evidence?" and "What's the data?" No longer are things true simply because Professor X says so. Today, proof is needed, Scientifically, *DSM-III* has its deficiencies, but these stem far more from gaps in scientific knowledge than from inadequacies in *DSM-III* itself.

Some people consider a *scientific* psychiatry a dehumanized psychiatry. The author could not disagree more. As long as therapists treat people-with-illness, instead of illnesses-that-happen-to-be-in-people, clinical practice necessitates artistry, intuition, philosophy, ethics, and science—each making its own special contribution. The distinct contribution of science is that, when properly conducted, it yields the most reliable predictions, and therefore, affords patients the greatest chance of receiving treatments most likely to work. Offering patients anything less is hardly humanistic.

There is, of course, far more to proper clinical assessment than diagnosis, and any clinician who evaluates a patient's condition _solely_ in terms of whether it meets _DSM-III_ criteria is a jerk. (The jerk would also be misapplying _DSM-III_ and misunderstanding diagnosis.) Proper clinical assessments also require a knowledge of the patient's psychosocial network, upbringing, genetic patterns, physical health, current stressors, psychodynamics, and so on. Still, good care requires accurate diagnosis.

DSM-III is the first nosology widely used by _all_ mental health disciplines. That's fortunate, for the essentials of psychopathology should be understood not just by psychiatrists, but by all physicians, psychologists, nurses, social workers, psychotherapists, and counselors. In 1985, _conservative_ estimates were that mental and addictive disorders afflicted 30–45 million Americans. Aside from their emotional costs, these disorders annually cost the nation $20 billion in direct health-care expenditures and another $165 billion in the indirect costs of social services, crime control, lost productivity, etc. These amounts are similar to those for heart disease and cancer, which strike about 45 million and 6 million Americans, respectively. Of all patients with mental disorders, about half (54.1%) are treated by primary care physicians, a quarter (24.4%) by mental health professionals, and another quarter (21.5%) go untreated. Thus, recognizing and healing psychopathology is an everyday task for every helping professional.

Essential Psychopathology presents the current, collective thinking of the experts. Although stressing the new, the book does not abrogate the old. Time-tested concepts and practices are included. When the author's views differ from the experts' consensus or from _DSM-III_, or when no consensus exists, the book says so. It examines some of these disagreements with the hope that students don't view psychiatric diagnosis as embedded in stone, but as alive, open to question, and fluid. Robert Spitzer, the chief architect of _DSM-III_, insists that _DSM-III_ is far from the last word in diagnosis, and when the author asked him, "What happens if a clinician doesn't want to diagnose using _DSM-III_ criteria?" Spitzer replied, "Then don't! It's a free country. People wrote _DSM-III_, not God."

That's why the American Psychiatric Association will release a revision of _DSM-III_ named _DSM-III-R_ around Spring, 1987. Because this book is being published before _DSM-III-R_, it tries to include information that will _pro-_

bably appear in *DSM-III-R*. Few of the changes in *DSM-III-R* will be major and anything here pertaining to *DSM-III-R* is tentative.

Essential Psychopathology is a "no-nonsense" book. Many psychiatric texts are written as if students were idiots, not to be "subjected" to anything more than the "most basic facts." As for concepts, forget it! "Everybody knows" that students are "antipsychiatry," and therefore, to prevent students from being turned off to psychiatry, psych texts should be as simple-minded as possible. The author disagrees. This text will not pander. Diagnostic psychopathology is essential to clinical evaluation, and if a student doesn't wish to learn the subject and know it well, he might ask himself why he chooses to provide inferior care.

In this book, people with *major* mental disorders will be called "patients" instead of "clients." As discussed later, referring to patients with *severe* mental disorders as "clients" not only is euphemistic but may unwittingly trivialize the burden of having a disorder like schizophrenia. Calling these people "patients" is purely descriptive, and certainly no sign of disrespect. In contrast, those who seek help for problems other than serious mental disorders (e.g., adjustment reactions, marital difficulties) are called, quite properly, "clients." This book will also employ "he" and "she" in the traditional manner, except when discussing a mental disorder which primarily affects women, in which case "she" will be used.

This text aims to be concise, to give students of all ages and levels of experience a brief, relatively jargon-free, and readable blend of the newest and most fundamental information in this rapidly evolving field. For convenience, less important material appears in smaller type. Nonetheless, in striving to be concise, many interesting details have been left out, and only references to material whose accuracy the reader might question have been included; this approach saves space, but doesn't allow for citing the major works in diagnostic psychopathology. The author hopes that *Essential Psychopathology* leaves students fascinated by the subject, encourages them to question whatever they read, to pursue the topic further, to chuckle every now and then, and most of all, to help patients.

The author begs students to avoid self-diagnosis. With "medical student's disease," future physicians "catch" diabetes while studying medicine, cancer while studying surgery, and schizophrenia while studying psychiatry. Everybody has some features of a mental disorder, but that hardly means one has a mental disorder. Hemophiliacs bruise, but everyone who bruises isn't a hemophiliac. So too with mental disorders. If the reader is concerned that he, or a loved one, has a mental disorder, consult an expert.

Perhaps I should thank my friends and relatives for their essential psychopathology, but instead I would like to thank, most genuinely, Drs. Marc Galanter, Steve Hyler, Fred Kass, Ron Rieder, Lawrence Sharpe, Michael Sheehy, and Andrew Skodal for their invaluable suggestions on parts of this text. Being the quintessential professional, Susan Barrows belongs to that handful of editors who've produced the major works in our field; seeing her edit this book shows me why. The deficiencies in this text are mine, and only mine. To paraphrase Montaigne, "It's only a fool who never suspects he could be foolishly mistaken."

* * *

To respect patients' confidentiality, I have changed their names, ages, sex, religion, city, occupation, and marital status, as well as presenting composites of real people and events. When altering the truth to protect confidentiality, I've tried to maintain the spirit of that truth. Any resemblance between the pseudonyms I've assigned to patients and to actual individuals with the same name is purely coincidental.

Essential
Psychopathology

SECTION I

Diagnostic Psychopathology

CHAPTER 1

Psychopathology

Such is man that if he has a name for something it ceases to be a riddle.
— I. B. Singer, "Property"

AT 58, AMY'S LIFE stopped. Although it had been five months since her mastectomy and she had been declared cancer-free, she remained paralyzed by depression and insomnia. Amy had withdrawn from family and friends, quit work, become addicted to sleeping pills, and contemplated suicide. Once an avid movie fan, she hid in bed ruminating about "it." (She was afraid to say "cancer.") Diligently, she attempted relaxation exercises to overcome insomnia, yet she was unable to concentrate—the harder she tried, the more she failed, and the less she slept. Her demoralization pervaded all.

Amy "knew" that, because the reasons for her symptoms were understandable, only time could heal. To be sure, having cancer and a mastectomy is an understandable reason for sadness and insomnia. Yet this misses the point: Amy had an additional problem—a mental disorder called "major depression."

It was only after her psychopathology was recognized and she received the proper antidepressant medication that her life returned to normal. She still worried about her mastectomy—who wouldn't?—but as a "normal" person, not as a depressed one. Amy continued to fret about her former cancer, but now she could get her mind off of it. Without major depression impeding her concentration, she was able to perform the relaxation exercises. She stopped taking sleeping pills, slept well, started socializing, went to the movies, returned to work, and so forth. No matter how "understandable" her symptoms, Amy was helped only *after* her major depression was diagnosed.

Critics would charge that to diagnose her condition is to "label," and thus

3

dehumanize, her. Yet it was only when a therapist recognized that Amy was suffering from more than the normal post-mastectomy demoralization that her humanity returned. Explained Amy, "For months I'd assumed there wasn't *really* anything wrong with me, and that if I only had the 'right' attitude, I'd feel fine. After all, other people get over their mastectomies, why couldn't I? It had to be my fault — or so I thought. As soon as I learned there really *was* something wrong with me, and that it had a name, my guilt stopped. So did the mystery. Now something could be done: Depression could be treated. But you can't treat what you can't name." When used with clear goals in mind, psychiatric diagnosis is not mere labeling, nor a meaningless academic exercise, nor a clinician's "power trip." (When diagnosis is abused in these fashions, the culprit is the therapist, not diagnosis.)

THE PURPOSES OF A PSYCHIATRIC DIAGNOSIS

Psychiatric diagnosis serves two main purposes (see Spitzer, 1976), the first being to *define clinical entities* so that clinicians have the same understanding of what a diagnostic category means. Although patients with a particular (medical or psychiatric) diagnosis need not exhibit identical features, they should present with certain cardinal *symptoms*. The disorder should have a similar *natural history* — a typical age of onset, life course, prognosis, and complications. A diagnosis should reflect the condition's *etiology* and *pathogenesis*. (Etiology refers to how a disorder originates, pathogenesis to how it develops.) The same disorder may arise in more than one way, but a diagnostic category should indicate whether a mental disorder consistently runs in families, is genetically transmitted, initiated by psychosocial forces, and exacerbated or aggravated by specific biological and environmental conditions.

The other main purpose of a psychiatric diagnosis is *to determine treatment*. Having diagnosed Amy's condition as "major depression," the clinician knew that antidepressant medications were indicated; yet no antidepressants would have been prescribed if her condition were diagnosed as unhappiness and insomnia. Diagnosis, although most useful in determining biological treatments, also influences the choice and conduct of psychotherapy.

How well a diagnosis defines a disorder and guides treatment depends on its validity and reliability. When a diagnostic category represents a genuine entity — that is, when patients with the same diagnosis have similar clinical features, natural histories, etiologies, pathogeneses, and responses to treatment — the category is said to have "high *validity*." The more clinicians agree on a diagnosis when examining the same patient, the greater its "(interrater) *reliability*."

DEFINING PSYCHOPATHOLOGY

Psychopathology is defined as the *manifestations* of mental disorders. (It also refers to the *study* of mental disorders — their manifestations, causes, and processes.) Psychopathology involves deviance and distress, but not all deviance and distress are psychopathology. Being an atheist, punker, or drag queen is deviant, but not psychopathological. Being starved, broke, or lonely is distressing, but not psychopathological.

Although it's usually easy to distinguish psychopathology from normality, sometimes it's difficult. Critics like Thomas Szsaz argue that because the line between psychopathology and normality is hazy, psychopathology must be a myth. That's nonsense. Day and night clearly exist, even though at dusk it's hard to know which it is. Psychopathology is relative, but no less real. *DSM-III*'s definition of mental disorder does not imply that there are sharp distinctions between a mental disorder and normality or between different mental disorders.

Mental disorders, according to *DSM-III*, must produce *distress* or *disability* in one's personal, social, or occupational life. Biological changes may or may not be involved. *DSM-III* (p. 6) states:

> . . . a mental disorder is conceptualized as a clinically significant behavior or psychologic syndrome or pattern that occurs in an individual and that typically is associated with either a painful symptom (distress) or impairment in one or more important areas of functioning (disability). In addition, there is an inference that there is a behavioral, psychological, or biological dysfunction, and that the disturbance is not only in the relationship between the individual and society. (When the disturbance is *limited* to a conflict between an individual and society, this may represent social deviance, which may or may not be commendable, but is not by itself, a mental disorder.)

DSM-III classifies *mental disorders*; it does not classify *individuals* with mental disorders. Patients diagnosed the same are not the same in every important respect. Just as the only similarity among diabetics is having symptoms of diabetes, the only similarity among schizophrenics is having symptoms of schizophrenia. Otherwise, some schizophrenics (and diabetics) are delightful, some obnoxious, some brilliant, and some stupid. When, for brevity's sake, a patient with schizophrenia is called a "schizophrenic," it should be done with the understanding that a disorder is an attribute of a person, and never his totality.

Many terms resemble "mental disorder." A *syndrome* refers to any cluster of signs and symptoms. Clinicians often use *mental disease* and *mental illness* as synonyms for mental disorder, especially for the more severe ones clearly involving biological changes, such as schizophrenia and manic-depression. Technically, this is inaccurate: In medicine, "disease" refers to a condition's specific physical disturbances, whereas "illness" refers to the total experience of a condition, including physical disturbances. In *DSM-III* diagnostic categories are always called "disorders" and never "diseases" or "illnesses."

Laymen use *insanity* and *nervous breakdown* to mean mental disorder. Neither term has psychiatric meaning: Insanity, which is a legal term whose definition varies between states, refers to a defendant's lacking criminal responsibility due to a mental disorder or defect. A nervous breakdown is a laymen's vague word for any severe incapacitation due to emotional or psychiatric difficulties.

The term *problems in living* is often a euphemism for mental disorder. To have a mental disorder is surely a problem in living, but it is far more than that: To equate the two is to err in categorization and to trivialize the pain of mental disorders. "Problems in living" connote the difficulties of everyday life: losing a job, squabbling with children, undergoing a divorce, fearing rejection, evading the bill collector, dealing with low self-esteem. Problems in living can be miserable, yet they are vastly different in magnitude and type from mental disorders. Problems in living consist of "*issues*,"[1] whereas mental disorders consist of psychopathology.

Symptoms, Signs, and Issues

Psychopathology manifests as *symptoms* and *signs*. Symptoms cannot be observed, are experienced subjectively, and must be reported by the patient; signs can be observed and documented objectively. Symptoms include pain, hallucinations, appetite loss, paranoid thinking, and anxiety, whereas signs include phobic behavior, restlessness, weight loss, and paranoid speech. Depressed mood is a symptom, crying a sign; chest pain is a symptom, heart failure a sign. Mental health professionals sometime ignore this distinction and refer to "signs" as "symptoms." (For literary convenience, this book does likewise, except when lumping them together clouds clinical thinking.)

People may have a symptom (e.g., anxiety, insomnia) without having a mental disorder. By itself, a symptom rarely constitutes a mental disorder. A symptom only reflects a mental disorder when it is a part of a specific symptom constellation.

Most symptoms are beyond the pale of routine experience; unlike issues (or problems in living) symptoms are not everyday occurrences. Everybody contends with issues, only some with symptoms. Patients with mental disorders have both symptoms *and* issues, whereas clients with problems in living have issues solely.

---

[1]This use of the term "issues" is the author's, and not part of the standard psychiatric lexicon.

Issues contain ideas, symptoms do not, even though symptoms convey issues. Just as mail transmits ideas, symptoms can express issues. The ideas patients communicate when they manifest symptoms reflect the issues concerning them. For instance, two men with the severe mental disorder of major depression may have the symptom of overwhelming hopelessness. The first, an elderly, devout Catholic, insists he is hopeless "because I sinned 20 years ago by cheating on my wife." The second, a young, up-and-coming actress, feels equally hopeless because "I'm not a star." Both patients have psychopathology — that is, hopelessness — yet, since their issues are so different, each expresses hopelessness quite differently.

As very broad generalizations, biological factors primarily cause symptoms, whereas psychosocial factors primarily determine issues. Because symptoms usually arise from an altered *brain*, biological therapies usually correct them; because issues mainly derive from an altered *mind*, psychosocial therapies usually rectify them. Since patients with mental disorders present with symptoms and issues, their treatment frequently involves medication and psychotherapy. Since clients with problems in living present with issues but not symptoms, they only receive psychotherapy.

Phenomenology is that aspect of psychopathology which deals with a person's consciously reported experiences (see Jaspers, 1923). It's also that branch of philosophy which studies occurrences or happenings in their own right, and posits that behavior is determined not by an external objective reality, but by a person's subjective perception of that reality. Phenomenology contributes largely to both existential and descriptive psychiatry.

TWO DIAGNOSTIC APPROACHES

There are two major approaches to diagnostic psychopathology. The first is called *descriptive*, because it bases diagnosis on relatively objective descriptive phenomena, which require nominal clinical inference; these phenomena are usually signs, symptoms, and natural history. The second is called *psychological*, because it bases diagnosis primarily on inferred psychological causes and mechanisms. The psychological approach also considers descriptive phenomena, but as merely superficial manifestations of more profound underlying forces.

The descriptive approach focuses on the *what* of behavior, the psychological on its *why*. Amy's case illustrates the common mistake of confusing the two. What was wrong (viz., major depression) had been ignored because people dwelled on why things were wrong (viz., having cancer and a mastectomy). Not distinguishing the "what" from the "why" of psychopathology is the novice's first big mistake. For example, a hallucinating, disheveled youth convinced of being Jesus Christ told beginning medical students that his parents stifled his creativity, poisoned his food, and robbed graves. Once he left the room, the students were asked, "What do you think is wrong with him?" "Nothing," they replied, "The problem is that he has lousy parents." Yet, even assuming he has dreadful parents (the "why"), he is no less delusional and hallucinatory (the "what").

Both descriptive and psychological approaches are valuable, since each addresses a different aspect of psychopathology. Take a delusion. The descriptive approach would detail its characteristics: Is it fixed? Vague? Paranoid? Circumscribed? The psychological approach would focus on inner mechanisms (e.g., projection), which produce the delusion.

The name of Emil Kraepelin (1856–1926) is virtually synonymous with descriptive psychiatry — sometimes called "Kraepelinian psychiatry" — because he devised the first major psychiatric nosology based on descriptive criteria. He examined thousands of delusional and hallucinating inpatients, dividing those without obvious brain damage into two groups according to prognosis and age of onset. The first he diagnosed as "dementia praecox," with "dementia" referring to their progressively downhill course and "praecox" referring to the appearance of symptoms in their teens or twenties. The second group he diagnosed as "maniacal depression" — today called "manic-depression." These patients typically returned to normal and were initially hospitalized in their thirties and forties. Thus, in creating a descriptively-based nosology, Kraepelin added natural (or "longitudinal") history to current (or "cross-sectional") symptoms. His textbook (1915) is *the* classic in descriptive psychiatry, and his approach the one which has dominated European psychiatry to this day.

The psychological approach was launched by the Swiss psychiatrist Eugen Bleuler (1857–1939). In *Dementia Praecox, or the Group of Schizophrenias* (1911), Bleuler introduced the term "schizophrenia" to signify that the disorder's basic defect was a split of psychic functions — that is, disorganization and incongruency between thought, emotion, and behavior. Bleuler felt these splits gave rise to schizophrenia's fundamental symptoms — flat or inappropriate *a*ffect, profound *a*mbivalence, *a*utism, and disturbed *a*ssociations of thought — the "4A's." These splits are inferred psychological mechanisms of causation, and thus, fundamentally different from Kraepelin's noninferred descriptive criteria.

Until *DSM-III* (1980), the psychological approach dominated American psychiatry, largely because it dovetailed with Freudian thought, which has always enjoyed more popularity in the United States than anyplace else. Indeed, Bleuler's psychological approach paved the way for diagnoses based on psychoanalytic criteria, such as "poor ego boundaries," "polymorphous perversity," "oral regression," "projection," and "primary process." The more psychiatrists focused on these inferred phenomena, the more they recognized that, to various extents, *everybody* had them. This belief helps to explain three key differences between psychological and descriptive diagnoses.

First, the psychological view holds that, as a price for civilization, everyone has some degree of psychopathology; with the descriptive approach, only a minority has psychopathology. Second, psychologically-derived diagnoses follow a *"unitary model,"* in which there is essentially one mental disorder, whose name is a matter of degree, not type—from the least severe to the most: neuroses, personality disorders, manic-depression, and schizophrenia. As in physical medicine, the descriptive approach follows a *"multiple model,"* in which disorders are distinct and numerous. Third, the psychological view considers patients to have more severe psychopathology than does the descriptive view. Patients diagnosed as "neurotic" by psychological criteria would have "no mental disorder" by descriptive criteria, whereas those diagnosed as "schizophrenic" by psychological criteria would be diagnosed as "manic" or "depressive" by descriptive critera.

THE DESCRIPTIVE REVIVAL

The psychological approach pervaded *DSM-I* (1952) the first official psychiatric nomenclature for the United States. (All *DSM*s, or *Diagnostic and Statistical Manual of Mental Disorders*, are created by the American Psychiatric Association.) *DSM-I* diagnoses were loosely defined and emphasized psychological etiologies by calling them "reactions," such as "schizophrenic reactions," "paranoid reactions," and "psychoneurotic reactions."

The main reason for writing *DSM-II* (1968) was to rectify *DSM-I*'s failure to conform to the World Health Organization's *International Classification of Diseases*. *DSM-II* eliminated "reactive" from most diagnostic labels, thereby inching away from an etiologically-based nosology.

Yet in trying to be flexible, *DSM-II*'s diagnostic categories were often vague, idiosyncratic, and susceptible to bias. For instance, studies revealed that patients with the same clinical features would receive the more benign diagnosis of manic-depression if they were white, but the more ominous diagnosis of schizophrenia if they were black. Without objective diagnostic standards, a nosology based on inferred psychological phenomena often said more about the clinician's orientation than about the patient's attributes. *DSM-II* suffered from low interrater reliability. The "US/UK" study showed that, unlike the descriptively-oriented British psychiatrists, American psychiatrists frequently reached different diagnoses after observing the same videotape of the same patient being interviewed by the same psychiatrist (Cooper et al., 1972). *DSM-II*'s diagnoses also lacked validity: The categories did not define disorders having predictable symptoms, natural histories, or responses to treatment. In theory, the chief virtue of the psychological approach was that it indicated a disorder's cause, but since the etiologies of most mental disorders were unknown, American psychiatry was moving away from the psychological tradition and returning to Kraepelin.

Other factors contributed to this descriptive revival and to the emergence of *DSM-III*. Different classes of *medications* were discovered that would alleviate or eliminate symptoms of one disorder, but not of another. As a result, correct diagnosis became essential for choosing the correct medication. Researchers increasingly applied the same *scientific methods* (e.g., double-blind conditions, matched controls, statistical proof) used in other branches of medicine to study mental disorders. Data began to show which mental disorders ran in families, which had predictable life courses, which afflicted various populations, which improved with specific therapies, etc. To make sure they were studying patients with similar disorders, researchers devised explicit, readily verifiable, and *specific diagnostic criteria*, which after adjustment for clinical purposes became *DSM-III*'s most distinctive innovation.

DSM-III: INNOVATIONS AND LIMITATIONS

DSM-III differs from previous *DSM*s in seven major respects:

1. Whenever possible, scientific evidence, not theoretical hypotheses, determine diagnostic categories.
2. The descriptive, instead of the psychological, approach is the foundation for diagnosis. Consequently, *DSM-III* employs a nonetiological framework and a multiple, rather than unitary, nosological model.
3. Diagnoses are defined by clearly delineated, objective, and readily verifiable criteria.
4. *DSM-III*'s diagnostic definitions recognize that most patients with the same mental disorder do not have identical clinical features. Patients usually share one or two core features; beyond that, they have a variety of different symptoms which are all consistent with the disorder. Thus, in making any diagnosis, *DSM-III* insists on some diagnostic criteria, while offering a choice among others.
5. *DSM-III* employs a multiaxial diagnostic system.
6. Technical terms are defined.
7. *DSM-III* is the first *DSM* to be field-tested prior to publication.

To illustrate some of these innovations, Table 1-1 shows how *DSM-II* and *DSM-III* define what is essentially the same kind of moderately severe depression. *DSM-II* calls it a "depressive neurosis," *DSM-III*, a "dysthymic disorder."

Whereas *DSM-II* merely indicates that depressed patients are depressed (!),

TABLE 1-1
DSM-II* and *DSM-III* Definitions of a Moderate Depression

[Note: This book's clarifications are in brackets, the *DSM*'s, in parentheses.]

DSM-II: DEPRESSIVE NEUROSIS

This disorder is manifested by an excessive reaction of depression due to an internal conflict or to an identifiable event such as the loss of a love object [i.e., a person] or cherished possession.

DSM-III: DYSTHYMIC DISORDER

[Note: In *DSM-III*, a patient has a mental disorder only if he satisfies *all* criteria—in this case, A through F.]

A. During the past two years (or one year for children and adolescents) the individual has been bothered most or all of the time by symptoms characteristic of the depressive syndrome but that are not of sufficient severity and duration to meet the criteria for a major depressive [i.e., very severe] episode. . . .

B. The manifestations of the depressive syndrome may be relatively persistent or separated by periods of normal mood lasting a few days to a few weeks, but no more than a few months at a time.

C. During the depressive periods there is either prominent depressed mood (e.g., sad, blue, down in the dumps, low) or marked loss of interest or pleasure in all, or almost all, usual activities and pastimes.

D. During the depressive periods at least three of the following symptoms are present:

    (1) insomnia or hypersomnia

    (2) low energy or chronic tiredness

    (3) feelings of inadequacy, loss of self-esteem, or self-deprecation

    (4) decreased effectiveness or productivity at school, work, or home

    (5) decreased attention, concentration, or ability to think clearly

    (6) social withdrawal

    (7) loss of interest in or enjoyment of pleasurable activities

    (8) irritability or excessive anger (in children, expressed toward parents or caretakers)

    (9) inability to respond with apparent pleasure to praise or rewards

    (10) less active or talkative than usual, or feels slowed down or restless

    (11) pessimistic attitude toward the future, brooding about past events, or feeling sorry for self

    (12) tearfulness or crying

    (13) recurrent thoughts of death or suicide

E. Absence of psychotic features, such as delusions, hallucinations, incoherence, or loosening of associations [i.e., speech in which thoughts seem unconnected].

F. If the disturbance is superimposed on a preexisting mental disorder, such as Obsessive Compulsive Disorder or Alcohol Dependence, the depressed mood, by virtue of its intensity or effect on functioning, can be clearly distinguished from the individual's usual mood.

DSM-II, p. 40; *DSM-III*, pp. 222–223.

DSM-III specifies the symptoms of this type of depression and shows how dysthymic disorder differs from normality and from other mental conditions. Because *DSM-III*'s criteria (e.g., crying and insomnia) are relatively objective and explicit, they are far easier for clinicians to identify and to agree on; in contrast, *DSM-II*'s inferred psychological mechanisms (e.g., internal conflict) produces a much lower interrater reliability. Whether *DSM-III*'s criteria for a dysthymic disorder are optimal or valid can be disputed; yet because they are precise, when a therapist states that "patient X meets *DSM-III* criteria for dysthymic disorder," clinicians know what's meant.

Despite the exactness of *DSM-III*'s criteria, their use still requires clinical judgment. In criterion "D," for instance, how much sleep loss (#1) is needed for "insomnia"? And how much pessimism qualifies for subcriterion #11? In practice, as clinicians gain experience, they develop norms to answer such questions. Moreover, as illustrated by the two-year requirement in criterion "A," a *DSM-III* diagnosis calls for a clinical judgment of the patient's past history as well as of her current condition.

In respect to etiology, *DSM-III* is "atheoretical." Except in obvious cases (e.g., "cocaine intoxication," "adjustment reaction"), its diagnostic criteria are free of etiological considerations — biological, psychoanalytic, social, or behavioral. On the other hand, in defining depressive neurosis, *DSM-II* requires an internal conflict or major loss.

DSM-III adopted a *multiaxial* system so that a diagnosis could include more than a primary clinical syndrome, such as schizophrenia or phobic disorder. *DSM-III*'s system uses five axes, as described and illustrated in Table 1-2. Axes I-III are required; Axes IV and V are optional.

The major reason *DSM-III* introduced multiaxial diagnosis was to underscore the distinction between mental and personality disorders or traits. *Personality*, or *character*, refers to a person's long-standing, deeply engrained patterns of thinking, feeling, perceiving, and behaving. Everybody has personality *traits*, which are prominent behavioral features and not necessarily psychopathological. In contrast, only some people have personality *disorders*, which occur when personality traits are so excessive, inflexible, and maladaptive that they cause sufficient distress or disability. Mental disorders (Axis I) tend to be more acute, florid, and responsive to treatment than personality disorders (Axis II), which are more chronic, consistent, and resistant to treatment. When patients present with both a mental and a personality disorder, the multiaxial system helps the clinician to focus on the diagnostic and therapeutic differences between the disorders.

Despite its many advances, *DSM-III* is not diagnostic dogma, but a *guide*. Remember — even those who created *DSM-III* are now rewriting it. Controversies rage over whether some of its diagnostic categories describe genuine disorders in people or just meaningless labels on paper. After all, nosologies

TABLE 1-2
***DSM-III*'s Multiaxial Diagnostic System**

AXIS	CONTENT	EXAMPLE
I.	Mental disorder/Clinical syndrome	Dysthymic Disorder
II.	Personality disorder/trait (or developmental defect)	Compulsive Personality Disorder
III.	Physical disorder/symptom	Diabetes
IV.	Severity of psychosocial stressors on the patient (Rating and description)	Severe—Divorce
V.	Patient's highest level of functioning during the past twelve months (Rating and description)	Good—Effective worker and parent; few friends and leisure-time activities

other than *DSM-III* exist, and on occasion this text will draw on them. Thus, when evaluating patients, clinicians should not twist, and selectively "hear," information from the patient to make him conform to a *DSM-III* diagnosis.

Although *DSM-III* diagnoses have improved treatment planning, they remain inadequate. This partly results from their dubious validity; yet, even if totally valid, no psychiatric (or medical) diagnosis would be sufficient by itself to determine treatment. Other factors must be considered: the patient's ability to introspect, his defenses, his family, his current stressors, his compliance with treatment, etc. Clinical evaluations that ignore such factors or are solely checklists of *DSM-III* criteria cannot lead to a treatment plan, since they overlook that it is a patient, and not a diagnosis, that is being treated! This text certainly stresses diagnosis, but clinical assessment clearly involves more than diagnosis.

AN OVERVIEW OF PSYCHIATRIC EPIDEMIOLOGY

Psychiatric epidemiology is the science that studies the frequency and distribution of mental disorders within various populations. By knowing the presence or absence of a mental disorder in a specific group, such as one defined by age, sex, race, socioeconomic class, inpatient status, health, diet, other illnesses, etc., the epidemiologist provides clues about a disorder's etiology, pathogenesis, prevention, and treatment.

The two measures cited most often are incidence and prevalence. For a specific interval and population, *incidence* refers to the number of *new* cases, whereas *prevalence* refers to the number of *existing* cases. These terms are usually expressed as percentages and calculated as follows:

$$\text{Incidence rate} = \frac{\substack{\text{\# persons} \\ \text{developing the disorder}}}{\text{Total number at risk}} = \text{Per unit time}$$

$$\text{Prevalence} = \frac{\substack{\text{\# persons with disorder} \\ \text{during a period of time}}}{\text{Total number in group}}$$

If 2,000 new cases of a disorder arise in one year in a population of 100,000, the incidence rate is 2% (2,000/100,000). *Prevalence* means how many cases exist during a period, which can vary from a month, to six months (i.e., "six-month prevalence"), to a lifetime (i.e., "lifetime prevalence").

Incidence and prevalence can convey very different pictures of a disorder's frequency. Incidence (new cases) is not affected by treatment; prevalence (existing cases) is affected by treatment. Unlike incidence, prevalence depends on a disorder's duration, frequency of recovery, and death rate. That's why acute disorders generally have a higher incidence than prevalence, whereas for chronic disorders it is just the reverse.

The frequency of a mental disorder varies enormously depending on how the disorder is defined, which populations are surveyed, and what assessment instruments are employed. For instance, older epidemiologic surveys were usually based on the unitary model of mental disorders and would invariably yield higher prevalence rates than surveys based on the multiple model—on average, 25% versus 18%, respectively.

The value of an epidemiologic survey depends on the sensitivity and specificity of its diagnostic instruments. A test is *sensitive* when it accurately detects the *presence* of a disorder in a person who *has* the disorder. A test is *specific* when it accurately detects the *absence* of a disorder in a person who does *not have* the disorder. Remember when a "handwriting expert" would examine a person's writing and then tell him, "Underneath you have feelings of insecurity"? Of course he's insecure! Who isn't? This test demonstrates high sensitivity, but low specificity.

A major advance in defining mental disorders came when Feighner et al. (1972) first listed specific signs and symptoms as diagnostic criteria. Called the "Feighner criteria," they were used mainly for research and led to the Research Diagnostic Criteria (RDC) developed by Spitzer and colleagues. The RDC, which added duration, severity, and life course as diagnostic criteria, became the foundation for the more clinically-oriented *DSM-III.*

With the development of RDC and Feighner criteria, it became possible to conduct more accurate epidemiologic surveys using *structured interviews.* These are a series of preset, standardized questions that systematically determine if the subject meets specific diagnostic criteria. Two structured interviews widely used in research are the "Schedule for Affective Disorders and Schizophrenia" (or "SADS") and the "Diagnostic Interview Schedule" (or "DIS"). The DIS can make over 30 diagnoses, which blend diagnostic criteria from Feighner, RDC, and *DSM-III.*

Using the DIS, researchers from the National Institute of Mental Health (NIMH) interviewed over 10,000 adults — the largest survey ever — to determine the six-month and lifetime prevalences of 15 mental disorders. These findings remain tentative; an additional 10,000 adults will be interviewed. This project is known as the Epidemiologic Catchment Area, or ECA, and will be referred to as such throughout this book.[2]

Table 1-3 contrasts the ECA's six-month prevalence rates of mental dis-

TABLE 1-3
Frequency of *DSM-III* Mental Disorders

DISORDERS*	SIX-MONTH PREVALENCE IN GENERAL ADULT POPULATION† (in percent)	ESTIMATED NUMBER OF AMERICANS† (in millions)	FREQUENCY AMONG PSYCHIATRIC PATIENTS+ (in percent)
ANXIETY/SOMATOFORM	8.3	13.1	4.9
Phobic	7.0	11.1	0.9
Obsessive Compulsive	1.5	2.4	0.5
Panic	0.8	1.2	1.3
Somatization	0.1	0.1	1.1
SUBSTANCE USE	6.4	10.0	11.0
Alcohol Abuse/Dependence	5.0	7.9	5.9
Drug Abuse/Dependence	2.0	3.1	5.1
AFFECTIVE	6.0	9.4	24.6
Dysthymic Disorder	3.2	5.1	2.7
Major Depression	3.1	4.9	12.8
Manic-Depression	0.7	1.0	7.1
SCHIZOPHRENIAS	1.0	1.5	25.3
Schizophrenia	0.9	1.4	18.2
Schizophreniform	0.1	0.1	2.4
COGNITIVE IMPAIRMENT (Mainly Organic Mental Disorders)	1.0	1.6	4.1
ANTISOCIAL PERSONALITY	0.9	1.4	1.9

*Schizoaffective disorders [2.5%] and atypical psychoses [1.6%] were subsumed under schizophrenic disorders. Borderline personality disorder [12.3%] is not listed.

†Adapted from Myers, J. K., Weissman, M. M., Tischler, G. L., et al. (1984). Six-month prevalence of psychiatric disorders in three communities. *Archives of General Psychiatry, 41*, 959–967.

+Adapted from Koenigsberg, H. W., Kaplan, R. D., Gilmore, M. M., & Cooper, A. M. (1985). The relationship between syndrome and personality disorder in *DSM-III*: experience with 2,462 patients. *American Journal of Psychiatry, 142*, 207–212.

[2]ECA findings from the first 10,000 adults are reported in the *Archives of General Psychiatry, 41*, 931–989, 1984.

orders in the general population (Myers et al., 1984) with those of 2,462 patients seen on inpatient (28%), outpatient, emergency, walk-in, and consultation-liaison services from 1979 to 1981 in New York City (Koenigsberg et al., 1985). Comparing these figures illustrates that clinicians deal with psychopathology that is not representative of the general population.

As seen on Table 1-3, the ECA revealed that during a *six-month* period, anxiety disorders were the most prevalent *class* of mental disorders in the general population, affecting 13.1 million Americans; next came substance abuse, affective, and then, schizophrenic, disorders. Table 1-4 rank orders the *lifetime prevalence* of *specific* mental disorders in the general population according to the ECA. Unlike most psychiatric epidemiologic reports, this one includes the two most frequent mental disorders — tobacco use and psychosexual disorders. Excluding these, alcoholism is America's most common mental disorder (Robins et al., 1984).

The ECA also showed that less than one person in five with a *DSM-III-* defined mental disorder seeks treatment in a six-month period, and, of those

TABLE 1-4
Rank-ordered Lifetime Prevalence of *DSM-III* Mental Disorders

DISORDERS	LIFETIME PREVALENCE RATES* (in percent)
1. Tobacco Use Disorder	36
2. Psychosexual Disorders	24
3. Alcohol Misuse	13.7
4. Phobic Disorders	8.2
5. Drug Misuse other than alcoholism	5.5
6. Major Depressive episodes	5.0
7. Dysthymic Disorder	3.0
8. Obsessive Compulsive Disorder	2.5
9. Antisocial Personality Disorder	2.5
10. Schizophrenia	1.5
11. Panic Disorder	1.4
12. Cognitive Impairment (severe) (Organic Mental Disorders)	1.2
13. Manic episodes	1.0
14. Anorexia Nervosa and other eating disorders	0.1
15. Schizophreniform Disorder	0.1
16. Somatization Disorder	0.1

*Summarized from: Robins, L. N., Helzer, J. E., Weissman, M. M., Orvaschel, H., Gruenberg, E., Burke, J. D., & Regier, D. A. (1984). Lifetime prevalence of specific psychiatric disorders in three sites. *Archives of General Psychiatry, 41*, 949–958.

who do, more consult general practitioners than mental health specialists. Among those with a recent DIS disorder, women seek treatment more often than men, and 18-to-24-year-olds do so more often than those ages 25 to 64.

This landmark investigation also corrected the long-held notion that women generally have higher rates of mental disorders than men. Previous surveys concentrated on depression and phobias, conditions which occur more often in women. In contrast, because the ECA also tracked alcoholism and antisocial personality disorder, which mainly afflict men, the overall rates of mental disorders are seen to be equal for the sexes.

The ECA found that 29.4 million (18.7%) Americans had some type of *DSM-III* mental disorder. Thus, during any six-month period, almost one of five adults suffer from a mental disorder. These figures are startling, especially in light of their conservatism; they show that a knowledge of psychopathology is essential for all mental and medical health professionals.

CHAPTER 2

Assessment

WOULD A PATIENT with severe stomach pain receive surgery or medication without obtaining an evaluation? Hopefully not. Yet in psychiatry, that has been the norm: Too many patients had chosen, and then received, specific treatments without being formally assessed or diagnosed. The unitary model of mental illness rendered diagnosis almost academic, and since there was basically one "decent" treatment – psychoanalytic psychotherapy – the treatment was a foregone conclusion. If performed at all, assessments blended imperceptibly into psychotherapy. Today, however, primarily because of the greater number and efficacy of contemporary biological and psychosocial treatments, *every* patient must receive a formal diagnostic assessment (i.e., evaluation) *before* treatment begins.

Assessment may be defined as: *a time-limited, formal process that collects clinical information from many sources in order to reach a diagnosis, to make a prognosis, to render a biopsychosocial formulation, and to determine treatment*. This definition emphasizes that assessment is a specific task that is distinct from therapy. Indeed, some superb therapists are lousy diagnosticians, and vice versa. Clinicians continue to reassess patients as treatment proceeds, but the *formal* assessment ends before *formal* treatment begins.

The patient interview is usually the principal source of data, but it is not the only source. Information may be gathered from family, friends, physical examinations, laboratory and psychological tests, and observations of the hospital staff. Patient interviews generally require one to three, hour-long sessions, although for patients with impaired concentration, sessions should be shorter and more frequent. Conversely, for healthier outpatients, the initial meeting is often 90 minutes.

The primary objective of these initial interviews is to obtain information

18

that will determine the patient's diagnosis, prognosis, psychodynamics, and treatment. These interviews should also make the patient feel comfortable and foster trust, yet these valuable objectives remain secondary.

This chapter shows how to obtain this information. How a clinician seeks, selects, and sorts out all the facts, figures, and fears patients present is no easy task. Essential for mastering this task is to use a standardized format, which often consists of eight steps: (a) obtaining a *history*, (b) evaluating the patient's *mental status*, (c) collecting *auxiliary data*, (d) summarizing *principal findings*, (e) rendering a *diagnosis*, (f) making a *prognosis*, (g) providing a *biopsychosocial formulation*, and (h) determining a *treatment plan*. Table 2-1 details these steps and presents an outline for reporting the formal assessment. The sequence for *conducting* and *reporting* these eight steps varies to some extent.

Whether oral or written, the report should be clear, succinct, and systematic. Although the exhaustively detailed history, or *anamnesis*, is still used in psychoanalysis, most patients will benefit more from a briefer history, since it is more likely to be read. A major challenge in reporting a patient's evaluation is to convey the germane data in the fewest words. Chapter 6 illustrates a recorded assessment.

THE HISTORY

The patient's history begins with *introductory information* (II) about the patient, followed immediately by his *chief complaint* (CC). The II is the patient's age, sex, marital status, occupation, religion, race, and if pertinent, nationality and sexual orientation (e.g., homosexual). The CC is a sentence or so which describes the *patient's*, not the therapist's, view of the main problem, preferably in the patient's exact words. If the patient's CC is senseless (e.g., "I need a new dress"), the therapist can add his own version of the CC (e.g., For three weeks the patient has had visual hallucinations).

History of Present Illness (HPI)

The HPI describes the major symptoms, issues, and events that brought the patient to treatment. For each major problem, the HPI chronicles when it began, what initiated or exacerbated it, what increased or decreased its severity, what problems existed concurrently, how it affected the patient's functioning, how the patient tried to resolve it, when it ended, why it ended, and what its subjective meaning was to the patient. When a problem emerged gradually, the time of onset should be estimated. If the patient has had repeated episodes of the same disorder, the HPI starts with the most recent episode.

TABLE 2-1
An Outline of the Psychiatric Assessment

I. HISTORY
   A. Identifying information (II)
   B. Chief complaint (CC)
   C. History of present illness (HPI)
   D. Past and family histories (PH and FH) [Table 2-2]
   E. Medical history (MH) [Appendix B]

II. MENTAL STATUS EXAMINATION (MSE)
   A. Appearance
   B. Behavior [including impulse control]
   C. Speech
   D. Emotion
      1. Mood
      2. Affect
      3. Congruency
   E. Thought processes
      1. Stream of thought
      2. Continuity of thought
      3. Content of thought
      4. Abstraction
   F. Perception
   G. Attention
   H. Orientation
      1. Time
      2. Place
      3. Person
   I. Memory
      1. Immediate
      2. Recent
      3. Remote
   J. Judgment
   K. Intelligence and information
   L. Insight

III. AUXILIARY DATA
   A. Interviews with relatives and friends
   B. Complete medical history and physical examination
   C. Laboratory tests [Table 2-3]
   D. Psychological tests [Table 2-4]

IV. SUMMARY OF PRINCIPAL FINDINGS

V. DIAGNOSES (DSM-III) [Appendix A]
   A. Axis I: Mental disorder
   B. Axis II: Personality (or developmental) disorder/trait

TABLE 2-1
(Continued)

C. Axis III: Physical disorder or symptoms
D. Axis IV: Severity of psychosocial (or medical) stressor (optional)
E. Axis V: Highest level of adaptive functioning past year (optional)

VI. PROGNOSIS

VII. BIOPSYCHOSOCIAL FORMULATION

VIII. PLAN
    A. Additional data gathering (e.g., interviews, tests, consultations)
    B. Treatment goals (immediate, short-term, long-range)
    C. Treatment plan
        1. Immediate management
        2. Short-term interventions
        3. Long-term therapies

Any and all "entrances" and "exits"—that is, people or events entering a patient's life (e.g., a newborn) or exiting from it (e.g., leaving for college)—are noted. Changes of all kinds are important to identify, even ostensibly good ones. For instance, on obtaining a long-desired promotion to vice-president of a major corporation, a man became severely depressed—now he had to boss his former peers, now he had to travel in a faster social set, now his wife demanded mink coats.

The therapist should ask why the patient comes for help *now*. A 37-year-old single designer sought treatment for, as she said, "an inferiority complex." When asked why she came now, all she could think of was that a friend suggested it. Yet by pursuing the "Why now?" question, the therapist discovered that it was the day after the patient's mother married her fifth husband that the patient began ruminating "What's wrong with me?" and finally decided to act on her friend's suggestion to seek treatment.

The clinician should never assume that the patient's use of a technical term is the same as his own: Patients will say "depression" and mean anxiety, "paranoia" and mean unhappiness, "nervousness" and mean hallucinations. If a clinician is at all unsure of what a patient means by a word, he should ask the patient to describe it more fully or to give an example.

During "intake" interviews, clinicians notoriously avoid three topics which demand immediate attention: (a) drug and alcohol use, (b) violent or homicidal tendencies, and (c) suicide. The reasons for this avoidance vary. Without realizing it, a therapist may not inquire about these problems because if they exist, he might not know how to intervene; it's "safer" not to ask in the first place! A therapist may not inquire to avoid embarrassing the patient. This embarrassment, however, is the therapist's more than the patient's: Most patients expect clinicians to ask "embarrassing" questions—it's the clinician's job—and if the clinician doesn't, some patients will feel the clinician is being slipshod or not taking their case seriously. In any case, patients will not be embarrassed if questions are posed tactfully and in a way that makes deviance "understandable." For example, "Given all the disappointments you've suffered, I wonder if you've ever contemplated suicide?"

Suicide must be evaluated, or at least considered, with *every* patient. Not only is it the tenth leading cause of death in the United States, but its frequency has skyrocketed among all age groups, especially youth. Although officially 30,000 Americans kill themselves each year, 100,000 is a more realistic figure. (More people die from suicide than from homicide.) If there is any question of suicide, the clinician *must* ask, "Have you thought about harming or, perhaps, killing yourself?" Asking patients about committing suicide does *not* make people commit suicide or "introduce suicidal thoughts into somebody's head." Most potentially suicidal patients are relieved when a therapist raises the subject. Contrary to myth, people who talk about suicide *do* commit suicide. Although Kovacs and Beck (1976) reported that communicating suicidal intent may be related more to personal style than to attempting suicide, until proven otherwise any patient who conveys suicidal intent should be carefully evaluated and monitored.

The risk of suicide escalates as the frequency and intensity of the patient's *thoughts* about suicide increase. Everyone has had suicidal thoughts, but only the suicidal ruminate about them. More dangerous is when the patient has a *plan*, especially if he has settled on one plan, can detail it, and has begun to implement it. Contrary to myth, people who *attempt* suicide are more likely to commit suicide; the more serious the attempt, the greater the risk of the patient's killing himself. The severity of an attempt depends on the potential lethality of the method, whether the patient acted on impulse or after long planning, how readily he could have been (or was) discovered after the attempt, and whether he signaled for help prior to the attempt.

In addition to being elderly, unemployed, unmarried, and living alone, high-risk factors include: (a) a threatened financial loss; (b) being unreligious in the formal sense; (c) sleeping longer; (d) a current weight gain or a 1%-9% weight loss; (e) ideas of persecution or reference; (f) a recent loss or death; (g) drug, and especially alcohol, misuse; (h) major depression, schizophrenia, or a previous psychiatric hospitalization; (i) a notable physical illness; (j) a family history of suicide, depression, or alcoholism; (k) suddenly giving away prized possessions; (l) recent visits to a physician ostensibly for medical problems; (m) a history of previously unsuccessful psychiatric treatments; (n) being an active bisexual or an inactive homosexual male; and (o) negative reaction of interviewer to patient (Motto et al., 1985).

Menninger (1938) observed that patients who commit suicide do so from not one, but three, wishes: the wish to die, the wish to kill, and the wish to be killed. Many people might want to die, yet few are prepared to kill, and even fewer, to be killed; the latter two require a degree of violence, anger, and physical pain that only the "truly" suicidal could endure. Finally, the patient should be asked why he wants to *live*? Nonsuicidal people can usually come up with some reason, such as "I love my children."

The HPI often ends with "significant negatives," which are symptoms, issues, experiences, or events that have *not* occurred, even though they frequently accompany problems like those of the patient. For example, significant negatives for a severely depressed patient might include a denial of suicidal thoughts, no recent losses, an unchanged libido, and no family history of affective disorders. When significant negatives are omitted, other professionals cannot tell whether these negatives are absent or the interviewer did not ask about them.

Past History (PH)

The past and family histories may be integrated or separate, whichever is clearer. The PH describes previous episodes in the patient's life that resemble the current episode, including each episode's duration, treatment, and outcome. The PH presents the patient's long-standing personality traits and characteristic ways of dealing with problems. Because it helps in setting treatment goals, the patient's highest level of functioning during his life *and* during the past year should be determined.

Although an exhaustive developmental history is usually unnecessary, it is valuable to cover the highlights, especially when they illuminate the present illness. Table 2-2 lists possible topics in the developmental history. Two quick ways to identify critical information is to ask patients (a) to name the three or four most crucial turning points in their life, and (b) to describe the most significant or memorable event during each developmental period.

Family History (FH)

Through a *genogram* or a traditional narrative, the clinician indicates the "dramatis personae," and how they're related, employed, and involved with the patient. The FH specifies who the patient lives with (if anyone), sees the most, trusts the most, and in a crisis, depends on the most. This section covers any family history of psychopathology and psychiatric hospitalizations and

TABLE 2-2
The Developmental History*

I. PRENATAL
    —Pregnancy: planned? desired?
    —Health of mother
    —Complications during pregnancy and birth
    —Full-term?
    —Breast-fed?

II. INFANCY (First 18 to 24 months)
    —Physical illnesses
    —Temperament, especially in comparison to siblings
    —Time of onset for teething, talking, walking, toilet training, and other developmental milestones
    —Attachment (child's behavior toward mother) and bonding (mother's behavior toward child)
    —Stranger anxiety (usually from 6 to 15 months)
    —Separation anxiety (usually from 10 to 27 months)
    —Family: stable?

III. CHILDHOOD (2 years to onset of puberty)
    —Illnesses, especially high fevers and convulsions
    —School: Phobias? grades, especially in reading, writing, and mathematics? learning impairments?
    —Symptoms: Enuresis (bedwetting), sleepwalking, thumb-sucking, nail-biting, night terrors, nightmares, cruelty to animals, fire-setting?
    —Social: Friends? shy? nicknames? family relations? interests and hobbies?
    —Familial: Child abuse? molestation? stable environment?
    —Earliest memory (i.e., "screen memory")

IV. ADOLESCENCE (Puberty to roughly 18 years)
    —Illness, school, and social histories (as above)
    —Menstruation: Time of onset? regularity, duration, and amount? pain? how dealt with or explained by family members? date of last period?
    —Sexual inclinations, practices, fantasies, and concerns; masturbation; social pressures; dating; homosexuality?
    —Drug and alcohol misuse
    —Identity problems?

V. EARLY AND MIDDLE ADULTHOOD
    —School: How much formal education? going away to college and why? (or why not?), grades?
    —Occupations: First job? dates of each job? performance patterns? likes and dislikes? work disabilities? discrepancy between ability, education, and present work? ambitious? current job? economic circumstances?
    —Military service: Combat experience? type of discharge? disability benefits?
    —Social: Dating? recreation? activities?

TABLE 2-2
(Continued)

—Family of origin: Separated from? If so, when and how? if not, why not? feelings toward them?
—Marriage: When? why? how many? quality of relationship? quality of sex life? money (who manages it? disputes over?) "faithfulness"? divorce?
—Children: Dates of miscarriages, including abortions; names, dates of birth, personalities of, and feelings toward children
—Religion: Its effect, if any, on the patient; conversion? exacerbates or alleviates psychiatric problems? spiritual beliefs?
—Standards: moral, political, social, aethestic, ethical

VI. LATE ADULTHOOD
—The "seven losses": How the person prepares for, adapts to, or surmounts each of them:
(a) loss of work (unemployment);
(b) loss of financial security (insecurity);
(c) loss of familiar surroundings, including home and community (dislocation);
(d) loss of physical health and ability to function (incapacitation);
(e) loss of mental abilities (incompetence);
(f) loss of people, especially spouse (isolation);
(g) loss of life (death)

---

*This table suggests topics for inquiry; it is not a comprehensive outline of development.

briefly describes how the patient's family normally functions (Walsh, 1982).

A description of routine family functioning may include information about who plays which roles in the family, who manages the money, who sets the day-to-day rules, and who makes the big decisions. Family snapshots are valuable, as much for how they are selected and discussed as for what they portray. Then, considering the family as a system — that is, as a totality in which each member's actions affect all others — how does the patient normally perpetuate or try to alter the family system, and how does the family as a whole contend with crises?

The FH documents how the patient's family members have influenced, and have been influenced by, the patient's illness. The clinician's opinion about these influences is saved for the biopsychosocial formulation; only the opinions of relatives, whether "correct" or not, are reported here. How the relatives (or friends) have tried to solve the patient's difficulties should also be mentioned.

Of great importance in modern psychopathology are all data regarding a history of mental disorders, including antisocial behavior and alcoholism, within the family. Because diagnoses by professionals, especially before 1980, are based on criteria different from those in *DSM-III*, and because laymen do not employ diagnostic terms in the way professionals do, therapists should place little weight on diagnoses ascribed to family members, and rely more on objective characteristics, such as speaking incoherently or being hospitalized for seven years. Since the response to medication is to some extent genetically transmitted, if a mentally ill relative received medication, the clinician should inquire about the type, duration, and results.

In gathering the FH, the clinician should note if information from family members varies depending on whether the patient is present. Although the clinician should never assume that one family member speaks for all, many families will present as a monolith, unless the therapist explicitly asks each member to state his or her own view of the problem. Finally, once a month a clinician on every inpatient service exclaims, "I've just interviewed the world's craziest family." Perhaps, but psychiatric crises are highly traumatic for relatives, and so one should not rush to conclusions about family members' typical behavior based on how they act during a crisis.

The Medical Assessment

The medical history, physical examination, and laboratory tests (Table 2-3) are performed sequentially; they comprise the medical assessment, whose chief goals are to detect medical causes for psychiatric symptoms, to identify physical states that will alter how psychiatric meds are prescribed, to discover previously undiagnosed medical diseases (which are disproportionately high among psychiatric patients), to alert therapists to substance abuse, and to monitor blood levels of various psychotropic agents.

Whether the medical assessment should be done by the patient's psychiatrist or family physician depends on several factors, one being who's the most qualified to perform it. In most cases, that's a family practitioner or internist. In any case, all psychiatric inpatients are required to receive a complete medical assessment, but whether all outpatients should have one remains controversial. Commonly used guidelines include: (a) Any patient with signs of organicity (see Chapter 7), psychosis, or incapacitation should receive a complete medical workup. (b) If in doubt, always get expert medical opinion. (c) All patients should have a complete medical examination once a year. (d) Clinicians of all mental and medical health disciplines may wish to have all new patients fill out a questionnaire, such as the Medical-Psychiatric History Form in Appendix B.

THE MENTAL STATUS EXAMINATION

The *mental status examination* (MSE) describes the patient's appearance, behavior, emotions, thinking, and perceiving. Whereas the psychiatric history is primarily a *subjective* account by the *patient* about *past* events *unwitnessed* by the therapist, the MSE is an *objective* report of the patient's *current* mental

TABLE 2-3
Laboratory Tests for Psychiatric Assessment

A. *Routine screening tests*:
  1. Complete blood count
  2. Urinalysis
  3. Electrolytes, calcium, parathyroid tests, glucose
  4. Hepatic and renal function tests
  5. Thyroid function tests, free T-4, TSH
  6. B-12 and folate levels
  7. FTA-ABS or MHA-TP for syphilis (not VDRL)
  8. Toxicology screen for blood and urine

B. *Relatively inexpensive, low-yield tests*:
  1. Sedimentation rate (Westergren)
  2. Skin testing (for infectious diseases)
  3. Stools for occult blood
  4. EKG
  5. Chest and skull x-rays

C. *With evidence of an Organic Brain Syndrome*:
  1. EEG, including sleep tracings
  2. CT scan
  3. Lumbar puncture

D. *Serum levels of psychotropic drugs* (where appropriate)

state as *observed* by the therapist. Because it is collected firsthand, the MSE is the most reliable part of the assessment; consequently, *every* patient's mental status must be ascertained.

There are two types of MSEs — informal and formal. Clinicians gather the *informal* MSE while taking a history; for most patients, these observations will suffice. The *formal* MSE is given to all patients with possible organic or psychotic disorders. The therapist conducts the formal MSE by asking the patient a series of standardized questions that assess memory, thought processes, attention span, and so on.

In reporting a MSE the clinician should present concrete illustrations to justify every conclusion. It's not enough to just *say* a patient is delusional; *show* how: "The patient is convinced that penguins read his mind." Saying a patient has a "depressed mood" is a conclusion and as such requires substantiation — "The patient moved slowly, cried throughout the interview, and never laughed."

This last statement shows how some information in the MSE could fit into a variety of categories. Should the description of this forlorn patient belong in the category called "Appearance," or "Behavior," or "Speech," or "Emotion," or should it be split among all of them? No single answer exists. Where information is reported is less important than how it is reported: It should be well-organized, coherent, and clear.

This section on the MSE, as well as the glossary of signs and symptoms in Appendix C, presents much of the language of psychopathology. These technical terms do give professionals a shorthand for communication, but they can also be abused. Jargon can mislead one into thinking he knows more than he does. To know the definition of "catatonia" does not mean that one knows anything else about catatonia. In reporting the assessment, descriptions in plain English are often more informative, and less ambiguous, than professional terminology.

At the same time, technical terms are not mere words; they also represent concepts, and so when terms are used carelessly, concepts get muddled. For instance, when clinicians interchange the terms "shame" and "guilt," they're missing an important conceptual distinction: Shame is an *interpersonal* phenomenon involving embarrassment; guilt is an *intrapsychic* phenomenon involving the violation of one's conscience or superego. Given this different focus, when therapists overlook this distinction, treatment suffers. As Wittgenstein (1958) observed, "philosophical problems arise when language goes on a holiday" (p. 3).

Once acquired, a professional vocabulary can shape how a professional thinks. That's okay, but the "learned" beware. Terms become mental categories, and being human, clinicians will fit their observations into these categories and tend to adjust their observations when they don't quite fit. With a clinical vocabulary, one is more likely to see the world *solely* through the goggles of psychopathology. People no longer "forget" things, they "repress" them; shy persons are now "schizoid"; people aren't even people—they're "objects." The dangers are more than "psychobabble" and the rudeness of "psychoanalyzing" everybody: To view people as only psychopathology and to ignore all their other aspects—ethical, political, religious, artistic—is not only bad manners, it's bad psychiatry. Therapists do not treat psychopathology, but people with psychopathology.

Appearance

This section portrays how the patient looks: his clothes, posture, bearing, grooming, etc. Clothes are costumes; what people wear is what people choose to communicate. The patient's level of consciousness (i.e., alertness) should be described. Is he in a coma, a stupor, with clouded consciousness, or alert?

"Palm reading" may reveal if the patient is frail, a hard laborer, or a nail-biter. Shaking hands with the patient at the outset of the interview does more than convey respect: It provides data. Is the patient's handshake crushing or wimpy? Do his palms sweat? Are his hands rough or smooth?

Behavior

In the MSE, the category on behavior refers to the patient's motor activity: his gait, gestures, twitches, tics, other muscular movements, and impulse control. Psychomotor agitation and retardation, including their extreme manifestations (viz., catatonia), are described here. Problems with impulse control refer to how the patient handles immediate aggressive, sexual, and suicidal wishes. If difficulties with impulse control arise during the interview (as opposed to only reported in the history), they also should be reported here. Examples: A patient smashes the clinician's ashtray when the interview is interrupted by a telephone call; a patient dashes from the office on hearing a distressing comment.

Speech

This category describes the *manner*, but not the content, of speech. Speech can be rapid, pressured, slowed, hesitant, slurred (i.e., dysarthria), monotonous, etc. Foreign or regional accents belong here.

Emotion

Emotion is usually divided between *mood*, which is a pervasive and subjectively experienced feeling state, and *affect*, which refers to instantaneous, observable expressions of emotion. In psychopathology, affects are overt and moods are covert. (In psychoanalysis, affects refer to unconscious, and therefore, covert emotional states.) Moods affect how people feel about themselves and their world; affects do not. People complain about their mood, but not about their affect. Moods persist; affects don't.

In reality, distinguishing moods from affects can be hard. For example, is anger a mood or an affect? It could be either, and which it is doesn't matter all that much. *What does matter is that the clinician provides clear, specific descriptions of the patient's emotions.* "He cries one moment, and laughs the next." "His expression never varies." "He says he feels 'like an emotional robot . . . the living dead'." "When first mentioning his wife, he pounded the table." As in this last example, what is occurring or being discussed during an emotional display may be worth reporting.

A normal range of affect is labeled "broad." Other affects include "flat," "blunt," "constricted," "labile," and "inappropriate." A normal mood is called "euthymia." Moods can also be high or low. On the up side, as one gets higher, moods go from "elevated," to "euphoric," to "expansive." On the down side, "dysphoria" is any mood the patient finds unpleasant, including anxiety, apprehensiveness, dysthymia, and irritability. "Dysthymia" will be used throughout this text to mean the *symptom* of depression, so as to distinguish it from the various *syndromes* of depression.

Mood-congruency refers to whether a patient's delusions and hallucinations are consistent with his mood. If consistent, the delusions or hallucinations are "mood-congruent"; if not, they're "mood-incongruent."

Thought Processes

Since no one can directly know another's thought processes, to evaluate them therapists must infer from the patient's speech and behavior. A patient may *say* he is God, which doesn't necessarily mean he *thinks* so: The style and context of delivery will determine if this is a put-on or a delusion. Whenever a claim of pathological thought is made, the clinician should present examples.

Psychiatrists traditionally used the term *thought disorder* to describe any communication that arose from pathological thought. Yet, because the term is so nonspecific, *DSM-III* discourages its use in favor of more precise descriptions of pathological thought: These can be divided into four general categories, each dealing with the stream, continuity, content, or abstractness of thought:

1. *Stream of thought* refers to the quantity of thought (e.g., overabundant, slowed). When the patient's speech is restricted to a few words or syllables, it's called "poverty of speech"; this should be distinguished from "poverty of content of speech," which is discussed below.

2. *Continuity of thought* refers to the associations between ideas. Some of these disturbances are always pathological, such as clanging, echolalia, neologisms, perseveration, and word salad. Others, such as looseness of associations, flight of ideas, blocking, circumstantiality, derailment, and tangentiality, are usually pathological unless they result from a transient, overwhelming affect (e.g., anger, fright), sarcasm, humor, limited intelligence or education, or differences in culture or language. The following quotation illustrates looseness of associations.

> Watching television is sun-worship: Our species has always stared into light and allowed it to enter us. Angie never fixes anything, and she's as old as they come. Age affects all of us.

That television shines light into people is being discussed, when the speaker shifts inexplicably to Angie. The connection may be clear in the speaker's mind, but not to anybody else. Laymen will often "read in" connections so as to understand—or to think they understand—the patient. Yet clinicians should not pretend to be mind readers, but ask the patient to explain what links the two thoughts. If the patient says, "Angie is an anthropologist who's been studying similarities between ancient rituals and modern culture," then the connection makes sense and is not a loose association. If no reasonable connection is presented, loose associations are reported along with verbatim illustrations. The following shows flight of ideas:

> I was so dejected about Reagan's election; it proves the insanity of the electoral college. You know his son was a ballet dancer, and should have gone to college, but that's the trouble with America: Too many dancers and not enough nurses.

Unlike looseness of associations, links clearly exist between these thoughts, despite the "tangentiality" (i.e., digressions which don't return to the point) and "punning" (e.g., electoral college and "real" college).

3. *Content of thought*, when disturbed, can result in delusions, overvalued ideas, illogical thinking, and magical thinking. Delusions (and hallucinations) called "Schneiderian First-Rank Symptoms" (FRS) involve the patient's experiencing his actions, thoughts, feelings, and perceptions as not his own, or somehow imposed on him. Although no longer considered pathognomonic of schizophrenia, FRS are often found in schizophrenia. (A sign or symptom is *pathognomonic* if it exists in only one disorder.)

"Illogical thinking" is another disturbance in thought content:

> People's bodies conform to the shape of their clothes, so that my mother's body must be a rectangle because she's wearing a chemise, and when my brother wears bell-bottoms, his legs become large, double-edged razors.

This patient also said that by getting dressed he could induce his father, via telepathy, to take a shower — that's "magical thinking."

Whereas in "poverty of speech" the patient utters only a few words or syllables, in "poverty of content of speech" the patient's words are sufficient and his individual sentences may even make sense, but the sum total says nothing. For example, when asked what religion meant to him, a patient replied:

> All that church stuff. Amazing Grace, Amazing Grace. "I know that my redeemer liveth, and that he shall stand at the latter day upon the earth." (Job 19:25) It is personal, very personal. I understand what you mean, you who live in God's grace.

"Incoherence" is a general, but often useful, term to describe incomprehensible speech in which the specific type of disturbed thinking is hard to identify, or in which there is a mixture of the thought disturbances mentioned above. Incoherence describes the response of a patient who was asked, "Do you fear anything specific?":

> That's just it. A doctor told me not to put a stamp on me. The Secretary of the Treasury is not part of it. People say to you, "Isn't it too bad that you're sick." It feels like I was very obstreperous. I couldn't communicate at any level.

My inside couldn't make sense of my outside. All the anxieties, and all the (pause), and all the rococo themes of psychiatric uh, uh, uh (pause) illness played back upon me again and again.

Obsessions, which are persistent unwanted *thoughts*, are another type of disturbed content. Because compulsions are "senseless," repeated *deeds*, they are behaviors, but since they arise from obsessions, the two may be reported together.

4. *Abstraction* refers to the patient's abilities to think symbolically, to generalize, and to conceptualize. The patient's behavior during the interview usually gives the clinician enough data to judge his ability to abstract. If there is any reason to question this ability, especially with evidence of psychosis or organicity, two specific clinical tests should be performed.

(Before describing these specific tests, some general pointers: Too much stock should not be placed in any single answer or on any clinical tests in general, since at best they are only rough measures of a patient's abilities; they do, however, provide some relatively objective data. Whenever formal clinical testing is done, the clinician should record not only his conclusion—e.g., "the patient's similarities were concrete"—but also what the patient actually said.)

The first test of abstractive ability involves whether the patient can recognize *similarities*. Questions are asked, such as, "What is the similarity between a poem, novel, and sculpture?" Or, "What is the similarity between a table, desk, and chair?" To the latter question, a properly abstracted answer would be, "They are all furniture." A concrete answer would be, "All are made of wood"; even more concrete would be, "I don't see any similarity." A bizarre answer would be, "They're all more human than humans."

The second test involves the patient's ability to interpret *proverbs*. Ideally, the proverbs asked the patient should (a) contain words and ideas within the patient's educational and cultural background, and (b) not be ones the patient has heard many times before. If the patient knows them, asking what they mean may test prior learning, not the capacity to abstract. For instance, "Water seeks its own level." Or, "The opera's not over till the fat lady sings." With the fat-lady proverb, an abstract response would be, "Nothing is resolved until everybody does their thing." A concrete response would be, "An opera is never finished until a fat woman sings." A bizarre response would be, "Fatso opera singers like sex." A personalized response would be, "I'm not fat!"

Perception

This category describes abnormalities in the five senses—hearing, seeing, touching, tasting, and smelling. These abnormalities, which include hallucinations, illusions, depersonalization, derealization, déjà vu, are often, but not always, psychopathological. Technically, dreams are hallucinations, but they are not reported as perceptual disturbances. Most people have brief experiences with derealization, depersonalization, and déjà vu.

Although some patients will readily admit they are hallucinating, many will not. Patients may be hallucinating when their eyes dart from side to side, when they stare at "nothing," or when they seem preoccupied, as if they were listening to voices. Because some patients will refer to their own thoughts as "voices," if auditory hallucinations are suspected, the clinician should ask the patient if the voices come from inside or from outside his head.

In general, auditory hallucinations occur in functional disorders, whereas these and other hallucinations occur in organic disorders. The hallucinations of patients with affective disorders tend to be mood-congruent; those of schizophrenics mood-incongruent.

Attention

"Attention" is the ability to sustain a focus on one task or activity. Impaired attention can usually be detected during a routine interview. "Distractibility" is when a patient's attention is frequently directed to unimportant or irrelevant external stimuli. If attention seems impaired, or if its immediate cause is unclear (e.g., due to anxiety, hallucinations, or to other psychotic preoccupations), formal clinical testing should be performed.

The most widely used test is *"serial 7's,"* whereby the patient is asked to subtract 7 from 100 without stopping as far as possible. The patient's educational background or infrequent use of mathematics may interfere with performance. A more informative test is *serial 1's*, in which the patient is asked to "count backwards by 1's from 57 and stop at 22." Because it requires no math skills, serial 1's is a purer test of concentration, and by noting if the patient stops at 22, the clinician also tests immediate memory.

Orientation

As patients become progressively more "disoriented," they are unable to indicate the current time, then their current location (place), and last, their own name (or person). To test for orientation to time, the clinician sees if the patient can identify the date, the day of the week, or how long he has been hospitalized. Therapists may be astonished to discover a seemingly normal patient who, when asked directly, says the current year is 1703.

Disturbances in orientation, memory, and judgment usually suggest organicity, which may arise from substance misuse or from toxicity from medication, especially antidepressants. Impaired orientation, memory, and judgment may also occur in schizophrenic, paranoid, psychotic, affective, and dissociative disorders.

Memory

In the MSE memory is divided into remote, recent, and immediate. *Remote* memory refers to many years ago; *recent* memory to the past several days to months; *immediate* memory to the past several minutes. When people lose their memory, immediate memory usually goes first, and remote memory last.

Remote and recent memory can be assessed by how well the patient recalls historical and current events. Immediate memory is best evaluated by formal testing: For example, the clinician names five (single-word) objects (e.g., book, umbrella, elephant, car, and toothpick), and then has the patient immediately repeat them to insure they "registered." He then tells the patient that in five minutes he will ask him to rename the five objects. Most patients can recall four out of five; remembering three raises doubts, and below three suggests organicity.

Sensing their failing memory and disorientation, many organic patients feel embarrassed and will try to conceal it by "confabulating." For instance, a 63-year-old professor with a slow-growing brain tumor had become adept at bluffing with charm to hide his inability to remember simple facts. When asked to name the year, he replied, "The year, well, it is the year of our discontent. Who cares about the year? It's but time, and time is relative."

Judgment

This section describes the patient's ability to deal with social situations, which includes acting appropriately during the interview and understanding the consequences of his action. Although judgment is largely assessed during the interview, if the patient's judgment is in question, the clinician should ask what he would do in a hypothetical situation: "What would you do if you found a stamped, addressed envelope lying on the street?"

Intelligence and Information

The only precise measure of *intelligence* comes from an IQ test, such as the Wechsler Adult Intelligence Scale (WAIS). By definition, IQ is whatever an IQ test measures, the average IQ being 100. Most people reading this book will not know anybody in their personal life with an IQ below 90. The diagnosis of mental retardation requires an IQ below 70 as determined by an IQ test. (See Appendix F.) IQ scores, and hence intelligence, reflect the cultural enrichment of a person's inborn biological potential. Thus, people exposed to the best schools are far more likely to have higher IQs.

The assessment of intelligence includes examining the patient's general fund of *information*; that's why intelligence and information are usually linked in the MSE. Both are affected by the patient's culture, education, performance anxiety, and psychopathology, especially organicity. Because the initial interview can only reveal gaping deficits, intelligence may be clinically tested by having the patient perform simple math (e.g., "Multiply 7×12"), or by having him read something and then tell the examiner what it meant. Evaluating the patient's fund of information involves questioning the patient's general knowledge and awareness of current events. Such questions should be geared to the patient's background. "Who wrote Hamlet?" "Who won last week's election for governor?"

Insight

In the MSE "insight" refers to whether the patient is aware of his chief problem. A delusional patient who claims he came for treatment to get Ma Bell to stop ringing in his ears lacks insight. The patient's level of insight is a rough predictor of how much he will cooperate with treatment and benefit from insight-oriented psychotherapy; the latter can be predicted further by offering the patient several interpretations during the assessment—not for therapy, but to see how the patient reacts to an interpretation.

AUXILIARY DATA

Information gathered outside the patient interview is considered auxiliary data; it brings in a tenth to a third of the information needed to determine the patient's diagnosis and treatment. As discussed already, two major sources of auxiliary data are interviews with friends or relatives and results from the medical assessment.

Psychological Tests

Time-consuming, costly, and requiring sophisticated interpretation by a psychologist, these tests should not be used routinely, unless they are needed to address *specific* questions whose answers may alter the patient's treatment. Specific questions might be: "What is the patient's IQ?" "How tenuous is the patient's contact with reality?" "Which conflicts most trouble the patient?" "How much control does the patient have over his aggressive impulses?" "Does the patient have organic impairment? If so, which functions are affected and to what extent?" Table 2-4 outlines the most commonly used psychological tests.

Most psychological tests were developed before *DSM-III*, and some psy-

TABLE 2-4
Psychological Tests

I. *Achievement tests*: Also known as "proficiency tests," they try to measure the outcome of systematic education and training.

II. *Aptitude tests*: They try to measure potential ability in specific areas or careers, such as music, medicine, and accounting.

III. *Intelligence tests*: These tests include the WAIS, the Stanford-Binet, and the Wechsler Intelligence Scale for Children (WISC). Beside measuring IQ, they can detect psychotic and organic impairments.

IV. *Personality tests*: These assess personality traits, and are of two general types:
   A. *Structured*: In these, largely quantitative, tests, the patient's response is compared to a "right" or "normal" response. Examples include the Minnesota Multiphasic Personality Inventory (MMPI), and parts of the WAIS.
   B. *Projective*: In these, largely qualitative, tests, there is no "correct" answer, but the subject projects his ideas to finish a task. Whereas with structured tests the subject relies heavily on previous knowledge and abilities, projective tests generally present the subject with unfamiliar situations and tasks. Projective tests include the Rorschach ("inkblot"), the Thematic Apperception Test (TAT), and the Figure Drawing Test.

V. *Neuropsychological tests*: These tests, such as the Halstead-Reitan Battery and a variety of scales from the WAIS and WISC, specifically evaluate brain impairment. These quantitative tests can determine if cerebral damage exists and whether it is diffuse or localized. Many tests can be used to assess specific types of brain functioning, such as:
   A. reasoning and problem solving
   B. memory
   C. orientation
   D. perceptual, motor, and visuospatial tasks
   E. language
   F. flexibility and speed of response, and
   G. attention and concentration

---

chologists still hold a psychological, instead of a descriptive, diagnostic approach. As a result, patients are more likely to be diagnosed as schizophrenic and borderline by psychological tests than by *DSM-III* criteria. With these reservations in mind, the clinician should delineate specific questions and then ask the psychologist whether testing can answer them. The choice of tests is the psychologist's and not the referring clinician's.

Amytal Interviews

Although popularly known as "truth serum," amytal does not make people tell the truth, and some patients even confabulate while receiving it. Consequently, amytal interviews have little place in the routine assessment. On occasion, they help to retrieve lost memories, to differentiate organic from functional disorders, to distinguish schizophrenic from affective disorders, and to unblock a stuck psychotherapy.

Neuroendocrine Batteries

A battery of neuroendocrine tests has recently emerged, which, when interpreted by *experts*, may help in diagnosis. At present, most, but certainly not all, psychiatrists believe these neuroendocrine tests lack sufficient sensitivity and specificity for a place in the routine assessment.

The Dexamethasone Suppression Test (DST) is the most widely used neuroendocrine test, partly because it is simple to administer and relatively inexpensive. Dexamethasone is a synthetic steroid, which the patient ingests as a tablet at 11:30 p.m. At four the following afternoon, the patient's blood is taken to measure the adrenal gland's cortisol. Normally dexamethasone decreases or suppresses the release of adrenal cortisol, but not in the severely depressed. In other words, a "positive" DST shows the "nonsuppression" of cortisol and is associated with depression. A positive DST, however, is also found in nondepressed patients, and a negative DST in depressed ones. Therefore, the DST must be interpreted with caution and only by those who understand it.

SUMMARY OF PRINCIPAL FINDINGS

After the history, MSE, and auxiliary data are reported, the clinician's next task is to highlight the major findings in a paragraph or two. This summary must indicate if there is an immediate threat to life, such as suicide, assaultiveness, or homicide. This summary does not include the patient's diagnosis, prognosis, biopsychosocial formulation, or treatment plan: These are all conclusions (of sorts), and a clear workup distinguishes findings from conclusions.

CHAPTER 3

Diagnosis and Prognosis

> Di-agnostic? . . . Lessee . . . agnostic means "one what don't know" . . . an' di is a greek prefix denotin' two-fold—so the di-agnostic team don't know twice as much as an ordinary agnostic . . . right?—Pogo, *New York Post*, August 11, 1966

ON THE PUBLICATION OF *DSM-III*, its chief architect, Robert Spitzer, began summarizing its major accomplishments by citing this unimpeachable source: Pogo knows that diagnostic labels may imply more knowledge than actually exists (Spitzer et al., 1980, p. 151). Despite their increased reliability and validity, *DSM-III*'s diagnostic categories are not eternal truths, but state-of-the-science hypotheses to be used with caution, but used nonetheless. For unless the clinician makes the correct diagnosis, no effective treatment can be launched and no accurate prognosis can be estimated.

Considering *DSM-III*'s 210 diagnoses, making a diagnosis has become an increasingly complex task, if only because over the years the number of diagnoses has skyrocketed. In 1840 there was but one psychiatric diagnosis: idiocy (or insanity). In 1880 there were seven: mania, melancholia, monomania, paresis (syphilis of the brain), dementia, dipsomania, and epilepsy. Over the next 100 years, the number of psychiatric diagnoses has risen at an average rate of two per year. This is progress.

DEFINITIONS

Differential diagnosis is the process of choosing the correct diagnosis from among conditions with similar features. Traditionally, differential diagnosis began with two general questions: (a) Was the patient's condition organic or

38

functional? (b) Was it a psychosis, neurosis, or personality disorder? In large measure, the first question addressed an *etiological* distinction, the second, a *descriptive* distinction.

Organic mental disorders are constellations of psychiatric signs and symptoms due to known anatomical, physiologic, or biochemical changes in the brain, such as a brain tumor or an amphetamine psychosis. *Functional disorders* are "nonorganic," meaning that no organic cause is known and implying that the primary etiology is psychosocial. The adjective "functional" does not exclude biological processes from operating, since the brain must be involved to produce any behavior. Moreover, this definition does not mean that no organic cause exists, merely that no organic cause has been *clearly* established, as *necessary* to produce the disorder. Thus, schizophrenia, panic disorder, and anorexia nervosa are functional disorders, even though biological factors play some role in these conditions. (Conversely, disorders are still called "organic," even though psychosocial factors influence their production.)

Psychosis exists when reality testing is grossly impaired. *Reality testing* is the ability to evaluate the external world objectively and to distinguish it from inner experience. Delusions, hallucinations, and massive denial are indicative of impaired reality testing and, therefore, of psychosis. Minor distortions of reality are not considered psychotic, such as transitory derealization or a man who overestimates his attraction to women. Psychosis is usually inferred when a patient's behavior is grossly disorganized—e.g., incoherent speech, "senseless" violence," total inattentiveness to the environment. Psychosis may be experienced as distressful and alien (i.e., ego-dystonic) or as an acceptable and integral part of one's normal self (i.e., ego-syntonic).

Neurosis is an ego-dystonic, nonpsychotic syndrome, which can be very disabling, but in general does not paralyze the individual's functioning nor violate social norms. In *DSM-III, neurotic disorder* is a purely descriptive term, without etiological or theoretical associations, whereas *neurotic process* refers to the unconscious mechanisms that produce neurotic symptoms. Unless stated otherwise, this text will use "neurotic," "neurosis," and "neurotic disorders" descriptively.

Personality disorders are long-standing conditions with "inflexible and maladaptive patterns of sufficient severity to cause either significant impairment in adaptive functioning or subjective distress" (*DSM-III*, p. 366). Unlike psychoses and neuroses, personality disorders are *always* chronic, even though their intensity may fluctuate. As a rule, they are nonpsychotic and ego-syntonic, but exceptions exist. Exemplifying the rule is antisocial personality disorder, a nonpsychotic state in which the patient doesn't mind his thievery, but his victims do. Two exceptions are the painful shyness seen with avoidant personality disorder and the transient psychosis of the borderline personality disorder.

TWO BASIC DIAGNOSTIC PRINCIPLES

DSM-III stresses two fundamental, yet related, principles: parsimony and hierarchy. The principle of *parsimony* is that clinicians should seek the single most elegant, economical, and efficient diagnosis that accounts for *all* the available data; when a single diagnosis is insufficient, the fewest number of diagnoses is sought. The principle of *hierarchy* is that mental disorders generally exist on a hierarchy of syndromes, which tend to decline in severity from top to bottom: Organic > Psychotic > Affective > Anxiety > Somatic > Psychosexual > Personality > Adjustment > No Mental Disorder.[1] Thus, when a patient's symptoms could be attributed to several disorders, the most parsimonious diagnosis belongs to the most severe category on this hierarchy. The decision tree in Figure 3-1 illustrates how these two principles guide differential diagnosis.

For instance, *without* these principles, the diagnosis of a patient with auditory hallucinations, persecutory delusions, apprehensiveness, and somatic preoccupations could range from schizophrenia to a paranoid, generalized anxiety, and somatoform disorder. *With* these principles, there is but one diagnosis — schizophrenia — and that's because it is the highest ranking disorder on the hierarchy which could account for *all* these symptoms.

SEVEN STEPS FOR PSYCHIATRIC DIAGNOSIS

Among the several perfectly good ways of reaching an Axis I or Axis II diagnosis is a seven-step procedure. The first two, *collecting data* and *identifying psychopathology*, are performed during the assessment and were discussed in Chapter 2.

3. *Evaluating the reliability of data*: Not all information is equally reliable. Not all informants are equally reliable. Present information is more reliable than past information, since memories fade and current moods often color past recollections. Information garnered during a crisis must be taken extra cautiously. Signs are more reliable than symptoms, because signs can be seen, whereas symptoms can't. Objective findings are more reliable than intuitive,

---

[1]Contemporary writers in the psychological tradition (e.g., Kernberg, Kohut, Masterson) consider personality disorders to be more severe than anxiety syndromes. Even descriptively, some personality syndromes, such as borderline personality disorder, impair more than many anxiety syndromes, such as social phobia and panic disorder. Yet considering *all* personality disorders and *all* syndromes, the *DSM-III* hierarchy is a reasonable *generalization*.

FIGURE 3-1
An Overview of Differential Diagnosis*

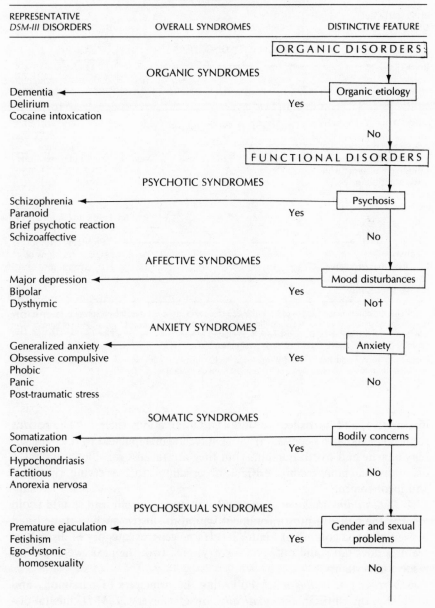

REPRESENTATIVE DSM-III DISORDERS	OVERALL SYNDROMES	DISTINCTIVE FEATURE

ORGANIC DISORDERS

ORGANIC SYNDROMES

Dementia ◄——————————————— Organic etiology
Delirium   Yes
Cocaine intoxication

No

FUNCTIONAL DISORDERS

PSYCHOTIC SYNDROMES

Schizophrenia ◄——————————————— Psychosis
Paranoid   Yes
Brief psychotic reaction
Schizoaffective   No

AFFECTIVE SYNDROMES

Major depression ◄——————————————— Mood disturbances
Bipolar   Yes
Dysthymic   Not

ANXIETY SYNDROMES

Generalized anxiety ◄——————————————— Anxiety
Obsessive compulsive   Yes
Phobic
Panic   No
Post-traumatic stress

SOMATIC SYNDROMES

Somatization ◄——————————————— Bodily concerns
Conversion   Yes
Hypochondriasis
Factitious   No
Anorexia nervosa

PSYCHOSEXUAL SYNDROMES

Premature ejaculation ◄——————————————— Gender and sexual
Fetishism   Yes   problems
Ego-dystonic
  homosexuality   No

(continued)

FIGURE 3-1
(Continued)

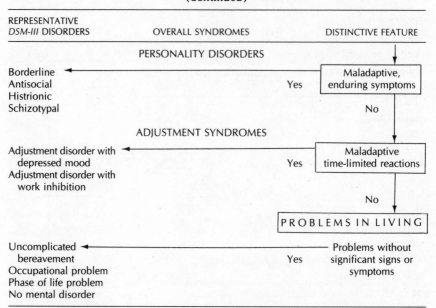

REPRESENTATIVE DSM-III DISORDERS	OVERALL SYNDROMES	DISTINCTIVE FEATURE
	PERSONALITY DISORDERS	
Borderline ◄— Antisocial Histrionic Schizotypal	Yes	Maladaptive, enduring symptoms No
	ADJUSTMENT SYNDROMES	
Adjustment disorder with depressed mood ◄— Adjustment disorder with work inhibition	Yes	Maladaptive time-limited reactions No
		PROBLEMS IN LIVING
Uncomplicated ◄— bereavement Occupational problem Phase of life problem No mental disorder	Yes	Problems without significant signs or symptoms

*In placing the differential diagnosis of *DSM-III*'s 228 categories into a manageable perspective, this overview contains some inaccuracies and oversimplifications. The left column presents sample *DSM-III* diagnoses. The middle column lists general syndromes, which are clusters of signs and symptoms. The right column indicates the most distinctive overall feature of each syndrome.

†Because of recent evidence, *DSM-III-R* may specify that anxiety syndromes may be diagnosed if they are unrelated to, instead of being ruled-out by, a higher-ranked syndrome.

interpretive, and introspective findings. Observations such as "The patient seems to be hiding a depression," or "I'm feeling manipulated by the patient," may be true and worth pursuing, but they are far less reliable in making a diagnosis than more readily verifiable observations, such as crying, slow gait, and incoherence.

4. *Determining the overall distinctive feature*: The clinican should try to identify the patient's most prominent symptom cluster, such as those listed in the righthand column of Figure 3-1. If one general category of distinctive features does not stand out, don't worry, pick two: the next two steps will resolve uncertainty.

5. *Arriving at a diagnosis*: Following the principles of parsimony and hierarchy, the clinician *systematically* considers every *DSM-III* mental disorder which exhibits the patient's overall distinctive feature. This task is not

easy: *DSM-III* lists 210 diagnoses, divided into 16 general categories for Axis I and two for Axis II; all 18 are summarized in Table 3-1.

Making a diagnosis from among all those in *DSM-III* is greatly facilitated by using *decision trees*. As illustrated in Figure 3-1, a decision tree is an algorithm, or flow chart, which uses branching logic to hone in on the most likely diagnosis.[2] But whether the clinician uses decision tree in a book or one in his mind, each possible diagnosis must be systematically considered.

6. *Check diagnostic criteria*: Having gone out on a diagnostic limb, the clinician should confirm the decision tree's diagnosis by seeing if the patient's characteristics meet the *DSM-III* diagnostic criteria for this disorder. To demonstrate: Table 3-2 lists *DSM-III*'s criteria for panic disorder. (Note how criteria C and D illustrate the principle of hierarchy.)

These criteria are guides, not laws. A patient, for instance, might have a genuine panic disorder even if her condition doesn't quite replicate *DSM-III*'s definition. The dozen symptoms listed under "B" do not include "an overwhelming sense of impending doom" or "an imminent fear of world destruction," and yet these commonly occur in panic disorder. If a patient's condition only approximates the criteria, the clinician may write, "The patient meets *DSM-III* criteria for panic disorder, but has had only *two* weeks of panic attacks, and only *three* symptoms in B." By using *DSM-III* as a *reference* point, the clinician is speaking the diagnostic language of his colleagues, while not being locked into its use. If a clinician has a good reason not to use *DSM-III*, he should specify which criteria he is using (e.g., Feighner. RDC).

A digression: Rote memorizing of *DSM-III* criteria is a long and pointless endeavor to be avoided; knowing specific criteria comes best with clinical experience. However, when this text presents a disorder, students should still examine its *DSM-III* criteria to (a) obtain an overall picture of the disorder, (b) learn its defining characteristics, (c) see examples of its common symptoms, and (d) understand the meanings of the technical terms which describe it.

7. *Resolve diagnostic uncertainty*: If at this stage one diagnosis (per axis) doesn't suffice, or if some evidence is inconsistent with other data, or if the diagnosis remains unclear for any reason, the most likely culprits are (a) inadequate data, (b) premature closure, (c) atypical presentations, or (d) multiple disorders.

Inadequate data may stem from too few facts. For instance, although *DSM-III*'s brief reactive psychosis must immediately follow "a recognizable

---

[2]*DSM-III*'s Appendix A presents seven decision trees; each starts with a general category of distinctive features (e.g., psychosis, bodily complaints) and "prunes" down to a specific diagnosis. Janicak and Andriukaitis (1980) have offered more detailed decision trees for all diagnostic categories in *DSM-III*.

TABLE 3-1
***DSM-III*'s General Diagnostic Categories**

AXIS I

1. *Disorders Usually First Evident in Infancy, Childhood or Adolescence*
   This category includes most, but not all, of the disorders which arise before adolescence, such as attention deficit disorders, bulimia, infantile autism, and mental retardation.

2. *Organic Mental Disorders*
   These disorders are temporary or permanent dysfunctions of brain tissue caused by diseases or chemicals. Examples are delirium, dementia, and amnestic syndrome. In *DSM-III*, this category also includes the harmful *consequences* of using substances (i.e., drugs and alcohol), such as amphetamine intoxication, phencyclidine (PCP) delirium, and alcohol withdrawal; in *DSM-III-R*, these disorders are catalogued as substance use disorders.

3. *Substance Use Disorders*
   This category refers to the *maladaptive* use of drugs and alcohol. Mere consumption and recreational use of substances are not disorders. This category necessitates an abnormal pattern of *use*, as with alcohol abuse and cocaine dependence.

4. *Schizophrenic Disorders*
   The schizophrenias are characterized by psychotic symptoms (e.g., grossly disorganized behavior, nonmood-congruent delusions and hallucinations) and by over six months of behavioral deterioration.

5. *Paranoid Disorders*
   These disorders, of which paranoia is the most common, are characterized by persecutory delusions in the absence of other psychotic symptoms. In general, these patients are less impaired than schizophrenics.

6. *Psychotic Disorders Not Elsewhere Classified*
   A grab bag of psychotic disorders, which usually have a briefer course and better prognosis than paranoid and schizophrenic disorders, this category includes schizophreniform disorder, brief reactive psychosis, and schizoaffective disorder.

7. *Affective Disorders*
   The cardinal feature of affective disorders is a disturbance of mood. Patients may, or may not, have psychotic symptoms, but when they do, delusions and hallucinations are often mood-congruent. These disorders include major depression, bipolar disorder, and dysthymic disorder.

8. *Anxiety Disorders*
   These disorders are characterized by physiologic signs of anxiety (e.g., palpitations) and subjective feelings of tension, apprehension, or fear. Anxiety may be acute and focused (panic disorder) or continual and diffuse (generalized

44

TABLE 3-1
(Continued)

anxiety disorder). This category also includes phobic, obsessive compulsive, and post-traumatic stress disorders.

9. *Somatoform Disorders*

These disorders are dominated by somatic symptoms which resemble physical illnesses. Their symptoms cannot be accounted for by an organic disease or by a pathophysiologic mechanism. There *must* also be strong evidence that these symptoms are produced by psychological factors or conflicts. This category includes somatization and conversion disorders, and hypochondriasis.

10. *Dissociative Disorders*

These disorders all feature a sudden, temporary alteration or dysfunction of memory, consciousness, identity, and behavior, as in depersonalization disorder, psychogenic fugue, and multiple personality.

11. *Psychosexual Disorders*

Psychological factors play major etiological roles in all of these disorders. There are four basic types: gender identity disorders (e.g., transsexualism), paraphilias (e.g., necrophilia), sexual dysfunctions (e.g., premature ejaculation), and ego-dystonic homosexuality.

12. *Factitious Disorders*

In these disorders (e.g., Munchausen syndrome), physical or psychological symptoms are produced voluntarily for no apparent or ulterior motive other than being ill.

13. *Disorders of Impulse Control Not Elsewhere Classified*

These disorders involving poor impulse control include pathological gambling, kleptomania, and pyromania.

14. *Adjustment Disorders*

These relatively mild disorders occur within three months of a clearly identifiable psychosocial stressor. Disorders are classified according to the predominant symptom, such as adjustment disorder with depressed mood or adjustment disorder with academic inhibition.

15. *Psychological Factors Affecting Physical Condition*

Once called "psychosomatic disorders," this category refers to psychological factors that initiate, exacerbate, or aggravate an identifiable medical illness. (The medical illness should be indicated on Axis III.)

16. *Conditions Not Attributable to a Mental Disorder That Are a Focus of Attention or Treatment*

This category covers malingering, marital problems, or phase of life difficulties.

(continued)

TABLE 3-1
(Continued)

AXIS II

17. *Personality Disorders*
These disorders are patterns of personality traits that are long-standing, mal-adaptive, and inflexible, and cause impaired functioning or subjective distress. Examples include: borderline, schizoid, and passive-aggressive personality disorders.

18. *Specific Developmental Disorders*
These are disorders of specific developmental areas which are not due to another disorder. Delayed language development would be classified here, unless it was secondary to another (Axis I) disorder, such as infantile autism.

TABLE 3-2
DSM-III* Criteria for Panic Disorder

A. At least three panic attacks within a three-week period in circumstances other than during marked physical exertion or in a life-threatening situation. The attacks are not precipitated only by exposure to a circumscribed phobic stimulus.
B. Panic attacks are manifested by discrete periods of apprehension or fear, and at least four of the following symptoms appear during each attack:
    (1) dyspnea [shortness of breath]
    (2) palpitations
    (3) chest pain or discomfort
    (4) choking or smothering sensations
    (5) dizziness, vertigo, or unsteady feelings
    (6) feelings of unreality
    (7) parathesias [tingling in hands or feet]
    (8) hot and cold flashes
    (9) sweating
    (10) faintness
    (11) trembling
    (12) fear of dying, going crazy, or doing something uncontrolled during an attack
C. Not due to a physical disorder or another mental disorder, such as Major Depression, Somatization Disorder, or Schizophrenia.
D. The disorder is not associated with Agoraphobia.

*DSM-III, pp. 231–232.

psychosocial stressor," the clinician could not explain why a patient had every symptom of a brief reactive psychosis without being subjected to any particular stressor. More data solved the puzzle: When the patient's urine was positive for amphetamines, his diagnosis was changed to amphetamine psychosis.

Sometimes inadequate data exist because the therapist hasn't been talking to the right people. After conducting two months of stalemated couples treatment, a therapist insisted on seeing the couple's five-year-old daughter to learn more about the family. Until then, mother and father had colluded in a secret, which, in childhood innocence, their daughter spilled, "How come daddy stumbles around every night he comes home?"

Premature closure refers to jumping the diagnostic gun, without proper differential diagnosis. A common trap is the "five-minute diagnosis," in which the clinician doesn't realize that his first diagnostic impression has become immutable. After interviewing a patient for five minutes, the therapist "unconsciously" reaches a diagnosis and then inadvertently distorts, converts, and selectively seeks information that confirms this initial diagnosis. Call it human nature, but *every* clinician is prone to see what he "wants" to see. What distinguishes the skilled professional is that he makes sure to double-check his diagnosis by repeating the previous six steps.

One of the author's lesser moments came when he diagnosed a patient in the emergency room as having a major depression. The diagnosis seemed obvious: The patient's face was blank, his gait slow, his movements agitated; he felt sad and lonely. He even said he was depressed! Yet soon after the patient was admitted, the author was called by a supervisor who said the patient's diagnosis was Parkinson's disease, not depression. The author's mistake was that he saw a depressed-looking person and stopped thinking: He assumed the patient was depressed, did not perform a systematic differential diagnosis, and only saw what he expected to find.

An *atypical presentation* causes diagnostic confusion, because some patients lack the decency to conform to classic textbook descriptions. For instance, patients with major depression usually feel sad, yet some don't feel sad at all, but complain of bodily aches and pains. Another advantage of using *DSM-III*'s decision trees is that they often detect atypical cases.

Multiple diagnoses—that is, more than one diagnosis per axis—may be indicated, even though clinicians should first try to ascribe a patient's symptoms to a single diagnosis. Just as medical patients can have more than one disorder, so can psychiatric patients. To not consider multiple diagnoses risks missing a disorder and messing up treatment.

If diagnostic uncertainty persists, the clinician should use the most applicable *DSM-III* lable: "diagnosis deferred," "unspecified mental disorder," or "provisional diagnosis." Finally, the patient may have "no mental disorder," a most underutilized diagnosis.

MULTIAXIAL DIAGNOSIS

In 1947, multiaxial diagnosis was first proposed in Sweden; although it was rejected, five years later Danish psychiatrists adopted an official "biaxial" system that separated symptoms from etiology. After two decades of promotion by the World Health Organization, the concept surfaced in America in 1975, when John Strauss suggested a multiaxial approach with an axis for social functioning. In 1980, *DSM-III* incorporated multiaxial diagnosis in order to clarify the complexities and relationships between the patient's biopsychosocial difficulties, and thereby, facilitate treatment planning. *DSM-III* uses five axes.

Axis I: Clinical Syndromes (e.g., Mental Disorders); Conditions Not Attributable to a Mental Disorder That Are a Focus of Attention or Treatment
Axis II: Personality Disorders/traits and Specific Developmental Disorders
Axis III: Physical Disorders/symptoms that pertain to current problem
Axis IV: Severity of Psychosocial Stressors affecting the patient's current problem
Axis V: Highest Level of Adaptive Functioning Past Year

The main advantage of separating Axis I and II is to prevent the typically more florid presentations of Axis I mental disorders from overshadowing, or becoming confused with, the more chronic and subtle Axis II personality disorders. Distinguishing between these axes may clarify what therapy can reasonably accomplish, since treatment is more likely to alleviate Axis I than Axis II disorders. Therapists (and clients) who fail to separate mental from personality disorders are frequently disappointed, however unjustifiably, when only the former remits with brief treatment.

Axis III lists only physical disorders or symptoms that are "potentially relevant to the understanding or management of the individual" (*DSM-III*, p. 26). Some nonphysicians are reluctant, or deem it inappropriate, to list an Axis III diagnosis; that's unfortunate, since a patient's diagnosis should be complete. When writing an Axis III diagnosis, many nonphysicians like to add, in parenthesis, the source of this diagnostic information (e.g., the patient's doctor, the patient, the chart). For example:

Axis I: Panic disorder
           Psychological factors affecting physical condition

Axis II: No personality disorder
Axis III: Crohn's disease (Dr. Sachar)
Axis IV: Stressors: Loss of job (acute) and failing marriage (enduring); Severity: 4 — Moderate
Axis V: Highest functioning during past year: 2 — Very Good

Axes IV and V are optional. That's because they are relatively new and untried, potentially bulky and inconvenient, and, although the interrater reliability of Axis V is good, it is only fair for Axis IV (Spitzer et al., 1980; Williams, 1985). Moreover, using Axes IV and V diagnoses may risk violating a patient's confidentiality by needlessly giving sensitive personal information anytime an official diagnosis must be sent to an insurance company, government agency, employer, etc.

Axis IV rates the severity of psychosocial stresses on the patient in terms of how much they would affect an "average" person in the same circumstances and with the same socioeconomic values. The ratings go from "none" (level 1) to "catastrophic" (level 7). As illustrated above, specific stressors (e.g., promotion, death) should be indicated, and, as *DSM-III-R* will probably recommend, whether they were predominately acute events (duration less than six months) or enduring circumstances (duration greater than six months). This distinction may help in rendering a prognosis and in planning treatment, since problems triggered by acute stressors tend to resolve sooner and respond faster to treatment than problems which develop insidiously.

In one of the few investigations to evaluate the validity of Axis IV, Zimmerman and co-workers (1985) studied 130 depressed patients and concluded that, in general, it was valid. But valid in what ways? After all, stressors have many qualities. Zimmerman's group found that Axis IV stressors were more highly correlated with (a) undesirable than desirable events, (b) "exits" more than "entrances," (c) time-limited rather than chronic occurrences, (d) greater risks for alcoholism, (e) more prevalent personality disorders, and (f) a greater likelihood of attempted suicide during the present episode. This research also showed that the degree of change induced by a stressor and whether or not it is under the patient's control were *not* correlated with the patient's condition. Thus, in rating Axis IV, all of these findings should be considered.

Axis V indicates the patient's highest level of adaptive social and occupational functioning (for at least a few months) during the past year. The ratings go from "superior" (level 1) to "grossly impaired" (level 7). Specifying the patient's highest level of functioning helps to determine prognosis and treatment, since patients who previously functioned at a higher level usually recover at a higher level. To illustrate: With everything else being the same, and with Tom and Jerry being equally delusional — one's certain he's a cat, the other, a mouse — if before becoming ill Tom had a solid marriage, good job, and satisfying hobbies, and Jerry did not, then after recovery Tom would probably function better than Jerry. Treatment goals should reflect these different expectations.

Instead of indicating the patient's highest level of functioning during the *past year*, the clinician may deviate from *DSM-III* by rating either the patient's *current global*, or his *highest premorbid* (predisorder), level of functioning. The period of time rated should be the one that will most help in determining prognosis and treatment. However, to avoid confusion, anytime a clinician deviates from *DSM-III*, he should say so.

A frequent criticism of *DSM-III*'s multiaxial system is that it doesn't convey enough useful information. Additional axes have been proposed for psychophysiologic variables, defense mechanisms, substance abuse, nutrition, grooming, social interactions, work performance, relational systems, and family functions of leadership, boundaries, affectivity, communication, and task-oriented performance. If incorporated, however, might not an ever-growing number of variables eventually bury a multiaxial system? Is it also possible that too much is being expected of a formal diagnosis? Regardless of one's views, experts all agree that diagnosis *by itself* is never enough to determine prognosis or treatment, for it is also necessary to consider historical, auxiliary, etiological, and treatment-response data.

PROGNOSIS

A patient's prognosis, or outcome, hinges on: (a) the natural course of the patient's disorder, (b) his highest prior level of functioning, (c) the duration of the present illness — the longer the duration, the bleaker the outlook, (d) the abruptness of onset — the more acute the onset the better the prognosis, (e) the age of onset — the earlier in life the poorer the outcome, (f) the availability of effective treatments, (g) treatment compliance, and (h) having a supportive social network. In different ways, each *DSM-III* axis sheds light on prognosis.

How disturbed a patient is during an acute episode is *not* always a good predictor of long-term outcome. A 20-year-old patient who has deteriorated over six years from schizophrenia and who now displays mild social withdrawal and flat affect has a far worse long-term prognosis than a 50-year-old patient who always functioned well until a month ago when she became wildly manic, insisting she was the reincarnation of Queen Victoria, throwing hundred-dollar bills out the window, and speaking with nonstop flight of ideas.

The clinician should be clear about *which* prognosis he is determining. Is it for a short-term (e.g., posthospitalization) or a long-term (e.g., a year after discharge) outcome? Is it for an Axis I or an Axis II disorder? Is it a forecast of something more specific, such as relapse, suicide, assault, social functioning? Therefore, when a clinician dispenses prognostic information to patients and their families, he should describe these various types of outcomes, instead of simply indicating a single, and less meaningful, prognosis.

CHAPTER 4

Etiology

AFTER REPORTING THE history, mental status, diagnosis, and prognosis, the clinician presents a *biopsychosocial formulation*—that is, a discussion of the etiology and pathogenesis of the patient's current problems. In general, "etiology" refers to what *originates* a disorder, whereas "pathogenesis" refers to *all the mechanisms* which ultimately produce it. In this chapter, the term *etiology* will encompass pathogenesis and include everything that has caused the patient's presenting difficulties.

Etiology plays an unusual role in psychiatry, since psychiatry is the *only* medical specialty that, virtually by definition, treats disorders without clearly known causes (or definitive cures). At the turn of the century, the most prevalent mental illness was general paresis (i.e., syphilis of the brain). Other common psychiatric disorders were "myxedema madness" (a type of hypothyroidism), the epilepsies, and psychoses due to vitamin deficiencies and brain infections. Yet as soon as the cause for each of these conditions was discovered, the job of treating them shifted to physicians *other* than psychiatrists, such as internists and neurologists. Therefore, that psychiatrists don't know the cause of mental illness is less an indictment of psychiatrists than a reflection of how medicine assigns diseases among its specialists.

Indeed, a major reason *DSM-III* switched to a nosology based on descriptive, instead of on etiological, criteria was because the etiology of most mental disorders is unknown. Exceptions exist, as when a disorder's etiology is both obvious and inherent to its definition, such as amphetamines in producing amphetamine intoxication, or psychosocial stressors in producing a post-traumatic stress disorder. Otherwise, *DSM-III* eschews etiological hypotheses— biological as well as psychosocial.[1]

---

[1]"Idiopathic" refers to unknown causation, whereas "iatrogenic" refers to physician-induced illness (e.g., drug side effects).

Although the etiologies of most mental disorders are unknown, more is understood about etiology today than ever. Most dramatized have been advances in psychobiology and epidemiology, but less heralded (and equally important) has been the growing appreciation of how intrapsychic, familial, and social influences interact with biology to produce mental disorders. As a result, the clinician's "*psychodynamic* formulation" has been superseded by a "*biopsychosocial* formulation"; the former was limited to psychological, largely intrapsychic, influences, whereas the latter is a synthesis of psychodynamic, biological, familial, and social etiologies (see Engel, 1977).

THE DIMENSIONS OF "CAUSATION"

To speak of "*the* cause" of a mental disorder is naive; it's akin to patients who enter treatment and say, "I want to get to the root of my problem." This "root myth" assumes that a lone root has caused their problem, and that unearthing it will cure them. There is, however, no such thing as *the* root to a problem; at most, there are root*s*, with many sprouting variegated phenomena. Formulations, therefore, consider diverse etiological influences, such as following:

What *initiates* a disorder usually differs from what *perpetuates* it. Many teenagers begin smoking to feel grownup. However, if they're still smoking when they reach 30, it's hardly to be adult; at this point they're smoking from habit. What originates and maintains a problem may also differ from what *exacerbates* a disorder. Stress may rekindle a smoking habit in somebody who previously stopped.

When determining causation, clinicians should be careful to delineate these three levels of causation. Many theories of mental illness are originally proposed as initial causes of a disorder, whereas subsequent data show these theories are more relevant to what maintains or aggravates a disorder. For instance, the hypothesis that "double-bind" communication initially produces schizophrenia has been largely refuted, yet growing evidence suggests that it does perpetuate and exacerbate schizophrenia.

Clinicians should also distinguish between what is *inherent* to a disorder and what is a *consequence* of it: Both may profoundly affect the patient and feed into the other. The importance of this distinction may become apparent by carefully examining the sequence of events. For example, a novice may err by assuming that a job loss caused a depression, whereas in reality the patient's depression caused him to get fired.

Causes may be categorized as (a) necessary and sufficient, (b) necessary but not sufficient, or (c) facilitating or predisposing but neither necessary nor sufficient (Goodwin & Guze, 1984). Few diseases have causes that are necessary and sufficient; one example is Huntington's Chorea, a progressive and fatal dementia, in which having the gene is all that's needed to produce the illness. Alcoholism illustrates the second type; although alcohol is necessary for the disorder, other factors are required to produce it, since everyone who drinks doesn't become an alcoholic. These other factors may include psychonoxious environments, poor nutrition, and predisposing genes. Many causes fall into the third category; loss of parents during childhood fosters most mental disorders, even though it is neither necessary nor sufficient to produce any of them. Consequently, a disorder's harmful effects may be reduced or prevented by rectifying facilitating or predisposing causes (e.g., poverty, stress), even when they are not a necessary or sufficient cause.

Because mental disorders have multiple, rather than single, causes, and because some of these causes are facilitating or predisposing, *multicausality* has been misconstrued as *omnicausality*—that is, anything can cause anything, as long as there is a tenuous connection; if a passive father has a schizophrenic son, than passive fathers are deemed a cause of schizophrenia. That's stupid; it's like saying milk is a cause of schizophrenia because a schizophrenic drank milk. Omnicausality falters because it equates a *casual*, with a *causal*, association between two events, a confusion that can only be clarified by studying the matter with scientific *controls* (Goodwin & Guze, 1984).

Some diagnostic categories, such as schizophrenia, consist of not one, but several, psychiatric entities, which all share similar cardinal features. The entities may be defined by the most prominant symptom, as in the various *subtypes* of schizophrenia—paranoid, catatonic, etc. Each subtype may involve different etiological factors. Conversely, entities which present with the same clinical picture may have arisen by different etiological routes. For instance, genetics clearly produces some depressions, but not others; many antihypertensive medications induce some major depressions, bereavement triggers others, and "learned helplessness" causes others. The reason these depressions may present with the same symptoms is because no matter what their origin, at some point a specific series of changes was launched within the brain—that is, a "final common pathway," which produced the characteristic symptoms of major depression.

Symptoms and *issues* usually arise from different causes. Symptoms may be hallucinations or insomnia, while issues entail what symptoms mean and symbolize to the patient, how he copes with them, how he feels toward authorities, and so on. (See Chapter 1, pp. 6–7). Symptoms and issues, although related, are of a different order. Goodwin (1985, p. 171) aptly quoted Donald Hebb's observation on whether intelligence was due to heredity or environment: "Each is *fully* necessary. . . . To ask how much heredity contributes to intelligence is like asking how much the width of a field contributes to its area."

For 15 years a middle-aged man had the occasional delusion that people were sneaking itching powder into his food. Since his divorce 20 years ago, homosexual urges had frightened him. When he felt close to another man—or to use his words, "get the itch for somebody"—his delusion would arise. The man's symptom was a delusion, and many patients have delusions. The man's issues about itching powder and homosexuals were idiosyncratic; they derived from his life experience, were symbolically meaningful to him, and erupted in circumstances stressful for him.

Symptoms have *form* while issues have *content*. Symptoms are to issues as videotape is to programming. For instance, two patients may present with major depression; both complain of severe guilt, hopelessness, and insomnia. Their symptoms are the same, yet their issues vary. The first patient, a young, successful TV executive, insists her sleeplessness stems from her being "a total failure," while the second, a retired Baptist postal clerk, is sure his sleeplessness is a punishment from God. Both patients suffer from the biologically-induced insomnia of major depression. Yet the issues the patients bring to their insomnia—that is, what it means to them and how they deal with it— differ according to their life experiences.

In general, biology determines symptoms and psychosocial influences shape issues. How a patient expresses a mental disorder greatly depends on his personality. When drunk or "stoned," some giggle, some babble, some dance, some cry, some withdraw; some get the munchies, and others become violent. They all have an organic mental syndrome, yet how it manifests varies according to the individual's personality. (The same holds for medical illness. For example, coronary patients contend with heart attacks in many different ways depending on their personality.)

Like intoxication, mental disorders tend to magnify personality. During a major depression, a lifelong worry-wart frets nonstop, a chronically suspicious man becomes downright paranoid, and a mild hypochondriac becomes a severe one. Consequently, the cause of a patient's behavior can never be fully attributed to either psychology *or* biology, since both are responsible for behavior, albeit in different ways—a truism recognized long ago by Hughlings Jackson: "There is no physiology of the mind anymore than there is a psychology of the nervous system." As long as people have minds *and* brains it's hard to imagine how one could function without the other!

Given that mental disorders neither "overpower" personality nor make it disappear, being mentally ill or taking LSD, PCP, or alcohol neither "explains" nor "justifies" committing antisocial acts. (Mental illness is no excuse for bad manners.) Statements like "Peter beat up Sally because Peter was drunk," or "Darlene's schizophrenia caused her to drown her child," imply that the patient/criminal has nothing to do with the act, as if the drug or the mental illness *made* him commit the crime. As a group, schizophrenics are no more or less violent than any other group; being schizophrenic *per se* does not make one violent. Being acutely psychotic may diminish normal social restraints or magnify preexisting violent tendencies, but that's quite different from dissociating the person from his crime by totally blaming the illness.[2]

---

[2]The night before Sirhan Sirhan appeared before a parole board, he developed a dreadful toothache. When he learned that no dentist was available, he threatened to kill the prison dentist. Now most people with Sirhan's predicament would be upset, yet they would not threaten to *kill* a dentist. Sirhan did—not because his tooth hurt, but because that's his nature. (If he had murdered the dentist, would he have invoked "the dental defense"?) Thus, the manifestations of physical and mental disorders are substantially determined by the individual's personality.

VOLITION

"Volition" means the act of willing, and how much a patient "wills" or determines his behavior during a mental disorder may confuse the observer. The first question, to be blunt, is "Can people fake mental illness?" The answer is "Yes, but not for long." If one has doubts, try it! Actors can fake "madness" for three hours a night and twice on Wednesdays and Saturdays, yet not much longer. Only those with mental disorders can pace for hours, shadow box for days, and dwell on rotting bladders and stinking bowels. It's too exhausting to sustain. Nor can one hallucinate at will, unless he has taken a funny chemical or is snuggled in a sensory-isolation chamber.

Nevertheless, the question of people faking mental illness stubbornly persists, partly because some patients seem to respond to the environment according to what's "convenient" or "necessary." When clinicians must decide whether to permit a floridly psychotic inpatient to attend the funeral of a loved one, they find that most patients pull themselves together, go to the funeral, and do just fine. How come? Because, like the intoxicated, the mentally ill can still modify their behavior depending on the situation and on the severity of their illness. When a tipsy student receives a telephone call from his parents, he can "get his act together," as long as the call is not too long and he is not too drunk. Likewise, if they are not too ill and not required to act "properly" for too long, the mentally ill can usually "normalize" their behavior. Therefore, highly disturbed psychiatric patients are not helpless automatons, for they can exert some control over their disorder.

Conversely, just as being intoxicated makes it extremely difficult to perform routine tasks, so does being mentally ill. Like everyone else, the mentally ill must contend with problems in living, but unlike everyone else, they must do so with the added burdens of psychiatric symptoms. Interviewing for a job is hard enough; doing so while certain the interviewer is Satan doesn't help. Writing a term paper can be stressful, but imagine doing so with racing thoughts and taunting hallucinations. Mental illness makes everything harder. Simple chitchat isn't so simple when one's sure a bomb will explode in one's stomach. Given all their symptoms, what amazes is not how poorly the mentally ill do, but how well.

EXPLAINING VERSUS UNDERSTANDING

In the formulation, the clinician should seek to understand, as well as to explain, the patient's difficulties. Unfortunately, many clinicians are unaware of the difference between "explaining" and "understanding." In this context, "understanding" is not being used in the *explanatory* sense of "I understand *why* Jim hates his mother," but rather in the *descriptive* sense of "I understand *how* Jim hates his mother."

To explain is to view from the outside; to understand is to view from within. Explaining relies on logic and intellect, understanding on experience and empathy. Explanations try to be objective, whereas understanding can only be subjective. Explanations address the "why" of behavior, understanding the "what" of behavior. For different reasons, both explaining and understanding are crucial for clinical care. One is not better than the other; they're different.

Clinicians often say they're "understanding" when they're actually "explaining." Consider Karen, a psychiatric inpatient, who was convinced she had no legs. When her psychiatrist went on vacation, she walked up to the staff and complained, more intensely than ever, of having no legs. Every time this occurred, her substitute therapist would reply, "You're walking, so that proves you have legs. But even so, you're obviously worried about having no legs because your doctor is on vacation." Karen was infuriated; she claimed the staff "doesn't understand me." The staff responded, "But we do understand: Your psychiatrist has gone away and you're understandably upset." Patient and staff talk past each other. The patient (accurately) felt she was being "explained away." The staff (mistakenly) believed they were showing understanding, when they were actually giving a (correct) explanation. Another psychiatrist demonstrated understanding when he said to Karen, "You must feel like a paraplegic. It's frightening to feel you have no control over your legs, or they don't work properly, or they don't belong to you. No wonder you're upset!" Feeling that somebody was finally on her "wavelength," Karen was ready to consider the explanation about her therapist's being away.

It's not that clinicians never understand their patients; to various degrees, they all do. Yet to the degree the clinician does understand, it's more a product of his being a *person* than of his being a *professional*. Therapists are essentially no better or worse than anyone else at understanding people. Indeed, a good novelist reveals a thorough understanding of a character's psychology without ever using a psychological term.

In contrast, by learning etiological theory, clinicians are far more adept at explaining behavior. They can learn how the unconscious does this and how the id does that; they can learn how the brain's chemicals affect this and how the person's environment affects that. Therefore, although clinicians are experts at explaining, but not necessarily at understanding, both explaining and understanding are important and belong in the formulation. The following sections will introduce explanatory theories, since they, unlike understandings, lend themselves to didactic presentations.

NEURONS AND NEUROTRANSMITTERS

The fundamental unit of biologically-derived behavior is the nerve cell or *neuron*. The brain has one trillion neurons; each consists of a microscopic *cell body* (or "head") which trails off into an *axon* (or "tail"), with an extremely narrow width, but a length of up to several inches or feet. By definition, axons take electrical impulses *away* from the cell body, whereas *dendrites* bring them *toward* it. Electrical impulses originate in cell bodies and run through these axons until they are conveyed to hundreds, or even thousands, of other nerve cells.

Neurons are the only cells in the body which are anatomically separate from one another. Therefore, to reach a nearby neuron, these electrical impulses do not travel over continuous tissue, but flow through the spaces between neurons. As illustrated on Figure 4-1, this passage is accomplished by chemicals called *neurotransmitters*, which transmit messages over these tiny spaces called *synaptic clefts*.

Neurotransmitters are synthesized inside the neuron and actively transported to the axon's end or *presynaptic terminal*; from here neurotransmitters swim across the synaptic cleft, binding onto *receptors* on the membranes (or edges) of adjacent cell bodies. By doing so, neurotransmitters can trigger or inhibit the receptor's firing. The nerve cell acts like a wet sponge: When it fires, it contracts to release its fluids of neurotransmitters; when not firing, it expands and reabsorbs them.

Whether a nerve cell fires mainly depends on the quantity and arrangement of neurotransmitters reaching its receptors at any instant. Many factors determine whether a neuron fires. The rate of synthesis and release of a neurotransmitter from the first cell could vary. Increases and decreases in the sensitivity of the receptors on the second cell will influence whether it discharges. Something could diminish the first cell's ability to reabsorb neurotransmitters, thereby increasing their concentration at the second cell's receptors. Drugs also exert effects. In pharmacology, *agonists* are substances that enhance or potentiate the firing of neurons, whereas *antagonists* are drugs that block or reduce the effects of an agonist.

During the past decade many types of receptors have been discovered, including some for benzodiazepines, the group name for diazepam and flurazepam. Since the body does not seem to produce its own benzodiazepines, the natural purpose of these receptors is unknown. Also identified have been receptors for enkephalins, the body's own opiate-like narcotics for mediating the perception of pain. The jogger's "high" may partly reflect a buildup of these enkephalins.

Most receptors are affected by one type (or subtype) of neurotransmitter. Symptoms of mental disorders appear to arise from changes in these receptor-neurotransmitter systems, of which six seem especially influential: dopamine (DA), norepinephrine (NE), serotonin (SE), acetylcholine (AC), histamine (H), and gamma-aminobutyric acid (GABA). Table 4-1 lists the *primary precursors* (i.e., major chemical antecedents) and *primary metabolite* (i.e., major breakdown product). Dopamine and NE are *catecholamines*; SE is an *indoleamine*.

Although a great deal more evidence is needed before it is clear how

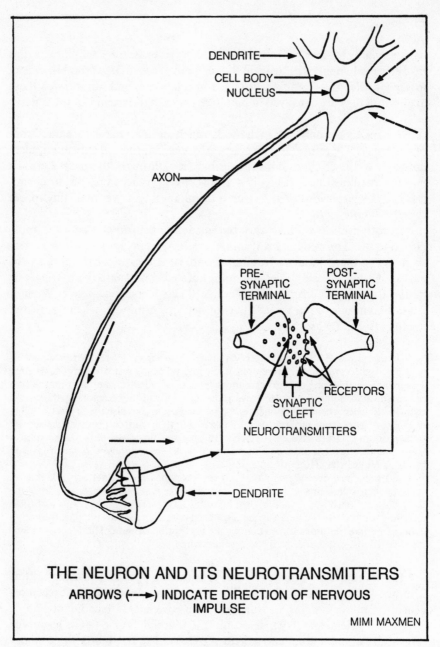

THE NEURON AND ITS NEUROTRANSMITTERS

ARROWS (‹--›) INDICATE DIRECTION OF NERVOUS IMPULSE

MIMI MAXMEN

FIGURE 4-1
The Neuron and Its Neurotransmitters*

*From Maxmen, J. S. (1986b). *The new psychiatry: How modern psychiatrists think about their patients, theories, diagnoses, drugs, psychotherapies, power, training, families, and private lives.* New York: Mentor, p. 141.

TABLE 4-1
Neurotransmitters: Precursors and Metabolites

NEUROTRANSMITTER	PRIMARY PRECURSORS	PRIMARY METABOLITES
Dopamine (DA)	Tyrosine L-Dopa	Homovanillic acid (HVA)
Norepinephrine (NE)	Tyrosine L-Dopa	Methoxyhydroxyphenylglycol (MHPG)
Serotonin (SE) or (5-HT)	Tryptophan	5-Hydroxyindoleacetic acid (5-HIAA)
Acetylcholine (AC)	Choline	No specific metabolite
Histamine (H)	Histidine	No specific metabolite
Gamma-aminobutyric Acid (GABA)	Glutamic acid	Succinic acid

neurotransmitters help to produce mental disorders, some of the more widely touted hypotheses are as follows: Schizophrenia seems to involve excessive activity in the DA-receptor systems. The "catecholamine hypothesis" of depression holds that a functional underactivity of NE causes severe depression, whereas a functional overactivity of NE causes mania. Others contend that depression stems from a high ratio of AC to catecholamine (e.g., DA or NE), whereas mania erupts with the ratio reversed. Sleep and perhaps mood are affected by changes in the SE-receptor system. When stimulated, GABA receptors inhibit neurons and induce calm, and thus anxiety increases when this system becomes less active. Abrupt opiate, and sometimes tobacco, withdrawal apparently accelerates the firing of NE from the *locus coeruleus*— a densely populated area of neurons that produces a majority of the brain's norepinephrine.

PSYCHOENDOCRINOLOGY

Psychoendocrinology is the study of the relationships between the brain, hormones, neurotransmitters, and behavior. Unlike neurotransmitters, which act close to their origin, *hormones* are produced by glands, secreted into the blood stream, and often act far away from their origin. Historically, psychoendocrinology merely focused on hormonal actions outside the brain. Recently, more sophisticated technologies have made it possible to study the *pituitary* as a "window" into the brain, by examining how neurotransmitters, hormones, and the brain interact to produce mental disorders.

The *hypothalamus* is a part of the brain directly above the pituitary gland; considerable psychoendocrine activity transpires on this "hypothalamic-pituitary axis."

For example, the biological or vegetative signs of depression (e.g., disturbances in sleep, appetite, sex) are mediated in the hypothalamus, the chief connecting station where neurotransmitters and hormones affect each other. That's why the vegetative signs of depression are called "hypothalamic signs."

Clearly established is that an underactive thyroid can cause depression and that too many steroids can induce depression or trigger psychosis. Conversely, during major depression, the adrenal gland releases excessive amounts of cortisol. Nonetheless, advances in psychoendocrinology are relatively new, few, and promising. In the near future, for example, psychoendocrinology will surely clarify the many controversies over "premenstrual syndrome."

TECHNOLOGY AND ETIOLOGY

Throughout history, etiological knowledge has only been as advanced as the methods available to study it. For example, psychodynamic etiologies always reflected the patients and the society that were investigated. Freud revealed the pathogenic power of repressed sexuality in a sexually repressive society. Jung's patients were not sexually inhibited, but religiously troubled, and his theories focused on philosophical, cosmic, and religious themes. Adler, not surprisingly, uncovered the inferiority complex when dealing with ambitious, middle-class patients (Wender & Klein, 1981).

More recently, an explosion in biomedical technology has uncovered alterations in the brain's anatomy, chemistry, and physiology that were previously undectable. Introduced in 1973, *computerized tomography* (CT) provides a two-dimensional anatomical image by contrasting the specific gravities of various brain tissue. Even newer is *magnetic resonant imaging* (MR); its images reflect the chemical properties of tissues by measuring the resonances of a certain atom (e.g., phosphorus) within those tissues. At present, because of technical limitations, MR can't measure neurotransmitter and metabolic defects, yet unlike the CT scan, it can distinguish brain tissues with similar densities but different chemistries (e.g., white matter versus gray matter, a tumor versus normal brain tissue, a multiple sclerosis plaque versus white matter). *Positron emission tomography* (PET) can measure the metabolic activity of a compound (e.g., glucose) at various sites in the brain. By labeling a psychotropic drug, such as haloperidol, PET can measure the number and alterations of dopamine receptors.

This "new alphabet technology" is helping to invalidate the traditional Cartesian distinction between *organic* and *functional* disorders. These technologies are demonstrating that many "functional" disorders involve changes in fine neuronal tissues and in cerebral ventricles; altered glucose metabolism and neurochemical changes are coming to light. In short, the organic-functional distinction has little basis in fact; it survives largely as a semantic convenience.

"ENVIRONMENTAL BIOLOGY"

"Environmental biology," the author's neologism, is the study of the two-way relationship between environment and biology in the production of mental disorders. Three of these relationships deserve comment: (a) biological trauma from the environment, (b) psychosocial trauma inducing biological changes, and (c) genotypes and phenotypes.

Biological Trauma From the Environment

Environmental stress and psychosocial stress are *not* synonymous, since the environment can also generate biological stress. During pregnancy, if not afterward, viruses, drugs, malnourishment, physical abuse, or premature birth could produce a mental disorder in the child or, at least, predispose him to one. In comparison to normals, schizophrenics have a higher rate of birth complications, and some evidence points to a ("slow") virus as the culprit in a few of these cases.

Light, natural and artificial, appears to be another biological (or physical) force that contributes to mental disorders. Some patients with affective disorders, especially manic-depression, become depressed every fall and winter and recover every spring and summer. These patients' depressions improve with a prolonged exposure to bright artificial light. The antidepressant effect of light is given further credence by the finding that people are more likely to have depressions the farther they live from the equator (Rosenthal et al., 1984).

Psychosocial Trauma Inducing Biological Changes

Biological changes do not necessarily have biological origins; they may be produced psychosocially. Kandel (1983), for instance, has demonstrated how psychosocial stress can alter the brain's anatomy and biochemistry to produce anxiety. He uses the marine snail *Aplysia*, because it has a relatively simple nervous system with large and easy-to-visualize brain cells.[3] By conditioning the *Aplysia*, and then by photographing its neurons, Kandel can observe the actual anatomical changes in a brain cell caused by a specific psychosocial environment.

The brain does not mature independently of the environment, and once developed it is still influenced by the environment. Being continually unable

---

[3]The *Aplysia* weighs up to 4 pounds, consists of only 20,000 cells, and has the largest neurons in the animal kingdom — up to 1 mm in diameter. Whereas a simple human behavior typically involves hundreds of thousands of brain cells, simple behaviors of an *Aplysia* involve less than 50.

to cope—so-called "learned helplessness"—can induce biological changes in depression. As another example, patients with Parkinson's disease can hardly walk, but if they are in a movie theater that catches on fire, they will race to the exit. The *do* have brain disease, yet how their diseased brains function depends on the environment.

Genotype and Phenotype

Having a gene and having it produce visible effects are two different things. The gene itself is a *genotype*; whether the gene is expressed—that is, if it becomes manifest—is a *phenotype*. If there is a gene (or genotype) for an ulcer, whether it develops into an ulcer (the phenotype) depends on environmental factors, such as diet, stress, and smoking. Therefore, to ask whether a mental disorder is caused by genes *or* environment is naive. When a person inherits the genotype for a mental disorder, how the environment affects that gene determines the degree, form, and existence of that disorder.

Genetic theory does not mean behavioral predestination. If a person inherits the genotype for a mental disorder, biological and psychosocial interventions can still alleviate or prevent the disorder.

THE GENETICS OF MENTAL DISORDERS

Genetic factors are prerequisites for most, but certainly not all, cases of schizophrenia, manic-depression, and somewhat less, for major depression. Heredity partly contributes to panic and obsessive-compulsive disorders, but does not seem to produce generalized anxiety disorders. These conclusions mainly derive from researching twins and adoptees.

Twin Studies

By comparing identical or *monozygotic* (MZ) twins with fraternal or *dizygotic* (DZ) twins, investigators can assess the relative contributions of nature and nurture in causing a mental disorder. Identical (MZ) twins have identical genes; the genes of fraternal (DZ) twins are like those of any other pair of siblings. A *concordance rate* is the percent of twins who both exhibit the same phenotype. Because MZ and DZ twins usually share the same environment, the difference in concordance rates between MZ and DZ twins largely reflects genetic influences.

For example, on average the concordance rate for schizophrenia among MZ twins is 45%; this means that when one twin of a MZ pair has schizophrenia, 45% of the time both members do. In contrast, DZ twin-pairs have a concordance rate of 10% for schizophrenia (Weiner, 1985). (If one sibling is schizophrenic, each of his siblings has a 10% chance of becoming schizophrenic.) The statistically significant difference between 45% and 10% would indicate that genes transmit schizophrenia. At the same time, these figures also demonstrate an important role for nongenetic factors. If genes alone were involved, one might expect that if one member of a MZ pair were schizophrenic, then his twin *must* also be schizophrenic. In other words, the MZ concordance rate would be 100%. But it's not; it's only 45%.

Geneticists attribute this 55% difference to *penetrance*, a term used to account for why the genotype does not become the phenotype 100% of the time. Penetrance may occur because the abnormal genes were "too weak," or they were interfered with by other genes; spontaneous genetic mutations, viral infections, and *in utero* difficulties may also explain penetrance.

A potential limitation of twin studies might be that, if identical twins were treated differently from fraternal twins, this might alter their concordance rates. However, two findings do not support this contention. First, MZ twins who are physically dissimilar have the same concordance rates as those who look the same. Second, identical twins who grew up with everybody, themselves included, assuming they were fraternal twins end up with concordance rates of identical twins.

Adoption Studies

To further clarify the nature/nurture question, various methods of the adoption approach have been conducted. The first major adoption studies of mental disorders occurred in 1963. They were conducted in Denmark, because the government had a register of every adoption, including those infants who were separated when they were less than three months old from their biological parents and then legally adopted.

As illustrated in Figure 4-2A, one method of using these records is to compare the biological and adoptive parents of adult schizophrenic adoptees. Because biological parents gave the child away so early in life, their psychosocial influence on the schizophrenic adoptee was probably nil; only genetic influences would persist. Therefore, if schizophrenia were genetically transmitted, the biological parents should have a much higher incidence of schizophrenia than the adoptive parents. On the other hand, if schizophrenia is produced psychosocially, just the opposite should occur. The results were striking: Repeatedly, the schizophrenic adoptee's biological parents were schizophrenic, whereas the adoptive parents were "normal."

In another adoption strategy (Figure 4-2B), children of schizophrenic biological parents were reared by adoptive parents and contrasted to a matched control group of adoptees whose biological parents had no family history of

FIGURES 4-2A AND 2B
Adoption Strategies

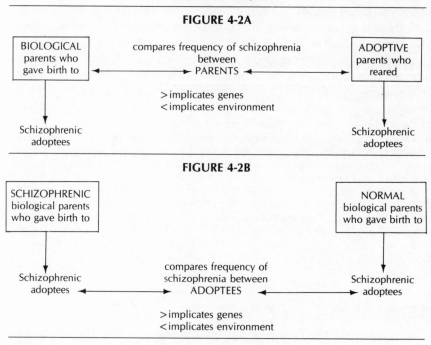

FIGURE 4-2A

BIOLOGICAL parents who gave birth to

compares frequency of schizophrenia between
PARENTS

ADOPTIVE parents who reared

>implicates genes
<implicates environment

Schizophrenic adoptees

Schizophrenic adoptees

FIGURE 4-2B

SCHIZOPHRENIC biological parents who gave birth to

NORMAL biological parents who gave birth to

Schizophrenic adoptees

compares frequency of schizophrenia between
ADOPTEES

Schizophrenic adoptees

>implicates genes
<implicates environment

mental disorders. Once again, genetic interpretations prevailed, since schizophrenia-like disorders were far more common among the offspring of the biologically ill than among those of "normal" parents. These and similar findings provide overwhelming evidence that in most cases genes are a principal source of schizophrenia.

Subsequent research suggested that what is genetically transmitted may not be a single gene for schizophrenia, but a gene for "schizophrenic-spectrum disorders." Beside schizophrenia, this spectrum includes several disorders which are like, but not identical to, schizophrenia, such as the schizotypal personality disorder. The concept of *genetic spectrum disorders* may apply to other syndromes. For example, evidence indicates there may be a gene for "depressive-spectrum disorders," which may include major depression, manic-depression, alcoholism, drug abuse, panic disorder, phobia, and antisocial personality disorder.

Finally, even when genes are implicated, this concept of spectrum disorders underscores the need to specify *what* is being inherited. Is it a predisposition to one disorder or to a series of disorders? Is it a particular trait, such as shyness or the inability to synthesize information? Or is it a vulnerability to certain psychosocial stressors, such as a chaotic family life, loss, or intense emotions? Some of these answers may involve psychosocial influences.

PSYCHOSOCIAL THEORIES

Numerous psychological and social factors influence the course of a mental disorder, and the many ways they do so can be divided into seven general models:[4]

1. *Developmental models.* Three developmental models are of particular etiological significance: Freud's *psychosexual*, Erikson's *psychosocial*, and Bowlby's *attachment* models. Each model presents a series of overlapping stages (or "passages") and claims that an "arrest" or "crisis"[5] at a stage may induce psychopathology associated with that stage. Tables 4-2A and 2B outline the psychosexual and psychosocial models of development, respectively.

Bowlby considered *attachment* behaviors the observable actions of a child that facilitate closeness to the primary caregiver, usually the biologic mother. In theory this attachment behavior serves the evolutionary purpose of protecting the child from predators. *Bonding* refers to the mother's relationship to the child. Disturbances in attachment and bonding may produce insecurity, anxiety, dysthymia, distrust, fear of loneliness, etc. A significant loss during childhood, usually of a parent, may be of special etiological significance, especially in depression.

Development does not stop with adolescence; it continues through life. The patient's presenting problems may result not only from an immediate precipitant, but also from a phase-of-life, or developmental, crisis. A 40-year-old may be fired and develop acute overwhelming anxiety. Losing his job is clearly the prime precipitant, yet why he was fired and why he is *that* devastated may be secondary to a "mid-life crisis."

2. *Defense mechanisms.* Sometimes called "coping mechanisms," defense mechanisms are relatively involuntary patterned feelings, thoughts, or behaviors that arise in response to an internal or external perceived psychic danger

---

[4]Some important models are not mentioned here, partly because their direct application to diagnostic psychopathology has (as yet) been limited. These include (a) the *existential* model, which focuses on the purpose and meaning of life; (b) the *humanistic* model, which concentrates on fulfilling or actualizing one's potential, and Piaget's *cognitive* model, which portrays the stages of development of a child's thought processes.

[5]A developmental *crisis* is not a catastrophe or an emergency; it is the normal developmental challenge posed by each psychosocial stage, which becomes a "necessary turning point, a crucial moment, when development must move one way or another, marshaling resources of growth, recovery, and further differentiation" (Erikson, 1968, p. 16).

TABLE 4-2A
Freudian Psychosexual Development*

| AGE (YEARS) | STAGE | RESOLUTION | |
		SUCCESSFUL	PATHOLOGICAL
0–1½	ORAL Primary gratification from mouth, lips, and tongue.	Self-reliance; self-trust; trust in others; capacity to give and receive without dependence and envy.	Needy; demanding; dependent on others for self-esteem; pathological optimism or pessimism; jealousy; [narcissistic].
1½–3	ANAL Primary gratification from sphincter control; aggressive, sadistic, and libidinal impulses.	Autonomy; independence; capacity to cooperate.	Excessive orderliness, stubbornness, and willfulness; miserly; heightened ambivalence; obsessive-compulsiveness; [immature].
3–6	PHALLIC Primary gratification from genital area; oedipal issues.	Basis for sexual identity; drives constructively redirected; superego established.	Castration fear in boys, penis envy in girls; failure to identify with same-sexed parent; neurotic disorders; [neurotic].
6–12	LATENCY Relative quiescent sexual drives.	Integration and consolidation of prior psychosexual gains; basis for love, work, and play.	Lack or excessive inner controls; poor sublimation; precociousness; premature closure of personality; [neurotic].
12–18	GENITAL Reawakening of libidinal drives; sexual maturation.	Full and satisfying genital potency; consolidation of prior accomplishments; [mature].	Any of the above problems; impaired ability to love and work; neurotic disorders; [neurotic].

*General class of defense mechanisms, as categorized by Vaillant (1971) shown in brackets. (See specific defenses on Table 4-3.)

in order to reduce or avoid conscious or unconscious stress, anxiety, or conflict. Whether a defense mechanism is adaptive depends on the defense and the circumstance. Projection is almost never adaptive, whereas sublimation is always adaptive; denial is usually maladaptive, but when the person is dealing with an overwhelming, acute stress, denial may help to maintain psychic equilibrium. Table 4-3 describes the major defense mechanisms.

3. *Intrapsychic conflict.* Freud divided the *topography* of the mind into three levels: the *unconscious*, whose mental content is rarely in awareness;

TABLE 4-2B
Eriksonian Psychosocial Development

AGE (YEARS)	PERIOD	TASKS	VALUES
0–1	Infancy	Trust vs. mistrust	Hope
1–3	Toddler	Autonomy vs. shame and doubt	Will
3–6	Preschool	Initiative vs. guilt	Purpose
6–12	School-age	Industry vs. inferiority	Skill/competence
12–20	Adolescence	Identity vs. identity diffusion/confusion	Fidelity
20–30	Young adulthood	Intimacy vs. isolation	Love
30–65	Adulthood	Generativity vs. stagnation	Care
65+	Late adulthood	Integrity vs. despair/disgust	Wisdom

the *preconscious*, whose mental content is not immediately in awareness, but can be readily recalled by conscious effort; and the *conscious*, whose mental content is in awareness. Freud also identified three psychic *structures*: the *id*, which harbors instinctual sexual and aggressive drives; the *superego* or conscience; and the *ego*, which mediates between these psychic structures, and between the person's inner needs and the environment. Defense mechanisms are ego functions. Intrapsychic conflict involves struggles between these various levels and structures of the mind.

4. *Stress*. The body's response to any demand on it for adaptation is called *stress*, and the demand, a *stressor*. By itself, stress is neither good nor bad: Without stress, people stagnate, they atrophy; with too much stress, people become overwhelmed. The stressor may be acute or chronic. When it's acute and severe, people react in a series of steps as sketched on Figure 4-3 (and detailed on Figure 12-1); these reactions may be normal or pathological, but even when normal, they may temporarily impair functioning. One need only recall the assassination of John Kennedy to remember how most people immediately reacted with either "outcry" or "denial." Chronic stressors, such as a failing marriage, may be less severe at any one moment, but eventually "wear a person down" and lead to a deteriorating mental state.

5. *Behavioral*. Traditionally, the behavioral (or "learning") model focused exclusively on how identifiable environmental forces influenced the produc-

TABLE 4-3
Defense Mechanisms*

Acting-out is the direct expression of impulses without any apparent reflection, guilt, or regard for negative consequences. (Whereas "acting-*up*" is a lay term for any misbehavior, acting-*out* is a misbehavior that is a response to, and a way of coping with, stress or conflict.) After breaking up with his girlfriend, a teenager acts-out by impulsively overdosing. [Immature]

Altruism is when the person dedicates himself to the needs of others, partly to fulfill his own needs. [Mature]

Denial is the lack of awareness of *external* realities that would be too painful to acknowledge. It differs from repression (see below), which is a "denial" of *internal* reality. Denial operates when a woman says, "I'm sure this lump on my breast doesn't mean anything." Denial may be temporarily adaptive. [Narcissistic]

Devaluation is when the person demeans another or oneself by the attribution of exaggerated negative qualities to them. By constantly ridiculing his competence, a patient devalues a therapist to avoid facing her sexual feelings toward him. [Immature]

Displacement is the discharge of pent-up emotions, usually anger, onto objects, animals, or people perceived as less dangerous than those which originally induced the emotions. Kicking the dog. [Neurotic]

Fantasy is the excessive retreat into daydreams and imagination to escape realistic problems or to avoid conflicts. Also called "autistic fantasy" or "schizoid fantasy." [Immature]

Humor is when the person uses irony or humor to reduce what otherwise might be unbearable tension or fear. Hawkeye Pierce in "M*A*S*H". [Mature]

Idealization is when the person unduly praises another or oneself by exaggerating virtues. "Better" to idealize a spouse than to see the jerk for what he is and be a very lonely divorcée. [!mmature]

Identification is the unconscious modeling of another's attributes. It differs from role modeling or imitation, which are conscious processes. Identification is used to increase one's sense of self-worth, to cope with (possible) separation or loss, or to minimize helplessness, as with "identification with the aggressor," as seen in concentration-camp prisoners who assumed the mannerisms of their Nazi guards. [Immature]

Intellectualization is the overuse of abstract thinking, which unlike rationalization (see below), is only self-serving in aiming to reduce psychic discomfort. Alcoholics use intellectualization when they quibble over the definition of alcoholism as a way of avoiding their drinking. [Neurotic]

TABLE 4-3
(*Continued*)

Introjection is the incorporation of other people's values, standards, or traits to prevent conflicts with, or threats from, these people. Introjection may also serve to retain a lost loved one, as when people adopted John Kennedy's accent after his death. [Immature]

Isolation of affect is the compartmentalization of painful emotions from their events. It involves the experience or recollection of an emotionally traumatic situation, without the anxiety customarily or originally associated with it. A soldier may kill without experiencing—that is, by isolating—the terror or guilt he would otherwise feel. [Neurotic]

Projection is the unconscious rejection of unacceptable thoughts, traits, or wishes by ascribing them to others. [Narcissistic when delusional; immature otherwise]

Rationalization is the self-serving use of plausible reasons to justify actions caused by repressed, unacceptable emotions or ideas. Psychotherapist: "I charge a lot so therapy will be meaningful to the patient." [Neurotic]

Reaction formation is preventing the expression or the experience of unacceptable desires, by developing or exaggerating opposite attitudes and behaviors. "The lady doth protest too much." [Neurotic]

Regression is retreat under stress to earlier or more immature patterns of behavior and gratification. On hearing terrible news, an adult begins sucking his thumb. [Immature]

Repression is the exclusion from awareness of distressing internal feelings, impulses, ideas, or wishes. Repression is unconscious, suppression (see below) is conscious. A man is unaware that he resents his more successful wife. [Neurotic]

Somatization is reacting to psychologically stressful situations by an excessive preoccupation with physical symptoms. [Immature]

Splitting is when the person views himself or others as all good or all bad, as opposed to being a balance of positive and negative attributes. In splitting, the person frequently alternates between idealization and devaluation. [Immature]

Sublimation is the gratification of a repressed instinct or unacceptable feeling by socially acceptable means. Better a surgeon than a sadist. [Mature]

Suppression is the conscious and deliberate avoidance of disturbing matters: Scarlett O'Hara: "I'll think about it tomorrow." [Mature]

(continued)

TABLE 4-3
(*Continued*)

Turning against the self is when the person takes a hostile thought or impulse aimed at another and inappropriately redirects it onto himself. He experiences less distress by blaming, hurting, or even mutilating himself, than by feeling guilty for being furious at the other person. [Immature]

Undoing is behavior or thoughts designed to cancel a previous act or thought associated with a painful idea, event, or emotion. A person prays to ward off distressing sexual thoughts, or crosses his fingers when telling a lie. [Narcissistic when delusional; otherwise neurotic or mature depending on circumstances]

*As indicated in brackets, defense mechanisms reflect various levels of psychological organization, which Vaillant (1971) has categorized from the least to the most mature: narcissistic, immature, neurotic, mature.

tion of observable behaviors. This model has expanded to include "inner behaviors," which were environmentally-induced, yet nonobservable, such as thoughts and feelings. Unlike before, behaviorists are recognizing the unconscious and integrating psychodynamic with behavioral principles. Even still, behaviorism focuses on how the environment creates, shapes, or alters the frequency of a behavior. The formulation should indicate whether the pa-

FIGURE 4-3
Responses to Acute, Severe Stressors*

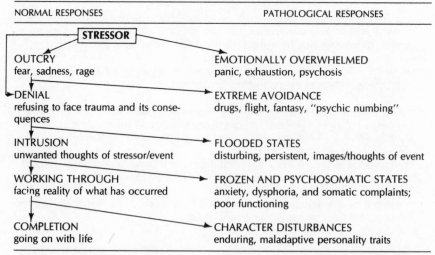

NORMAL RESPONSES	PATHOLOGICAL RESPONSES
STRESSOR	
OUTCRY fear, sadness, rage	EMOTIONALLY OVERWHELMED panic, exhaustion, psychosis
DENIAL refusing to face trauma and its consequences	EXTREME AVOIDANCE drugs, flight, fantasy, "psychic numbing"
INTRUSION unwanted thoughts of stressor/event	FLOODED STATES disturbing, persistent, images/thoughts of event
WORKING THROUGH facing reality of what has occurred	FROZEN AND PSYCHOSOMATIC STATES anxiety, dysphoria, and somatic complaints; poor functioning
COMPLETION going on with life	CHARACTER DISTURBANCES enduring, maladaptive personality traits

*Modified from: Horowitz, M. J. (1985). Disasters and psychological responses to stress. *Psychiatric Annals*, *15*, 161–167. (Figure 12-1 provides more details of the normal and pathological responses to trauma.)

tient's difficulties are being encouraged — that is, *positively reinforced* — by the environment.

6. *Family systems*. In this model, the family is viewed as a *system*, which is a complex of interacting elements. Systems theory holds that one cannot fully understand a system (e.g., organization, family, person) by only examining its parts. What happens in one part of a system eventually reverberates and affects the others; no man is an island. In the family systems model, the patient's behavior is viewed less as the product of a mental disorder and more the result of intrafamilial disturbances. This does not necessarily deny the existence of mental illness, but that how it is maintained, exacerbated, and perhaps initiated depends on a confluence of forces within the family.

7. *Sociocultural*. The pathogenic role of social, cultural, political, economic, religious, racial, and sexual aspects are often given short shrift; that's partly because ideology tends to overwhelm the few facts that exist. Sociologists examine these matters, but usually lack training in psychopathology to place them in context, whereas mental health professionals usually lack sociological sophistication. Therefore, clinicians should be especially careful when attributing mental pathology to social "pathology." On the other hand, when social factors are culpable, their influence (for good or ill) should be recorded in the patient's biopsychosocial formulation.

CHAPTER 5

Treatment

THE MOST IMPORTANT factor in deciding treatment is the patient's diagnosis. Other factors—psychological, medical, sociocultural, ethical, intellectual, financial—influence the choice and conduct of treatment, but, except for emergency interventions, no treatment should begin without a diagnosis. Conversely, although diagnosis may serve other ends, its chief purpose is to help in determining treatment. Therefore, when clinicians debate a patient's diagnosis, it is important to know how a change in diagnosis will alter the patient's treatment.

WHAT DO TREATMENT
PLANS INCLUDE?

Every patient should have a *treatment plan*—that is, an organized program of one or more treatments for helping the patient achieve specified objectives. The clinician should indicate the type, amount, focus, goals, and timing of each treatment.

1. The *type*(s) may be group therapy, psychoanalysis, recreational therapy, lithium, "suicide precautions," "seclusion room," "school consultation," and so on.

2. The *amount* of treatment refers to its frequency and duration. Will psychotherapy be once or thrice a week? Will it be for six weeks or six months? The dose, frequency, and duration of medication should be indicated.

3. The *focus* refers to the specific problem(s) that treatment will address. Treatment does not, and cannot, concentrate on everything; choices and priorities must be set. Is it better to focus on a patient's alcoholism or his

depression? Should the etiologic focus be on childhood trauma, ongoing familial problems, or precipitating stressors?

4. The *goals* (or objectives) of each treatment should be specified; otherwise, clinicians and patients cannot know where treatment is going, when it should end, and whether it has succeeded. A goal of "helping the patient function better" is too vague, because it does not indicate the areas in which the patient should function better. It borders on poverty of content to say chlorpromazine is for "treating the patient's schizophrenia." Is the goal to eliminate hallucinations or to stop him from talking about his hallucinations? Is it to stop his delusions, diminish his agitation, increase his social interactions, leave the hospital, or function at work? No drug should be prescribed without first specifying its target symptoms and functions.

At times, the objectives are clear, but unrealistic: "To help the patient like her (thoroughly obnoxious) mother." In establishing goals, two generalizations should apply: (a) The briefer the treatment, the less ambitious the goals. (b) The more recent the problem, the fuller and faster it will improve with treatment.

Outlining the goals *on paper* heightens the clinician's awareness of them; if he can't write them, he can't know them. Discussing these goals with the patient before treatment starts helps the patient make a more informed judgment about entering treatment and reduces his unrealistic expectations of it. (Overexpectations of therapy may be the greatest cause of malpractice suits.) When patient and therapist explicitly agree on the goals of treatment, they are more likely to be on the same wavelength during therapy. Clearly delineating goals also minimizes inpatient staff's working at cross-purposes, as when an individual therapist tells a teenager "to liberate himself from parental domination," while the family therapist tells his parents "to set limits on their kid."

5. The *timing* of therapies—that is, when, and in what sequence—generally follows these guidelines: Treatment should rectify biological changes before psychosocial influences, symptoms before issues, acute crises before chronic problems, and psychosis before neurosis; psychotic patients should receive supportive psychotherapy; only later, when nonpsychotic, can they benefit from insight-oriented psychotherapy.

Treatments cannot happen all at once, nor should they. For instance, patients with major depression view all information in the worst possible light; they use insights not for self-improvement, but for self-punishment. During insight-oriented psychotherapy, a very proper 55-year-old woman recalled a long-forgotten affair from 30 years earlier. But instead of using this insight to unburden herself of a long-repressed guilt (as would "normal" people), she berated herself: "This proves I'm a whore and deserve to die." Like most severely depressed patients, she could benefit from insight only *after* antidepressant medications alleviated her symptoms.

THREE LEVELS OF TREATMENT

Psychiatric treatment occurs in three stages: biological, psychosocial, and moral-existential. First, if needed, the psychiatrist prescribes medication to rectify *biological* abnormalities. Second, the therapist performs psychotherapies to address *psychosocial* problems. Third, he uses the clinician-patient relationship to demonstrate that he values the patient as a person, the *moral-existential* dimension of therapy (Abroms, 1983).

This three-stage model holds that biological and psychosocial treatments are both valuable, albeit in *different* ways. To argue that talk therapy is better than drug therapy (or vice versa) is pointless; they serve different functions. Group therapy frequently helps diabetics cope with their illness, yet nobody would suggest that groups regulate blood sugar; conversely, insulin regulates blood sugar, yet nobody would suggest it helps diabetics cope with their illness. Just as group therapy and insulin help patients with diabetes in different ways, so do psychotherapies and biotherapies help patients with mental disorders. Excellent therapists can have very different interests (e.g., psychoanalysis, medications), but still appreciate that each treatment serves a distinct purpose.

In general, biological therapies eliminate or alleviate *symptoms*, such as a depressive's insomnia, a schizophrenic's delusions, or a manic's spending sprees; psychosocial therapies usually address *issues*, such as coping with job losses, a failed marriage, or an illness — physical or mental.

When used properly, biological and psychosocial therapies do not inhibit, but facilitate, one another. Repeated evidence shows that medications do not increase a patient's passivity, decrease his motivation, or diminish his involvement in psychotherapy. Correctly medicated patients gain more from psychotherapy. Wildly hallucinating schizophrenics feel so bombarded by stimuli that they cannot focus sufficiently to benefit from psychotherapy; once medicated, they can.

Conversely, psychotherapies can accomplish what drugs cannot. They can teach patients about their mental disorders — their symptoms, dangers, causes, and precipitants. Talk therapies can alert patients to situations which are likely to retrigger an episode. Psychotherapies can help patients to understand what their condition means and symbolizes to them. Psychotherapies can improve a patient's willingness to adhere to a therapist's treatment plan (e.g., taking medication); they can facilitate social adjustment, interpersonal relationships, leisure-time activities, and occupational skills. They can heighten self-esteem, guide ambition, and enhance well-being. They can reveal how previous experiences affect current difficulties. When a patient cannot figure out why terrible things keep happening to him — why people are rude to him, why women avoid him, why nobody will hire him — only psychotherapy can show him why these events happen, what he can do about them, and how to regain control over his life.

The moral-existential dimension of therapy does not involve particular treatments or occur during specified periods. Instead, it prevails throughout therapy, pervading both biological and psychosocial treatments. To quote Abroms (1983), moral-existential interventions involve the "realm of pure value, where the ultimate aim is integrity of the person. . . . [They entail] moral qualities of trust and gratitude, of loyalty and devotion, and above all, of respect . . . the therapist becomes firm in the resolve to stand by the patient, even to tolerate a measure of moral failure."

GENERAL GUIDELINES FOR SELECTING TREATMENT

Treatment selection should be based primarily on pragmatic, rather than on etiologic, considerations. Some of the major difficulties of linking treatment with an etiological theory are as follows: (a) The cause of most mental disorders is unknown. (b) The treatment must then be consistent with the theory, which may determine what can and cannot be treated. For example, Freud's early feelings about schizophrenia excluded this disorder from psychoanalytic therapy. (c) A total commitment to any single etiological theory and its accompanying treatments limits the therapist's range of interventions. (d) The goals of therapy often become the fulfillment of a theory rather than what the patient needs or desires. (e) Even if a disorder's etiology is known, therapies addressing it are unlikely to rectify the patient's current disorder. For example, a man who is chronically depressed because he was deprived (or depraved) as a child might find that further insight into his childhood cannot alter the many self-destructive patterns that he has developed over the years.

When theory prevails over pragmatism, therapists will insist that a patient who feels and functions substantially better has not "really" improved, because he has not accepted the oedipal origins of his problem, and that as long as he continues to "resist," he shall never improve. In other words, the patient can't get better unless he buys his therapist's theory.

To serve up pragmatically-based treatments, one should follow (Bill) *Tilden's Law*: "Never change a winning game." If a treatment works, don't change it; if a treatment doesn't work, do change it. Tilden's Law does not mean that clinicians should alter treatments every time the patient has a setback, but it does mean that if a patient fails to improve following an ample trial with a particular treatment, another treatment should be tried. For example, even if a patient "should" respond to antidepressant medications, if he doesn't, he doesn't, and a different treatment should be attempted. Or, if a patient has failed to improve after three trials of insight-oriented psycho-therapy with three different therapists, chances are that a fourth trial of in-sight-oriented therapy won't help; however, another treatment, such as be-havior, cognitive, or drug therapy, might help.

When pragmatically-chosen treatments are based on scientific evidence, instead of on intuition or theory, they have the greatest chance of being ef-fective. For instance, studies show that if a patient's biological relative has improved with a particular drug, so will the patient. "Scientific," however, is not synonymous with "biological"; although medications are more amenable to scientific investigation, over 400 well-controlled, quantified studies have evaluated psychotherapy.

Scientific studies of social relations can also guide the treatment of patients. For example, before discharging an inpatient, staff must decide how much the patient should change his life during the immediate posthospital stage; one investigation in-dicates the answer is "very little." It revealed that discharged psychotic patients go through two stages: First, there is a period of *convalescence*, in which they mainly see themselves as "ex-patients" and maintain contacts with hospital staff and former patients. During the second stage of *rebuilding*, these patients view themselves more as members of society and less as "ex-patients"; key relationships are with people in the community instead of with former hospital associations. In general, patients fare much better when therapy fosters stability during the convalescence stage and does not encourage the patient to make changes until he enters the rebuilding stage (Breier & Strauss, 1984).

Most acutely *psychotic* patients benefit more from psychotherapeutic con-tacts that are relatively simple, clear, and brief. They are frequently over-whelmed by external stimuli, have troubles distinguishing reality from fantasy, often confuse their outer with their inner world, and have short attention spans. Thus, insight-oriented therapies rarely help, and frequently harm, the acutely psychotic; reality testing is more beneficial. If a patient says, "I'm the worst sinner on earth," the therapist empathizes with the patient's emotional state, but still tests (or clarifies) reality, "I understand how miserable you feel, but I don't think you're a sinner." Sessions should be shorter and more fre-quent: An extremely psychotic patient with a short attention span may profit more from five, 10-minute contacts a day, than from a once-a-day, 50-minute hour.

Acutely ill patients should also be discouraged from making any important life decisions, especially if irreversible. This does not mean that therapists should run their lives, nor does it imply that *all* patients in therapy should place major decisions on hold. Therapists should only step in when a patient's judgment is severely impaired by a mental disorder.

Every axis in *DSM-III* highlights a key issue for planning treatment. In setting treatment goals, clinicians distinguish between Axes I and II, since diagnoses on Axis I usually respond more readily to treatment than those on Axis II. These plans address the stressors in Axis IV and use the highest level of functioning on Axis V for determining treatment goals.

Axis III disorders should not be overlooked, especially by nonpsychiatrists: Depending on the study, physical problems are the *chief* cause of psychiatric symptoms among 9% to 18% of psychiatric outpatients and among 5% to 28% of psychiatric inpatients; an additional 25% of patients have medical problems which *aggravate* their psychiatric problem; as many as 42% of psychiatric outpatients and over 50% of psychiatric inpatients are physically ill. In comparison to the general public, not only are psychiatric patients afflicted by more medical problems, but more of these problems go undiagnosed, and for many reasons: Psychiatric patients give poorer medical histories, have more trouble using medical services, and if they look sloppy or crazy, physicians are less likely to examine them closely. What's more, when it comes to psychiatric patients, mental and medical health professionals tend to ignore physical problems (Hoffman & Koran, 1984).

PSYCHOLOGICAL CLUES

During assessment, clinicians should sprout antennae especially for seven psychological clues that facilitate planning both biological and psychosocial treatments.

1. *Locus of responsibility*: Patients who always view others as responsible for their difficulties — so-called "externalizers" — do poorly in psychotherapy and are less cooperative in taking medication. Patients can change themselves much more readily than they can change others.

2. *Habitual view of "helping" figures*: How patients feel about other "helping" figures — doctors, nurses, teachers, parents — may predict how they will behave toward the therapist. Some patients are highly suspicious of helping figures. The paranoid wonders, "What's the *real* reason this therapist claims he wants to help me?" With suspicious patients, therapists should keep a safe psychological distance to prevent what the patient might experience as phony intimacy; these patients are also allergic to interpretations that are too frequent or too probing, viewing them as too intrusive and the therapist as a "mind-fucker." On the other hand, for patients who view helping figures as omnipotent, unending sources of gratification and dependency, therapists should avoid becoming swamped by their needs by limiting phone calls and by not scheduling too many sessions at the outset of treatment. (Sessions can always be added.)

3. *Defense mechanisms and coping patterns*: Patients who rely on more immature defenses, such as projection and massive denial, are more likely to not benefit from, and to be harmed by insight-oriented psychotherapy. Because past behavior is often the best predictor of future behavior, the

therapist should ask, when the patient has previously faced a major problem, has he avoided it, denied it, overcompensated for it (i.e., reaction formation), or intellectualized it away? These responses often predict "flights into health," in which, after several sessions, the patient dramatically improves and wants to stop therapy; yet his first blush of relief, quickly pales as he discovers his old problems remain.

4. *Patient expectations of treatment*: Although knowing what patients expect of therapy affects treatment planning, there is surprisingly little evidence confirming the popular assumption that therapy's outcome is directly related to these initial expectations (Bloch et al., 1976; Wilkins, 1973a, 1973b). Thus, just because a patient anticipates a treatment won't work, that doesn't automatically mean it will fail. (Of course, negative expectations are no guarantee of success!)

If the patient or the therapist is unsure if psychotherapy holds promise, the clinician may recommend an initial *trial period* of (roughly) six, once-a-week sessions. Each party can see if the particular approach and the "chemistry" between them are likely to be therapeutic. A formal trial period allows both participants to begin therapy without feeling committed to "years" of treatment. As long as the therapist does not make the patient feel he is "on trial," a trial period allows each person a graceful way to terminate treatment.

5. *Follow the affect*: By noting what is being discussed *when* the patient's affect abruptly changes, the therapist can discern, from among many issues, the ones of prime import to the patient. For instance, a man claims he's gotten over a divorce yet breaks down and weeps on mentioning his former wife. Usually nonverbal, these telltale affective switches may be subtle—a tear is shed, a cigarette lit, a leg moved, a body tensed. Therapists may gain considerable information by pursuing any topic that suddenly triggers an intense affect.

6. *Follow the associations*: When patients jump to an apparently unrelated topic, or when they keep returning to the same topic, that topic deserves attention. To illustrate: While continually harping about his daughter's not applying to medical school, a 72-year-old man kept raising the topic of his own retirement. Initially, although the connection between these two concerns was unclear, exploring the association revealed that the man's rage at his daughter for "giving up" arose from his own fear that by retiring he too was "giving up."

7. *The therapist as "emotional barometer"*: How a therapist feels toward a patient is often, but not always, a good guide as to how most people feel about the patient. If a therapist is constantly irritated by a patient, even if the therapist doesn't know precisely how or why, the patient is probably irritating. (If the therapist is irritated by *all* his patients, then the problem lies

with the therapist, not the patient.) The therapist's reactions to a patient are not irrelevant feelings, but germane clinical data. For instance, when a paranoid patient emotionally attacks a therapist, the paranoid may be unconsciously conveying to the therapist how he always feels under attack in the "real" world.

"ALL THAT'S THERAPY ISN'T THERAPEUTIC"

This dictum of Thomas Detre's receives too little attention. All treatments have "side effects," and that includes psychosocial treatments. Abraham Kardiner (1977, p. 69) wrote, "Freud was always infuriated whenever I would say to him that you could not do harm with psychoanalysis. He said, 'When you say that, you also say that it cannot do any good. Because if you cannot do any harm, how can you do good?'" Clinical experience confirms Freud's observation: An upsurge of repressed thoughts or primitive feelings can exacerbate psychotic, neurotic, and affective symptoms. Patients may become overly dependent on a therapist or become "addicted" to therapy; they may substitute therapists for friends, therapy for living. For some patients, "insight" becomes an excuse to avoid change, while others use "insight" for punishment not learning. Thus, in devising treatment plans, clinicians should weigh a therapy's potential hazards and benefits, and for some patients conclude that "no treatment" is the prescription of choice.

Sometimes no treatment is the best treatment, not because therapy would harm, but because it would most likely fail. Therapy does not help most patients with "psychosomatic" problems and personality disorders, especially antisocial personality disorder. The same often applies to the "unmotivated,"[1] and to those seeking compensation, disability, or a lawsuit. Some people, like those seen initially during bereavement or an acute crisis, will improve without therapy. Thus, don't assume that every patient needs, or benefits from, treatment, and don't forget that a failed treatment hurts more than no treatment.

A SUMMARY OF
PSYCHIATRIC TREATMENTS

Despite the ever-increasing number of therapies—over 250 by one recent count—in reality, the commonly used treatments of any enduring importance have not changed very much over the years. These treatments are listed in Table 5-1, and briefly described below.

---

[1]Clinicians should think twice when claiming a treatment failed because the patient was "unmotivated." The patient may be unmotivated, but it is the therapist's job to motivate him!

TABLE 5-1
Modern Psychiatric Treatments

I. BIOLOGICAL THERAPIES

A. Medication
   1. Antipsychotics (e.g., chlorpromazine, haloperidol)
   2. Antidepressants
      a. Tricyclics (TCAs) (e.g., imipramine, amitriptyline)
      b. Monoamine Oxidase Inhibitors (MAOIs) (e.g., phenelzine)
      c. Others (e.g., trazodone)
   3. Lithium
   4. Hypnosedatives (e.g., barbiturates)
      a. Antianxiety agents (e.g., diazepam, chlordiazepoxide)
      b. Hypnotics (e.g., flurazepam, temazepam)

B. Electroconvulsive Therapy (ECT)

II. PSYCHOSOCIAL THERAPIES

A. Individual Treatments
   1. Psychoanalysis
   2. Insight-oriented Psychotherapy
   3. Supportive Psychotherapy
   4. Short-term Psychotherapies

B. Group Treatments
   1. Psychotherapy
   2. Self-help (e.g., Alcoholics Anonymous, Recovery)

C. Couples and Family Treatments
   1. Counseling
   2. Therapy
   3. Multiple Family (or Couples) Group Therapy

III. BEHAVIOR THERAPIES
   1. Biofeedback
   2. Relaxation (e.g., progressive relaxation)
   3. Systematic Desensitization
   4. Operant Conditioning (e.g., token economy)

IV. COGNITIVE THERAPIES

V. HYPNOTHERAPY

VI. NO TREATMENT

BIOLOGICAL TREATMENTS

There are five major classes of psychiatric (i.e., psychotropic) medications: antipsychotics, tricyclic antidepressants, monoamine oxidase inhibitors, lithium, and hypnosedatives.[2] (Appendix D lists the names and doses of the most frequently prescribed medications, and Appendix E, their side effects.)

Modern psychopharmacology began in 1954 with the release of chlorpromazine (Thorazine), an antipsychotic. Before then, only hypnosedatives (mainly barbiturates) were used. Regardless of the patient's disorder, hypnosedatives have virtually the same effect on everyone: They calm people, quell anxiety, and induce sleep. (Of these five types of psychotropic medications, *only* hypnosedatives can addict.) In contrast, the other four types of psychoactive drugs affect *specific* symptoms of mental disorders. For example, unlike hypnosedatives, chlorpromazine eliminates the schizophrenic's hallucinations and delusions. Similarly, tricyclic antidepressants, such as imipramine (Tofranil), help patients with major and bipolar depressions, but they do not make normal people feel happier or alleviate everyday human sadness. When "normals" take lithium, they become irritable, yet when manics take lithium, their frenetic activity and grandiosity diminish. Thus, the value of psychotropic agents is restricted to particular symptoms of particular mental disorders.

In general, antipsychotics treat schizophrenia and sometimes mania. Tricyclic antidepressants treat major and bipolar depressions; they also prevent panic attacks. Monoamine oxidase inhibitors help patients with major and "atypical" depressions. Lithium prevents and attenuates the highs and lows of bipolar disorder. Hypnosedatives reduce anxiety, induce sleep, and decrease nocturnal awakenings. Electroconvulsive therapy treats severe depressions.

Psychosurgery and *megavitamin therapy* are two biological treatments almost never used in psychiatry. When neurosurgeons perform psychosurgery, they cut small segments of the brain to reduce intractable violence, compulsions, obsessions, or pain. (A *lobotomy* is an operation in which a lobe, or large section, of the brain is removed; it's rarely performed today.) Although psychosurgery was widely used during the 1950s, in the latest year surveyed, 1973, 57 American neurosurgeons conducted 167 psychosurgeries (Donnelly, 1978).

---

[2]Some of these classes go by other names: Antipsychotics are also known as "neuroleptics" and "major tranquilizers," the latter term being a misnomer since tranquilization is not their chief function, and many of them do not even tranquilize. Tricyclic antidepressants have been labeled "psychostimulants"; that's unfortunate, because "stimulants" is the name for another class of drugs, which includes amphetamines and cocaine. Hypnosedatives are also called "minor tranquilizers," which falsely implies they are less powerful versions of "major tranquilizers." The pharmacological distinction between antianxiety agents and hypnotics is slim, which accounts for their collective label of "hypnosedatives."

Despite the many anecdotal claims that tons of vitamin C, niacin, pyridoxine, and vitamin B-12 do wonders for mental illness, unfortunately all controlled scientific studies refute these assertions (American Psychiatric Association, 1973). ("Unfortunately" because it would be wonderful to cure mental illness with relatively harmless vitamins.)

PSYCHOSOCIAL TREATMENTS

With so many psychosocial treatments (and so many defended passionately), one can readily overlook their similarities. Overtly and implicitly, psychosocial treatments all involve a contract and a degree of rapport and trust between a supposed expert and a patient or client with emotional or behavioral problems. Whether or not the patient has symptoms, all treatments seek to combat demoralization by restoring the patient's sense of mastery. They all derive from a particular theory or set of principles in which all parties have some faith.

Individual Psychotherapies

There are three basic types of psychotherapies that involve a single patient: psychoanalysis, insight-oriented psychotherapy, and supportive psychotherapy. (For clarity, the following distinctions between these therapies are somewhat overstated.)

Psychoanalysis. "Free association" is the cardinal rule of psychoanalysis—that is, without self-censorship, the patient should say whatever comes to mind, including dreams, fantasies, early memories, current experiences, or feelings about the analyst (i.e., transference). Psychoanalysis aims to heal by uncovering as much as possible about how the patient's mind functions. The patient lies on a couch; behind him sits the analyst so that his nonverbal signals won't influence the patient's associations. By deliberately acting as a "blank screen" and not as a "real person," the analyst assumes that everything the patient attributes to him is a projection of the patient instead of a quality of the analyst.

Psychoanalysis requires three to five meetings a week. It is prescribed for "problems in living," and mild to moderate depression, anxiety, and obsessiveness, which does not interfere with more than one main area of functioning—familial, occupational, and recreational. The patient must be bright, introspective, usually under the age of 50, a good abstract thinker, nonpsychotic, and in general, able to pay roughly $14,000/year.

Insight-oriented psychotherapy. In what is also called *psychodynamic* or *psychoanalytic psychotherapy*, clinicians address the patient's difficulties by primarily relying on insight—in the sense of bringing unconscious or unclear material into sharp awareness. In comparison to psychoanalysis, in psychodynamic psychotherapy the patient faces the therapist, meets once or twice a week, does not free associate, pays more attention to his current realities than to his dreams and childhood. The patient must be nonpsychotic, introspective, intelligent, and capable of abstract thought.

Psychoanalytic psychotherapy works best for "problems in living," "neurotic" symptoms, and ego-dystonic character traits. Like psychoanalysis, a successful insight-oriented therapy does not eliminate every problem or bestow "perfect mental health." Problems are inherent to the human condition and perfect mental health doesn't exist. By therapy's end, however, the patient should develop more realistic and flexible ways of dealing with personal needs and environmental demands; psychic pain, especially when the patient produces it "unnecessarily," should be reduced; he should leave understanding why "bad things" were happening to him so that he can avoid similar pitfalls in the future; he also should have acquired a framework for continued self-reflection and problem-solving.

Supportive psychotherapy. Whereas psychodynamic psychotherapy stresses insight, supportive psychotherapy emphasizes advice, education, persuasion, reason, and other appeals to conscious processes to alleviate current and practical life difficulties. Therapists support the patient's adaptive capacities and discourage his maladaptive behaviors. To gain, patients need not be introspective, intelligent, or able to think abstractly, but they do need a willingness to change, to examine themselves, and to show up for usually one to four sessions a month.

During an acute psychosis, supportive psychotherapy is the verbal therapy of choice; it provides reality testing, emotional comfort, and help in distinguishing between sensible and senseless ideas, feelings, and actions. After an acute episode, supportive psychotherapy can show patients how to avoid situations which are likely to precipitate symptoms and how to prevent a relapse. For instance, following several bouts of major depression, many patients become so adept at identifying its earliest symptoms that when they do arise these patients can avert (9–12 months of) a full-fledged relapse by quickly calling their psychiatrist, getting back on tricyclics antidepressants, and having their concerns placed into perspective.

Short-term therapy. This is a time-limited treatment (usually 8–20 sessions) that focuses on a clearly delineated problem which has erupted recently (e.g., within the past two months), and whose goals are specified and agreed on from the outset. There are numerous models of short-term therapy, including behavioral and cognitive.

Depending on whether it suppresses or provokes anxiety, short-term psychotherapy may stress support or insight. When supportive, short-term psychotherapy helps people get over an acute problem, maintain the psychological status quo, or acquire a specific skill. When combined with other biological or psychosocial treatments, it becomes part of a *crisis intervention* program. Insight-oriented, short-term psychotherapy typically examines a "focal conflict"—a recent and well-defined wish that conflicts with the person's enduring traits. For instance, Ernest Borgnine's ("What are we going to do tonight?") Marty suddenly faces a focal conflict when he meets a woman and must choose between mom or marriage. Anxiety-provoking short-term psychotherapy would focus on this choice, but not on other related yet more peripheral, issues in Marty's life, such as his painfully low self-esteem.

Group Treatments

Group psychotherapy. More than any other treatment, group therapy is ideally suited to address *interpersonal* difficulties. Methods vary, but in general the patient can learn how he affects others and can practice better ways of relating to people. Once patients have become comfortable using these new behaviors in the safety of the group, they can try them out in the "real" world. A typical session lasts 60–90 minutes, occurs once a week for outpatients, (three to five times a week for inpatients), has six to ten members, and is led by one or two therapists.[3]

Surveyed patients claim that groups help most by giving them a sense of belonging and by showing them they are not the only ones in world facing difficulties. On the other hand, psychotic patients and those who are extremely sensitive to personal slights or to feelings of persecution are likely to panic or to become further disorganized if the group becomes too intense.

Self-help groups. Alcoholics Anonymous, Recovery, and various drug programs run self-help groups, which focus on a single problem. These groups are unique in that the helper and the beneficiary are peers, and that every member can be both—two factors of enormous benefit. On the other hand, some professionals criticize these groups for their dubious efficacy, evangelistic nature, lack of trained leadership, and avoidance of scientific scrutiny. Nonetheless, many self-help groups assist patients, such as alcoholics and drug addicts, whom many therapists don't like or can't help. (To obtain information about any self-help group, contact the National Self-Help Clearinghouse, 33 West 42nd St., New York, NY 10036, 212-840-1259.)

---

[3]Group psychotherapy differs from (a) *"encounter groups,"* which help "normals" with "consciousness-raising" and "self-actualization," and (b) *"T-groups"*—the "T" stands for "training"—which teach "normals" how groups function (i.e., group process) by having them participate in the group.

Couples and Family Treatments

With these treatments, a convenient distinction is between "counseling" and "therapy." This distinction hinges on the clinician's view of where psychopathology mainly exists: If it primarily rests within the patient, treatment with the patient's spouse or family is *counseling*; if it primarily resides within the couple or the family, treatment is *therapy*.

Whether or not the family plays a major role in producing the disorder, counseling starts on the basic assumption that there is a patient with a mental disorder, which disrupts family members, who in turn may act "neurotically," unwisely, or harmfully. Family members are viewed not as victimizers, but as victims. Counseling usually helps to solve problems, to deal more constructively with the patient's disorder, and to minimize psychological trauma to other family members.

In therapy, the clinician thinks of the patient as an "identified patient," implying that the real patient isn't the patient, but the family, and that the identified patient is merely its most vulnerable member. In this view, the family is as much an unwitting victimizer as a victim. Therapy tries to rectify distorted communications and relationships within a couple or a family as a means of helping the entire family, including the "identified" patient.

Multiple family group therapy. MFGT generally consists of four to seven families meeting with two or more therapists, for 60 to 90 minutes. These families typically come together by dint of having a hospitalized relative on the same unit. These meetings occur once or twice a week and usually include the patient.

In many respects, MFGT offers something other treatments cannot: It affords relatives a chance to see that they are not alone in the world, to share mutual problems with a uniquely sympathetic audience, to learn how other families cope with similar problems, and to feel more hopeful by observing other patients' improvement. Conversely, MFGT enables inpatients to see what other patients' families are like; as a result, when patients talk to one another outside of MFGT—informally or in group therapy—they can speak with firsthand knowledge of their families.

BEHAVIOR THERAPIES

Behavior therapy is any treatment that alters quantifiable behavior, whether external (e.g., smoking) or internal (e.g., thoughts, feelings), by systematically changing the environment which produces it. Generally speaking, in behavior therapy changed behaviors lead to changed feelings (and attitudes), whereas in psychotherapy changed feelings (and attitudes) lead to changed behaviors. Take an oversimplified example of a patient with an elevator phobia: In behavior therapy, he would be gradually led, first mentally and then physically, into an elevator, and *after* each step, he would discuss his new feelings and attitudes. In insight-oriented psychotherapy, at first the same patient would explore how he feels about elevators and what riding them unconsciously represents (e.g., independence); only then, would he begin to ride an elevator

The distinctions between behavior therapies and psychotherapies are more semantic than real, more professional than clinical. Psychotherapies arose from a medical (and thus, psychiatric) tradition, whereas behavior therapies came from experimental psychology. In all therapies, new behaviors always change feelings, and vice versa. To various extents, all psychotherapies address behavior, and all behavior therapies address feelings. As behaviorism, psychoanalysis, and even psychobiology increasingly influence each other, techniques are often called "behavioral" more from tradition than from anything else.

In *biofeedback* an electronic instrument informs the patient about changes in one or more physiologic variables that he normally does not perceive, such as brainwave activity and blood pressure. A patient with tension headaches, for example, can identify tension in his facial muscles while hearing beeps from a biofeedback machine, which reflect the degree of this tension. He then experiments with different mental activities (e.g., fantasizing lying on a beach, humming "Oooooooooommmmm") to see which decrease the frequency of beeps, and thereby, diminish facial tension and headaches. Biofeedback is mainly used to treat psychophysiologic disorders.

In *relaxation* techniques, such as "progressive relaxation," a patient systematically contracts every muscle in his body and then fully relaxes them. These exercises, which resemble meditation, can reduce anxiety and induce sleep. They also are used in conjunction with another behavioral technique for treating phobias, *systematic desensitization*, in which the patient is gradually exposed to a hierarchy of feared images. After the patient relaxes, the therapist has him mentally picture the phobic object or situation, and when the patient can imagine it without feeling anxious, the therapist presents the next object up the hierarchy. Eventually, the same steps are repeated in reality instead of fantasy.

Operant conditioning is a process of systematically rewarding or reinforcing positive behaviors. An *operant* is a behavior shaped by its consequence. *Positive reinforcement* is a procedure that uses consequences for increasing operant behaviors. For example, by repeating his routine, a stand-up comic learns which jokes get laughs, and which don't: The audience's laughter, which is a consequence, positively reinforces certain jokes, which become operants.

Token economies are programs that systematically apply operant conditioning. They are used most often to prepare chronically hospitalized schizophrenics for living in the community. When these patients display adaptive behaviors, they receive tokens, which they can exchange for desired goods (e.g., candy) and privileges (e.g., watching TV). This positive reinforcement supposedly conditions patients so they eventually will perform desired behaviors (i.e., operants) in response to society's natural rewards (e.g., praise), but without needing tokens.

COGNITIVE THERAPY

Cognitive therapy blends elements of psychotherapy and behavior therapy. "Cognition" means "the process of knowing or perceiving." Cognitive theory assumes that a patient's faulty perceptions and attitudes about the world and himself precede and produce pathological moods — anxiety, depression, worry, guilt, etc. In cognitive therapy, whether a glass is half-empty or half-full all depends on one's goggles.

The cognitive therapist identifies the habitual ways that patients distort information: They make mountains out of molehills, or project their own fears onto others, or see things in the worse possible light. These patterns, which are called "automatic thoughts," are accompanied by "automatic emotions," such as dread, worry, and tension. The cognitive therapist teaches the patient to recognize his usual patterns of automatic thoughts, the emotions that go with them, and the situations that produce them; he then shows the patient more rational and healthy ways to view the same information.

A student social worker entered cognitive therapy for a moderate depression that intensified when she started her placement on a psychiatric inpatient service. A typical exchange was:

PATIENT: [situation] On my very first day on the ward, a patient asks me if his medication should be changed. I freaked.
THERAPIST: When you were freaking, what did you think about?
PATIENT: [automatic thoughts] I felt like an idiot. That I can't even answer a simple question, and if I can't do that, then maybe I shouldn't be a therapist. [automatic emotions] I felt terrible, filled with shame and guilt.
THERAPIST: [pointing out a more rational thought] But you're a social work student, not a physician; why should you know about his medication?
PATIENT: [automatic thought] Maybe, but then the patient asked me when he'd be discharged, and I felt like a fool for not knowing the answer.
THERAPIST: In retrospect, do you believe your feeling was justified?
PATIENT: [rational thought] No. That's silly! Why should I know when he'd be discharged: I just arrived on the ward two hours earlier. He's not even my patient!!

Cognitive therapy most often treats mild to moderately severe depression, but it also helps anxiety and phobias. Throughout the typical 15 to 25 once-a-week sessions, patients record episodes at home that led to troublesome feelings and thoughts, and at the following session, the cognitive distortions creating them are examined.

HYPNOTHERAPY

Hypnosis is a state of hypersuggestibility in which the patient is relatively oblivious to everything except the hypnotist's voice. Hypnosis is *not* sleep, but a form of intense restricted alertness. The "power" of hypnosis lies within the subject, not the hypnotist. When a person says, "You can't hypnotize me," he is correct. Psychological, and probably neurological, variables affect the patient's ability to enter a trance. The hypnotist cannot, and does not, "control" the patient.[4]

Although laymen often view hypnosis as a magic trick that, without any time or effort, will remedy every human affliction, its clinical efficacy is far more limited than generally presumed. Nonetheless, hypnosis may help in treating habits, such as overeating and smoking. When psychotherapy gets "stuck," hypnosis may accelerate information-giving. Hypnosis is generally ill-advised for patients who are currently or potentially psychotic.

DOES THERAPY WORK?

Strange how people say, "I don't believe in psychiatry." No one says, "I don't believe in surgery." That's because everyone knows that surgery helps sometimes, but not at other times: It depends on the patient, the illness, the goals of surgery, and the surgeon. Yet the same holds for psychiatric treatment: Whether it helps depends on the patient, the disorder, the goals of treatment, and the therapist.

Weird how people say, "I don't believe in psychiatry," as if it were a matter of theology, as in "I don't believe in God." Patients should evaluate their therapy not as a matter of faith, but as a matter of trusting their own judgment; they can ask themselves if, given reasonable expectations and sufficient time, treatment is helping or not helping.

And what's meant by "I don't believe in psychiatry"? Surely, people do believe that psychoactive drugs can treat some problems, and surely they believe that talking to a relatively neutral, objective, and skilled professional who's uninvolved in the patient's personal life can affect how the patient views himself and the world.

To ask, "Does psychotherapy work?" is akin to asking, "Does a restaurant work?" No one would compare McDonald's with Maxim's. Each is splendid

---

[4]Most people have been hypnotized without realizing it. In driving a long distance at night on a superhighway, they will "glaze over," and then will suddenly jerk awake to attention. When "glazed over" the driver is in a light hypnotic trance, focused on the road, and oblivious to everything else.

at what it does. The same for psychotherapy. It does what it does, as long as what's expected of it is appropriate, and as long as the therapist, like the restauranteur, knows his stuff. And just as whether a restaurant "works" depends on who's making the judgment, so too with therapy. In evaluating if a patient has improved, who's the best judge? The patient? The therapist? A researcher? A family member? A friend?

Therefore, the proper question is not does psychiatry work, but which treatments work for which disorders, in which patients, toward which goals, under which conditions, and according to whom. Section II will present some of these answers.

CHAPTER 6

Sample Case History: Sherlock Holmes

In *The Seven-Percent Solution*, Nicholas Meyer revealed that Sigmund Freud evaluated Sherlock Holmes, yet not until now has Freud's initial writeup of the case come to light. Quite remarkably, Freud's presentation illustrated a standard approach used 90 years later![1]

2 JUNE 1891

IDENTIFYING INFORMATION

The patient, Mr. Sherlock Holmes, is a 41-year-old, white, single, protestant, private detective, referred for cocaine misuse, depression, and bizarre behavior by his friend and colleague, Dr. John H. Watson. (*Informant*: Quotations are from the patient, while all other information, unless specified to the contrary, is from Dr. Watson, a reliable historian.)

CHIEF COMPLAINT

"I have applied all my will to banishing this (cocaine) habit and I have not been able to do so. . . . once a man takes the first false step, his feet are set forever on the path to his destruction."

---

[1]This case history is modified from one composed by Drs. Lawrence Sharpe and Jerrold S. Maxmen, based partly on material from Meyer, N. (1974). *The seven-percent solution*, New York: Dutton.

90

HISTORY OF PRESENT ILLNESS

The patient was apparently well until 24 April 1891, when late at night he snuck through the back door of Watson's home, appearing agitated, perspiring, gaunt, and pale. His eyes roved restlessly, but nothing seemed to register. He started to close and bolt every shutter in the room, but suddenly stopped and began to pace until Watson persuaded him to sit. Holmes then launched into a rambling story that people with airguns were after him because he had penetrated the defenses of a Professor Moriarity, an ex-University Professor of Mathematics with "incredible mental prowess and hereditary diabolic tendencies." He insisted that Moriarity is the "Napoleon of crime, the organizer of half the evil in the world and the center of a web of malefactors."

After an hour of standing, and sitting, and pacing, Holmes' excited speech slowed into inarticulate mutterings, followed by whisperings. He slept for two hours and awoke with a blank stare. He did not recognize the name Moriarity when it was mentioned, but insisted that before he slept, he was discussing an entirely different subject. Although earlier Watson had mentioned that his wife was away, Holmes requested that she be thanked for an excellent dinner (which never existed).

The next day, Holmes would not admit Watson to his room, fearing he was Moriarity in disguise. Holmes questioned Watson about items that only Watson would have known. Once inside, Watson noted there were new shutters of heavy iron and new locks on the doors. Holmes rambled on about Moriarity.

Later that day, Watson was approached by Professor Moriarity, who teaches math at a small school, but had privately tutored Holmes and his older brother Mycroft, when both were children. Moriarity claimed that for the previous five weeks, Holmes had been harassing him by standing outside his house all night, dogging his footsteps, telling his superior that he was a master criminal, and sending him telegrams with warnings such as, "Your days are numbered." The Professor was contemplating legal action to prevent this harassment, but was dissuaded from doing so by Watson's reassurances.

Mrs. Hudson, Holmes' landlady of many years, told Watson that around the end of February Holmes began spending his days locked in his study-bedroom; he would barricade the doors, bolt the shutters, see no one, and refuse all meals. Late at night, he'd sneak out to spy on the Professor.

Watson believes that Holmes has episodically snuffed cocaine for at least five years, but that only recently has this use escalated to where it totally impairs occupational and social functioning. He now intravenously injects himself with unknown (but increasing) amounts of a 7% solution of cocaine circa 3-4 times a day. Holmes only makes wild accusations about Moriarity during cocaine intoxication; at other times on cocaine Holmes becomes grandiose, saying such things as, "It is very dangerous for me to leave London for any length of time. It generates in the criminal classes an unhealthy excitement when my absence is discovered." He denies and conceals his cocaine use, but without his usual meticulousness and caution — syringes are left in open drawers, his shirt sleeves are rolled up, thereby exposing puncture marks, etc.

Two weeks ago, at Watson's insistence, Holmes stopped cocaine, and within a day, felt extreme despair, gloom, and boredom — extreme even for Holmes. He has stopped working on any other case, believing that no other criminal in Europe is clever enough to bother with. He has lost all interest in his usual activities, has no appetite, shed ten pounds, looks pale, and stays in bed most of the day. Watson has never heard Holmes speak of suicide. Being concerned about his worsening state, Dr. Watson, in collusion with Mycroft Holmes and Professor Moriarity, tricked the patient into leaving London for treatment here in Vienna.

PAST AND FAMILY HISTORY

Little is known of the patient's early childhood. His mother was involved in an illicit love affair, which Holmes' father discovered. He then shot her to death. Moriarity, then Holmes' tutor, was the one who told the patient the news. There is no information as to his behavior prior to, or immediately after, this catastrophe. Sherlock was an intelligent child and went through college with high grades. His income derives from family land-holdings and from a thriving detective practice.

Watson thinks the patient's father died years ago, but knows nothing of the circumstances. The patient's sole living relative is his older brother Mycroft, who is also a bachelor. Watson claims that Mycroft is even more intelligent, reclusive, and eccentric than the patient, living in London's highly traditional Diogenes Club, whose main qualifications for membership are shyness and misanthropy, and whose main distinction is that members' chairs are all back-to-back so that nobody speaks with each other. Watson is unaware of any mental illness in the family.

Dr. Watson describes the patient as a "deeply private person, whose reclusivity reaches major proportions" at times . . . and who behaves "as a 'thinking machine,' impassive, aloof, and austere and not in direct contact with the sordid realities of physical existence." Holmes once observed, "Watson, I am a brain." Nonetheless, Watson contends that underneath Holmes is a deeply compassionate man, who regards his emotions as interfering with his mental processes. He tries, Watson maintains, to suppress his emotions by indulging in intellectual pursuits, such as chemical experiments and violin improvisation for hours on end, or by practicing shooting at the walls of his room. Except for a brief attraction to an Irene Adler, women have been conspiciously absent in the patient's life.

Watson considers Holmes to be an ill-mannered eccentric, who is easily bored when not confronted with an interesting problem to solve. Holmes confirmed this by saying, "I abhor the dull routine of existence, I loathe stagnation." On occasion, he becomes demoralized, sad, and hopeless; he lacks energy, sleeps 10-12 hours/day (normally he sleeps under five hours/day), socially isolates himself, loses interest in everything. These depressive periods occur once or twice a year, last from several days to weeks, but no longer than two to three months. Some of these periods end when Holmes gets a new and challenging case, some end for no apparent reason, and some because Holmes binges on cocaine for a week or two. When confronted with an interesting problem, he would stop cocaine, but return to it when bored or depressed. Except for some prior experimentation with morphine injections, Holmes has not used any drug except cocaine.

MEDICAL HISTORY
AND PHYSICAL EXAMINATION

Although a physical examination was not performed, the patient was observed to be malnourished, had dilated pupils, puncture marks on both arms, and a weak pulse.

MENTAL STATUS EXAMINATION

[Formal testing not performed.]

Appearance: Gaunt, sallow, malnourished, tired-looking, and appeared to have lost weight.

Behavior: Entered office slowly, weak handshake, dry palms, and sat throughout the 80-minute consultation. His movements were a bit slow, although when speaking of Moriarity he became fidgety and spoke with more animation.

Speech: He said very little, and spoke only when asked a direct question. His speech was hushed, moderately slow, but not slurred.

Emotion: Patient said he was despondent, had no interest in things, and nothing brought him pleasure. His facies was glum, his general look, bored. His affect and mood were appropriate to what was said. There were no signs of anxiety.

Thought processes: During the middle of the interview, he said that he thought I was Moriarity in disguise, and that his brother and Watson had concocted a sinister plot to deliver him into the clutches of his enemies. Yet, when confronted, Holmes abandoned this idea, and apologized. When asked if he still believed that Moriarity was a master criminal, he said he would rather not discuss the matter. Despite these apparently overvalued ideas, there is no evidence of actual delusions, ideas of reference, incoherence, phobias, obsessions, or compulsions.

Perception: Although not tested specifically, there were no indications of a perceptual disturbance.

Attention: His mind seemed to wander on occasion, but not while speaking.

Orientation: Knew the date, time, place, his name, Watson's name, and my name.

Judgment: No apparent functional disturbance.

Intelligence and Information: Extremely high.

Insight: On confrontation, he admitted to cocaine addiction and that it was a serious problem.

DIAGNOSIS

Axis I:	305.62	Cocaine abuse
	296.30	Major depression (Provisional, rule out)
	296.60	Bipolar disorder (Provisional, rule out)
Axis II:	301.40	Compulsive personality disorder (Provisional, rule out)
Axis III:		None
Axis IV:		Psychosocial stressors: None apparent
		Severity: 1 – None
Axis V:		Highest level of adaptive functioning past year: Excellent work functioning, but few relationships. Level: 2 – Very good.

PROGNOSIS

Guarded prognosis for cocaine abuse, especially in view of (a) the disorder's natural course, and the patient's (b) history of depressive symptoms, (c) current reluctance to abandon cocaine, and (d) characteristic unwillingness to place himself under the care of others.

BIOPSYCHOSOCIAL FORMULATION

The patient's heavy cocaine abuse produces grandiosity, persecutory and overvalued ideas, and agitation. Holmes' particular choice of cocaine may partly be to self-medicate an underlying depression (especially given Holmes's unusual intolerance of boredom), and partly because he is very attracted to the sense of sharpened intellect cocaine affords. Stopping cocaine brings on and/or aggravates depressive symptoms, especially dysthymia, anhedonia, hypersomnia, psychomotor retardation, and social isolation. Totally unclear is why the patient's use of cocaine sharply increased late last February, since no precipitant has been identified.

The diagnosis of cocaine abuse is firm. In addition, in light of current information, his symptoms strongly suggest an affective disorder, even though they fall short of meeting *DSM-III* criteria. Because his depressive symptoms are episodic, a dysthymic disorder is highly unlikely, whereas a major depression is a distinct possibility. Slightly more probable would be bipolar disorder, since his periods of enormous energy resemble hypomania and his hypersomniac depressive intervals suggest bipolar depression. In lieu of his long-standing meticulousness, perfectionism, excessive use of logic and intellect at the expense of emotion, mild self-righteousness and suspiciousness, a compulsive personality disorder should be considered.

Psychodynamically, *repression*, supplemented by other defenses, appears to have played a major role in shaping Holmes' preoccupations and behavior. His *repressed* rage at his father for killing his mother seems to have been *displaced* onto Moriarity, the man who informed Holmes of the murder. *Introjecting* rage intended for his father may have compounded Holmes' depression. His repressed rage at his mother's unfaithfulness and her subsequent "abandonment" of young Sherlock may have contributed to his disinterest in women — his viewing them as untrustworthy, immoral, and not dependable. By *sublimation*, Holmes excelled in detective work "to punish the wicked and see justice done."

PLAN

1. Withdrawal from cocaine.
2. Observation; look for hidden cocaine use.
3. Evaluation of affective and personality disorders.
4. Encourage involvement in pursuits that usually bring him pleasure, such as violin playing, attending Wagnerian opera, chasing criminals.
5. Next appointment: Tuesday, 16:00

Sigmund Freud, M.D.

SECTION II

Mental Disorders

CHAPTER 7

Organic Brain Syndromes

"Like trees, we grow old from the top," says Gore Vidal's Emperor Julian. Although most would agree, they're barking up the wrong tree: Dementia—or what laymen call "senility"—is *not* inherent to aging, but a set of illnesses that strikes 15% of elderly Americans. To assume that "growing old from the top" is natural and inevitable stereotypes the elderly and causes many curable dementias to go untreated.

As the age of the population increases, so does the importance of dementia. In 1970, Americans over age 65 numbered 20.1 million and comprised 9.8% of the population; by the year 2000, these figures will climb to 34.9 million and 13%, respectively. In 1980, three million had dementia; by 2000, four million will have it. Dementia afflicts 58% of the 1.2 million elderly now residing in nursing homes, at a cost of $12 billion a year. Over half of all hospitalized elderly mental patients have dementia, and over half of them have Alzheimer's disease—the fourth or fifth leading cause of death in the United States. All in all, about 1% of adults have some type of organic brain syndrome.

Organic brain syndromes (OBS), including the dementias, are constellations of psychological or behavioral signs and symptoms, which are proven (or reasonably presumed) to be produced by a medical, neurological, or biochemical alteration in the brain's structure or function.[1] The cardinal symptoms of OBSs are memory impairment, disorientation, poor judgment, confusion, and a general loss of intellectual functions. Also common are halluci-

---

[1]To state that OBSs have *known*, or strongly assumed, biological changes does not imply that functional disorders are without biological changes; it simply means they are not as obvious. (See pp. 39,60.) Patients with OBSs still have psychodynamics.

nations, illusions, delusions, personality changes, and secondary emotional reactions (e.g., depression and persecutory ideas).

By definition, organic *brain syndromes* (e.g., dementia, delirium) refer to conditions without a specific etiology, whereas organic *mental disorders* (OMD) refer to OBSs with a specific etiology (e.g., alcohol withdrawal delirium or Alzheimer's disease). *DSM-III* presents both.

This chapter will examine two types of OBS: *delirium*, whose primary characteristic is a clouding of consciousness (i.e., a reduced awareness of the environment), and *dementia*, whose chief feature is a deterioration of intellectual functions.

Two other types of OBSs, *intoxication* and *withdrawal*, are discussed in the chapter on substance abuse (as *DSM-III-R* is scheduled to do). *DSM-III* also lists five OMDs that are all without clouding of consciousness, and whose name depends on their main characteristic: For *amnestic syndrome* it's memory loss, for *organic hallucinosis* it's hallucinations, for *organic delusional syndrome* it's delusions, for *organic affective syndrome* it's mood changes, and for *organic personality syndrome* it's personality changes, such as emotional lability (e.g., sudden crying, temper tantrums), poor impulse control (e.g., shoplifting, exhibitionism), marked apathy or indifference, suspiciousness, or paranoid ideation. *DSM-III-R* may add an *organic anxiety syndrome*.

DELIRIUM

Clinical Presentation

Delirium—from the Latin *delirare*, meaning to rave, to be crazy—is characterized by clouding of consciousness, disorientation, and recent memory loss. These signs arise abruptly (e.g., several hours to days), become worse at night or in the dark (i.e. "sundowning"), and rarely persist for more than a month. Often appearing frightened and agitated, delirious patients frequently have illusions, hallucinations (in any of the five senses), incoherent speech, and disrupted sleep-wake cycles. The *DSM-III* diagnostic criteria for delirium are listed in Table 7-1.

Disorientation is usually first to time: At midnight, the patient may say it's noon, or that the year is 1737. As delirium worsens, the patient becomes disoriented to place (e.g., thinks he's at a country club), and later, to person (e.g., misidentifies his spouse); immediate memory dwindles first, followed by ten-minute, and then by remote, memory. If either disorientation or recent memory loss is absent, the diagnosis of delirium is doubtful. Lucid intervals and symptoms becoming worse at night are also virtually diagnostic of delirium.

TABLE 7-1
DSM-III **Criteria for Delirium***

A. Clouding of consciousness (reduced clarity of awareness of the environment), with reduced capacity to shift, focus, and sustain attention to environmental stimuli.

B. At least two of the following:

(1) perceptual disturbance: misinterpretations, illusions, or hallucinations
(2) speech that is at times incoherent
(3) disturbance of sleep-wakefulness cycle, with insomnia or daytime drowsiness
(4) increased or decreased psychomotor activity

C. Disorientation and memory impairment (if testable)

D. Clinical features that develop over a short period of time (usually hours to days) and tend to fluctuate over the course of a day.

E. Evidence, from the history, physical examination, or laboratory tests, of a specific organic factor judged to be etiologically related to the disturbance.

DSM-III, p. 107.

Clinical Course and Complications

Anytime there is a sudden, unexplained behavioral change or psychosis, delirium must be suspected. It usually arises quickly, from several hours to days, depending on its cause. The onset may be dramatic, as when patients begin thrashing about, tearing out IVs, or fighting. When the onset is subtle, and the symptoms exaggerations of normal personality traits, delirium may go undetected. For instance, a normally perfectionistic physician recovering from heart surgery started to cuss at nurses for not washing their hands. Initially, the staff said, "Everybody knows doctors make the worst patients," and missed the delirium. At first, delirious patients may simply appear a bit confused, mistake a night nurse for a relative, or not find their room. Nurses' reports may be the first clue to a delirium, especially when they describe a calm patient by day and a confused one by night (i.e. "sundowning"). Frequent, around-the-clock mental status testing is often needed to spot a delirium.

Accidents are common in delirium. The patient may fall out of bed or step in front of a truck. Otherwise, the patient will either recover soon or die soon. The longer delirium continues, the greater the chance of permanent brain damage. Delirium rarely persists for over a month—by then, the patient is either demented or dead.

Etiology and Pathogenesis

Most delirious patients have an underlying medical, surgical, chemical, or neurological problem; it may be an infectious disease, drug intoxication or withdrawal, congestive heart failure, fluid and electrolyte imbalance, or stroke. Sometimes the *first* sign of a medical illness will be a delirium. Psychotropic drugs, especially tricyclic antidepressants, monoamine oxidase inhibitors, and antiparkinsonian medications frequently cause delirium because of their substantial anticholinergic properties. The elderly are especially susceptible, since they are prone to depression and extra-sensitive to anticholinergics. Fortunately, some newer antidepressants (e.g., trazodone) and antiparkinsonian agents (e.g., amantadine) are not anticholinergic.

Another cause of delirium is sensory isolation, as happens in intensive and cardiac care units ("ICU" or "CCU psychoses"). The monotony of a weird and unfamiliar setting leads patients to see walls quiver, mistake technological noises for human voices, hallucinate taps on their shoulders, etc.[2] How much of an individual patient's delirium stems from sensory isolation or from the disease, medical complications, and treatment which brought him to an ICU or CCU is often unclear and varies depending on the circumstances.

Differential Diagnosis

Delirium can be distinguished from accentuated *normal personality traits* by the presence of lucid intervals and "sundowning." Unlike *dementia*, delirium has an abrupt onset, fluctuating course, and clouding of consciousness.

When *schizophrenia* erupts, although the patient's hallucinations and apparent confusion can resemble a delirium, the patient will not have the disorientation, memory loss, and diurnal pattern seen in delirium. *Generalized anxiety disorder* and delirium may both present with agitation, yet the former is without disorientation, confusion, and memory loss.

Management and Treatment

The first priority is to keep the patient alive; a close second is to prevent brain damage; third is to stop the patient from self-harm. Quickly identifying a delirium and its cause is critical to these goals.

In sequence, these medical interventions should be a done immediately: (a) Administer 50 ml of 50% glucose IV to prevent hypoglycemic brain damage. (b) Prevent

---

[2]The curious can experiment with a drug-free delirium by lying for thirty minutes in a sensory-isolation chamber. They can hallucinate lights that twinkle, wave, change color, or flash; they can have pins-and-needles sensations, surges of warmth and cold, and restlessness—all for $30.

hypoxia and anoxia by addressing its causes. (c) Severe hyperthermia (> 105°), which can be the cause or consequence of delirium, also produces brain damage and death. Regardless of its etiology, the fever must be treated vigorously with ice packs, aspirin, fans, and alcohol sponges. (d) A thiamine (vitamin B-1) deficiency, unless corrected promptly (with thiamine 100 mg IV immediately and 50 mg IM every day for a week), can cause brain damage.

Careful nursing care is essential, and often lifesaving. Because medically hospitalized delirious patients fall out of bed, wander off, trip, break bones, develop concussions, rip out IVs, hurl IV bottles, and so on, these patients need constant observation, and sometimes, physical restraints.

Delirious patients should be frequently oriented by health-care professionals wearing white uniforms for obvious identification. Their contacts with the patients should be brief and numerous (e.g., three minutes four times an hour), always telling the patient, the date, the place, the staff member's name, and what he or she is doing. The patient should be reassured as to his safety and reality-tested. Pictures of family members, a clock, and a calendar showing the date should be seen by the patient. The best treatment for an ICU psychosis is removal from the ICU. If that's medically unsafe, all the above measures should be taken.

Before the underlying cause of the delirium is rectified, the patient may be initially helped by small doses of antipsychotic drugs, such as haloperidol 2 mg to 5 mg. Some authors (Wells & McEvoy, 1982) claim that antianxiety agents (e.g., diazepam 5 mg to 10 mg, chlordiazepoxide 25 mg to 50 mg, oxazepam 15 mg to 30 mg) are as helpful and safe as antipsychotics, while other authors (Goodwin & Guze, 1984) opine that too many delirious patients become even more agitated and disorganized on antianxiety drugs; they, therefore, recommend antipsychotics. The elderly should receive one-half to one-third of these doses. They may benefit most from oxazepam, because it is not conjugated into other medically active compounds, has a relatively short half-life, and accumulates less (Shull et al., 1976).

More important than the choice of drug is the dose: Too little and the delirium gets worse and more dangerous; too much and coma and respiratory depression may follow. Because errors on either side of this delicate balance can lead to death, remember that *more* of a drug can always be given, but not *less*! If the initial doses mentioned above are insufficient or wear off, they may be repeated hourly, as long as the patient is checked before each new dose is administered.

DEMENTIA

Clinical Presentation

Dementia — from the Latin *demens*, meaning "out of one's mind" — is characterized by a loss of intellectual abilities, especially memory, judgment, abstract thinking, impulse control, and language skills, and marked changes in personality. Most dementias begin gradually (e.g., months to years), but may erupt suddenly, as after a cracked skull. Unlike delirium, dementia occurs without clouding of consciousness. Table 7-2 lists *DSM-III's* diagnostic criteria for dementia.

Initially, *memory loss* is for recent events: Ovens are left on, keys misplaced, conversations forgotten. Retained, and often dwelled on, are details from childhood (e.g., "Rosebud"). *Personality changes* are often intensifications or exact opposites of preexisting character traits. A gregarious grandpa retreats to a corner and daydreams. A mildly suspicious and self-righteous woman begins calling the cops every night accusing her neighbors of performing abortions in their basements. *Impaired judgment* and *poor impulse*

TABLE 7-2
DMS-III Criteria for Dementia*

A. A loss of intellectual abilities of sufficient severity to interfere with social or occupational functioning.

B. Memory impairment.

C. At least one of the following:

   (1) impairment of abstract thinking, as manifested by concrete interpretations of proverbs, inability to find similarities and differences between related words, difficulty in defining words and concepts, and other similar tasks
   (2) impaired judgment
   (3) other disturbances of higher cortical [brain] function, such as aphasia (disorder of language due to brain disfunction), apraxia (inability to carry out motor activities despite intact comprehension and motor function), agnosia (failure to recognize or identify objects despite intact sensory function), "constructional difficulty" (e.g., inability to copy three-dimensional figures, assemble blocks, or arrange sticks in specific designs)
   (4) personality change, i.e., alteration or accentuation of premorbid traits

D. State of consciousness not clouded (i.e., does not meet the criteria for Delirium or Intoxication, although these may be superimposed).

E. Either (1) or (2):

   (1) evidence from the history, physical examination, or laboratory tests, of a specific organic factor that is judged to be etiologically related to the disturbance
   (2) in the absence of such evidence, an organic factor necessary for the development of the syndrome can be presumed if conditions other than Organic Mental Disorders have been reasonably excluded and if the behavioral change represents cognitive impairment in a variety of areas

DSM-III, pp. 111–112.

control are common: Patients may start speaking crudely, exhibit genitals, or shoplift. A normally cautious businessman invested $5,000 with an enterprising, 19-year-old botany student who claimed she could make millions growing purple tangerines.

Intellectual abilities deteriorate. Patients may have trouble naming objects (agnosia). They may have difficulties understanding language (aphasia); speech is stereotyped, slow, vague, and filled with irrelevant detail, as these patients increasingly are unable to concentrate, to follow conversations, or to distinguish the germane from the trivial. Words are misused, chosen more by sound than by sense. They cannot perform simple motor tasks (apraxia); driving, cooking, handling money, and using tools become too complicated. They find it hard to draw a simple house, copy the placement of four matchsticks, or assemble blocks.

In response to these impairments, patients usually become ashamed, anxious, demoralized, irritable, and dysthymic. Hypochondriasis increases. Energy and enthusiasm decline. Some patients display *"catastrophic reactions"* — they respond to stimuli by excessive laughing, hostility, and weeping, or by readily becoming dazed, evasive, or immobile. Also common is *confabulation* (i.e., the fabrication of stories to hide memory loss); so too are suspiciousness and paranoid ideation, especially when the patient has trouble hearing or seeing. Fear invades a vacuum: Forgetting where he left his wallet, he assumes it was stolen and may accuse others, including loved ones.

The patient's deterioration may go unrecognized for months to years, and for many reasons: Intellectual decline is usually insidious. Memory loss is dismissed as "normal aging." The patient's impaired judgment and poor impulse control are explained away as "folks naturally get 'crusty' and 'cantankerous' with age." If granddad starts making lewd gestures to teeny-boppers, he's a fun-loving "dirty old man." (Dirty old women don't exist.) Inappropriate jocularity (*witzelsucht*), which arises from impairments of the brain's frontal lobe, are dismissed as "being in good spirits." The patient's loss of sharpness, or intellect, or wit may be too subtle or slow to be noticed. The patient does "all the right things," but on scrutiny, he's a beat behind: Grace notes become eighth notes.

When presenting clinically, demented patients may move slowly or fidget. They may look glum, bored, or tense. On a formal mental status examination, they show recent memory loss and disorientation, and usually have difficulty subtracting serial 1's or 7's and performing abstractions.

Subtypes

There are three major subtypes of dementia: (a) About half of all demented patients have *primary degenerative dementias*, chiefly Alzheimer's disease (AD). (This category also includes Pick's, Huntington's, and Jakob-Creutzfeldt diseases, as well as the one-third of Parkinson's patients who live long enough to develop dementia.) (b) *Multi-infarct dementias* (MID), accounting for 10% to 25% of dementias, are mainly caused by hypertension or emboli.[3] Contrary to popular belief, MID is not caused by arteriosclerosis (i.e., "hardening of the arteries"). A combination of AD *and* MID account for another 20% to 25%. (c) *Secondary dementias*, which produce 5% to 15%, result from other conditions, most often alcoholism and head trauma, but also from infectious diseases, hypothyroidism, and drug use.

The single most crucial fact about dementia is that, unlike AD and MID, most secondary dementias are reversible. Everyone who presents with a dementia *must* receive a thorough medical and neurological examination to determine if he is one of the roughly 10% of demented patients who can be cured either medically or surgically. Table 7-3 lists these reversible dementias.

On her 70th birthday, widowed, modest Mrs. Kass moved to Miami. Unlike her "normal self," she launched her first of many sexual flings; "life is short," she informed her relatives. Hotly debated was whether Mrs. Kass belonged in a motel or mental hospital. While the family was paralyzed by worry, Mrs. Kass was thrilled and active. She'd laugh at anything, so much so that one night a policeman noticed her on a fishing pier, lost, confused, and giggling. When he asked her where she was, she burst into "Swanee River," until she forgot a lyric and began weeping all the way to the hospital. Her dementia, initially attributed to AD, was due to a benign (frontal lobe) brain tumor, which was surgically removed. After a full recovery, she regained her normal temperament and settled down with a retired businessman.

Clinical Course

Although it usually arises during old age, AD has been known to emerge as early as a person's forties, as it did in the case first described by the German neurologist Alois Alzheimer in 1906. Its stealthy onset typically manifests with memory loss and intellectual decline, often *preceded* by irritability, fatigue, moodiness, shortened attention span, and distractibility. In general, Alzheimer's patients do not have marked diurnal changes and gradually deteriorate.

During end-stage AD, the patient's memory is almost totally gone. He cannot recognize his closest relatives; everyone becomes a stranger. Speech is reduced to a phrase or two. He cannot dress nor feed himself. Bladder and bowel control fails. Muscles deteriorate. Insomnia plagues. At the very end, full nursing care is required. The patient is bedridden, disoriented, oblivious,

---

[3]Emboli are small blood clots, which break off from the heart or a carotid artery in the neck, flow to the brain, block part of its blood supply, and cause the death (or infarct) of those brain cells.

and incoherent. Alzheimer's patients may survive up to 15 years, but they usually expire in seven to ten years, dying most often from malnutrition, dehydration, infections, pneumonia, or heart failure.

In contrast to the slow, generalized deterioration of AD, MID begins abruptly, progresses in a stepwise fashion, spares personality until the end, occurs in patients with histories of strokes and cardiovascular disease, and causes "patchy" neurological signs, such as inarticulate speech, small stepped gait, abnormal reflexes, and specific weak muscles.

Complications

The demented patient is susceptible to medical illness and delirium. His work and social functioning gradually declines, and as his condition worsens, he may get lost wandering away from home. If his mind wanders, he may fall off a ladder or trip on a curb; if he smashes his head and loses consciousness, he may suffer a potentially fatal subdural hematoma.[4] Although dementia often induces severe despair and depression, it rarely leads to suicide.

Epidemiology

The incidence of Alzheimer's disease increases with age, arising most often between 70 and 80 years. At age 65, about 5% have AD; by age 80, about 20%. Women are affected more than men. At present, two million Americans have AD. In 50 years, AD's prevalence is expected to triple.

Etiology and Pathogenesis

In general, the biological factors which produce a dementia vary according to the subtype of dementia, whereas the psychosocial influences depend more on the individual's personality and circumstances. Alzheimer's disease seems to result from a genetically predisposed brain affected by an unknown physical or chemical agent. In contrast, an autosomal dominant gene appears sufficient to cause another dementia, Huntington's chorea ("Woody Guthrie's disease").

During the early stages of most dementias, patients respond with either exaggerations of their normal personality traits or their exact opposite. As discussed later, those close to the patient may also influence the patient's experience and quality of life.

---

[4]A subdural hematoma is a sudden or gradual bleeding under the outer lining (or dura) of the brain. The patient may lose consciousness immediately, yet more often there is a fluctuating course of drowsiness, headache, and confusion that persists for weeks to months until the patient finally loses consciousness.

During the later stages, most dementias "take over," irrespective of psychosocial influences.

Genetic. First-degree relatives (e.g., brother, mother, daughter) of patients with AD have three to four times the prevalence of AD as the general population. The incidence is even higher among relatives of those few who develop AD before age 60. Some researchers believe that an autosomal dominant gene is *a* (not *the*) culprit; it may come from either sex. If one parent has the gene, his child has a 50% chance of having AD; this chance is 75% if both parents have the gene. Children tend to get AD at the same age as their parents did. In other cases, genetic vulnerability to AD is less clear. Down's syndrome also predisposes to AD.

Medical. In addition to the etiologies of (reversible) dementias listed on Table 7-3, some dementias are probably due to "slow" viruses and immunologic deficiencies. Alcohol aggravates all dementias. High-risk factors for MID include hypertension, cigarette smoking, obesity, and heart disease.

Physiological. In normal aging, although the blood supply to the brain decreases, the brain extracts oxygen more efficiently. In AD, however, the brain's blood supply is also diminished, but the brain extracts *less* oxygen and glucose. Moreover, the enzymes which both synthesize and metabolize acetylcholine are deficient. On autopsy, the neurons of Alzheimer's patients display twisted clumps of protein called "neurofibrillary tangles," while coating the outside of blood vessels are remnants of dead cells called "neur*i*tic plaques" (not neur*o*tic!). Whether these anatomical changes are the cause or the consequence of biochemical changes is unclear.

Differential Diagnosis

As discussed earlier, dementia must be distinguished from *delirium*. Because delirium presents with disorientation and memory loss, dementia cannot be diagnosed until *after* a delirium clears. In *normal aging* there is some memory loss; names and dates are forgotten, papers misplaced, new learning becomes harder, thinking becomes slower, and problem-solving gets tougher. These changes do not substantially interfere with occupational or social functioning, whereas AD and other dementias do. Some intellectual deterioration may occur in *chronic schizophrenia*, but it is milder than in dementia.

The second most important fact about dementia is that clinicians must distinguish it from "pseudodementia," a form of *major depression*, which is highly treatable. From 10% to 33% of old people with pseudodementia will be misdiagnosed as having dementia, since both disorders may present initially with memory loss, confusion, disorientation, apathy, and hypochondriasis.

On careful examination the two conditions can be readily distinguished. Pseudodementia's onset is more abrupt, easier to pinpoint, and more obvious to family members; its symptoms escalate more rapidly. In dementia, patients *have* a poor memory; in pseudodementia, they *complain* of a poor memory. When pressed, demented patients really can't remember five objects named five minutes earlier, whereas after considerable fussy helplessness, depressed patients recall them. Pseudodemented patients frequently respond to ques-

TABLE 7-3
The Reversible Dementias

A. INFECTIONS
　1. Abscesses
　2. Encephalitis
　3. Meningitis, chronic
　4. Syphilis of the brain

B. LUPUS ERYTHEMATOSUS

C. MECHANICAL DISORDERS

　1. Normal pressure hydrocephalus
　2. Subdural hematoma (acute or chronic)

D. METABOLIC DISORDERS

　1. Hypothyroidism (myxedema)
　2. Hyponatremia (diminished sodium)
　3. Hypocalcemia (diminished calcium)
　4. Hypoglycemia (diminished blood sugar)
　5. Porphyria
　6. Wilson's disease
　7. Uremia (kidney failure with toxicity)
　8. Hepatic encephalopathy (liver failure with toxicity)

E. NEOPLASMS, BENIGN

　1. Gliomas
　2. Meningiomas

F. POISONS

　1. Alcohol
　2. Barbiturates
　3. Belladonna alkaloids
　4. Bromides
　5. Carbon monoxide
　6. Metals (e.g., arsenic, manganese)
　7. Organic phosphates

G. PSEUDODEMENTIA (?)

H. VITAMIN DEFICIENCIES
　1. B-1 (Wernicke's encephalopathy, Wernicke-Korsakoff syndrome)
　2. B-12 (pernicious anemia)
　3. Folic acid
　4. Niacin (pellagra)

tions with silence or by saying, "I don't know"; demented patients answer with numerous near-misses. Demented patients will struggle to accomplish a task; depressed patients won't try. Social skills are retained more in dementia than in pseudodementia. The demented patient wants company, whereas the depressed patient will say, "Leave me alone!" Patients with pseudodementia often have a prior, or family, history of affective disorder (Charatan, 1985). The ultimate test is whether the patient improves with biotherapies—antidepressants or ECT.[5] Antidepressants must be used with caution, since demented patients are prone to become delirious on them.

Although pseudodementia is widely viewed as a functional disorder that mimicks an organic disorder, a minority view is that pseudodementia is a depression-induced organic mental disorder. The distinction between these views may be more semantic than real, more of outlook than of practice, since the treatment of pseudodementia is the same in either case. Still, considering pseudodementia a depression-induced OMD would account for why psychological tests reveal organicity in both pseudodementia and in true dementia and, therefore, are not useful in differentiating them.

Management and Treatment

Because the care of the demented falls mainly to loved ones and custodians, they must become partners in the patient's treatment plan. For family members, being a caretaker is usually a novel experience; it is difficult and draining, demoralizing and devastating. Relatives need support and practical instruction, and a major task of the physician or therapist is to provide both.

Psychosocial Interventions

Patient. The primary goal is to make the demented patient's life as comfortable as possible. The environment should be kept simple. Clocks, calendars, labels, lists, familiar routines, short-term tasks, brief walks, and simple physical exercises (to prevent muscle atrophy)—such are the elements which improve the patient's quality of life and maintain his self-respect.

The patient should be allowed and encouraged to do what he can, but *only* what he can. Pressing too hard, as by trying to preserve memory by exercizing it, leads to frustration and resentment. Demented patients dislike abdicating such tasks as handling money, driving, cooking, and later on, bathing, dressing, using the toilet, and living alone. Attempts to help them may be greeted with insults, complaints, annoying questions, tears, or rage. Responding with hostility is pointless and harmful; distracting and calming the patient work better. These patients often lose things and blame others for stealing them;

---

[5]That ECT *increases*, instead of diminishes, the memory of patients with pseudodementia suggests that ECT does not harm brain cells.

instead of refuting the accusation, which is pointless, it is better to offer to look for the lost items. Reassurance repeated several times each hour is never too much. Later, as words fail, touch may still reassure. The patient's sleeping area should be made safe, since he is likely to become more confused at night, wander about, and hurt himself.

Moving to a senior citizen's apartment, sheltered housing, or a nursing home is usually necessary when the patient is dangerous to himself, hallucinates, loses bowel or bladder control, or makes life impossible for his caretaker. The reasons for such a move should be calmly reiterated; the patient will forget the explanation, but the *repeated reassurance* is what counts.

Family counseling. When dementia is first diagnosed, relatives often deny the patient's illness (e.g., "Everybody grows old") or blame him for being "deliberately difficult" (e.g., "He remembers when he wants to!"). In time, family members feel overwhelmed and helpless; they may become angry at professionals for "not doing enough." They may take out their frustrations on each other, and latent family tensions may surface under the strain of caring for a demented relative. A son or daughter may feel guilty about resenting their demented mother or father; the children may be ashamed of the parents or think they would be better off dead. The professional must care for the caretakers, who must be told that caring for the demented is an impossible, no-win, and thankless task, over which the family members must not destroy themselves. Loved ones often benefit from a self-help group, the Alzheimer's Disease and Related Disorders Association, Inc. (70 East Lake St., Chicago, IL 60601, 1-800-621-0379).

Biomedical Interventions

For calming agitation and alleviating insomnia, psychoactive drugs should be used cautiously, since they can also aggravate the patient's confusion and generate intolerable side effects. The patient, and especially his family, should be questioned about other drugs used medically or surreptitiously that might compound (or produce) the patient's symptoms. Anticholinergic agents, including those sold over-the-counter or prescribed for glaucoma, are common culprits. During the earlier stages of AD, a few medications may improve memory and concentration, albeit mildly. Lecithin, which contains choline, has been slightly useful for a third of patients.

If the patient has a MID, then removing the risk factors of hypertension, cigarette smoking, etc., is essential. If they help at all, cerebral vasodilators (e.g., Hydergine, Pavabid, Cyclospasmol) may be useful during the initial, but not later, stages of MID.

By diagnosing and treating pseudodementia and reversible dementias, by removing risk factors, and by helping families help the patient, today's clinician can offer enormous assistance to the demented patient and his family.

CHAPTER 8

Substance Abuse

SUBSTANCE ABUSE IS as old as the substances abused.[1] Rock carvings in caves from the fourth millennium B.C. display workmen making beer from barley. In 2285 B.C. a gentleman in China was allegedly banished for getting soused on a rice beverage. Individuals and religions of every era have sought to suspend people's realities and to alter their moods by the simplest and quickest way possible—"better living through chemistry."

The current frequency of this "better living" is hard to assess epidemiologically: The drug scene constantly changes, users are reluctant to mention their drug-taking, antidrug/alcohol groups have vested interests in exaggerating dangers, definitions of drug misuse vary considerably, and it's unclear which substances are deemed problematic—e.g., tobacco?, caffeine?, alcohol? Having said this, eight facts are worth noting: (a) The ECA survey of substance abuse by adult Americans revealed six-month and lifetime prevalence rates of 6.4% and 19.2% respectively—two-thirds from alcohol, one-third from other drugs. (b) These figures do not include the most frequent mental disorder among Americans, tobacco use disorder, whose lifetime prevalence is 36%. (c) Substance abuse is greatest among 18- to 24-year-olds. From 1975–1979, about 65% of high-school seniors reported using at some time in their life at least one illicit drug—most often, marijuana. During middle age, alcoholism is more of a problem. (e) After age 44, substance misuse

---

[1]"Substance" is a general term, encompassing alcohol, recreational drugs, and medications. "Substance," "chemical," and "drugs" are employed interchangeably. Nonpsychoactive drugs (e.g., insulin) are also abused, but, like *DSM-III*, this book solely discusses *psychoactive* substances. Unless otherwise specified, *this* text uses (or abuses) "misuse" and "abuse" synonymously.

112

declines for both sexes. (f) Substances are abused more by men than women, more by inner-city residents than country dwellers, more by nongraduates than college graduates. (g) Whites and blacks have the same overall rate of substance abuse. Table 8-1 presents the generic, brand, and street names of the commonly misused substances.

Definitions

DSM-III distinguishes *recreational* drug use (which merely produces a "high," verbiosity, giggling, or slurred speech), from an actual mental *disorder* (which requires impaired social or occupational functioning in addition to an OBS). The mental disorders defined in *DSM-III* fall into two categories: *substance-induced organic mental disorders*, in which the drug's acute or chronic effects directly disrupt the nervous system, such as in amnestic disorders, hallucinosis, intoxication, and withdrawal; and *substance use disorders*, in which the sustained consumption of a chemical causes drug dependency.

Intoxication and withdrawal are the most prevalent substance-induced OMDs. *Intoxication* is a substance-specific syndrome of maladaptive behavior that arises during or shortly after ingesting a substance. Intoxication generally disturbs perceptions, wakefulness, sleep, attention, judgment, emotionality, and movement. *Withdrawal* is a substance-specific syndrome that follows when a chronic intake of a substance has been abruptly stopped or greatly diminished. Withdrawal usually manifests as restlessness, apprehension, anxiety, irritability, insomnia, and impaired concentration.

Intoxication and withdrawal involve two pharmacological phenomena: *Tolerance*, which is the necessity to increase a drug's intake to attain its original effects, and *cross-tolerance*, which occurs when a drug exhibits tolerance to other drugs, usually in the same class. For example, patients tolerant to diazepam are tolerant to barbiturates, but not to heroin. In general, the more an individual's tolerance to a drug, the worse the withdrawal and the more he must take of a drug in the same class to become intoxicated.

DSM-III subdivides substance use disorders into substance *dependence* and substance *abuse*.[2] *Drug dependence* is the repeated, nonmedical use of a substance that harms the user or others, and involves psychological and/or physical dependence. *Psychological dependence* or *habituation* involves the compulsive misuse of a substance, intense craving, and a preoccupation with

---

[2]Because substance abuse and dependence have so many overlapping features, *DSM-III-R* plans to dump this distinction; it also may replace the term "substance use disorders" with "psychoactive substance dependence disorders."

TABLE 8-1
Names of Misused Substances

CATEGORY	TYPE	GENERIC NAME	BRAND NAME	STREET NAMES
Alcohol				
Anticholinergics		atropine	Butabell	
		belladonna	Donnatal	
		benztropine	Cogentin	
		trihexyphenidyl	Artane	
Cannabis (THC)	Hashish	Cannabis (female) resin		hash
	Marijuana	Cannabis leaves, stems		ganja, grass, reefer, pot, weed, smoke
Hallucinogens ("Psychedelics")	Amphetamine-like	DMT, DET, DOM, MDA		businessman's special,
	Others	LSD		blotter, acid, sunshine, purple haze, windowpane
		mescaline		peyote cactus,
		myristicin		nutmeg
		psilocybin		magic mushroom, buttons
Hypnosedatives (See Appendices C & D)	Barbiturates	amobarbital	Amytal	downers, barbs blues, lilly
		pentobarbital	Nembutal	yellow jackets
		phenobarbital	Luminal	purple hearts
		secobarbital	Seconal	reds, pink lady
	Barbiturate-like	chloral hydrate	Noctec	Mickey Finn
		ethchlorvynol	Placidyl	(with alcohol)
		glutethimide	Doriden	
		mebrobamate	Equinil Miltown	
		methaqualone	Quäälude Parest	ludes, Q, sopors, lemmons
		methyprylon	Noludar	
	Benzodiazepines (short-acting)	alprazolam	Xanax	
		lorazepam	Ativan	
		oxazepam	Serax	
		temazepam	Restoral	
		triazolam	Halcion	
	(long-acting)	chlordiazepoxide	Librium	libbies
		clorazepate	Tranxene	
		diazepam	Valium	Vitamin V
		flurazepam	Dalmane	
		prazepam	Centrax	
MDMA		3,4-methylenedi-oxymeth-amphetamine		ecstasy, XTC

114

TABLE 8-1
(Continued)

CATEGORY	TYPE	GENERIC NAME	BRAND NAME	STREET NAMES
Opiates		codeine	Empirin with codeine	
		diphenoxylate	Lomotil	
		heroin		smack, skag, H, snow, horse
		hydromorphone	Dilaudid	lords, dL's
		meperidine	Demerol	
		methylmorphine	(codeine)	
		methadone	Dolophine	dollys, amidone
		morphine		dope, M, Miss Emma, morpho
		opium (tincture of)	Paregoric	PG, licorice
		oxycodone	Percodan	percs
Pentazocine			Talwin	
Phencyclidine (PCP)			Ketamine Sernyl	angel dust, killer weed, crystal, hog, peace pill
Solvents	(Inhalants)	amyl nitrite		amys, pears
		butyl nitrite	Rush, Locker room	poppers, snapper
		carbon dioxide		wippit
		ether		
		ethyl chloride		Ethel
		nitrous oxide		laughing gas
		toluene		
Stimulants	(Major) Amphetamines	dextroamphetamine	Dexadrine	uppers, speed brownies, wake-ups, black beauties
		dextroamphetamine/amobarbital	Dexamyl	greenies
		dL-amphetamine	Benzadrine	bennies, A's, jelly beans, peaches
		methamphetamine	Desoxyyn, Methedrine	meth, crystal
	Cocaine			coke, flake, toot, snow, crack freebase
	Cocaine with heroin			speedball, white tornado
	Misc.	methylphenidate	Ritalin	
		pemoline	Cylert	
	(Minor) Caffeine		Vivarin, No Doz, Coke, coffee	
	Nicotine		Marlboro	

obtaining it, often at the expense of occupational, social, medical, or financial considerations. *Physical dependence* is the repeated use of a drug to avert withdrawal. Psychological and physical dependencies may coexist.

In *DSM-III*, a *substance abuse disorder* requires a pattern of (a) pathological use, such as daily intoxication, inability to cut down or stop, or on-going use of a substance despite a serious physical disease, (b) impaired functioning (e.g., missing work, being arrested for drug-related activity, can't study as necessary, disrupted interpersonal relations), and (c) substance misuse lasting over one month. *Substance dependence disorders* include all the criteria for substance abuse, plus tolerance *or* withdrawal. In *DSM-III*, substance *misuse* encompasses all drug and alcohol problems. Table 8-2 compares the major pharmacologic of commonly misused substances.

THE ASSESSMENT OF
SUBSTANCE MISUSE

Many factors complicate the diagnosis and treatment of substance abusers. They give unreliable histories. Unlike most patients, their objectives differ from the therapist's: Abusers want their habit or, as a heroin addict said, "If I had to choose between smack and castration, I'd take smack." Denial and lying are their norm; at times, even the addict doesn't know which he's doing. Outright lying is common to avoid detection and to hasten discharge. On admission, however, the already-discovered addict may exaggerate his intake to garner more of the drug during detoxification. For all these reasons, clinicians should favor objective signs and social behaviors over subjective reports, and corroborate and supplement this information by interviewing family and friends.

Because these patients frequently lie and deny, manipulate professionals, and relapse, they habitually frustrate and infuriate clinicians. Therefore, therapists should constantly check their own angry and moralistic feelings towards these patients. Moreover, therapists should not take these patients' provocations and relapses personally: They are part of the natural history of substance abuse. Guidelines for evaluating substance abusers are listed in Table 8-3.

Complicating the assessment is that patterns of substance abuse constantly change. During the past decade, the use of marijuana, LSD, nicotine, and hypnosedatives has declined, while the use of opiates, cocaine, amphetamines, and phencyclidine (PCP) has increased. (Alcohol misuse has remained constant.) As soon as clinicians get on top of one drug problem, another pops up, resulting in a constant information-lag about drug abuse. More serious is that *polydrug abuse* has shot up. In comparison to single drug abusers, polydrug abusers have more severe withdrawals and bleaker

TABLE 8-2
Phamacology of Misused Substances

DRUG	PSYCHOLOGICAL DEPENDENCE	PHYSICAL DEPENDENCE	TOLERANCE	LETHAL OVERDOSES
ALCOHOL	mild to marked	mild to marked	some	+
AMPHETAMINES and other stimulants	mild to marked	mild	marked	rare
BARBITURATES and some other hypnosedatives	mild to marked	mild to marked	substantial	+
BENZODIAZE-PINES	mild to moderate	mild to moderate	minimal	rare
CAFFEINE	mild	mild	little, if any	–
CANNABIS	mild to moderate	little, if any	(?) at * higher doses	–
COCAINE	mild to marked	yes (mild withdrawal)	yes	rare†
HALLUCINO-GENS	mild to moderate	none	mild to marked; rapid,* reversed*	rare
MDMA	none	none	? rapid	once
OPIATES	moderate to marked	marked	marked	+
PHENCYCLIDINE	?	some	moderate	+
SOLVENTS and INHALENTS	mild to moderate	little, if any	moderate	+
TOBACCO	mild to moderate	mild to moderate	nominal	–

*Tolerance for hallucinogens varies considerably, depending on the specific drug. For some, tolerance develops rapidly (e.g., after two to three doses). As with some marijuana smokers, some hallucinogen users develop a "reverse tolerance"—"the cheap date"—in which the more a drug is used, the *less* is needed to obtain the original effects.

†As with John Belushi, "speedballs"—IV cocaine and heroin—are often fatal.

prognoses. They are harder to diagnose and treat, especially in emergencies, since they present a more confounding mix of signs and symptoms than single substance abusers. Not uncommonly an inpatient is being successfully treated for an opiate intoxication, when four days later he suddenly convulses from barbiturate withdrawal. The lesson— polydrug abuse must be evaluated for every substance abuser.

TABLE 8-3
The Assessment of Substance Misuse

I. HISTORY

A. *Substance(s)*
1. Name(s) (e.g., diazepam, cocaine)
2. Polydrug use: Indicates names and preferred combinations
3. Special preparations (e.g., freebasing)

B. *Route* (e.g., ingestion, inhalation, injection)

C. *Amount*
1. Typical dose, frequency, and duration of drug use
2. Dose and duration of drug use during past 10 days
3. The time and amount of the most recent drug use

D. *Patterns of Use*
1. Self-medication: for physical, psychiatric, or emotional problems
2. Identifiable events or stresses that increase or decrease the use of a substance (e.g., drinking before sex, "chipping" heroin before job interviews, smoking after meals)
3. History: How did substance abuse begin? Why does it continue? Are there conditioned relapses? What began and ended the patient's longest drugfree period?
4. Timing: How early in the day does the patient first use the substance?
5. Style (e.g., sneaking drugs, hiding bottles, boasting, running away, using substances with others or by himself)

E. *Acquisition*
1. Sources: legal, illegal, prescription, theft, "mobsters," friends
2. Time and money spent obtaining substances

F. *Network*
1. Family and friends: Which exert beneficial and harmful influences on the patient?
2. Family history of antisocial personality, substance misuse, and affective disorder.

G. *Functioning*
1. Interference with social, occupational, recreational, academic, and familial functioning
2. Adverse influence on physical health, appearance, finances, and self-image
3. How does the patient feel *without* the drug?
4. Impaired organic functioning, such as forgetting location of "stash," poor concentration, impaired judgment
5. Does patient become suicidal or assaultive on the drug?

H. *History: Medical and Psychiatric*
1. Drug-related medical illnesses: hepatitis, infections, insomnia, allergies, cirrhosis, TB, AIDS, epilepsy
2. All recently-taken prescribed and over-the-counter drugs. Does the patient use these medications differently from the way they were prescribed or intended? Does the patient take or sneak other people's or family members' medications? (Have family bring all medications in the patient's home.)

118

TABLE 8-3
(Continued)

3. History of psychiatric symptoms or mental illness prior to his substance misuse
4. History of substance-related syndromes: flashbacks, delirium, idiosyncratic intoxication, hallucinosis

I. *Prior Treatment*
  1. Type, duration, degree of participation, including experiences with community agencies and self-help groups
  2. Results, as seen by (a) the patient, (b) his relatives, and (c) his therapists

J. *Current Motivations to Change*
  1. Why the patient is seeking treatment *now*?
  2. Current threat of jail, divorce, etc.

II. COMMON SYMPTOMS AND SIGNS
[With special signs among students in brackets]

A. *Prodromal Phase*
  1. Increased tolerance
  2. Sneaking chemicals [frequenting odd places, such as closets or storage rooms during school, to take drugs]
  3. Temporary amnesia
  4. Preoccupation with chemical use
  5. Avoids talking about personal use
  6. More frequent loss of memory

B. *Crucial or Basic Phase*
  7. Time lost from work [or changes in school attendance, grades, or discipline]
  8. Loss of control [unusual or apparently unmotivated temper outbursts]
  9. Alibis [especially about not doing homework]
  10. Increased extravagance—time, money, advice; being a "know-it-all"
  11. Aggressive or abusive behavior
  12. Persistent remorse
  13. Periodic abstinence
  14. Losing or changing friends
  15. Losing clients or position
  16. Persistent resentments
  17. Diminished self-care and unhealthy appearance
  18. Slovenly dress, sunglasses at inappropriate times (to hide dilated or constricted pupils and to diminish increased glare), and long-sleeved shirts (to hide needle marks)
  19. Borrowing money [and theft of small items from school] to buy drugs
  20. Escape—geographical, psychological, social
  21. Protecting supply [furtive looks to avoid stash being detected]
  22. Morning use of chemical(s)

C. *Chronic Phase*
  23. More-or-less continuous use over 10-hour period
  24. Ethical deterioration

(continued)

119

TABLE 8-3
(Continued)

25. Decreased tolerance
26. Sleeping at inappropriate times
27. Indefinable fears
29. Tangential or incoherent speech; inappropriate remarks
30. Tremors
31. Quest for spiritual needs

III. PHYSICAL EXAMINATION

A. *Rectal and pelvic examinations*:
    1. Critical, since substance abusers notoriously hide and smuggle drugs in weird places

B. *Physical signs*:
    1. Marks: scarring along a vein, tatooing over a vein, abscesses, ulcers, and needle tracks. The quantity and age of needle marks can be a rough check on the validity of the patient's history.
    2. Nose: Is it dripping? Are nasal membranes infected, swollen, or septum eroded from snorting cocaine?
    3. Pupils: Constricted (miosis) with opiates and PCP; Dilated (mydriasis) with amphetamines, anticholinergics, hallucinogens, and marijuana
    4. Signs of intoxication or withdrawal (Tables 8-4 and 8-7)

IV. LABORATORY EXAMINATIONS

A. *Urine screens* for drugs:
    1. Thin Layer Chemistry (TLC): highly inaccurate, and virtually useless (Cost: ca $10)
    2. Enzyme Immuno Assay (EIA) and Radio Immuno Assay (RIA): These two tests have relatively high degrees of sensitivity; the EIA is a qualitative test, the RIA, quantitative (Cost: ca $55 each)
    3. Gas Chromotography Mass Spectometry (GC/MS) The most reliable and informative of tests (Cost: ca $185)

B. *Serum levels*
    1. Abused substances (when urine tests are positive, or abused substances are already known)
    2. Other psychotropic drugs (e.g., antidepressants)

C. *Liver and renal function tests*

In general, withdrawal, intoxication, and dependence should be addressed in this sequence. The most dangerous acute problem is *hypnosedative* (including alcohol) withdrawal, since this can be lethal, whereas opiate withdrawal is, at most, uncomfortable. (Patients with a serious medical problem can die from opiate withdrawal.) When it's unclear whether the patient is intoxicated or withdrawing from hypnosedatives, err by treating withdrawal, since that poses a greater threat than intoxication.

Patients who are at high risk for being hypnosedative abusers may have any of the following: (a) histories of drug misuse, alcoholism, and polydrug abuse, (b) signs of hypnosedative withdrawal (see Table 8-4), (c) recent unexplained convulsions, and (d) insomnia the first night either off drugs or in the hospital. Health-care professionals are another high-risk group. Hypnosedative withdrawal can occur up to *ten days after the last dose.* If there is any question of hypnosedative misuse, a test dose of pentobarbital should be given to *estimate* the patient's tolerance (Table 8-5).

Once the total daily tolerance level to a pentobarbital-equivalent is determined, the patient can be tapered from any hypnosedative, 10% less per day. Chlordiazepoxide is preferred for alcohol withdrawal; pentobarbital, given in three equal doses, works fine for withdrawing other hypnosedatives. If the total daily tolerance to hypnosedatives is the pentobarbital-equivalent of 900 mg, the patient might receive 300 mg of (oral) pentobarbital three times a day. Two to three days before the end of withdrawal, pentobarbital can be replaced by phenobarbital, which creates a smoother withdrawal because of its longer half-life. If hypnosedative withdrawal is imminent and there is no time to perform a test dose, 200 mg of pentobarbital should be given immediately. If the patient is free of hypnosedatives or has been taking small doses, an hour later he will be asleep or show coarse nystagmus, unsteady gait, muscle incoordination, a positive Romberg, and slurred speech. If these signs are absent, then the patient is tolerant to hypnosedatives and must be withdrawn carefully.

According to the *self-medication hypothesis*, the patient's original choice of an abused drug is not random, but is partly made to alleviate a specific distressing symptom or affect. At first, he may try narcotics to mask pain, hypnotics to sleep, cocaine to eliminate depression, amphetamines to "get up," marijuana to join the crowd, or bourbon to rid boredom. Yet no matter how substance abuse begins, once it becomes habitual and stopping it causes severe distress, the patient is drug dependent. At this juncture his habit occurs less from original motives and more to quell a drug-induced biological imperative. Therefore, treating the initial cause is ineffective: Drug dependence must be treated first, and only then can the original problems be rectified.

Many of a substance abuser's problems, including conditions likely to prompt relapse, cannot be evaluated properly until the patient has been drugfree for ten days. (Some experts suggest one to three months.) For example, when hospitalized, a chronic alcoholic was very suspicious. After three weeks of "drying out" and having his "head clear," his suspiciousness disappeared; only then did it become apparent that marital problems greatly affected his alcoholism.

TABLE 8-4
Alcohol-Hypnosedative Withdrawal*

STAGE	SYMPTOMS AND SIGNS°	TIMING	PERCENT OF PATIENTS
I. "THE SHAKES"	Tremor, bad dreams, insomnia, morning sweats, apprehension, blepharospasm, agitation, ataxia, dilated pupils, increased blood pressure and respiration, nausea, vomiting, flushed, postural hypotension; atypically have transient hallucinations and illusions; rum fits—14%†	4–8 hours after last dose; peaks at 24 hours; may last 2 weeks; may occur on substance	80
II. HALLUCINOSIS	Auditory hallucinations both vague (e.g., buzzes, hums) and specific (e.g., accusatory voices); clear consciousness must exist; fear, apprehension, panic, tinnitus, atypically other hallucinations and some clouding of consciousness occur; rum fits—3%†	Onset may occur on drug or up to 12–48 hours (and infrequently, up to 7 days) after last dose; usually lasts one week, but can last over two months	5
III. SEIZURES ("Rum fits"†)	Single or multiple grand mal convulsions; occasionally status epilepticus; muscle jerks.	Appears 6–48 hours after last dose; peaks at 12–24 hours; seizures usually first arise 16 hours into withdrawal	10
IV. DELIRIUM TREMENS	Typical delirium: clouded consciousness, confusion, disorientation, fluctuating consciousness; loss of recent memory, illusions and hallucinations (of all types, often scary), agitation, emotional lability (e.g., laughing, crying, anger, fear), delusions of persecution, performing imaginary tasks, severe ataxia, coarse tremor; REM rebound (up to 3–4 months); rum fits—41%; 1–15% of DT patients die.	Appears 48–96 hours after last dose; persists 4–7 days without complications; convulsions first appear 16 hours into withdrawal, and psychotic symptoms, 36 hours into withdrawal.	15

*The withdrawal pattern presented here applies most to alcohol, barbiturates, and barbiturate-like hypnosedatives; these same symptoms and stages occur, albeit less frequently and severely, with benzodiazepines. These stages may evolve gradually or quickly, present typically or atypically. Any stage of withdrawal may be entered without passing through any prior stage.

°The three most objective signs of alcohol-hypnosedative withdrawal are (a) *insomnia*, (b) *postural hypotension* (with a corresponding pulse rise [over 12–15 beats] on standing), and (c) *blepharospasm*, which is illicited by rapidly tapping the glabella (point between eyes at top of the nose) with a finger. Normally, people respond with a few blinks and stop, but in blepharospasm they blink with increasing intensity, and can only stop by closing their eyes, staring at the examiner, or actively forcing themselves to not spasm. Sometimes they experience pain.

†"Rum fits" are convulsions that occur during any stage of withdrawal. They are most intense and frequent during stage III, which often heralds stage IV. About 20% of patients with DTs have already had a seizure.

TABLE 8-5
Test Dose to Estimate Tolerance to Hypnosedatives

I. Estimate the patient's total daily amount of the abused substance, and then convert this dose to pentobarbital-equivalents. For example, 100 mg of pentobarbital is equal to:

1. meprobamate (Miltown) .... 400 mg
2. flurazepam (Dalmane) .... 30 mg
3. diazepam (Valium) .... 10 mg
4. glutethimide (Doriden) .... 500 mg
5. most barbiturates .... 100 mg
6. whisky .... 3 to 4 ounces

II. The morning following admission, the patient receives 200 mg of pentobarbital. (A 300 mg test dose is better for patients known to take over a pentobarbital-equivalent of 1200 mg a day. For elderly patients, the test dose should be 100 mg.)

III. Examine the patient 50 minutes later. Signs of tolerance to a total daily dose of pentobarbital-equivalents are:

Tolerant to: >800 mg = no signs of intoxication
700–800 mg = nystagmus only*
500–700 mg = nystagmus, mild ataxia*, and possible dysarthria*
300–400 mg = coarse nystagmus, positive Romberg*, gross ataxia, sleepiness
<300 mg = sound sleep

IV. Inaccurate estimations of tolerance may occur if the patient hasn't taken the full test dose or has taken other drugs. Tolerance increases with greater anxiety or agitation.

Nystagmus is an involuntary rapid movement of the eyeball when the patient fixes a stare either horizontally or vertically. *Ataxia* refers to muscle incoordination. *Dysarthria* is slurred speech. A positive *Romberg* is when a patient's body sways when standing with feet together and eyes closed.

ALCOHOL

There are more English synonyms for "drunk" than for any other word. Benjamin Franklin was the first to publish them — 228; recently Flexner listed 353 and said he just scratched the surface. "Alcohol" comes from the Arabic "*alkuhl*," Arabs being the first to distill it in 600 A.D. Genghis Khan counseled his troops, "A soldier must not get drunk oftener than once a week. It would, of course, be better if he did not get drunk at all, but one should not expect the impossible" (Goodwin & Guze, 1984, p. 148).

Today, alcoholism is America's most serious drug problem, as it is for every other industrialized nation; it costs New York City alone a "mere" $1 billion a year. Alcoholism is an illness of "normal" people, not bums. The typical alcoholic is in his middle thirties and has a good job, home, and family. Less than 5% of alcoholics are on Skid Row.

A practical definition of alcoholism could be "when a person's alcohol consumption repeatedly interferes with his occupational or social functioning, emotional state, or physical health." This definition stresses whether alcohol impairs the individual instead of setting some arbitrary number, such as whether the person downs one or five or 50 drinks a week. People with a condition called *idiosyncratic intoxication* often become violent on a single drink; for them, one drink is alcoholism. In the service of denial, patients and relatives will nitpick over alcoholism's definition; by stating that alcoholism exists whenever problems with alcohol keep arising, the clinician circumvents semantic quibbling.

Clinical Presentation

Although alcoholics vary considerably, in general they suffer from apprehension, agitation, dysphoria, guilt, remorse, despair, hopelessness, futility, self-deprecation, and insomnia. Their symptoms are usually worse in the morning, when the patient hasn't drunk for hours. *The Lost Weekend*—a "must-see" movie for every clinician—portrays with bone-chilling accuracy the "typical" alcoholic's life: obsessed with drink, continually lying about it, hiding bottles, sneaking booze, and disappearing repeatedly. After "going on the wagon," they will reexperience anxiety or depression, and start drinking again; a vicious spiral of abstinence-dysphoria-drinking escalates until the alcoholic reaches "rock bottom."[3]

DSM-III lists nine mental disorders related to alcohol, and Table 8-6 enumerates the diagnostic criteria for the "big four": intoxication, withdrawal, abuse, and dependence. (The others are idiosyncratic intoxication, withdrawal delirium, hallucinosis, amnestic disorder, and dementia.)

Withdrawal, which is detailed in Table 8-4, is most critical, since 15% of alcoholics who develop delirium tremens ("DTs") die. The first and most common withdrawal symptom is tremulousness, which begins a few hours after stopping, or greatly reducing, alcohol intake. When transitory hallucinations occur, it's usually 12 to 24 hours after cessation of alcohol. By the second or third day, the alcoholic may undergo "rum fits," which are convulsions, and/or DTs. Days later, if the patient is hearing voices, he has probably

---

[3]The alcoholic's usual alternating between drinking to feel good and then drinking to not feel bad, may be related to the increase of serotonin that occurs while intoxicated and the subnormal levels that occur afterwards (Goodwin, 1985).

TABLE 8-6
DSM-III* Criteria for Major Alcohol Problems

ALCOHOL INTOXICATION

A. Recent ingestion of alcohol (with no evidence suggesting that the amount was insufficient to cause intoxication in most people).

B. Maladaptive behavioral effects, e.g., fighting, impaired judgment, interference with social or occupational functioning.

C. At least one of the following physiological signs:

(1) slurred speech
(2) incoordination
(3) unsteady gait
(4) nystagmus
(5) flushed face

D. At least one of the following psychological signs:

(1) mood change
(2) irritability
(3) loquacity
(4) impaired attention

E. Not due to any other physical or mental disorder.

ALCOHOL WITHDRAWAL

A. Cessation of or reduction in heavy prolonged (several days or longer) ingestion of alcohol, followed within several hours by a coarse tremor of hands, tongue, and eyelids *and* at least one of the following:

(1) nausea and vomiting
(2) malaise or weakness
(3) autonomic hyperactivity (e.g., tachycardia, sweating, elevated blood pressure
(4) anxiety
(5) depressed mood or irritability
(6) orthostatic hypotension

B. Not due to any other physical or mental disorder such as Alcohol Withdrawal Delirium.

ALCOHOL ABUSE

A. *Pattern of pathological alcohol use*: need for daily use of alcohol for adequate functioning; inability to cut down or stop drinking; repeated efforts to control or reduce excess drinking by "going on the wagon" (periods of temporary abstinence) or re-

(continued)

TABLE 8-6
(Continued)

ALCOHOL ABUSE

stricting drinking to certain times of the day; binges (remaining intoxicated throughout
the day for at least two days); occasional consumption of a fifth of spirits (or its
equivalent in wine or beer); amnestic periods for events occurring while intoxicated
(blackouts); continuation of drinking despite a serious physical disorder that the individual knows is exacerbated by alcohol use; drinking of nonbeverage alcohol.

B. *Impairment in social or occupational functioning due to alcohol use*: e.g., violence
while intoxicated, absence from work, loss of job, legal difficulties (e.g., arrest for
intoxicated behavior, traffic accidents while intoxicated), arguments or difficulties
with family or friends because of excessive alcohol use.

C. *Duration* of disturbance of at least a month.

ALCOHOL DEPENDENCE

A. Either a pattern of pathological alcohol use *or* impairment in social or occupational
functioning.

B. Either tolerance or withdrawal.

DSM-III Sources: Intoxication: p. 131; Withdrawal: pp. 133–134; Abuse: pp. 169–170; Dependence: p. 170.

developed a "chronic alcoholic hallucinosis," which can persist for over a
week.

Alcohol is one of the few drugs to cause "*blackouts*," a temporary (anterograde)
amnesia, in which short-term (but not long-term) memory is lost, while other intellectual and motor functions remain intact. To illustrate: The day after a "bender," an
alcoholic surgeon became angry at a nurse for allowing a tracheostomy to be done
on one of his patients without notifying him. She reminded the surgeon that he himself
did the procedure the day before. He apparently had a blackout, since he had no
recollection of doing it. As in this case, alcoholics may appear to function normally
and even perform complex tasks *during* a blackout. Research suggests the forgotten
material does not hold special psychological significance, but results from a neurological deficit in retrieving new information. Blackouts scare alcoholics, who are often
terrified of having committed violence they can't remember; blackouts also frighten
because they're dramatic proof—no pun intended—that alcohol is destroying the brain.
In truth, however, they have no prognostic significance.

Clinical Course

Male alcoholics usually begin heavy drinking during their late teens or
twenties, but only in their thirties, after a long and insidious course, do they
fully acknowledge their alcoholism. (Alcohol abuse rarely begins after age

45, and if it does, affective or brain disorders are the most likely culprits.) From ages 25 to 40, alcohol-related events typically unfold in this sequence: frequent drunks, weekend drunks, morning drinking, benders, neglecting meals, "shakes," job loss, separation, divorce, blackouts, joined AA, hospitalization, and delirium tremens. Although less is known about alcoholism among women, it appears to have a more variable course than among men, begins later, and has a lower rate of spontaneous remission.

Mortality rates of alcoholics are two or three times greater than for nonalcoholics. Because "spontaneous" improvement is more common than generally realized, *if the alcoholic can keep functioning when he reaches mid-life, his long-term prognosis improves considerably.* In other words, alcoholism is *not* hopeless!

Complications

Alcoholism is a major factor in 20% of divorces and 40% of problems brought to family court. Half of all police work, hospital admissions, homicides, and automobile fatalities are alcohol-related. One-fourth of suicides involve alcohol, especially in men over 35 who have suffered a recent loss. Suicide causes 5% to 27% of all deaths of alcoholics (Berglund, 1984).

Alcoholism assaults every organ; it causes anemia, muscle weakness, gastritis, diarrhea, ulcers, pancreatitis, "fetal alcohol syndromes," and birth defects. (Pregnant women should not drink.) Combined with poor nutrition, alcoholism may produce a fatty liver, cirrhosis, and the rapidly erupting *Wernicke-Korsakoff syndrome* of nystagmus, ataxia, and confusion. If W-K is not promptly treated with massive doses of thiamin and other B vitamins, in several days the patient may develop *Korsakoff psychosis*, a permanent dementia characterized by anterograde (short-term) amnesia and confabulation.

Epidemiology

Heavy drinkers are more often men (20%) than women (8%), from lower socioeconomic classes, less educated, black, and many (though not all) Native American tribes. The low rate of alcoholism among orientals may be due in part to the "oriental flushing phenomenon." When given a beer or two, 70% of orientals develop a flushed face and upper body, an uncomfortable warmth and queasiness, an increased heart rate, and lower blood pressure. This flushing is biologically-induced, since newborn orientals show it. Male alcoholics often have antisocial personality and other substance abuse disorders, while female alcoholics are prone to depression and phobia (Hesselbrock et al., 1985).

Prevalence rates for alcoholism are high among waiters, bartenders, longshoremen, musicians, authors, and reporters; they're low among accountants, postmen, ministers, and carpenters. It's a small sample, as Goodwin (1985) admits, but he says the highest alcoholism rate belongs to Americans who've won the Nobel Prize—five out of seven.

Etiology and Pathogenesis

About half of all hospitalized alcoholics have a family history of alcoholism. In contrast to "nonfamilial" alcoholics, these "familial" alcoholics become alcoholics earlier in life, have worse dependency, bleaker prognoses, and fewer nonalcoholic psychiatric problems, and are less able to maintain "controlled drinking." The best predictor of future alcoholism among adolescents is a family history of alcoholism (Goodwin, 1985).

Twin studies generally support this division, by showing that heredity plays a major role in some, but not all, cases of alcoholism. Whether reared by alcoholic biological parents or by nonalcoholic adopted parents, the sons of alcoholics have three to four times the normal rate of alcoholism, whereas daughters have the same rate as the general population. Twenty to 25% of sons of alcoholics become alcoholics; 5% to 10% of daughters become alcoholics. Affective disorders may run in the families of alcoholics, but this remains controversial.

Treatment and Management

The treatment of alcoholic dependence is the "standard AAA"—Abstinence, Antabuse, Alcoholics Anonymous. Since clinicians can't reliably predict which alcoholics belong to the 5% to 15% who can drink moderately, abstinence should be urged on all alcoholics; that's especially so for the first 6–12 months after hospitalization, when 70% to 90% of cases relapse. The longer patients remain dry, the sharper their thinking and the better their occupational, social, and sexual functioning.

Antabuse (disulfiram) helps many patients keep abstinent, because they know that if they drink while on the drug, they'll develop a flushed skin, nausea, tachycardia, and hypotension. The standard dose is 250 mg/day; higher doses offer no more deterrence and, if mixed with alcohol, are potentially lethal. Because Antabuse takes three to five days to be excreted, patients can take it only during the week, knowing its effects persist over the weekend. Nurses or family members can monitor the patient's use of Antabuse, especially during the postdischarge period.

Alcoholics Anonymous (AA) greatly benefits most alcoholics. AA doesn't go into *why* people drink, just that they *do*, and shouldn't; it stresses a "one-day-at-a-time" philosophy, which allows the alcoholic to deal with manageable units of time and end a "dry day" with a sense of accomplishment. On a trial basis at least, all alcoholics should attend AA meetings. Clinicians can help by finding a socially appropriate AA chapter for the patient, by not giving in to the alcoholic's rationalizations for why he can't go to this or that AA meeting, and by getting the patient linked up with an AA member who's on the same "wavelength" as the patient. AA also welcomes people with other drug problems, especially hypnosedative, marijuana, and cocaine dependence.

The clinician must also attend to the needs of the alcoholic's family. If one member drinks, the others shouldn't drown. Growing up with an alcoholic parent can be devastating; so is living with an alcoholic spouse. The clinician should make sure family members do not feel responsible for the alcoholic's drinking or obligated to "reform" him. Whether or not the alcoholic goes to AA, the patient's relatives should go to Alanon, a support group for family members, or to Alateen, which offers information and assistance to teenage alcoholics and to teenage relatives of alcoholics.

HYPNOSEDATIVES

Hypnosedatives quell anxiety, induce sleep, or both. Table 8-1 classifies the hypnosedatives into three groups: barbiturates, barbiturate-like, benzodiazepines. *Barbiturates* are the prototypic hypnosedative. The first barbiturate, Veronal—named after the tranquil Verona, Italy—was introduced in 1902 as a safe replacement for alcohol. *Benzodiazepines* are now the most widely prescribed hypnosedatives in the world. In the United States, 68 million prescriptions were written (in 1978) for benzodiazepines, with diazepam being the nation's fourth most frequently prescribed drug. (Hypnosedatives are described in Tables 8-2 and 8-4, and in Appendices D and E.)

When taken as an overdose, benzodiazepines are rarely lethal. Relative to barbiturates, less tolerance develops to benzodiazepines, withdrawal is infrequent, and potentiation by alcohol is minimal (Goodwin & Guze, 1984). Benzodiazepines, however, are not innocuous: The elderly are highly sensitive to them. Whether they produce birth defects remains unknown. Longer-acting benzodiazepines may insidiously slow thinking and moving. Psychological dependence may arise from ongoing use; in one survey, 58% of long-term users admitted they would have "difficulty" without them (Salzman, 1985). Four to six years after being hospitalized for hypnosedative dependence, 84% of patients were using hypnosedatives, 52% were abusing them, 42% had been rehospitalized for drug misuse, and 12% had had withdrawal convulsions (Allgulander, et al., 1984). Although benzodiazepine withdrawal is usually mild, it can be severe. If there is any question of physical dependency, a test-dose of pentobarbitol should be evaluated (Table 8-5).

According to *DSM-III*, hypnosedative (physical) dependence generally occurs on the frequent use of 600 mg a day of secobarbitol equivalents or 60 mg a day of diazepam equivalents. A mild benzodiazepine abstinence syndrome consists of anxiety, irritability, dry mouth, a choking feeling, hot and cold sensations, trembling, weak legs, hand tremors, diminished appetite, nausea, and mild dysthymia. Insomnia often persists for three to four days; normal sleep returns in a week. In more severe benzodiazepine withdrawal, patients have increased tension, poor concentration, weight loss, panic attacks, palpitations, muscular pains, and occasionally seizures.

Benzodiazepines are classified as "short-acting" or "long-acting," with half-lives of 8–12 hours and over 45 hours, respectively. (A drug's "half-life" is when 50% of it has become pharmacologically inactive.) More cases of benzodiazepine withdrawal have been reported with long-term, low-dose use than with short-term, high-dose use. For example, 15 mg of daily diazepam for two years apparently causes more physical dependence than 50 mg of daily diazepam for two months. Short-acting benzodiazepines, while causing less hangover, also cause more withdrawal.

On first prescribing any psychoactive agent, but especially a hypnosedative, the physician must warn the patient that, for a week or so, his "reflexes" might be a tad slow, and that he should be extra-careful around machines, crossing streets, and cooking. Nonalcoholic patients can drink on hypnosedatives (and other psychotropic drugs), but they should be told that "one drink will probably feel like two to three drinks."

STIMULANTS

Cocaine. Americans consume 50 metric tons of cocaine each year. Fifteen percent of high school students have snorted "coke," while 10% Americans have taken, as Cole Porter's (1934) lyric goes, "even one sniff" of cocaine. Chic in Porter's day, by the mid-1980s cocaine has so dropped in price that it's commonly used in all social classes. With growing use, there is a growing awareness of its hazards. Whereas *DSM-III* lists only cocaine intoxication and abuse, *DSM-III-R* plans to add cocaine withdrawal and delirium, as well as delusional, flashback, and residual disorders. Although psychological dependency is more striking, increasingly a moderate physical dependency is being seen.

A typical story starts with the curious paying $75 to $150 a gram for a white powder ("snow"), which is usually 30% cocaine and 70% adulterants (e.g., inactive sugars). After making a thin, two-inch line of the powder, the user snorts it with a straw or rolled up dollar bill. This launches a 30-minute high, which tapers off in 60–90 minutes. The user feels energetic, creative, talkative, attractive, excited, euphoric, and motivated; he flirts with grandiosity and feels "connected." Initial negative reactions include restlessness, agitation, anxiety, hyperexcitability, and hostility.

Habitual cocaine abusers gradually become obsessed with the drug and securing its supply. Not uncommonly, the user blows over $3,000 a week on the drug. A week, and then a day, cannot pass without that "extra boost." When high, the user can't sleep, and when asleep, he can't awake. "Freebasing" may start.[4] On crashing (i.e., withdrawing), he feels depressed, anergic, and unmotivated. Appetite's gone, weight drops, often to medically precarious levels. Noses drip and bleed continuously, exhausting endless supplies of gauze. Work is missed, jobs are lost, friends lose patience, and marriages die.

And yet, of those who actually called a cocaine hotline (1-800-Cocaine), most still preferred to continue their habit because it produced euphoria (82%), diminished boredom (57%), increased energy and self-confidence (48%), and stimulated sexuality (21%). Callers said cocaine was more important than food (71%), sex (50%), family activities (72%), and friends (64%). Among all the callers, 61% snorted the drug, 21% freebased, and 18% injected it. Half used the drug daily. On average, users spent $637 a week on cocaine (Gold, 1984).

Tentative evidence suggests that tricyclic antidepressants might help some cocaine-dependent patients, and that (the dopamine agonist) bromocriptine (0.6255 mg) exerts an anticraving effect in one to two minutes. By helping patients get off and stay off cocaine, these drugs might enable cocaine abusers to participate more effectively in rehabilitative treatments, such as Cocaine Anonymous or AA. As Sherlock Holmes' case illustrates (Chapter 6), cocaine's many "advantages" offer former abusers little incentive to remain drug-free. Therefore, therapy must help the patient find or rediscover interests that will "replace" cocaine in the person's life.

Amphetamines. Intoxications and withdrawals from cocaine and amphetamine are similar. As overdoses, both are potentially fatal. Their long-term use is associated with increased morbidity, mortality, criminality, as well as ongoing, diffuse suspiciousness and a chronic organic delusional syndrome.

Differences between the two drugs exist. Tolerance hardly (or doesn't) develop to cocaine, but it rapidly develops to amphetamines: In just three days, "speed freaks" can go from 15 mg to 2,000 mg a day to obtain the original effects. Whereas the acute effects of a single amphetamine dose lasts four to six hours, those from cocaine rarely extend beyond two hours. More often than cocaine, amphetamines may trigger a toxic psychosis resembling paranoid schizophenia.

Seven days before taking the Medical College Admissions Test (MCAT), Darlene was frantic. Night and day she crammed, with an hourly 5-mg "black beauty" (i.e., dextroamphetamine). Darlene was not only awake, she was flying. Never did she feel more alert and focused. After two days of nonstop studying, she began pacing ("because I can concentrate better"). By day three, she repeatedly told her roommate that the MCATs were "dumb" — an insight which Darlene considered brilliant — and by day four she began shouting this indictment out her apartment window. By nightfall, she was convinced the MCAT-people hired mobsters to break her arms and legs; already they were playing tricks on her eyes: One moment beatles were crawling in her hair,

---

[4]In freebasing, a highly flammable solvent (e.g., ether) is heated to separate the adulterants. The result is pure cocaine, aptly called "white tornado," because when smoked it produces an intense two-minute high, followed by extreme dysphoria, craving, and often by marathon "coke" binges of 24–96 hours, or until supplies run out.

the next moment they disappeared. The telephone rang, wrong number; surely the MCAT-mobsters. To protect herself, she bolted the door. Believing strangers in front of her apartment were also MCAT-mobsters, she hurled darts and dishes at them. As typically occurs, Darlene became psychotic on 60 mg a day, was psychotic for two weeks, and recovered fully. (Six months later she got high scores on the MCATs.)

During an acute stimulant intoxication, the patient's safety should be insured and he should be observed continuously. Physical restraints may be needed. If paranoid, the patient's environment should be simplified, as few people as possible should care for him, and anything he deems dangerous should be removed. An increasing body temperature indicates an increasingly dangerous toxicity. Antipsychotic drugs (e.g., haloperidol 2 mg to 5 mg orally or IM) are effective in treating intoxication.

Amphetamines have no place in dieting and a dubious role in depression. They do have two legitimate medical indications—treating narcoleptic sleep attacks and childhood hyperactivity. Even here they must be used cautiously, or, as rock star Frank Zappa warned, "Speed will turn you into your parents."

Nicotine. There are two "minor stimulants"—caffeine and nicotine. Caffeine's effects are presented in Chapter 12 and its sources on Table 12-3. Nicotine has always been controversial. The Turkish and German governments once considered smoking in public an offense punishable by death; the Russians preferred castration. Americans subsidized its growth and made it a mental disorder in *DSM-III*.

The essential features of tobacco dependence are its continuous use for over a month, plus *one* of the following: (a) the inability to stop or significantly reduce one's smoking, (b) the development of a tobacco withdrawal syndrome (with craving, irritability, anxiety, concentration difficulties, restlessness, headache, drowsiness, or GI disturbances), or (c) the existence of a cigarette-induced physical disorder.

Men smoke more than women, but are also more successful in stopping. The most effective treatment programs combine education, group support, and behavior modification; yet, even here 80% of patients relapse within a year. Hypnosis, nicotine gum, and gradual substitution with lower nicotine-containing cigarettes help only a few smokers. Recent studies of male heavy smokers undergoing nicotine withdrawal show that clonidine (0.2 mg) substantially decreases their craving and anxiety, whereas the benzodiazephine alprazolam (1.0 mg) only diminishes anxiety (Glassman et al., 1984).

HALLUCINOGENS

In 1938, while investigating ergot preparations for a pharmaceutical firm in Basel, Albert Hofmann synthesized the first LSD-25.[5] Five years later, he unwittingly absorbed it through his fingers and experienced a "not unpleasant

---

[5]The number 25 refers to nothing chemical, but to the date (2 May) Hofmann first produced LSD.

delirium." Several days later he swallowed 250 micrograms, and in 40 minutes he felt a "mild dizziness, restlessness, inability to concentrate, visual disturbance and uncontrollable laughter." His diary continues:

> . . . on the way home (a four mile trip by bicycle), the symptoms developed with a much greater intensity than the first time. I had the greatest difficulty speaking coherently and my field of vision fluctuated and was distorted like the reflections in an amusement park mirror. I also had the impression that I was hardly moving, yet later my assistant told me that I was pedaling at a fast pace. So far as I can recollect, the height of the crisis was characterized by these symptoms; dizziness, visual distortions, the faces of those present appeared like grotesque colored masks, strong agitation alternating with paresis [partial paralysis], the head, body and extremities sometimes cold and numb; a metallic taste on the tongue; throat dry and shriveled; a feeling of suffocation; confusion alternating with a clear appreciation of the situation; at times standing outside myself as a neutral observer and hearing myself muttering jargon or screaming half madly.
>
> Six hours after taking the drug, my condition had improved. The perceptual distortions were still present. Everything seemed to undulate and their proportions were distorted like the reflections on a choppy water surface. Everything was changing with unpleasant, predominately poisonous green and blue color tones. With closed eyes multi-hued, metamorphizing fantastic images overwhelmed me. Especially noteworthy was the fact that sounds were transposed into visual sensations (i.e., "synesthesias"] so that from each tone or noise a comparable colored picture was evoked, changing in form and color kaleidoscopically. (Coles, Brenner, & Meagher, 1970, pp. 44–45)

Hofmann apparently slept well, and the next day, felt "completely well, but tired" (Coles et al., 1970). Despite some differences (see Table 8-2), most *pure* hallucinogens (or "psychedelics") produce experiences like Hofmann's.

"Street acid," however, is rarely pure, usually consisting of anticholinergics, quinine, sugar, and PCP; it might even contain LSD. As a result, clinicians can't assume that a patient on a "bad trip" knows what drug he's taken. Therefore, it is safest to "talk the person down," by reassuring him the trip will end in a few hours, that he is safe, and that he's not going mad, shrinking, or becoming a zombie. The patient should not "fight" the experience, but "flow with it"; he should be encouraged to become curious about it, and if he wishes, talk about it. If a clinician doesn't have the time to "talk a person down," or if the patient remains terrified despite talk, diazepam 5 mg, taken orally every hour until the patient is reasonably comfortable or asleep, is safer than antipsychotics; diazepam causes less hypotension and fewer adverse drug interactions than antipsychotics.

Less than 5% of Americans have ever tried a psychedelic, and only 1% claimed they would take these drugs if they were legal. Hallucinogens can trigger "flashbacks," in which a person off drugs reexperiences his LSD trip days to months after taking it. What causes flashbacks is unknown. Psychedelics rarely, if ever, cause psychosis *de novo*, but they, as well as PCP and *high* doses of marijuana, can easily rekindle a preexisting psychosis. High-risk patients include those with borderline or schizotypal personality disorders, and those with a personal or family history of (drug- or nondrug-induced) psychoses. Clinicians should inform these patients about their increased risk: This is not moralizing; it is giving information.

CANNABIS

The hemp plant, *Cannabis sativa*, grows anyplace it doesn't freeze; marijuana comes from its stems and leaves, while hashish derives from the resin of female plants. The psychoactive substance in cannabis is THC (delta-9-tetrahydrocannabinol). With normal recreational use, marijuana intoxication peaks in 30 minutes, persists for three hours, and sometimes impairs driving for up to six hours. It stimulates appetite ("the munchies"), causes dry mouth, produces bloodshot eyes, elevates mood, intensifies experiences and perceptions, and heightens relaxation and apathy.

Given that over 60% of American adults and adolescents have smoked "grass" at least once, relatively few experience severe reactions after 24 hours of using the drug. Panic attacks, which account for 75% of all *acute* side effects, usually last two to six hours. Otherwise, heavier cannabis use can cause the "4 D's": depersonalization, derealization, déjà vu, and dysphoria; it can also exacerbate a preexisting psychosis. Marijuana's effects are greatly influenced by "set and setting"—that is, the user's "mind set" or attitudes toward the drug, and his environment's receptivity toward using it. Adverse reactions occur more often among those who smoke because of peer pressure or who have negative expectations of the drug. Less than 1% of university students at campuses with high marijuana use develop panic attacks, whereas 25% do so at rural Southern colleges where cannabis use is discouraged.

Longer-term problems associated with marijuana are relatively few. Only 9% of marijuana users meet *DSM-III* criteria for cannabis abuse. These criteria consist of over 30 days of pathological use (e.g., intoxication throughout the day, almost daily consumption) coupled with impaired social or occupational functioning. Marijuana hallucinosis and flashbacks may occur. Although an "amotivational syndrome" of laziness, apathy, and a lack of ambition has been attributed to marijuana, this finding is derived from biased samples of largely lower-class patients, and has not been supported by more recent surveys in countries where marijuana use is extensive—Jamaica, Costa Rica, and Greece. Medically, cannabis diminishes respiratory capacity, produces bronchial and pulmonary irritation (more than equal amounts of nicotine), causes tachycardia, and temporarily impairs cognition and recent memory.

Ever since *Reefer Madness* obtained cult-film status, the dominant question has been whether marijuana leads to the abuse of "heavier" illegal substances. The answer is a qualified "no." Repeated studies strongly suggest that the best predictor of illegal drug use is *legal* drug use. In other words, the chief "gateway" drug is not marijuana, but tobacco and alcohol (Rittenhouse, 1982). Moreover, marijuana use, which peaked in 1978, is on the decline. From 1978 to 1984, high school seniors using marijuana during the past month dropped from 37% to 25%, while daily usage dropped from 10.7% to 5%. Yet because patients are not statistics, the hazards of marijuana use must be evaluated in the light of each person's history.

PHENCYCLIDINE

Originally an animal tranquilizer, "hog" or phencyclidine (PCP) became a battlefield anesthetic in Vietnam. It resurfaced as a recreational drug in California during the late sixties, ironically rechristened as "angel dust." PCP produces a euphoric, floating, energized, invincible, other-worldly, and dream-like state, in which time is slowed, thinking is quickened, dreams come true, fantasies are dramatic, life is intensified, and reality goes on holiday.

Yet PCP is not the dust of angels. Having taken street doses, users are motionless and stare blankly. Myoclonic (leg) jerks and confusion are common. On large doses, patients may convulse, become stuporous, enter a coma, and convulse with gaping eyes. If they recover from the coma, they exhibit an agitated delirium, marked by persecutory delusions, hallucinations, illusions, disorientation, agitation, and *episodic* assaultiveness; they'll be asleep or calm one moment, and without warning, fanatically violent the next. For no apparent reason, they'll fight with police, wreck cars, commit suicide, or kill strangers. This violence may stem from the extreme suspiciousness and persecutory delusions produced by PCP. Being a "dissociative" anesthetic, PCP makes the user feel outside his body, so that damage to it is damage to something other than himself; the user doesn't perceive pain and is unaware and amnestic for the experience. This delirium can last a week. Some patients die, usually by respiratory depression, others by drowning, automobile accidents, falls, and fires.

Medically, PCP intoxication causes ataxia, nystagmus, and muscle rigidity. Whereas hallucinogens produce dilated pupils, PCP produces normal or small pupils.

Phencyclidine is often sprinkled on top of marijuana or parsley. When smoked, its effects arise in one to five minutes, peak after five to 30 minutes, remain high for four to six hours, and dwindle over the next 18 hours. Snorting PCP hastens its effects.

From 1979 to 1984, the percentage of high school seniors who have used PCP at least once has declined from 13% to 5%. Most users are polydrug abusers. They often drink while on PCP, even though it usually makes them dreadfully sick. Given the drug's horrors, PCP users typically say they take it because, "It's the perfect escape."

The treatment of acute PCP overdose includes cardiopulmonary resuscitation, treatment for seizures, acidification of the urine (to hasten PCP's elimination) with 500 mg to 1,000 mg ammonium chloride every three to five hours orally, until the urine's pH is below 5. Since patients are unpredictably violent and frequently combative when arising from a coma, physical restraints may be needed until the patient has been calm for several hours. Some clinicians recommend (as needed) hourly haloperidol 5 mg IM; others suggest diazepam 10 to 30 mg orally or IM. Most experts agree that phenothiazines should be avoided, since they may compound PCP's anticholinergic and hypotensive effects.

MDMA

Also known as "ecstasy" or "XTC," MDMA was synthesized in 1914. Yet it wasn't until the early 1970s that it quietly became a recreational and psychotherapeutic drug. In 1985, the popularity of this then legal drug was featured in *Time* and *Newsweek*, yet by June of that year the Drug Enforcement Agency "temporarily" made it illegal. Many opposed this decision, claiming that MDMA had been confused with the psychedelic MDA, that harm allegedly due to MDMA was really from adulterants (e.g., Borax!), and that research into a potentially therapeutic drug was being stymied. MDMA is the only drug discussed in this chapter which is not mentioned in *DSM-III*.

In recreational doses of 75 mg to 175 mg, MDMA produces a tranquil, floating, introspective, talkative, two-to-four-hour trip. Grinspoon and Bakalar (1985) claim it "invites rather than compels intensification of feelings and self-exploration." Although chemically related to amphetamines and mescaline (a psychedelic), ecstasy exerts no stimulant effects or hallucinogenic alterations of consciousness, perception, movement, or coordination. Unlike with psychedelics, information revealed during MDMA is more readily remembered and applied afterward. The person does not feel "stoned."

Physical side effects, which are dose-related, include dry mouth, increased blood pressure and pulse rate, anorexia, nystagmus (eye-wiggles), urinary urgency, blurred vision, loss of balance, and jaw-clenching. Fatigue may persist for a day or two. One fatal overdose has been reported. Bad trips, flashbacks, and psychotic reactions are rare. Once-a-week use is also rare. At present there are no cases of MDMA-induced craving or withdrawal. Nonetheless, as always occurs with psychoactive agents, the wider use of MDMA is likely to uncover some currently unknown hazards.

OPIATES

Junk is the ideal product . . . the ultimate merchandise. No sales talk necessary. The client will crawl through a sewer and beg to buy. . . . The junk merchant does not sell his product to the consumer, he sells the consumer to this product. — William S. Burroughs, *Evergreen Review*, Jan./Feb. 1960

Opiates are compounds with morphine-like properties. ("Opioids" are synthetic opiates.) Opium, the original opiate, derives from the head of the opium poppy *Papaver somniferum*, cultivated mainly in the Middle East, Southeast Asia, China, India, and Mexico. Although growing it in the United States is illegal, throughout the 1840s it was the most popular sleep aide in Kansas. Heroin is the only illicit opioid. Morphine is the prototypic opiate. (See Tables 8-1 and 8-2).

Clinical Presentation

In therapeutic amounts, morphine produces analgesia, induces tranquility, constricts pupils, and elevates mood. With higher doses, anorexia, nausea, and vomiting may occur (or, as Taylor Mead quipped, "Opium is very cheap considering you don't feel like eating for the next six days."). The user's skin itches, and his respiratory rate and other vital signs decline. Except for meperidine, opiates do not cause seizures.

Most opiate *intoxication* comes from shooting morphine or heroin IV. This produces a "rush," which is a strong flushing sensation coupled with an orgastic feeling in the belly. Waves of a pleasant, floating drowsiness ("the nod"), and dreams follow.

DSM-III defines opiate *dependence* as either tolerance or withdrawal, following over a month of pathological use, and impaired functioning (Table 8-3, Part II). Tolerance to opiates develops quickly. Table 8-7 outlines the overlapping stages or "grades" of opiate *withdrawal*. Morphine withdrawal peaks up to 72 hours after the last dose and subsides slowly. Most opiate withdrawal symptoms disappear within seven to ten days, although some craving, restlessness, weakness, and fitful sleep may persist.

Clinical Course

Although infrequently seen by professionals, many "chippers" use heroin in a controlled fashion. Otherwise, about half of all opiate abusers become opiate dependent. Whether this opiate dependency becomes chronic depends on the setting. For example, only 2% of American heroin-dependent soldiers in Vietnam continued their habit after returning home; most who continued were heroin abusers *before* Vietnam. Vaillant found that 98% of (nonVietnam) patients at the federal addiction treatment center in Lexington returned to opiate use within a year of discharge. One of them, Danny, returned to his old New York neighborhood after six months of abstinence. Yet as soon as he passed a street corner where he once shot heroin, he immediately developed goose bumps, diarrhea, and hot flashes. As with Danny, such *conditioned withdrawal symptoms* often trigger a relapse.

The annual death rate of heroin addicts is between 1.6% and 3%. Addicts usually die from accidental and intentional overdoses, allergic and acute toxic reactions, infections from unclean needles, a lowered immunologic resistance,

TABLE 8-7
Opiate Withdrawal in Sequence

		HOURS AFTER LAST DOSE WHEN SIGNS AND SYMPTOMS ARISE*			
GRADE	SIGNS AND SYMPTOMS	PARE-GORIC/MOR-PHINE	HEROIN	MEPERI-DINE	CODEINE
0	Craving (e.g., pleading, manipulation, faking, and demanding for drug) Anxiety	6	4	2–3	8
1	Yawning Perspiration (warm and sweaty) Tearing (lacrimation) Runny nose (rhinorrhea) "Yen" sleep (light, restless, fitful sleep) "Miserable feeling" Severe sneezing	14	8	4–6	24
2	[Increase of above signs and:] Mydriasis (large or dilated pupils) Gooseflesh (piloerection, from which "cold turkey" derives) Muscle twitches (from which "kick the habit" derives) No appetite (anorexia) and nausea Hot and cold flashes, chills Aching bones and muscles, muscle spasms Vomiting, abdominal cramps, diarrhea Insomnia Increased blood pressure	16	12	8–12	48

and from murder. The hopeful point to remember is that if they can survive to their mid-thirties, their opiate misuse usually declines, and if they make it to 40, they often stop completely.

Epidemiology

Although accurate epidemiologic data on opiate misuse are especially elusive, household surveys during the 1970s revealed that under 1% of adults over age 25 had used an opiate at least once for nonmedical reasons. Among high-school seniors, the lifetime prevalence of heroin use has dropped from

TABLE 8-7
(Continued)

		HOURS AFTER LAST DOSE WHEN SIGNS AND SYMPTOMS ARISE*			
GRADE	SIGNS AND SYMPTOMS	PARE-GORIC/MOR-PHINE	HEROIN	MEPERI-DINE	CODEINE
3	Fever (1–2° F.) Increased breathing rate and depth Increased pulse rate Restlessness Severe nausea	24–36	18–24	16	—
4	[Increase in above plus]: Spontaneous erection, spontaneous orgasm (both sexes) Menstrual bleeding (menorrhagia) Hot, flushed, febrile facies Severe vomiting and diarrhea Dehydration, weight loss (5 lb. daily) Hemoconcentration causing increased blood sugar, hematocrit, white blood cells, and eosinophils Fetal position, often on hard floor (to alleviate stomach cramps)	36–48	24–36	—	—

*These signs and symptoms don't always evolve in this sequence, and not all signs are necessary to diagnose a particular grade.

2.2% in 1975, to 1.1% in 1979 (Johnston et al., 1981). In 1984, although 11.2% of seniors had taken opiates other than heroin at least once, only 1.3% had done so during the past month (Galanter, personal communication, 1985).

The "demographic" heroin addict is male, from the inner cities of either coasts, nonwhite, and with a teenage history of truancy, poor school performance, and delinquency. Immediate availability of opiates greatly increases the number of *new* cases of heroin misuse, whereas *chronic* misuse depends less on neighborhood access. All the sorrows of social blight and communal disorganization — poor housing, sanitation, health, nutrition, employment and educational levels, family cohesiveness, and cultural morale — correlate with opiate misuse.

Except for antisocial personality disorder, there is little evidence that psychiatric illness accompanies opiate dependence. Many opiate addicts are polydrug abusers, especially with "downers" like alcohol and hypnosedatives. For heroin addicts, polydrug abuse is a bad prognostic indicator.

Treatment and Management

No single program works for a majority of opiate abusers, and controversy remains over the preferred approach. In general, there are two schools of thought: The "soft" pro-methadone school, and the "tough" anti-methadone school.

Methadone is an opioid with a long (12-hour) half-life that exerts pleasant effects when ingested. Because methadone is cross-tolerant with other opiates, once signs of opiate withdrawal begin, clinicians can initiate *methadone substitution* by giving roughly 10 mg three times daily, and then withdrawing the patient by gradually diminishing the dose; a typical schedule would be total daily doses of 30-30-20-15-10-5-0-0 mg. With medical complications — e.g., high fever, cardiac failure — slightly higher and more frequent doses are indicated, such as 45-45-35-25-15-10-5-0-0 mg. Methadone should not be withdrawn at faster than 20% a day. It is rare for more than 15 mg to be needed at any one time.

During opiate withdrawal, patients should be in a low bed; only if they are observed should they be allowed to smoke (cigarettes!); they may need assistance when ambulatory to avoid injury. Small doses of diazepam may be given temporarily for insomnia. If the patient convulses, he is probably also withdrawing from alcohol or hypnosedatives, and a pentobarbital test dose (Table 8-5) should be performed immediately.

The loudest argument against methadone substitution is that using it makes withdrawal too easy, and therefore, fails to "teach the patient a lesson." No scientific evidence indicates that having this "lesson" prevents relapse.

The rationale for *methadone maintenance* (MM), which begins following opiate withdrawal, is that ingested methadone usually blocks the euphoria of injected opiates. Because methadone is taken orally and daily, MM diminishes the addict's daily search for heroin and his crimes to pay for it; the user becomes a better worker and family member. Without needles, there are far fewer medical complications and deaths.

Although studies repeatedly support these findings and show that MM produces the best overall results, critics charge that in MM one narcotic is merely being replaced for another, that many addicts sell methadone illicitly, that many studies favorable to MM included only patients with initially good prognoses, that some addicts get a high from shooting up on methadone, and that many patients on methadone can overcome the blockage by taking high doses of heroin. These objections are significant, yet studies indicate that, after four years of MM, a majority of ex-addicts live productively and 94% no longer commit crimes to obtain "smack."

With or without MM, the usefulness of psychosocial treatments, including self-help groups, therapeutic communities, and drug treatment centers, remain unknown. The more restrictive the program, the more patients quit. The effectiveness of any therapy for opiate dependence varies largely on the characteristics of various subgroups.

Addiction is also a "family matter." As important as it is to help the patient, educating, supporting, and counseling relatives may be the therapist's most valuable and enduring contribution. It's also a "family matter" in another sense: Health care professionals are at high risk for addiction, and they and their relatives are also "our family."

CHAPTER 9

Schizophrenic Disorders

Of all the functional disorders, schizophrenia devastates as no other, for no other disorder causes as pervasive and profound an impact — socially, economically, and personally. Schizophrenic patients occupy one-quarter of all American hospital beds and, excluding geriatric patients with organic brain syndromes, two-thirds of all psychiatric beds. In 1983, schizophrenia cost the United States $48 billion — 60% from lost productivity, 20% for public assistance, and 20% for treatment. Conservatively, costs for schizophrenia equal 2% of the nation's gross national product. On any single day, there are two million schizophrenics in the United States, and in any one year, there are two million new cases arising worldwide.

Parents of schizophrenics endure years of uncertainty, guilt, dashed hopes, rage (at, and from, the patient), financial burdens, self-doubt, and futility. Siblings resent the schizophrenic's getting "all" the attention, berate themselves for feeling resentful, and constantly worry if they too will go crazy.

Yet, nobody suffers more than the schizophrenic. When Bleuler (see Chapter 1) invented the term "schizophrenia," he did not mean a "split personality" (i.e., multiple personality), but a *shattered* personality. Whereas patients with other severe mental disorders may have one or perhaps two symptoms of schizophrenia, the curse of the schizophrenic is to be plagued by virtually *all* of them. (After reading the following typical case, try to imagine — that is, to understand — how such a person might feel about himself and the world, and what it might be like for him to negotiate everyday activities.)

141

Case Illustration

David Sebastian, a 24-year-old single, Catholic, ex-divinity student, was hospitalized for a "convulsion." For 16 hours nonstop, it consisted of masturbatory movements accompanied by groans, prayers, flailing limbs, and head-banging. During these
"seizures," he was totally self-absorbed: If asked questions, he wouldn't respond; all
attempts to restrain him (for his own physical safety) were fiercely resisted. Eventually,
he slept.

On awakening, he stared and smiled at the nurse, who described him as "Rasputin
imitating the Mona Lisa." He accused the Pope of "fornicating nuns," "spreading diarrhea and gonorrhea," and "plotting to assassinate me [David]." He was convinced that
St. Christopher, the patron saint of travel, was removed from the universal church
calendar because David was having sexual thoughts while traveling. His thoughts
traveled incoherently from topic to topic. When asked if he feared anything, he replied
with a flat affect:

Nothing but the Pope wants slivers up his ass or my ass or he's an ass; you
know this is not me talking but a taped list recording of how you are today that
couldn't communicate at any level as a dialectical incongruence of spiritual
sexuality.

About a year ago, David began to change. Before then he was an outstanding
biology student, a jogger, a bit of a loner, and as his neighbors in Queens would
remark, "such a sweet boy to live with his parents." At age 23, however, his grades
began to slip and he became far more reclusive. Seven or so months later, and several
weeks before his sister's wedding, he spent days and nights making his sister's wedding gift: a stained-glass penis. Two days before the wedding, his father accidentally
knocked the gift off a table, and as it smashed into a million pieces, David did too.
For the next month he attacked his family for destroying him, turning him into a robot,
and sapping his vital fluids.

God's voice accused him of being too preoccupied with sex and proclaimed that
becoming a priest was his only salvation. This instruction gave renewed purpose to
life while permitting a rapprochement with his family. He enrolled in divinity school,
but a month later he could no longer concentrate. New and unfamiliar voices began
discussing his plight, with one saying that David's "prick doesn't work," and the other
saying, "If you [David] were a *real* man, you'd go out and use your prick." He did.
David picked up a coed and went to her apartment. They hopped into bed, but when
David was about to enter her, he started to "seize" on her naked body. Horrified, she
fled the room, called the cops, and David was admitted.

Repeated neurological exams and tests revealed no evidence of epilepsy or of any
other physical disorder. He was placed on antipsychotic medication, and over the next
ten days, his "seizures" (catatonic excitement with negativism), delusions, hallucinations, incoherence, paranoia, and self-referential ideas gradually disappeared. Three
days after admission, he joined group therapy, but within minutes he began to shake.
Pointing to the nine people in the room, he exclaimed, "Eighteen eyes haunting my
head, changing its size, televising my mind, eating it, bleeding it, feeding it. You
gyrating Judases, how dare. . . . " Suddenly silent, slowly he left the room. Days later
he said he had felt besieged by the other members, and that he left the room to escape

this bombardment and to stop "embarrassing myself." Once his psychotic symptoms abated, David actively participated in group and supportive individual psychotherapy. In meetings with the family, his parents ventilated their frustration, were told "the facts" about catatonic schizophrenia (David's diagnosis), and discussed how they could all live more peaceably together. After three weeks of inpatient care, he was discharged on medication and was to receive weekly psychotherapy.

For three months David worked at his father's grocery store, visited daily with a neighborhood priest, lived at home, read theology, painted a little, and saw friends. Then, when his father suggested that "maybe you should live away from home," David stormed out of the house, wandered the streets, and stopped his medication because "it was digesting my sex organs." Within weeks he looked like a rag picker. He kept to himself. Voices began mocking his scrawny figure and sexual inadequacies; they insisted he go out with prostitutes. After considerable guilt, he succumbed, but when he entered a prostitute's room, he'd extricate himself from the situation by having a "seizure." Later he told the therapist that he was in a "no-win" situation: If he did have intercourse, he was committing a sin; if he didn't, his voices were right, and he wasn't a man. The police found David "convulsing" on the steps of St. Patrick's cathedral and brought him to the hospital. David's second admission began.

David passed through the proverbial "revolving door" for three more hospitalizations; each occurred after a fight at home or a sexual confrontation triggered a "seizure," which would persist between two and 20 hours. Physicians were baffled by how, from a physiologic viewpoint, a person could "convulse" for so long. Neurological exams remained negative, and a trial of anticonvulsant medications had no effect. When his parents visited, he'd have a "mini-seizure" or accuse them of "warping" his penis; these meetings, however, would eventually calm down. On the other hand, whenever the staff tried to separate David from his parents, he would vegetate in a corner, stop talking, and starve himself; one time, he had to be physically restrained from jumping out the window. So after six tumultuous months, David returned home: He worked regularly in a bookstore, remained on moderate doses of antipsychotic drugs, and participated in weekly group therapy. He began a theology class, where he befriended a shy young lady who felt nobody would ever like her. David did. Three years later they are still seeing each other ("We'll marry when *he* can afford me!" she laughs); he works at the bookstore and lives at home. He remains on medication ("I go bonkers without it"), and although he stopped the group ("I outgrew it"), he continues to receive individual psychotherapy ("So my crazy ideas don't overwhelm me").

Clinical Presentation

In *DSM-III* the essential features of schizophrenia are (a) a history of acute psychosis with either delusions, hallucinations, incoherent speech, catatonia, or flat affect, (b) chronic deterioration of functioning, (c) duration that exceeds six months, (d) onset before age 45, and (e) the absence of a preexisting organic, substance use, or affective disorder. In general, schizophrenia has a chronic, episodically downhill course, but with modern treatment the patient's condition eventually stabilizes so he can be moderately independent and productive. Table 9-1 lists *DSM-III*'s criteria for schizophrenia.

TABLE 9-1
DSM-III Criteria[1] for a Schizophrenic Disorder*

A. At least one of the following during a phase of the illness:

   (1) bizarre delusions (content is patently absurd and has no possible basis in fact), such as delusions of being controlled, thought broadcasting, thought insertion, or thought withdrawal

   (2) somatic, grandiose, religious, nihilistic, or other delusions without persecutory or jealous content

   (3) delusions with persecutory or jealous content if accompanied by hallucinations of any type

   (4) auditory hallucinations in which either a voice keeps up a running commentary on the individual's behavior or thoughts, or two or more voices converse with each other

   (5) auditory hallucinations on several occasions with content of more than one or two words, having no apparent relation to depression or elation

   (6) incoherence, marked loosening of associations, markedly illogical thinking, or marked poverty of content of speech if associated with at least one of the following:

      (a) blunted, flat, or inappropriate affect
      (b) delusions or hallucinations
      (c) catatonic or other grossly disorganized behavior

B. Deterioration from a previous level of functioning in such areas as work, social relations, and self-care.

C. Duration: Continuous signs of the illness for at least six months at some time during the person's life, with some signs of the illness at present. The six-month period must include an active phase during which there are symptoms from A, with or without a prodromal or residual phase, as defined below.

   Prodromal phase: A clear deterioration in functioning before the active phase of the illness not due to a disturbance in mood or to a Substance Use Disorder and involving at least *two* of the symptoms noted below.

Criterion A indicates that schizophrenia's *active* or *positive symptoms* must persist for at least one week. (*DSM-III-R* may suggest two weeks.) The most prevalent of the florid, acute symptoms are delusions of persecution or of control, other bizarre delusions, and auditory hallucinations. Less frequent are incoherence, disturbed affect, and catatonia.

Schizophrenic *delusions* are often bizarre and mood-incongruent. One can readily empathize with the depressive's delusions, but not the schizophrenic's. His are weird, from "The Twilight Zone." They may be Schneiderian FRS (see Appendix C) such as delusions of control: "Martians have taken over my

TABLE 9-1
(Continued)

Residual phase: Persistence, following the active phase of the illness, of at least *two* of the symptoms noted below, not due to a disturbance in mood or to a Substance Use Disorder.

Prodromal or Residual Symptoms
(1) social isolation or withdrawal
(2) marked impairment in role functioning as wage-earner, student, or homemaker
(3) markedly peculiar behavior (e.g., collecting garbage, talking to self in public, or hoarding food)
(4) marked impairment in personal hygiene and grooming
(5) blunted, flat, or inappropriate affect
(6) digressive, vague, overelaborate, circumstantial, or metaphorical speech
(7) odd or bizarre ideation, or magical thinking, e.g., superstitiousness, clairvoyance, telepathy, "sixth sense," "others can feel my feelings," overvalued ideas, ideas of reference
(8) unusual perceptual experiences, e.g., recurrent illusions, sensing the presence of a force or person not actually present

Examples: Six months of prodromal symptoms with one week of symptoms from A; no prodromal symptoms with six months of symptoms from A; no prodromal symptoms with two weeks of symptoms from A and six months of residual symptoms; six months of symptoms from A, apparently followed by several years of complete remission, with one week of symptoms in A in current episode.

D. The full depressive or manic syndrome (criteria A and B of major depressive or manic episode), if present, developed after any psychotic symptoms, or was brief in duration relative to the duration of the psychotic symptoms in A.

E. Onset of prodromal or active phase of the illness before age 45.

F. Not due to any Organic Mental Disorder or Mental Retardation.

DSM-III, pp. 188–190.
'These criteria can be remembered by the code: A = Active; B = Below normal; C = Course/ Chronic; D = Depression/Differential; E = Emergence; F = Functional.

body." Persecutory delusions are common in schizophrenia, but, unlike when they appear in organic and affective disorders, in schizophrenia the menace is often an ill-defined and remote group or a vague "they."

Hallucinations are reported by 75% of newly admitted schizophrenics; they are usually in one sensory modality, with 90% being auditory. Fifteen percent of hallucinations are Schneiderian (Ludwig, 1985). Voices may whisper or shout, comment on the patient's actions, or demand he do a morally offensive act ("command hallucinations"). The voices may be from known people (e.g., a dead grandmother) or strangers; they may be verbose or just one or two words constantly repeated. (Because some people refer to their own thoughts as "voices," be sure to ask if the voices come from "inside or outside your head.") Visual hallucinations are weird, frightening, or threatening: snakes crawling out of skulls, blood dripping from dead relatives. Olfactory hallucinations are rare, most often disgusting smells from one's own body. Tactile (haptic) hallucinations are also uncommon; the patient may feel bugs scratching his testicles or ants crawling under his skin.

Initially, many schizophrenics present with an unshakable belief in their delusions and hallucinations. After months of confusion, schizophrenics will suddenly come up with a delusion that "explains" everything; this "insight" has enormous personal meaning, while it mystifies everyone else. In normal recovery occurring over several weeks, patients typically take increasing distance from their psychosis. They will go from, "The telephone company is poisoning my food," to "It seems like the telephone company is poisoning my food." As the psychosis melts further, the patient says, "I'm not so sure about that telephone company stuff." And later, "Every so often I think the phone company is poisoning my food. Isn't that crazy!"

Incoherent speech is the third major group A symptom. It usually manifests as loose associations, tangentiality, circumstantiality, and illogical thinking. Poverty of content may occur, but more often the patient seems flooded with ideas and unable to filter the relevant from the immaterial. Such an example unexpectedly came to the author, who picked up the phone, and to his astonishment heard a total stranger say in a monotonously pert voice (the author's responses are in brackets):

> Hello. I'm paranoid schizophrenic from Tampa. Are you the Dr. Maxim [sic] who wrote *The New Psychiatry*? [Yes.] Well, I'm 75 years old, but I grew up in the home of the very famous Dr. Zuckerman who graduated from P&S, your school. He was the Dr. obsessive-compulsive neurosis psychiatrist, who was a brilliant cardiologist, and I was his only psychiatric patient, and he never said he was my father, but my mother was a borderline butch lesbian personality, and Dr. Zuckerman was the first to take me to the Metropolitan Museum of Art because I have a tooth on the right side that's too big, just as in that Picasso painting, and I have a malformed skull, and a right leg also much longer than my left, and my daughter Infanta Marguerita Pequina lives in Chicago, but Dr. Zuckerman didn't rescue me from a terrible marriage from 1948 to 1966 in which a man beat and raped me in the Jewish community—Are you Jewish? [Yes] Dr. Zuckerman didn't end the marriage but I got out of it in 1962 and have been on Mellaril every since. [What happens if you stop the Mellaril?] My brain waves flash too fast, just as you said in your book, which I'm taking to my clinical psychologist, where I go three times a week, although Dr. Zuckerman

studied with A. A. Brill and Dr. Freud and belonged in psychoanalysis, but that couldn't help in my skull, which was genetically deformed and made worse by my sadist husband in the Jewish community. Do you see patients?

When incoherence is milder or first appears, many listeners will "read into" the patient's speech. Consider this example from a term paper written by an acutely disturbed schizophrenic college student.

> we see the stately dimension of godly bliss that marlowe's *dOctOr fA UstUs* dies and lives. lucifer — oh lucy, luck, lackluster, lazy lucifer — devilishly adorns all sanctifarious, all beauty, all evil. our world disolves into SACRED nihilism.

Individually, the sentences might make sense, but collectively, they're nonsense. Punning, as around "lucifer," is typical of schizophrenic speech; so too is the neologism "sanctifarious." The strange punctuation would seem to have a private meaning, a hunch later confirmed by the patient, who explained, "It's all about Christ. Don't you see. Marlowe's first name is Christopher. Christ. Get it?"

Affects, flat and/or inappropriate, typically develop insidiously and persist chronically. At times they arise acutely. Pathological affects are not, however, diagnostically specific: Depressed mood, drug-induced dullness, and akinesia (a side effect of antipsychotic drugs) can appear as flat affect; organic brain syndromes often produce inappropriate affects. A reasonable inference is that inappropriate affects emerge because the patient is responding more to internal, than to external, stimuli. He may cry when talking about the weather or laugh when hearing of a massive airplane crash. When schizophrenics giggle for no obvious reason, the listener's skin crawls. Their "humor" is not funny; it's tragically pathetic.

Catatonia is the final group A symptom. It presents as stupor or, as with David Sebastian, excitement.

Clinical Course

In most cases, schizophrenia first manifests during adolescence or early adulthood.[2] It presents either abruptly or slowly. One-fourth of patients have an abrupt onset with active, "positive," or "group A" symptoms. The majority have an acute episode only after a slow, insidious onset of schizophrenia's *chronic*, or *negative*, or "group C" symptoms: social withdrawal, markedly impaired functioning, poor hygiene, flat or inappropriate affect, vague

---

[2]*DSM-III* requires an onset before age 45, whereas recent evidence may lead *DSM-III-R* to scratch this requirement.

rambling speech, odd or magical thinking, ideas of reference, overvalued ideas, persecutory thoughts, and unusual perceptions, such as illusions, derealization, or depersonalization. When these chronic symptoms occur before the initial acute flairup, they constitute schizophrenia's *prodromal phase*; when they occur following this flairup, they constitute schizophrenia's *residual phase*. During these prodromal and residual phases, patients seem unmotivated and burned-out; they get labeled as "oddballs," "eccentrics," and "weirdos."

To diagnose schizophrenia, active and/or chronic symptoms must be present for at least *six months* (criterion C). This requirement rules out shorter and more benign psychoses, such as schizophreniform disorder and brief reactive psychosis. At some point, the patient's social or occupational functioning must be impaired (criterion B).

For most patients schizophrenia is a chronic illness characterized by exacerbations and remissions. Whereas the first several years are dominated by active symptoms and frequent hospitalizations, the condition eventually evolves into a nonpsychotic state with chronic symptoms of apathy, low energy levels, social withdrawal, and increased vulnerability to stress. At the worst end of the spectrum are schizophrenics who end up in the backwards of state mental hospitals; they can be seen huddled in a corner, body contorted, picking imaginary flowers, and repeatedly mumbling, "Mineral oil, mineral oil, mineral oil. . . . " Most schizophrenics, however, function in the community: They marry and work at moderate-to-low-level jobs. As with many chronic disorders, such as diabetes and heart disease, schizophrenia may require episodic rehospitalization.

Roughly half of all schizophrenic patients report depressive symptoms at some point during their illness. They'll complain of feeling depressed or of an "affectless" state, in which they'll claim "I don't feel," "I'm empty, numb." These depressive episodes are associated with an increased risk of suicide and relapse, poor social functioning, longer hospitalizations, and bleaker outcomes. They occur most often after an acute psychotic episode, and when they do it's called a *post-psychotic depression*. This is a particularly dangerous period in the schizophrenic's life, for he's apt to feel hopeless, abandon treatment, and kill himself. Whether these depressive symptoms are inherent to schizophrenia or a reaction to it is unclear. In either case, criterion D points out that to qualify as schizophrenia, symptoms of depression (or mania) must appear *after* the onset of psychosis.

How completely a patient recovers from an acute episode is *not* related to the severity of the psychosis. Instead, better prognoses are associated with (a) an acute onset, (b) a clear precipitant, (c) prominent confusion and disorganization, (d) highly systematized and focused delusions whose symbolism is clear and often related to the precipitating event, (e) being married, (f) good premorbid functioning, (g) a family history of depression or mania, and (h) no family history of schizophrenia.

Complications

If schizophrenia's symptoms weren't bad enough, its timing couldn't be worse: It strikes just when the individual is trying to establish himself in the world and to form an identity. Schizophrenia interferes with breaking away from home, performing at school, launching a career, and forming relationships. Schizophrenics have fewer children, marry less often, divorce and separate more frequently, and have higher rates of celibacy.

Schizophrenia's chief complication is *suicide*. About 10% of schizophrenics eventually commit suicide; about 20% attempt it. Of those who've already made an attempt, half will eventually kill themselves. In general, schizophrenics do *not* commit suicide during a psychosis, but rather in its immediate aftermath; 30% of outpatient suicides occur within three months of discharge, while 50% occur within six months of discharge. Their suicides usually arise from having a nondelusional awareness of their illness, feeling depressed, thinking treatment is futile, and believing the future is hopeless. In comparison to schizophrenics who do not commit suicide, those who do have better premorbid functioning and higher levels of education; these patients may have greater expectations of themselves, view schizophrenia as a greater obstacle to achieving their goals, and be less tolerant of a marginal existence. Patients on relatively low doses of medication, those who've abruptly stopped their medication, and those from relatively nonsupportive families are at a greater risk. Roughly 75% of these patients are male; they're usually unemployed, unmarried, isolated, and paranoid (Drake et al., 1985).

Schizophrenics do not commit *violent crimes* at a higher rate than the general population; if anything, they commit fewer crimes. Despite headlines, the insanity defense is used in merely 1% of violent crimes that go to court. On the other hand, schizophrenics are the victims of crime at a higher rate than the general populace. When schizophrenics are arrested, it's usually for vagrancy, disturbing the peace, and other misdemeanors.

Although *homelessness* is another complication of schizophrenia, its extent may be exaggerated because of the myth that deinstitutionalization has produced the homeless. Common wisdom is that state mental hospitals dumped hordes of chronic schizophrenics into the community without proper lodging and treatment. These patients, so the myth goes, roam streets and sleep in alleys. This gospel, however, rests on two fallacies:

The first is that most of the homeless are psychiatric patients. In 1981 a study of the homeless at New York City's men's shelters revealed that only a third were ever admitted to a psychiatric hospital, only 22% of the total had ever been admitted to a state mental hospital, and only 20% were currently homeless because of mental disorders. In contrast, one-third suffered from severe medical problems and two-thirds from substance abuse (New York State, 1982). Nationally, 30% of the homeless have severe psychiatric disturbances, 25% to 40% have substance abuse, and only a minority have ever been psychiatric inpatients (Mowbray, 1985). The second myth is that state hospitals suddenly flooded the community with large numbers of mental patients. Discharge planning may be crummy, but the bulk of discharged state hospital patients leveled off from 1968 to 1975, which is long *before* the "homeless problem" arose. For example, in New York State, deinstitutionalization was completed in 1973–74, the very same years that New York's homeless were at their fewest! Not until 1979 did their numbers rapidly escalate, and with 1982's reduction in federal social programs, their numbers shot up further (Hoffman et al., 1984). Schizophrenia and improper aftercare contribute to homelessness, but relatively little;[3] the homeless need housing and social support far more than Thorazine and therapy.

Subtypes

DSM-III lists five types of schizophrenic disorders, each based on the patient's most prominent feature. The *disorganized* type is characterized by marked incoherence along with flat, silly, or inappropriate affect. Formerly called "hebephrenic," these patients have an early and insidious onset, poor premorbid functioning, severe social impairment, and a chronic course.

The *catatonic* type, which is becoming rarer, primarily displays psychomotor disturbances. Patients with catatonia tend to have a more sudden onset, a better prognosis, a greater prevalence of affective disorders among first-degree relatives, and a better response to ECT — four features commonly associated with affective disorders. Pointing out that catatonic excitement and stupor may be severe psychomotor agitation and retardation, respectively, Ries (1985) and others claim that catatonia occurs as often in bipolar disorders as in schizophrenia.

Schizophrenics of the *paranoid* type have prominent persecutory or grandiose delusions or hallucinations. These patients are often unfocused, angry, argumentative, violent, and anxious. Stiff and mistrustful, they assume people can't be trusted and that anybody who likes them must be up to no good. "If I don't like me, why should they like me?" These patients live a "contained," highly structured existence. Unsure of their own gender identity, they may project these fears onto others and be terrified of homosexuals. Relative to the other schizophrenias, the paranoid type arises later in life, interferes less with social functioning, and displays a more stable course.

---

[3]When the oil crisis peaked during the late 1970s, people moved from suburbs to city, bought up the temporary lodgings and SROs which formerly housed the marginally adjusted, and the homeless had no place to go (Maxmen, 1986b).

Schizophrenics who don't fit the above three types are diagnosed as *undifferentiated* type if they are actively psychotic, and as *residual* type if, after an active phase, chronic symptoms predominate.

Epidemiology

The prevalence and incidence of schizophrenia tend to be the same regardless of political system, nationality, or historical period. Schizophrenia's lifetime prevalence is between 0.8% and 1%. With an incidence of 0.3 to 0.6 per thousand people, about 100,000 new cases of schizophrenia arise annually in the United States. The disorder afflicts men slightly more than women (Lewine, Burbach, & Meltzer, 1984), whites and blacks about the same, and urbanites more than country folk.

Lower socioeconomic classes have a disproportionate number of schizophrenics. To explain why, two theories are usually advanced: "social causation" and "drift." The former asserts that poverty causes stress which causes schizophrenia. The drift theory holds that because schizophrenia devastates social and occupational functioning, schizophrenics migrate to the society's lower socioeconomic echelons. A major problem in studying these theories is that the usual measures of social class—occupation, education, income, location of home—are themselves affected by schizophrenia. Nonetheless, most evidence points to the drift theory. For example, studies in four nations revealed that whereas the fathers of schizophrenics were equally distributed among social classes, their schizophrenic sons had drifted downward (Goodwin & Guze, 1984).

Etiology and Pathogenesis

These are generalizations surely, but the causes of schizophrenia can be summarized thusly: Schizophrenia involves disturbances of the brain's chemistry, anatomy, and physiology, which in turn distort how the person experiences himself and the world. Biology produces schizophrenia; environment alters its course. More specifically, genetic and other biological factors (e.g., slow viruses) create various degrees of vulnerability to schizophrenia; whether, and how severely, this predisposed individual becomes a schizophrenic depends on a mix of biological factors (e.g., severity of heredity) *and* psychosocial influences (e.g., traumatic childhood). Once the disorder exists, psychosocial factors (e.g., disturbed intrafamilial communication) substantially affect the extent of recovery, whether the patient relapses, his overall quality of life, and the symbolic meaning he will attribute to the disorder. These generalizations fit the modern, *DSM-III* definition of schizophrenia; they are neither "too biological" nor "too psychosocial," but supported by the following evidence.

Biological Theories

Mothers often observe that their schizophrenic child "wasn't right since birth"; in comparison to their other (normal) children, he was "fussier," "more temperamental," "distant," "tense," "aggressive," or "inhibited." Although one could discount such comments as biased retrospection, considerable data confirm what mothers have been saying all along. For instance, schizophrenics have a higher rate of complications during pregnancy and birth; so do the children of schizophrenic mothers. "Soft" neurological signs (e.g., abnormal reflexes, minor motor and sensory signs, EEG changes) frequently occur in schizophrenia, but rarely in affective disorders. Long before they're diagnosed, preschizophrenic children have more academic difficulties and lower IQ scores than siblings or controls.

Genetic. Schizophrenia runs in families. (See Table 9-2.) Overall, first-degree relatives of schizophrenics have a 10% chance of becoming schizophrenic, whereas second-degree relatives (e.g., cousin, aunt, grandson) run a 3% chance. Monozygotic twins have roughly three times the concordance rate

TABLE 9-2
Risk for Relatives of a Schizophrenic

SCHIZOPHRENIC PATIENT	PERSON AT RISK	PERCENT OF RISK
General population	Everybody	0.8–1.0
Father	Each child	1.8
Mother	Each child	10–16
Both parents	Each child	25–46
Child	Each parent	5
One sibling	Each sibling	8–10
Second-degree relative	Another second-degree relative	2–3
Monozygotic twin	Other monozygotic twin	40–50
Dizygotic twin	Other dizygotic twin	12–15
Adoptive parents (schizophrenic)	Adoptee with "normal" biological parents	4.8
Biological parents (schizophrenic)	Adoptee reared by "normal" adoptive parents	19.7

of dizygotic twins. Strong evidence for a genetic transmission in schizophrenia is also provided by adopted-away studies (see Chapter 4) of "schizophrenic-spectrum disorders" (SSD), which usually include schizophrenia, schizotypal personality disorder, and sometimes, borderline and paranoid personality disorders. They reveal that SSD is five to six times more common among biological, than among adoptive, parents of schizophrenic adults. Furthermore, if a schizophrenic adoptive parent rears an adoptee from biologically "normal" parents, the adoptee's risk of becoming schizophrenic is four times *less* than if the adoptee had a schizophrenic biological parent and was reared by "normal" adoptive parents. The more severe the schizophrenia, the greater its inheritability.

Biochemical. Most widely touted, the *dopamine hypothesis* states that the symptoms of schizophrenia arise from a relative excess of dopamine (DA) and from an overstimulation of DA receptors. (This theory does not necessarily mean that excessive DA is the "cause" of schizophrenia, but merely that it plays a role in producing schizophrenia.) Snyder (1981) demonstrated a positive correlation between how much an antipsychotic drug blocks DA receptors (in tissue cultures) and how much it reduces schizophrenic symptoms. Amphetamines, which produce a schizophrenic-like state, stimulate the release of DA into synaptic clefts; they also retard the inactivation of DA. L-Dopa, a direct precursor of DA, triggers schizophrenic symptoms. Despite such findings, the dopamine hypothesis is only supported by indirect evidence; direct evidence, such as abnormal levels of DA in schizophrenic patients, has not been found.

Anatomic and physiologic. The recent explosion in biomedical technology (see Chapter 4, p. 60) has uncovered changes in schizophrenia that were previously undetectable. For example, CT scans reveal that chronic schizophrenics have enlarged lateral, and perhaps third, ventricles. It's unclear whether these big ventricles are consequences of schizophrenia or of something associated with it, such as long-term incapacitation, medication, or incarceration. What is clear is that cerebral atrophy produces these enlarged ventricles, a finding magnetic resonant imaging (MR) confirms. MR also shows that schizophrenics have smaller craniums and smaller frontal lobes, while PET scans indicate that their frontal lobes take up and metabolize less glucose. Other new techniques suggest that schizophrenics have a reduced cerebral blood flow. Finally, although some patients with affective disorders have cerebral atrophy, most do not.

Psychosocial Theories

With an unusual consistency for scientific investigations of psychosocial influences, one finding stands out: *The amount of tension patients are exposed to within their family is the most critical psychosocial variable affecting the course of schizophrenia*. These American and British studies compare families with "high-expressed emotion" (HEE) to those with "low-expressed emotion" (LEE). HEE families are more openly critical of the patient, more hostile and dissatisfied toward him, convey little warmth or encouragement, and form overprotective and symbiotic relationships with him. Typical comments from HEE relatives toward the patient are: "You do nothing but bitch"; "I wish you'd just get out of my hair!"; "I worry so much about you, I don't think you should go out tonight."

Nine months after their initial discharge, schizophrenics living with HEE and LEE families relapsed at rates averaging 56% and 21%, respectively (Caton, 1984). Similar results occur two years following discharge. Those in HEE families who take or don't take their medication had relapse rates of 66% and 46%, respectively. Patients exposed to HEE families for more or less than 35 hours/week had relapse rates of 69% and 28%, respectively. In LEE families, use of medication and duration of contact did not affect relapse rates. Vaughn and Leff (1976) report that patients with the highest nine-month relapse rate (92%) had high exposure to HEE families and did not take their drugs, whereas patients with the lowest relapse rate (12%) took their meds and lived with LEE families.

Family. Before these studies on expressed emotion appeared, other investigators observed distorted communication and relationships in the families of schizophrenics. Whether these disturbances are a cause or a consequence of schizophrenia remains controversial.

Lidz and Fleck (1986) emphasized the dangers of blurred generational and gender boundaries. In other words, parents should be parents, and kids, kids; men should be men, and women, women: Blur these distinctions, and psychopathology ensues. They described two familial patterns: The *schizmatic* family is divided into two factions with each of the irreconcilable parents devaluing the other. The patient, usually a female, finds it hard to use the same-sexed parent as a role model, blames herself for the conflict, and if she tries to be neutral, alienates both parents. A *skewed* family is where everyone accommodates to the dominance of a single parent, usually the mother. The patient, most often male, becomes overly dependent on this demanding, intrusive, and overbearing mother, and in so doing, supplants his ineffectual father. The son's symbiotic relationship with his mother leads to a confused sexual identity, frightening incestuous feelings, absorption into his mother's psychopathology, and rejection by jealous siblings.

Wynne (et al., 1958) coined the term *pseudomutuality* to describe families which demand the appearance of a superficial harmony, but covertly insist on uniformity and "outlaw" individuality and separation. (Bowen [1978] depicts the "glob" mentality as an *undifferentiated family ego mass*.) *Double binds* are contradictory (or "double") messages that leave the recipient in a "no-win" situation. Consider a son who visits his mother and greets her with a hug. When the mother obviously tenses up, the son begs off. Mother then says, "Don't you love me anymore?" On seeing her son look guilty, mother continues, "Don't feel guilty; it's good to show your feelings." No matter what the son does, he's wrong. Double messages are not the problem: Everybody gives them. But when the person who delivers the double message refuses to *acknowledge* the contradiction in what he says, double messages become double binds, and problems ensue.

These distorted communications and relationships can also be viewed as other ways of describing HEE. For instance, consider the following example of a 20-year-old schizophrenic who telephones her suburban parents to say she will be spending the weekend in town with her boyfriend. The author's characterizations of each communication are in brackets.

FATHER: Don't you want to be with us? Your sister always brings her boyfriend here for the weekend. Aren't we good enough for you? [HEE critical comment]

DAUGHTER (sounding defeated): Okay, I'll visit you.

FATHER: Don't bother. I don't want you to feel obligated to your parents. We want you to be independent. [double bind]

MOTHER (interjecting): If you want dear, I'll bake the sponge cake you love. If that sponge cake hooked your father, it can hook your boyfriend! [HEE emotional overinvolvement]

FATHER: Mother's always interrupting, but it's always for your benefit. You're like your mother — you get upset way too easily. [HEE dissatisfaction and blame; schizmatic family?]

DAUGHTER: I know, dad. But why should you be upset that I stay in town once in a while? I've been home five weekends in a row.

MOTHER: Your father's not upset. [double-bind] It's just that when the whole family gets together we all have a wonderful time. [pseudomutuality]

Differential Diagnosis

Organic brain syndromes may present with delusions, hallucinations, incoherence, and flat, inappropriate, or labile affects. Yet even when they do, OBSs also show profound confusion, memory loss, fluctuating levels of consciousness, and disorientation. Schizophrenic hallucinations are invariably auditory; organic hallucinations involve any of the senses. Most schizophrenics defend their delusions, hallucinations, and bizarre behaviors as reasonable and valid, whereas most organic patients consider them inexplicable, crazy, and foreign — not their "real selves." If there is no family history of schizophrenia, or if schizophrenic-like symptoms first arise in a person over 40, the diagnosis is unlikely to be schizophrenia. (*Temporal lobe epilepsy* can simulate schizophrenia and so differential diagnosis may hinge on the age of onset, life course, and a family history of schizophrenia.)

Substance misuse, especially intoxication from amphetamines, cocaine, hallucinogens, PCP, cannabis, and alcohol may be indistinguishable from the active phase of schizophrenia. This similarity is usually temporary, and substance misuse is readily confirmed by urine screening. Although *alcoholic hallucinosis* typically stops within 48 hours of withdrawal, it may persist for weeks or months, and appear like acute schizophrenia. Yet in alcoholic hallucinosis, the hallucinations are usually visual, and the patient's response to these images is appropriate to their content, e.g., anxiety in response to frightening images. Of course, schizophrenics can also have a superimposed drug-induced psychosis.

Affective disorders often present with delusions and hallucinations, but they are often mood-congruent: Delusions of poverty, sin, and disease are common with depression; those of overconfidence and grandiosity are common with mania; patently bizarre, Schneiderian, and nonmood-congruent delusions are typically schizophrenic. Persecutory delusions occur in both affective and schizophrenic disorders. Indeed, distinguishing these two disorders is a frequent and difficult problem, since at some point over half of all schizophrenics have depressive symptoms, and affective patients can show deterioration, withdrawal, and psychosis. When the patient exhibits symptoms of both disorders, the timing and duration of symptoms are critical: Schizophrenia should only be diagnosed if (a) the full schizophrenic picture appears *before* the onset of the affective disorder, and (b) the active schizophrenic symptoms continue for at least several weeks. When the two disorders cannot be distinguished, diagnose *schizoaffective disorder*.

Paranoid disorders do not show the prominent hallucinations, incoherence, or Schneiderian delusions seen in schizophrenia, such as thought broadcasting or delusions of control. Paranoid disorders are characterized by delusions of persecution or jealousy in otherwise well-functioning people. Paranoid disorders are rare. *Schizophreniform disorder* meets all of *DSM-III*'s criteria for schizophrenia, except that it lasts between two weeks and six months; schizophrenia must persist for six continuous months. If the patient is psychotic for less than two weeks and returns to his premorbid level of functioning, the diagnosis is *brief reactive psychosis*.

Anxiety and somatoform disorders may resemble schizophrenia, but not for long. Obsessive and hypochondrical patients may be preoccupied with their concerns to a near-delusional intensity. Yet unlike the schizophrenic, the obsessive knows his obsessions are "silly" and the hypochondriac knows he's a hypochondriac.

Schizotypal, paranoid, and *borderline personality disorders* may present as psychosis and resemble the prodromal or acute phase of schizophrenia. Without schizophrenia, however, psychotic symptoms remit in hours or days. Severe *schizoid personality disorder* may produce a schizophrenic-like social withdrawal; these patients, however, rarely become psychotic. When a personality disorder and schizophrenia coexist, diagnose them on Axes II and I, respectively.

Management and Treatment

The goal of treatment of schizophrenic patients is not to *cure* them, but to improve their *quality of life*—to minimize symptoms, to prevent suicide, to avert relapses, to enhance self-esteem, to improve social and occupational functioning, and to reduce the pain for the patient's relatives. (Similarly, the goal of treating heart disease, diabetes, arthritis, and most physical ailments is not to cure, but to improve the patient's everyday life.)

Treatments vary depending on the stage of the patient's disorder. This section refers to *acute care*, which is the treatment of florid symptoms; *transition care*, which is treatment given before and after discharge from a psychiatric hospital; and *chronic care*, which is the community-based treatment of relatively stable, albeit impaired, patients.

Biological Treatments

With each of these three stages, overwhelming evidence demonstrates that the vast majority of schizophrenics benefit from antipsychotic medications. Although a few patients recover without medications and some become worse with them, it's hard to predict these patients in advance. Antipsychotics are most effective in eliminating schizophrenia's active symptoms, but they also diminish schizophrenia's chronic symptoms. When first prescribed, antipsychotics exert an *antipsychotic* action, which begins in roughly 30 minutes, peaks at around 24 hours, and persists substantially for 72 hours. *Some* neuroleptics also have a *sedative* effect, which manifests in 10–15 minutes, peaks around two hours, and subsides by six hours. Antipsychotic actions continue as long as the patient is on the drug; sedative effects wear off in seven to ten days.

Acute care. The clinician's first priorities are to prevent the patient from harming himself or others. If these dangers are imminent, observation, medication, and sometimes physical restraints are essential. Symptoms can be reduced quickest by "rapid tranquilization," during which the patient receives a small dose of an antipsychotic (e.g., 5 mg of haloperidol, 25 mg of chlorpromazine) every 30 minutes until his symptoms subside, he falls asleep, or he develops an incapaciting side effect (e.g., dystonia, orthostatic hypotension). To avert a hypotensive crisis, (a) the patient's blood pressures should be taken lying and standing before each dose, and (b) antipsychotics should be withheld if the patient is dizzy or light-headed on standing.

When a floridly psychotic patient's immediate safety is not at issue, antipsychotic medication should not be given until diagnoses other than schizophrenia have been ruled out. Since these drugs all exert the same antipsychotic effect, the choice of an antipsychotic depends primarily on its side effect profile. (See Appendix E.) In general, there is an inverse relation between parkinsonian side effects on one hand, and anticholinergic (e.g., dry mouth) and sedative side effects on the other. For example, the highly sedating thioridizine is the most anticholinergic and the least parkinsonian of antipsychotics. Thus, if sedation is desired or if the patient is at high risk for parkinsonian side effects, thioridizine might be a good initial choice. Patients should only receive as much sedation as required to insure their safety. A patient banging his head against a wall requires sedation, whereas a patient standing rigidly in the corner does not. Dosage (Appendix D) must be tailored to the individual patient.

Transition care. The patient should be discharged on the same dose and type of medication that proved necessary as an inpatient; decreasing it is a mistake. After living in the relative security of a hospital, the discharged patient must suddenly contend with all the environmental stresses that prompted his admission. To face these stresses, the patient "needs all the help he can get," including medication. Since transition involves so many psychosocial changes, if medication is also changed, it's hard to pinpoint which changes account for problems that might arise. If the patient continues in remission for roughly six months after his first hospitalization, his medication should be gradually stopped to prevent tardive dyskinesia (see below).

At no time, however, should the clinician imply that taking medication is a "crutch": That's akin to telling a diabetic that using insulin is a crutch. In reviewing all well-controlled studies, Davis (1975) found that of 3,609 patients sampled over four to six months, 20% relapsed on drug and 53% relapsed on placebo. Davis determined that the probability of this difference being due to chance is less than 10^{-87}. Thus, every effort should be made to insure that the patient receives his medication: This means educating the patient and his family about the medication, using injectible fluphenazine decoanate which persists for two to three weeks, having family members monitor the nightly intake of antipsychotics in liquid form, or having the patient receive his once-a-day dose in front of a nurse.

Chronic care. How long patients should remain on antipsychotic medications following *subsequent* hospitalizations depends on the illness's duration and severity. Although the beneficial effects of antipsychotic drugs are greatest during the acute stage, they control symptoms for at least a year and decrease relapses for many years.

Unfortunately, this long-term use of antipsychotics creates one of psychiatry's darkest problems — *tardive dyskinesia* (TD). About 10% to 40% of patients who take antipsychotics for over two continuous years (though it can be as little as six months) develop involuntary, bizarre movements of the mouth, limbs, and hips. Although a majority of cases are mild, severe impairment is common. Most often TD appears as "tobacco-chewing," lip-smacking, and "fly-catching" movements of the mouth and tongue; less often, as hip jerks or slow, undulating motions of the hands or feet. These grotesque movements typically erupt within a few days of decreasing or stopping antipsychotics; they subside only when the patient sleeps or is put back on the medication. TD's cause is unknown.[4]

Unless detected early, half the time TD is *irreversible*. Although other drugs may occasionally counteract it, once TD occurs, there is usually *no* good way to eliminate it. The risk and severity of TD may be reduced by maintaining patients on the lowest possible dose, and by periodically seeing if the drug can be discontinued. Yet because

---

[4]One popular theory holds that because antipsychotic drugs block dopamine (DA) receptors, these receptors eventually become "supersensitive" to DA, so that when antipsychotics are decreased or withdrawn, they can't handle the onslaught of DA; as a result, these receptors degenerate, resulting in tardive dyskinesia.

the only way to avoid TD is to avoid antipsychotics,[5] doctor and patient must decide, as with any medication, if the treatment is worse than the disease. At some point, most schizophrenics must choose between risking TD or madness and institutionalization. In reality, this choice isn't that dreadful, since slightly increasing the dose will temporarily suppress TD. In time, however, more severe TD will emerge, which only higher doses of medication can control; yet even here, the increase is usually small, the relief great, and the alternative terrifying.

For patients who are not sufficiently improving on antipsychotics, the first consideration is whether the drug is being taken, and if so, properly absorbed. These questions can be answered by obtaining serum levels. Fluphenazine decoanate can circumvent problems with drug compliance. The patient may not be improving because of misdiagnosis, or because he has developed affective symptoms that might improve with antidepressants or lithium.

Psychosocial Treatments

Acute care. When hospitalized, most actively psychotic schizophrenics have a short attention span, are overwhelmed by stimuli, and cannot easily discern reality; they often feel lost, alone, and frightened. Therefore, contacts with these patients should be no longer than the patient can tolerate; in one day most patients benefit more from, let's say, ten, five-minute contacts than from one, 40-minute contact. These frequent contacts should stress reality testing and reassurance, while avoiding psychologically sensitive material. They should be performed by as few staff as possible. As the patient's psychosis diminishes, the role of psychosocial treatment increases. At some point, individual supportive therapy should identify the stressors that led to hospitalization and prepare him to contend with similar stressors following discharge.

Hospitalization is also a major crisis for the family. Studies show that prior to hospitalization, most relatives deny or "explain away" the schizophrenic's symptoms (e.g., "It's normal for teenagers to lock themselves in a room." "Kids often fly off the handle.") When the patient is psychotic and finally admitted, families are shell-shocked: They might insist "nothing is wrong," telephone the ward 15 times a day, not leave the unit, etc. These are weird but *normal* responses to an acute and severe stress (Figure 4-3); they are not indicative of the "craziest family on earth." Only *after* the immediate crisis can the family's normal behavior be assessed.

Because schizophrenia is a chronic disorder, the family's long-term involvement as an extension of the treatment team is essential. On admission, most families are already guilty about "creating" a schizophrenic, and so their guilt is compounded when therapists blame them, either directly or euphemistically (e.g., "The family has problems communicating."). Not only do attempts to rectify a family's "communication

---

[5]Consequently, antipsychotics should only be used for schizophrenia. A draconian, but all-too-frequent, error is to treat chronic anxiety or depression with antipsychotics for more than five months.

problems" and "pathological relations" reinforce the family's guilt, but they don't work — at least during short-term hospitalizations. Similarly, studies show that separating the schizophrenic from his family is usually harmful.

On the other hand, near the outset of hospitalization, several members of the staff should begin forming a *collaborative* relationship with the family. Nurses should monitor visits to gather information. New families should be introduced to relatives of other schizophrenics so that the new family feels less alone, embarrassed, and guilty. Since research demonstrates that most acutely psychotic schizophrenics do as well, if not better, after three weeks, rather than three months, of hospitalization, discharge planning, which includes the family, should begin the day the patient is admitted.

Transition care. The patient's chance of relapse and suicide is greatest within the first six months, and especially within the first 14 weeks, following discharge. Suicide most often occurs when patients (a) have a post-psychotic depression, (b) are discouraged about their treatment, (c) believe their future is hopeless, (d) misconstrue a drug-induced akinesia for depression and futility, and (e) stop taking medication. Therapists should be alert to these specific warning signs, meet frequently with patients to check on them, and tell family members to also be aware of them.

In general, the patients who fare best during these 14 weeks are those with the most stability in their lives; those who fare worst have the most changes in their lives. Transition, therefore, is *not* the time to introduce major alterations in the patient's living arrangements, social life, medications, therapists, and so on. Some changes may be necessary, but they should be kept to a minimum. Considerable research (Caton, 1984) shows that discharge planning should focus on the five areas most likely to produce relapse:

1. *The failure to take medication* is the most frequent cause of readmission, and a common prelude to suicide. Because 24% to 63% of outpatient schizophrenics take less than the prescribed dose, *all* patients and their families should have the purpose and importance of medication explained to them.

2. *The failure to continue aftercare* stems less often from a lack of resources than from the patient's refusal to partake of available programs. Dropout rates from aftercare programs are as high as 75%. Good discharge planning insures that the patient has visited the aftercare facility, knows how to travel there, understands the nature and purpose of aftercare treatment, feels comfortable with the outpatient staff, and knows the time of his first aftercare appointment.

3. *Inadequate life-support*, especially in housing and income, but also in money management skills, hygiene, and medical care should be addressed in occupational therapy.

4. *Inadequate socialization and recreation* often prompt rehospitalization. If a bowler stops bowling, his bowling skills atrophy; so too with the schizophrenic's leisure-time and social skills. Recreational and group therapy should prevent further deterioration of these skills.

5. *High exposure to HEE families* can be avoided by using a "psychoeducational approach," whose effectiveness has been repeatedly demonstrated (Anderson, Hogarty, & Reiss, 1980). The approach aims to reduce the guilt, overresponsibility, confusion, and helplessness of families, and although its implementation varies between settings, it generally involves five steps: (a) The patient and his family are given "the facts" about schizophrenia, including information about its symptoms, natural course, genetics, etc. (b) The family and patient unload pent-up concerns about the illness and about each other, preferably with other families. (c) Families are taught about the psychonoxious effects of HEE environments. (d) Next they're trained to contain emotional outbursts, to avoid (or at least delay and mute) criticisms, to praise positive activities, to reduce unrealistic guilt and overresponsibility, and to be less judgmental. (e) If the family is, for whatever reason, an immutably HEE family, then the patient's amount of contact with the family should be reduced. Community-based self-help groups for the families of schizophrenics often provide a kind of psychoeducational approach over the long haul.

Chronic care. Contrary to many long-held assumptions, more therapy is not always better therapy. In the most thorough series of studies to date, Hogarty et al., (1974) found that supportive psychotherapy is more beneficial with patients who take medication, more likely to hasten relapse in non-medicated patients, and more effective the longer the patient has not been actively psychotic.

On the other hand, even at the very best of facilities (e.g., Chestnut Lodge), long-term, intensive psychotherapy is ineffective in treating schizophrenia. A 15-year follow-up showed that only 14% of these patients were functioning "good" or better (McGlashan, 1984). When long-term hospitalization is required, chronic schizophrenics obtain better results from token economies (Chapter 5) than from therapeutic communities (Maxmen, 1984). Chronically hospitalized patients function better in the community when they are *gradually* released from the hospital, often to halfway houses or to a group setting with patients they knew in the hospital.

Despite the severity and chronicity of schizophrenia, modern treatments can enable patients to live relatively satisfying lives. The author knows many patients who, after five to 15 years of being institutionalized, went on to become independent and productive with the help of sound and sensible treatment. These cases are not rare; patients and families should be made aware of this, if for no other reason but to combat demoralization.

CHAPTER 10

Paranoid and Miscellaneous Psychotic Disorders

THIS CHAPTER COMBINES two *DSM-III* categories of psychoses called "paranoid disorders" and "psychotic disorders not elsewhere classified." Paranoid disorders — renamed "delusional disorders" in *DSM-III-R* — are characterized by persecutory delusions or delusional jealousy without any other deterioration in functioning, thinking, perceiving, or behaving. The "other psychoses" is a residual category; it covers brief reactive psychosis, schizophreniform disorder, schizoaffective disorder, and the ultimate residual category: atypical psychosis.[1]

PARANOID DISORDERS

> O, beware, my lord of jealousy.
> It is the green-eyed monster which doth mock
> The meat it feeds on.
> — Othello, III.iii.165

Although Iago's "green-eyed" monster of jealousy mocks and feeds on its creator, in every other respect patients with paranoid disorders function quite

---

[1]Atypical psychosis is the name for all disorders that present with psychotic symptoms, but do not meet the diagnostic criteria for other *DSM-III* disorders (as those discussed in Chapters 7–11). An example is a "postpartum psychosis" not due to affective, schizophrenic, or other disorders.

well. Of course, most jealousies are not disorders but passions, and it is the clinician's task to distinguish the two. Iago, for instance, does *not* have a paranoid disorder. Most patients with paranoid disorders experience their problem as ego-syntonic; Iago doesn't: His "green-eyed" monster torments and consumes him.

Persecutory delusions *or* delusional jealousy lasting over a week are the chief features of paranoid disorders. The persecutory delusions are enduring, systematized, interrelated, and internally consistent. Their themes may be single or multiple, simple or complex: The patient may think he is being drugged, followed, conspired against, or maligned. Grandiose delusions may arise: The entire United Nations is spying on him or General Motors is harassing him. With delusional jealousy, a spouse's "unfaithfulness" is fabricated on tissues of evidence—a misplaced stocking, a misconstrued remark. Paranoid disorders do not present with prominent hallucinations. *DSM-III*'s criteria for paranoid disorders are indicated on Table 10-1.

Historically, paranoid disorders were considered a subtype of either schizophrenia or affective disorder, but now they are viewed as independent entities. In *DSM-III*, paranoid disorders cannot be diagnosed if schizophrenic (or organic) disorders are present. In contrast to the delusions in paranoid disorders, schizophrenic delusions are more bizarre, fragmented, vague, unsys-

TABLE 10-1
DSM-III Criteria for Paranoid Disorders*

A. Persistent persecutory delusions or delusional jealousy.

B. Emotion and behavior appropriate to the content of the delusional system.

C. Duration of illness of at least one week.

D. None of the symptoms of criterion A of Schizophrenia (Table 9-1)†, such as bizarre delusions, incoherence, or marked loosening of associations.

E. No prominent hallucinations.

F. The full depressive or manic syndrome (criteria A and B of major depressive or manic episode) (Tables 11-2, 11-3)† is either not present, developed after any psychotic symptoms, or was brief in duration relative to the duration of the psychotic symptoms.

G. Not due to an Organic Mental Disorder.

*DSM-III, p. 196.

†The corresponding tables in this textbook have been substituted for the corresponding pages in DSM-III.

tematized, and Schneiderian; schizophrenia also differs in having an earlier age of onset, prominent auditory hallucinations, flat or inappropriate affect, and disorganized behavior. Unlike affective disorders, with paranoid disorders the full picture mania or depression is (a) not present, or (b) develops *well after* the paranoid delusions have begun, or (c) is transitory.

Paranoid disorders usually begin insidiously with a plausible suspicion or grievance against an individual, government agency, or business. As the patient becomes increasingly frustrated in trying to rectify his complaint, he often develops psychotic fantasies and presses his demands for justice. He may bring legal action, recruit supporters, make public appeals, or send petitions. With growing self-importance and messianic zeal, he often displays the pressured speech seen with manics. Yet unlike mania or schizophrenia, *the hallmark of a paranoid disorder is that its psychopathology does not spill over into other areas of functioning.* Consider this example of delusional jealousy:

Flabbergasted, the author was confronted by a secretary who refused to type his paper on medical student activists. The secretary, Josefina Gomez, a 45-year-old, married Cuban exile, protested my passing reference to Ché Guevara being a physician and psychotherapist to lepers. She demanded to know if her husband had put me up to this. "No," I replied, "I don't know what you're talking about." In short order, she told me.

Five years before she had fled Cuba with her physician husband (Roberto) of 12 years. She claimed that two years ago Roberto had begun an affair, which she first detected on returning home to find *two* glasses on the kitchen table, when, as she insisted, "There should only be *one.*" She could not think of another plausible explanation, adding that her husband, who denied any affair, gave the "lame excuse" that he had used an extra glass by accident. Over the next few weeks, she detected more "evidence" of this affair: Roberto was watching more public television ("Where everybody has disgusting affairs."); he sometimes came home wearing surgical garb, even though he's a pediatrician ("He changes clothes in the hospital so I won't see lipstick on his shirts."). When Roberto became assistant chief of staff, she launched a letter writing campaign to hospital bigwigs, at first saying they had promoted "an immoral devil," and later claiming they and Roberto were converting the hospital into a brothel. Unaware that Josefina worked at the same hospital, the bigwigs dismissed her letters as "crank mail." That her husband was unfaithful and in cahoots with the hospital became "even clearer" when the hospital liberalized its abortion policy "simply to dispose of Roberto's bastard children."

Throughout her apparent paranoia — "apparent" only because diagnoses should only emerge from a formal workup — she actively participated in her church and performed her work impeccably (my paper, aside). She had no personal or family history of psychiatric care and saw no reason to get some. Josefina said that her "parents favored my brothers," that she left Cuba because "Castro betrayed the revolution," and that she would not type my paper since "Ché Guevera was a doctor with a mistress, just like Roberto." Subsequently, her relationship to the author was polite, yet chilly.

DSM-III describes three paranoid disorders: (a) *paranoia*, with over six months of chronic and stable persecutory delusions, and without folie à deux; (b) *shared paranoid disorder* (i.e., folie à deux), in which the patient adopts another person's persecutory delusion out of a close relationship with that person; and (c) *acute paranoid disorder*, which by definition lasts under six months.

Most cases of *paranoia* arise gradually during middle or late adult life, have chronic and stable courses with few remissions and exacerbations, and disproportionately affect those who are female, married, immigrants, and in lower socioeconomic groups. Paranoia constitutes 1% to 4% of all psychiatric hospital admissions, with an incidence of first admissions between 1 and 3/100,000 population per year. Its etiology is unknown. Watt's (1985) investigation does not support *DSM-III*'s contention that paranoid and schizoid personality disorders, as well as hearing loss, predispose to paranoia. Paranoia does not run in families. Social isolation and stress may foster paranoia in the elderly, while projection is its chief defense mechanism.

Given Freedman and Schwab's (1978) finding that 40% of psychiatric inpatients have paranoid symptoms, paranoia must be distinguished from *schizophrenia* and *affective disorders* as discussed above. *Organic delusional syndromes*, most often from amphetamine intoxication or brain tumors, may produce paranoid delusions. *Paranoid personality disorder* may exhibit paranoid ideation and pathological jealousy, but not delusions. If paranoid delusions develop on top of a preexisting paranoid personality disorder, both disorders should be diagnosed.

Since paranoia is usually ego-syntonic, these patients rarely seek treatment. If they do — and it's usually under coercion — a trial of antipsychotic medication is indicated, even though they are unlikely to take it. Since they are leery of psychotherapy, these patients' trust can only be acquired if therapy is pursued cautiously.

Shared paranoid disorder is quite rare, occurs 90% of the time in the same family, and most often affects two sisters. In a typical case, a woman became alarmed that the FBI was polluting the air with "liquid napalm," which made her skin peel. Her sister began noticing that her skin was also peeling and joined in her sister's delusion. About a quarter of the recipient partners are physical invalids. If the partners are merely separated, they abandon their delusions. Very often the partners reunite and the delusions return.

Acute paranoid disorder afflicts those whose world has drastically changed: immigrants, refugees, prisoners of war, military inductees, those who've left home for the first time, etc. Homosexual panic may trigger it in men. In contrast to the other paranoid disorders, acute paranoid disorder begins abruptly, rarely becomes chronic, may arise at any age, and may include mild hallucinations. Also, since it is ego-dystonic, patients are more amenable to treatment with antipsychotics (e.g., haloperidol 5 mg) and supportive psychotherapy. After the psychosis remits, most patients are reluctant to continue treatment.

BRIEF REACTIVE PSYCHOSIS

Whether *anybody* can become psychotic under sufficient stress is hard to prove, but when people do, *DSM-III* calls it a "brief reactive psychosis." This disorder has seven key features: (a) It must be triggered by an *acute psychosocial stressor*, which is obvious (not inferred) and severe enough to distress anybody (e.g., a loved one's death, discovering one has AIDS). There may be a series of major traumas that accumulate over a month or so, but in most cases there is a single devastating stressor. (b) There is *no increasing psychopathology prior* to these stressors, as often occurs in schizophrenic and paranoid disorders. (c) The patient is in *emotional turmoil* with rapid shifts of mood, perplexity, or confusion. (d) The patient has *psychotic symptoms*, such as incoherence, delusions, hallucinations, catatonia, or grossly bizarre or disorganized behavior. The patient may scream, curse, undress, chant, or defecate in public. Psychotic symptoms usually pertain to the precipitating stressor and must be foreign to the patient's subculture. (e) The psychosis must last *over a few hours, but less than two weeks*. Symptoms usually abate in three or four days, even though some patients have a secondary dysthymia for several weeks following the acute psychosis. (f) The patient returns to his *premorbid level of functioning*. (g) The symptoms are not caused by another disorder. *DSM-III* combines these seven features into five criteria (Table 10-2).

Marc, a 30-year-old hotel executive was at work, when a "moderate" earthquake toppled the hotel killing four occupants and injuring many others. Dazed but physically unharmed, Marc wandered away from the rubble, arrived home hours later, and kept mumbling that he was responsible for the hotel's collapse. Staring into space as if listening to someone, Marc would say, "The devil's saying, 'You're to blame, you're to blame. You'll fry in hell.'" At times Marc would sit and sulk, sometimes he was rigid and mute, while at other times he would pace the floor arguing loudly with the devil. Marc had no previous psychiatric difficulties and his mental state had been stable prior to the earthquake.

Marc's wife took him to the emergency room where a drug screen was negative. His brief reactive psychosis was treated with 5 mg of haloperidol stat, and 2 mg tid for the next two days. The day after the earthquake Marc's symptoms began to recede, and three days later he was back to normal.

If Marc's symptoms lasted less than two to three hours, his diagnosis would have been *atypical psychosis*; if they persisted over two weeks, his diagnosis

TABLE 10-2
DSM-III Criteria for Brief Reactive Psychosis*

A. Psychotic symptoms appear immediately following a recognizable psychosocial stressor that would evoke significant symptoms of distress in almost anyone.

B. The clinical picture involves emotional turmoil and at least one of the followng psychotic symptoms:

(1) incoherence or loosening of associations
(2) delusions
(3) hallucinations
(4) behavior that is grossly disorganized or catatonic

C. The psychotic symptoms last more than a few hours but less than two weeks, and there is an eventual return to the premorbid level of functioning. (Note: The diagnosis can be made soon after the onset of the psychotic symptoms without waiting for the expected recovery. If the psychotic symptoms last more than two weeks, the diagnosis should be changed.)

D. No period of increasing psychopathology immediately preceded the psychosocial stressor.

E. The disturbance is not due to any other mental disorder, such as an Organic Mental Disorder, manic episode, or Factitious Disorder with Psychological Symptoms.

DSM-III, pp. 201–202.

would be *schizophreniform disorder*. In contrast to *schizophrenia*, brief reactive psychosis usually has an acute precipitant, a rapid onset, delusions and hallucinations which pertain to the stressor, and a quick and complete recovery. Gradually increasing psychopathology before the florid psychosis characterizes schizophrenic and schizophreniform disorders, but not brief reactive psychosis. If the patient meets the full *DSM-III* criteria for *affective disorders*, brief reactive psychosis should not be diagnosed. *Malingering* and *factitious disorder with psychological symptoms* must be considered. *Organic brain syndromes*, especially delirium and (psychomotor or) *temporal lobe epilepsy*, can produce delusions, hallucinations, and repeated automatisms with fluctuating levels of consciousness, or without confusion (McKenna et al., 1985). EEG recordings should rule out epilepsies, including *petit mal*, which present as absence attacks. Finally, *substance misuse*, especially intoxication or withdrawal, is often the prime suspect, and the most important to diagnose promptly.

The priorities in treating brief reactive psychosis are: first, prevent suicide or assaultiveness; second, hasten recovery by prescribing antipsychotics. If the patient is imminently suicidal or dangerous, "rapid tranquilization" (see p. 157) may be indicated. Tapering medication should begin only after the patient is clearly recovering. Third, initial talking therapy emphasizes reality testing and repeatedly telling the patient he is safe and will improve soon. At this point, relatives and therapists should refrain from "psychologizing" the "meaning" of the psychosis with the patient. For instance, probing Marc's guilt over the earthquake would have further disorganized him. Fourth, *after* the psychosis resolves, some patients benefit from psychotherapy which addresses (a) the stressor and its personal meaning, or (b) incompletely resolved issues related to the psychosis. For example, on returning to his wife's grave a year after she died, a well-functioning man developed an acute psychosis which disappeared in a week. Sensing his psychosis indicated that he was more distressed by his wife's death than he had realized, he entered brief psychotherapy to examine this concern.

SCHIZOPHRENIFORM DISORDER

The *DSM-III* criteria for schizophreniform disorder and schizophrenia (Table 9-1) are identical, except for duration: Schizophreniform disorder must occur between two weeks and six months, whereas schizophrenia must exist over six months. This six-month cutoff point was chosen because it appears (for now) to be the single best predictor of which patients (viz., schizophreniform) recover and which become chronic (schizophrenic).

To differentiate these two disorders and to cast schizophreniform psychoses as having a favorable outcome, *DSM-III-R* plans to expand the disorder's diagnostic criteria to include the patient's having two of the following four indicators of a good prognosis: (a) onset of prominent psychotic symptoms within four weeks of first noticeable signs of illness; (b) confusion, disorientation or perplexity at height of the psychotic episode; (c) absence of blunted or flat affect; and (d) good premorbid social and occupational functioning. A further *DSM-III-R* criterion will be that the patient recovers to approximately his premorbid level of functioning. (While anticipating recovery, the clinician can still diagnose schizophreniform disorder, preferably accompanied by the *DSM-III* qualifier "provisional.")

Roughly half of patients *initially* diagnosed as having schizophreniform disorder will substantially improve or recover; in general, the longer the disorder persists, the worse the prognosis. Although findings conflict, most suggest that there is no increased prevalence of schizophrenia among relatives. The ECA survey (Chapter 1) found a lifetime prevalence of 0.1% for schizophreniform disorder in the general population. The disorder's etiology is unknown.

Schizophreniform disorder differs from *brief reactive psychosis*, which resolves in under two weeks and always follows a severe stressor. It differs from *schizoaffective disorder*, which has a strong affective component (see below). All the factors for differentiating *organic brain syndromes* and *affective disorders* from schizophrenia would apply to schizophreniform disorder. Schizophreniform disorders should be treated symptomatically, with observation, antipsychotic medication, supportive psychotherapy, suicide precautions, and family involvement.

SCHIZOAFFECTIVE DISORDER

In 1933, the term "schizoaffective disorder" was introduced to describe a psychosis with prominent schizophrenic *and* affective symptoms; since then the term's use has been equally "schizophrenic" and "affective." Experts have split over whether schizoaffective disorder is an actual disorder: Some claim it is not a true disorder, but a mere label, a fudge-factor, a provisional diagnosis to be used until the patient's real diagnosis—schizophrenia or affective disorder—becomes apparent. Others contend that schizoaffective disorder is a genuine entity which combines features of both disorders. The debate was so charged that schizoaffective disorder became the only disorder in *DSM-III* without diagnostic criteria; *DSM-III-R* plans to add them, suggesting that, at least in some patients, schizoaffective disorder is a genuine disorder.

A preliminary draft of *DSM-III-R* (10/5/85) lists three criteria for schizoaffective disorder: (a) At some point either a major depressive (Table 11-2) or a manic syndrome (Table 11-3) coexists with the active (group A) symptoms of schizophrenia (Table 9-1). (b) At least two weeks of delusions or hallucinations in the absence of prominent affective symptoms. (c) The disorder does not meet the criteria for schizophrenia or an organic mental disorder. *DSM-III-R* names two subtypes of schizoaffective disorder: *bipolar* (i.e., history of mania or hypomania) and *depressive*.

By these criteria, Fred, a 24-year-old librarian, would seem to have a schizoaffective disorder. At first, over a period of seven months, he developed typical signs of schizophrenia: He believed a nearby hospital was zapping his brain with x-rays, thereby controlling his actions. By stringing together the first letter of each book title returned to the library, Fred uncovered a secret code, which auditory hallucinations later informed him was part of a plot to destroy Dartmouth College. After a three-week hospitalization, including treatment with antipsychotics, Fred recovered, returned to work, and secretly stopped his medication. Within a week his delusions reappeared, but this time accompanied by symptoms of major depression: insomnia, anorexia, anhedonia, psychomotor retardation, and severe dysthymia. Did Fred have a post-psychotic depression (see p. 148)? Probably not, because in post-psychotic depression the patient feels hopeless, or anergic, or depressed—in other words, a *symptom*, instead of a *syndrome*, of depression. Fred had the syndrome (Table 11-2), and thus, a schizo-affective disorder.

When schizoaffective disorder is used as a temporary diagnosis awaiting further clarification, appending the term "provisional" clarifies the clinician's intention. In Fred's case, however, schizoaffective disorder was diagnosed as a "true" disorder. Little is known about this "true" disorder. It may be a heterogeneous entity with numerous etiologies. Some genetic studies show these patients have an increased family history of alcoholism and affective disorder. Apparently, it occurs more in women. Its age of onset, degree of recovery, natural history, and prognosis fall between schizophrenia's and affective disorder's. The longer the psychosis, the bleaker the outcome.

Treatment is symptomatic: Schizophrenic symptoms treated with antipsychotics, manic symptoms with lithium, depressive symptoms with tricyclic antidepressants. Some "schizo-manic" patients treated with lithium require lower doses of antipsychotics and some taking both drugs concurrently become extremely confused or parkinsonian; some do well on lithium without antipsychotics, which is the most desirable option since lithium has fewer side effects and does not cause tardive dyskinesia. When antidepressants are added to antipsychotics, a toxic psychosis with confusion and disorientation is common; it's partly due to excessive anticholinergic activity. The point is that because the treatment of schizoaffective disorders often requires two or more drugs, these patients' mental status should be frequently and formally tested.

CHAPTER 11

Affective Disorders

AFFECTIVE DISORDERS ARE the most common disorders seen by outpatient psychiatrists. Affective disorders, principally depression, are far and away the number one cause of suicide. What's more, with each successive generation in the 20th century, the prevalence of depression and suicide is apparently on the rise. Teenage suicides are increasing at an alarming rate. Most of these suicides, however, *are* preventable, and in doing so the first step is to learn about their chief cause — depression.

When laymen speak of depression, they usually refer to the *emotion* of feeling sad, blue, down-in-the-dumps, unhappy, demoralized — i.e., dysthymia. When clinicians speak of depression, they usually refer to a *syndrome*, or mental disorder, of depression, consisting of many symptoms and signs, including appetite loss, anhedonia, hopelessness, insomnia, and dysthymia. Whereas the emotion of depression affects everyone to some degree, the syndrome afflicts only some — a "mere" 15% of Americans during their life and a hundred million earthlings every day. (For clarity, in this text "dysthymia" refers to the emotion or symptom of depression while "depression" refers to the syndromes and disorders of depression. "Dysphoria" means any unpleasant mood, including dysthymia.)

Affective disorder is the overall category for entities whose predominant symptom is usually a pathological mood: dysphoria, euphoria, or both. (In *DSM-III-R*, affective disorders may be renamed "mood disorders," since they color one's entire outlook on life, which is a trait of moods, not affects.) In *DSM-III*, affective disorders which consist solely of "lows" are major depression, and its milder version, dysthymic disorder; those with a history of "highs" and "lows" are bipolar disorder, and its milder form, cyclothymic disorder.

171

Affective disorders have also been classified according to at least four different conceptual models (Table 11-1). First, the *endogenous versus reactive* model considers endogenous depression as a strictly biological event unrelated to any environmental forces, whereas reactive depression must be psychosocially triggered and devoid of any biological factors. This distinction unjustifiably assumes that a depression's etiology is (a) known and (b) either biological *or* psychosocial. Indeed, many "endogenous" depressions follow environmental stressors and many "reactive" depressions emerge without any obvious precipitant. Second, *primary and secondary* depressions differ in that secondary depressions are preceded by another physical or mental disorder (e.g., alcoholism, hypothyroidism, anxiety disorder), whereas primary depressions are not. Third, in the *unipolar versus bipolar* model, a bipolar disorder exists whenever a manic episode has occurred. Patients with bipolar depression must have a history of mania or hypomania while those with unipolar depressions don't. Fourth, historically *psychotic and neurotic* depressions were distinguished, with psychotic depressions being any severe depression, even when the patient wasn't psychotic. In *DSM-III*, however, a "psychotic depression" must display psychosis. Neurotic depressions are roughly equivalent to "atypical depression" or dysthymic disorder.

Until the mid-1970s, American psychiatrists tended to equate psychosis with schizophrenia, even though many, especially mood-congruent, delusions and hallucinations occur in depression and mania. Research also showed that many "acute schizophrenics" had symptoms, histories, clinical courses, prognoses, family histories, and responses to medication that more closely resembled affective disorders than schizo-

TABLE 11-1
Models of Depression

DISTINCTIONS BASED ON:	*DSM-III* CATEGORY		
	MAJOR DEPRESSION	BIPOLAR DEPRESSION	DYSTHYMIC DEPRESSION
ETIOLOGY: biological or psychosocial	*biological* Endogenous Depression	Endogenous Depression (i.e., melancholia)	*psychosocial* Reactive
HISTORY: (without) (with) other illness	Primary and Secondary	Primary and Secondary	Primary and Secondary
HISTORY: mania or hypomania	*without* Unipolar Depression	*with* Bipolar Depression	*without* Unipolar Depression
SEVERITY: moderate or severe	*severe* Psychotic Depression	*severe* Psychotic Depression	*moderate* Neurotic Depression

phrenia.[1] To reflect these findings, *DSM-III* expanded the definition of affective disorders and narrowed it for schizophrenia.

Nonetheless, diagnostic dogmas die hard: Some clinicians still equate psychosis with schizophrenia, thereby overlooking affective disorders, which have more effective and safer treatments, fewer and less severe symptoms, better prognoses, and a higher (6X) prevalence than schizophrenia. Thus, schizophrenia should never be diagnosed without *first* considering an affective disorder.

Clinical Presentation

Major depression. The first essential feature of major depression is *either* severe dysphoria *or* anhedonia — that is, a pervasive loss of interest or ability to experience pleasure in normally enjoyable activities. The dysphoria is usually dysthymic, but it can be irritable or apprehensive. Patients describe this dysphoria as "living in a black hole," "feeling dead," "overwhelmed by doom," or "physically drained." On the other hand, many patients with major depression do *not* feel depressed nor even dysphoric, but anhedonic. A baseball freak doesn't care about the World Series; a loving father loses interest in his child; a devoted nurse cares little for her patients. Just because a patient doesn't look unhappy or doesn't complain about being in the dumps, if anhedonic, she might still be depressed.

The other essential feature of major depression is the presence of at least four *biological signs of depression*, which generally include appetite loss, (unintentional) weight loss, insomnia or hypersomnia, psychomotor retardation or agitation, anhedonia, a lack of energy or fatigue, diminished libido, and constipation. In another common biological sign, "diurnal mood variation," the patient feels worse in the morning and slightly better by night; this pattern continues through weekends. Patients typically awake in the middle of the night (i.e., "middle insomnia") or in the early morning (e.g., "terminal insomnia"), finding it hard or impossible to return to sleep.

As presented on Table 11-2, *DSM-III*'s criteria for major depression require dysphoria *or* anhedonia *and* several biological signs of depression. *DSM-III's* criteria indicate that biological signs must exist nearly every day for at least two weeks, and that outside of depressive periods, bizarre behavior and mood-*in*congruent delusions and hallucinations should not be prominent. Moreover, as Amy's case of major depression (pp. 3–4) illustrates, the *DSM-III* diagnosis of major depression is based on symptoms and clinical course, and not

---

[1]Many psychotherapeutic "cures" for "schizophrenia" depicted in books, such as *I Never Promised You a Rose Garden*, occurred in patients with affective disorders who would have improved no matter what therapy they received (North & Cadoret, 1981).

TABLE 11-2
DSM-III* Criteria for Major Depressive Episode

A. Dysphoric mood or loss of interest or pleasure in all or almost all usual activities and pastimes. The dysphoric mood is characterized by symptoms such as the following: depressed, sad, blue, hopeless, low, down in the dumps, irritable. The mood disturbance must be prominent and relatively persistent, but not necessarily the most dominant symptom, and does not include momentary shifts from one dysphoric mood to another dysphoric mood, e.g., anxiety to depression to anger, such as are seen in states of acute psychotic turmoil. (For children under six, dysphoric mood may have to be inferred from a persistently sad facial expression.)

B. At least four of the following symptoms have each been present nearly every day for a period of at least two weeks (in children under six, at least three of the first four).

   (1) poor appetite or significant weight loss (when not dieting) or increased appetite or significant weight gain (in children under six, consider failure to make expected weight gains)
   (2) insomnia or hypersomnia
   (3) psychomotor agitation or retardation (but not merely subjective feelings of restlessness or being slowed down) (in children under six, hypoactivity)
   (4) loss of interest or pleasure in usual activities or decrease in sexual drive not limited to a period when delusional or hallucinating (in children under six, signs of apathy)
   (5) loss of energy; fatigue
   (6) feelings of worthlessness, self-reproach, or excessive or inappropriate guilt (either may be delusional)
   (7) complaints or evidence of diminished ability to think or concentrate, such as slowed thinking, or indecisiveness not associated with marked loosening of associations or incoherence
   (8) recurrent thoughts of death, suicidal ideation, wishes to be dead, or suicide attempt

C. Neither of the following dominate the clinical picture when an affective syndrome (i.e., criteria A and B above) is not present, that is, before it developed or after it has remitted:

   (1) preoccupation with a mood-incongruent delusion or hallucination
   (2) bizarre behavior

D. Not superimposed on either Schizophrenia, Schizophreniform Disorder, or a Paranoid Disorder.

E. Not due to any Organic Mental Disorder or Uncomplicated Bereavement

DSM-III pp. 213–214.

whether the disorder is, or is not, produced by environmental stressors.

Everything about these patients is slow — walking,[2] talking, thinking, eating, reacting. If asked their wife's name or their occupation, they may take 20–30 seconds to answer. Their concentration can be so impaired that they may be unable to sit through a sitcom or to read a simple paragraph. Their slowed thinking, impaired concentration, and low self-esteem paralyze decision-making. Readily overwhelmed by easy tasks, they no longer try to do anything. Although some patients have psychomotor retardation, others have psychomotor agitation: They fidget, they pace, they wring their hands. They may be suspicious, paranoid, or preoccupied with somatic concerns.

Depressed patients see the world through depressed glasses. To them, everything is bleak — their life, their world, their future, and their treatment. "I beg you to shoot me," a depressed woman pleaded, "If they'll put a sick horse out of his misery, why not a person?" They ruminate over personal failures — real or imagined — often making mountains out of molehills. With a nearly delusional conviction, they may feel utterly hopeless, helpless, worthless, or guilty. A severely depressed man insisted on shock treatment because "I deserve to be punished." (So much for "informed consent"!) A self-made millionaire declares he's a "financial flop" who's "forcing my family into the poorhouse." Whereas the unhappiness of everyday life comes and goes, the dysphoria of major depression never leaves: With everyday unhappiness, one can go to a movie and temporarily enjoy it; with major depression, the patient cannot be distracted by a movie. The suicidal preoccupations of depressed patients often come more from a wish to escape unrelenting dysphoria than to actually die.

Virtually diagnostic of major depression is that relatives will devote hours reassuring the patient, but to no avail; no matter how effective or frequent their pleas, nothing they say sticks for more than a minute. Loved ones soon become impatient or furious at the patient: They realize he's ill, but feel he's spurned their advice and does nothing to help himself. Depression is also "contagious": The patient's futility becomes the family's futility. People avoid depressed people — they're depressing. Although this withdrawal may aggravate the patient's depression, at other times it doesn't really matter, since the patient is too wrapped up in himself to care. For the patient, it's No Exit: He can't escape depression; he can't talk about and he can't not talk about it.

Bipolar disorder. Ten to 15% of major depressives eventually exhibit mania or its attenuated version, hypomania. By definition, a bipolar patient is anybody who displays mania, with or without a period of depression. Most

---

[2]Frame-by-frame analysis of movies shows that, in walking, depressed patients lift their thighs with their lower legs lagging behind, whereas most people propel their lower legs and feet forward.

patients, however, have both manic and depressive episodes in various sequences and frequencies.

An elevated, euphoric, expansive, or irritable mood is the cardinal feature of mania. These patients are hyperactive, highly distractible, and grandiose. They have flight of ideas, pressured speech, tangentiality, and a diminished need for sleep. They're prickly and quick to anger. As their disorganization worsens, they may develop persecutory and grandiose ideas of reference; these often become delusions. Generally speaking, persecutory delusions among schizophrenics are not aimed at anyone or anything specific, whereas manics feel harm comes from specific individuals or organizations. Sherlock Holmes' obsession that Professor Moriarty is interfering with his attempt to rid the world of evil is a typical manic persecutory delusion. About a quarter of manics develop hallucinations; they are usually auditory or visual, of shorter duration, and less compelling than those of schizophrenia. Disorganization may occur, but more briefly than with schizophrenia. Table 11-3 lists *DSM-III's* criteria for a manic episode.

Manics talk a blue streak, do "20 things at once," and launch outrageous projects. A manic spent $100,000 hiring city planners, attorneys, architects, and a guru to construct a 90-story building on one square foot of land. Another manic, a UCLA undergraduate, telephoned Krushchev to invite him to the Rose Bowl, and although Nikita didn't get the message, the student did reach a high Kremlin official (who declined). Manics often resemble fast-talking comics of the Henny Youngman genre. People laugh *with*, not *at*, the manic. Like Max Bialystock (Zero Mostel in *The Producers*), manics are supersalesmen. Caught unaware, I was visited by a manic salesman who almost sold me a set of encyclopedias for my children. I have no children. On the spur of the moment, a Dartmouth graduate who resided in California jumped on a plane and admitted himself to "the hospital of my alma mater." He arrived with four tennis rackets, three suitcases, a fishing rod, dozens of lollypops, and a swimsuit; it was winter. Five minutes after his grand entrance, he coaxed all the patients and staff into singing "The Yellow Rose of Texas."

But as eventually occurs in mania, things get out of control. When crossed, or when people don't go along with them, manics become irritable, nasty, and sometimes cruel. They may play the "manic game," in which they are constantly testing everybody's limits; they manipulate others' self-esteem, perceive and exploit people's vulnerabilities, and project responsibility. After wreaking havoc and infuriating everybody, they will blame everyone but themselves. For instance, the Dartmouth grad told a plump, insecure teenage inpatient, "You're a fat pig. No wonder boys don't like you." The girl dissolved in tears, and the other patients, urged on by the manic, rushed to the teenager's defense

TABLE 11-3
DSM-III Criteria for Manic Episode*

A. One or more distinct periods with a predominently elevated, expansive, or irritable mood. The elevated or irritable mood must be a prominent part of the illness and relatively persistent, although it may alternate or intermingle with depressive mood.

B. Duration of at least one week (or any duration if hospitalization is necessary), during which, for most of the time, at least three of the following symptoms have persisted (four if the mood is only irritable) and have been present to a significant degree:

(1) increase in activity (either socially, at work, or sexually) or physical restlessness
(2) more talkative than usual or pressure to keep talking
(3) flight of ideas or subjective experience that thoughts are racing
(4) inflated self-esteem (grandiosity, which may be delusional)
(5) decreased need for sleep
(6) distractibility, i.e., attention is too easily drawn to unimportant or irrelevant external stimuli
(7) excessive involvement in activities that have a high potential for painful consequences which is not recognized, e.g., buying sprees, sexual indiscretions, foolish business investments, reckless driving

C. Neither of the following dominate the clinical picture when an affective syndrome (i.e., criteria A and B above) is not present, that is, before it developed or after it has remitted.

(1) preoccupation with a mood-incongruent delusion or hallucination
(2) bizarre behavior

D. Not superimposed on either Schizophrenia, Schizophreniform Disorder, or a Paranoid Disorder.

E. Not due to any Organic Mental Disorder, such as Substance Intoxication.

*DSM-III, pp. 208–209.

and blamed the staff for allowing her to get so upset. On the slightest whim, manics will call total strangers and amass humungous phone bills. They'll walk down the street throwing money in the air. An 80-year-old woman whom I'd never met waltzed into my office, gave me the keys to her Cadillac, and wrote me a check for $1 million. (Yes, she could afford it, and yes, I returned the check.)

These patients develop reputations as normally being a Dr. Jekyll—upstanding, likeable, and productive—yet sometimes becoming a Mr. Hyde—outrageously excitable, intrusive, and demanding. "Unpredictable" is what some people call them: fine one month, profoundly depressed the next month. Because periods of high energy, creativity, and achievement are not recognized as hypomania, bipolar disorder may go undiagnosed. Clinicians find that a good barometer of these hypomanic periods is the patient's diminished need for sleep. At the same time, the adaptiveness of moderate hypomanic behavior contributes to bipolar patients' being among society's most accomplished individuals.

Bipolar disorder is more severe than major depression. Bipolar depressions last longer, relapse more frequently, display more depressive symptoms, show more severe symptoms, have more delusions and hallucinations, prompt more suicide, cause more hospitalizations, and produce more incapacitation (Coryell et al., 1985). Yet when a patient first presents with a severe depression, it's usually hard to tell if a bipolar or a major (or unipolar) depression exists. However, because the prognoses and treatments differ substantially, it's desirable to distinguish them as soon as possible: Table 11-4 lists some criteria for doing so. In general, bipolar depressives prefer to remain in bed and have what are termed "laying-down depressions," whereas unipolar depressives are usually out of bed and said to have "standing-up depressions."

Dysthymic disorder. Formerly called "depressive neurosis," dysthymic disorder presents with a chronic dysphoria or anhedonia, which is not severe enough to meet all the criteria for major depression. *DSM-III* requires that symptoms exist for at least two years. This dysphoria or anhedonia may be continual or episodic; euthymia may exist for several days to weeks, but no longer than several weeks. The diagnosis should not be made if an interval of normal mood lasts for more than a few months. Whereas many patients with major depression are unable to work or to socialize, those with dysthymic disorders function, though not at their peak. By definition, dysthymic disorders never present with delusions or hallucinations. When a major depression is superimposed on a dysthymic disorder, it's dubbed a "double depression." Table 11-5 lists *DSM-III*'s criteria for dysthymic disorder.

In contrast to major depression, dysthymic disorder is more relenting and less consuming: Patients may laugh and tell a joke; on occasion, they even enjoy themselves. Although loved ones find dysthymic disorders less infuriating and frustrating than major depressions, others become bored with the dysthymic patient's habitual moaning and "kvetching." Dysthymic patients often become upset over matters that others take in stride.

Carol Campanella, a 40-year-old married woman from a traditional Italian family, sought treatment because, "I'm anxious and shaky most of the time, especially at work. I can't be that way at home, ever since my mother-in-law moved in for good and I have to be on my best behavior when I'm around her." The patient said she's been unhappy most of her life, but much worse since her mother-in-law camped in five months ago. "She comes from the old country: She expects me to wait on her and nothing I do ever satisfies her. She complains; otherwise she does nothing. I return

TABLE 11-4
Characteristics Which Tend to Distinguish
Unipolar From Bipolar Depressions

UNIPOLAR DEPRESSION	BIPOLAR DEPRESSION
PRESENTING SYMPTOMS	
Psychomotor agitation	Psychomotor retardation
Anger, verbal	Less angry, quiet
Anxiety	Lethargy
Insomnia	Hypersomnia
Anorexia	Hyperphagia
Underweight	Overweight
Feel worse in morning and better as day goes on; ("diurnal mood variation")	Feel worse in evening and better in morning; ("reverse diurnal mood variation")
Psychosis less likely	Psychosis more likely
No history of mania/hypomania	History of mania/hypomania
Less severe and frequent suicide attempts	More severe and frequent suicide attempts
Less incapacitation	More incapacitation
Low to normal steroid production	High steroid production
Age of onset usually in mid-forties	Age of onset usually in early thirties
Untreated episode lasts three to six months	Untreated episode lasts six to nine months
LONGITUDINAL FEATURES	
Less college education	More college education
Less family history of affective disorders	More family history of depression and mania
Premorbidly obsessional, shy, inhibited, moralistic, insecure	Premorbidly outgoing, active, successful
No prior mania or hypomania	Prior mania or hypomania
No prior hospitalizations	Prior hospitalizations
Younger patients remain ill *briefer* than older ones	Younger patients remain ill *longer* than older ones
Lithium is not prophylactic and has not helped prior depressive episodes	Lithium is prophylactic and has helped prior manic or depressive episodes
Antidepressants have helped prior acute episodes	Antidepressants have not helped prior episodes

TABLE 11-5
DSM-III* Criteria for Dysthymic Disorder

A. During the past two years (or one year for children and adolescents) the individual has been bothered most or all of the time by symptoms characteristic of the depressive syndrome but that are not of sufficient severity and duration to meet the criteria for a major depressive episode (although a major depressive episode may be superimposed on Dysthymic Disorder).

B. The manifestations of the depressive syndrome may be relatively persistent or separated by periods of normal mood lasting a few days to a few weeks, but no more than a few months at a time.

C. During the depressive periods there is either prominent depressed mood (e.g., sad, blue, down in the dumps, low) or marked loss of interest or pleasure in all, or almost all, usual activities and pastimes.

D. During the depressive periods at least three of the following symptoms are present:

   (1) insomnia or hypersomnia
   (2) low energy or chronic tiredness
   (3) feelings of inadequacy, loss of self-esteem, or self-deprecation
   (4) decreased effectiveness or productivity at school, work, or home
   (5) decreased attention, concentration, or ability to think clearly
   (6) social withdrawal
   (7) loss of interest in or enjoyment of pleasurable activities
   (8) irritability or excessive anger (in children, expressed toward parents or caretakers)
   (9) inability to respond with apparent pleasure to praise or rewards
   (10) less active or talkative than usual, or feels slowed down or restless
   (11) pessimistic attitude toward the future, brooding about past events, or feeling sorry for self
   (12) tearfulness or crying
   (13) recurrent thoughts of death or suicide

E. Absence of psychotic features, such as delusions, hallucinations, incoherence, or loosening of associations

F. If the disturbance is superimposed on a preexisting mental disorder, such as Obsessive Compulsive Disorder or Alcohol Dependence, the depressed mood, by virtue of its intensity or effect on functioning, can be clearly distinguished from the individual's usual mood.

DSM-III, pp. 222–223.

exhausted from work and immediately prepare dinner; so what does she say? 'You made the carrots wrong; you should cut them at angles, not up-and-down.' When I ask my husband to do something about *his* mother, all he says is, 'You're overreacting.' I feel unappreciated and drained. I cry all the time, but only in private: I don't want anybody to see I'm weak."

For the first time, somebody did. Tears and words gushed out, as Carol revealed her darkest fear: "I'm terrified I'm turning into my mother. Our family lived near Rome, which is where my mother was hospitalized for shock treatment, but she was depressed most of her life. She would sit in the corner for hours and say nothing. At other times, she'd act crazy and speak nonsense; she'd talk to the dead and accuse the milkman of stealing. My mother wasn't mean to me; it was more like she was mentally absent. That's when I learned you can't rely on anybody to solve your problems but yourself. . . . When I was 16, my mother began to improve. Suddenly, I had the mother I always wanted. I loved it. Two years later though, she died of cancer. I still miss her, and I know I can't expect my mother-in-law to replace her, yet sometimes I do and that's nuts. Far worse is that I'm acting like my mother — snapping at people, never laughing, overly serious, avoiding people, not talking, and always hopeless. I'm frightened I'll be crazy like her."

Carol's marriage ("my ticket to America") was sexless and passionless ("All he does is eat."). Because of financial limitations, she quit premed and became a secretary. Over the years, she's been promoted to administrator, but far slower than "other women with less skill." She claimed to have "always" had initial insomnia and poor appetite. During the past year she shed 25 pounds, felt increasingly sluggish and restless during the day, preferred being alone, and seemed immune to praise. Carol had no history of hypomania or mania, nor did she ever contemplate suicide.

Her dysthymic disorder was treated with a tricyclic antidepressant, and after two weeks her sleep and appetite normalized and her dysthymia lifted. She could laugh and enjoy people. Although she still felt just as unappreciated at home and at work, she stopped fretting about it. After a month of treatment, her symptoms abated completely, but Carol refused to have any of her family meet with the therapist: "I will handle things myself." (Note: Another example of how Axis I problems resolve much more easily than Axis II problems.) Two months after her first visit, she observed, "I must have been depressed my entire life. Until now, I didn't know what it was like *not* to be depressed. . . . I feel like a new person, and yet, I still worry that someday I'll go crazy like my mother." It was only after eight months of psychotherapy that this fear disappeared.

Cyclothymic disorder. Cyclothymic patients have hypomanic *and* dysphoric periods which are not severe enough to qualify as a bipolar disorder. Moreover, whereas bipolar disorder is episodic, *DSM-III's* cyclothymic disorder is continual; it, like dysthymic disorder, must exist for at least two years without the patient's being euthymic for more than three months. *DSM-III's* criteria for cyclothymic disorder are listed on Table 11-6.

Atypical depression. In *DSM-III*, atypical depression is a residual category of affective disorders that do not meet the criteria for other disorders. However, "atypical depression" usually refers to an ill-defined syndrome characterized by (a) an episodic, yet long-term, course of (b) dysphoria and demoralization, (c) which is highly reactive to environmental events, with (d) frequent "neurotic symptoms" (e.g., phobias, panic attacks, eating binges), (e) "reverse biological signs of depression" (e.g., overeating, hypersomnia, initial insomnia, feel worse as the day goes on), and (f) principally affects women. (In this text, when "atypical depression" is in quotes, it refers to this use; when not in quotes, it refers to *DSM-III's* use.) "Atypicals" are often anxious, tremulous, fatigued, and complaining of physical problems. Many have histrionic and

TABLE 11-6
DSM-III* Criteria for Cyclothymic Disorder

A. During the past two years, numerous periods during which some symptoms characteristic of both the depressive and the manic syndromes were present, but were not of sufficient severity and duration to meet the criteria for a major depressive or manic episode.

B. The depressive periods and hypomanic periods may be separated by periods of normal mood lasting as long as months at a time, they may be intermixed, or they may alternate.

C. During *depressive* periods there is depressed mood or loss of interest or pleasure in all or almost all, usual activities and pastimes, and at least three of the following:

    (1) insomnia or hypersomnia
    (2) low energy or chronic fatigue
    (3) feelings of inadequacy
    (4) decreased effectiveness or productivity at school, work, or home

    (5) decreased attention, concentration, or ability to think clearly
    (6) social withdrawal

    (7) loss of interest in or enjoyment of sex
    (8) restriction of involvement in pleasurable activities; guilt over past activities

    (9) feeling slowed down
    (10) less talkative than usual
    (11) pessimistic attitude toward the future, or brooding about past events
    (12) tearfulness or crying

During *hypomanic* periods there is an elevated, expansive, or irritable mood and at least three of the following:

    (1) decreased need for sleep
    (2) more energy than usual
    (3) inflated self-esteem
    (4) increased productivity, often associated with unusual and self-imposed working hours
    (5) sharpened and unusually creative thinking
    (6) uninhibited people-seeking (extreme gregariousness)
    (7) hypersexuality without recognition of possibility of painful consequences
    (8) excessive involvement in pleasurable activities with lack of concern for the high potential for painful consequences, e.g., buying sprees, foolish business investments, reckless driving
    (9) physical restlessness
    (10) more talkative than usual
    (11) overoptimism or exaggeration of past achievements
    (12) inappropriate laughing, joking, punning

D. Absence of psychotic features such as delusions, hallucinations, incoherence, or loosening of associations.

E. Not due to any other mental disorder, such as partial remission of Bipolar Disorder. However, Cyclothymic Disorder may precede Bipolar Disorder.

*DSM-III, pp. 219–220.

borderline personality disorders. Some "atypicals" are said to have "hysteroid dysphoria," thereby spotlighting their histrionic qualities, which are the worst stereotypes of "female" behavior. "Atypical depression" most resembles major depression, except that "atypicals" display many "neurotic" symptoms, reverse biological signs, and an extreme reactivity to environmental events, which often manifests as "rejection sensitivity." The slightest rejection plunges these patients into dark despair, while the slightest good news induces ecstasy.

A typical (excuse me!) exhibition of rejection sensitivity occurred when Mary Rae's fiancé met her at the airport. He casually remarked to Mary Rae that a passerby was "attractive"; Mary Rae became incensed, opened her suitcase, threw clothes all over the place, spent 30 minutes screaming at him, and left the airport by herself. By evening she calmed down, yet for weeks she pouted that "The cluck doesn't realize I'm sensitive about my looks. Why couldn't he say something nice about *my* body?"

Clinical Course

Major depression. The age of onset is equally distributed throughout the adult life cycle; age 40 is the mean, and it can arise during childhood and infancy. Its appearance is usually over days or weeks, but it may erupt in a day or evolve over months or years. Anxiety, phobia, panic, or dysthymia may predate a major depression. The sequence of events leading to a depression should be precisely determined, since a mistake is to assume that, for example, a patient's being fired caused his depression, whereas it was his depression (and poor functioning) which caused his firing. Some depressions arise out of the blue, some after a precipitant. If biologically untreated, major depression usually persists three to six months.

Single and recurrent episodes of major depression may be slightly different species. Roughly half of all patients with a major depression never have another episode; about half do. Of those having a second episode, 50% have a third one, and so on. Patients with recurrent major depressions are more likely to become manic later on and to have more difficulties in between depressive episodes. Recurrence rates are greatest during the first four to six months after recovery; thereafter, the further away from the episode, the lower the chance of a recurrence. For patients with major (or bipolar) depression, the risk of future episodes increases further with a history of dysthymic disorder, a persistent dysthymia after a major or bipolar depression, a substance abuse or anxiety disorder, an older age of onset, and a greater number of previous episodes.

Roughly 20% of patients with major depression become chronically depressed; 80% recover fully. Thus, for the vast majority, major depression is an episodic condition; outside of distinct periods of illness, these patients are their normal productive selves. Of those having a recurrence, 22% will be depressed for over a year, especially if they delay getting treatment, are elderly, poor, and had a longer prior depressive episode (Keller et al., 1986).

Bipolar disorder. On average, bipolar disorder arises at age 30, although on rare occasions it may begin in octogenarians. Mania usually precedes depression, although the opposite is common. Whereas most bipolar depressions emerge over days or weeks, mania erupts suddenly. If biologically untreated, bipolar depressions typically persist six to nine months, manic episodes, two to six weeks.

The sequence and frequency of manic and depressive episodes vary: Some patients have three or four depressive periods before exhibiting mania; others alternate between highs and lows. Some have an episode every ten years, whereas others, known as "rapid cyclers," have three or more episodes of either mania or depression in a single year.

Bipolar disorder is divided into *bipolar I*, which meets the full diagnostic criteria for a major depressive and a *manic episode, and bipolar II*, in which there is a major depressive episode and *hypomania*, not mania; the patient's "highs" do not merit hospitalization. Although bipolar II disorder is generally considered to be a mild bipolar I, it may be an intermediate entity between bipolar I and major depression, or a completely distinct entity (Coryell et al., 1985).

The term "bipolar" is misleading. It implies that mania and depression are opposites and that euthymia occurs between them. Yet careful observation demonstrates that a continuum or a triangular model more closely approximates their behavior (see Figure 11-1). In both these models, mania and depression are closer to each other than to normality. For instance, it's common to see a depressive affect intrude on mania; a patient will be talking a mile a minute, when for no apparent reason he cries a eulogy to a long-departed mother, and then, just as suddenly, starts imitating Tina Turner. The continuum and triangular models more accurately depict the fact that unipolar depression is at least five times more frequent than bipolar depression, and why recovering manics often become depressed before they return to normal. When this happens, the clinician should not jump in with antidepressants: The patient is simply getting better and time is the best prescription.

Further support for a continuum or triangular model is that bipolar patients often undergo a "*switch phase*," in which, over a day or two, they go from being very low to very high. When treated with antidepressants, ostensibly unipolar depressed patients may switch into mania, thereby revealing a bipolar disorder. They need lithium, not antidepressants.

Dysthymic Disorder. This disorder typically emerges during early adult life, although it commonly occurs in children and adolescents. Its onset is gradual and often hard to pinpoint. Its course is chronic, its symptoms fluctuating.

Cyclothymic disorder. The age of onset for cyclothymic disorder is most often in early adulthood. It begins gradually and persists chronically. Intermixing or alternating, hypomanic and dysphoric symptoms may fluctuate within hours, days, weeks, or months. Intermittent euthymic periods may exist for up to three months.

FIGURE 11-1
Models of Bipolar Disorder

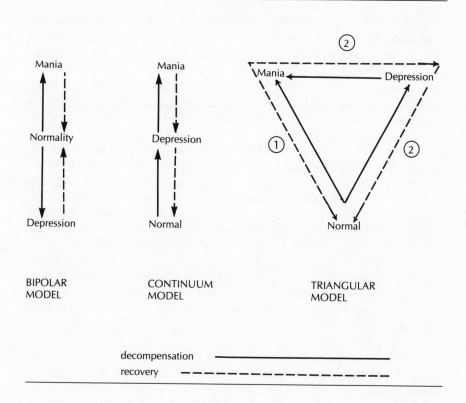

BIPOLAR MODEL	CONTINUUM MODEL	TRIANGULAR MODEL

decompensation ────────────────

recovery ── ── ── ── ── ── ── ──

Complications

Suicide is committed eventually by 15% of patients with severe—that is, major or bipolar—depression. (It rarely occurs with dysthymic and cyclothymic disorders.) Major and bipolar depressions account for 50% to 70% of suicides, making depression the chief cause of suicide. (Alcoholism is second.) Although the evaluation of suicide is discussed in Chapter 2 (pp. 22–23), it's worth repeating that, contrary to myth, those who talk about suicide are more likely to commit suicide.

Substance abuse, particularly from alcoholism, is a frequent complication in all affective disorders. Patients will "medicate" their dysphorias with alcohol, cocaine, amphetamines, and less often with marijuana and hypnosedatives. Convinced they're immune from danger and oblivious to their own limitations, hypomanic and manic patients take drugs to remain "up." *Death* from physical illness, especially cancer, is more prevalent among patients with major affective disorders.

Impaired judgment and *lousy decisions* are common. If a depressed patient thinks he's a terrible person, he may try to divorce a loving spouse; if he's sure he's incompetent, he may quit a perfectly good job. The manic may also initiate divorce and quit work, thinking he's too good for his spouse or job. Clinicians should inform patients that their pathological moods are distorting their judgment and that they should postpone major decisions until they've recovered. *Occupational and academic failures* result from poor judgment and more: Depressed patients function slowly, work inefficiently, and display little effort. Neuropsychiatric tests show their abstract thinking, attention spans, and short-term (but not long-term) memories are impaired. Depressed and manic patients often trap colleagues into covering for them.

Familial consequences, including an increased rate of marital difficulties, separation, and divorce, occur in major depression. Although the mechanisms are unclear, roughly 40% of children with a depressed parent develop major, long-standing impairments, especially affective, neurotic, and conduct disorders. Targum et al. (1981) found that after hospitalized bipolar patients and their spouses learned of the increased risk of inheritance and the long-term burdens of the disorder, 5% of patients and about half of the spouses confessed that, if given a second chance, they would not get married or have children.

Subtypes

Types and subtypes of affective disorders are important to identify for several reasons: Some imply different treatments; some often escape detection (and treatment) because they resemble other disorders; some suggest different etiologies; some have research implications. Some have already been mentioned: endogenous/reactive, primary/secondary, unipolar/bipolar, psychotic/neurotic. (Reader beware! The classifications presented above and below are commonly used but not fixed in stone.)

DSM-III's most important subtypes of major depression are those with "psychotic features" and "melancholia." (The two subtypes can, and often do, coexist.) *Psychotic depression* displays delusions, hallucinations, or depressive stupor (e.g., mute, unresponsive). Depressed patients rarely hallucinate without also having delusions. During the first six months psychotic depressions are more severe than nonpsychotic depressions, but by two years they're the same. The chief reason for distinguishing psychotic from nonpsychotic depressions is that they benefit from different treatments.

Melancholia is a severe major depression seemingly unaffected by the environment. Melancholia often features: (a) anhedonia, (b) lack of reactivity to usually pleasurable stimuli, (c) diurnal mood variation, (d) terminal insomnia, (e) psychomotor agitation or retardation, (f) anorexia or significant weight loss (over 5% of total body weight in a month), (g) no significant personality disturbance prior to first major depressive episode, (h) a complete or nearly complete recovery from a prior major depressive episode, and (i) a history of good response to biological treatment. (*DSM-III-R* requires five of the above to diagnose melancholia.) Despite its severity, melancholia is the most successfully treated of the major depressions.

Two subtypes of major depression may go undiagnosed because the patient's most striking feature is neither dysphoria nor anhedonia: pseudodementia and masked depression. *Pseudodementia* is a severe major depression that presents as dementia. Chapter 7 (pp. 108, 110) discusses its diagnosis and treatment.

Masked depression is a major depression dominated by physical complaints. It presents with a triad of (a) somatic preoccupations, (b) biological signs of depression, and (c) alexithymia, an inability to identify and articulate emotions. For these patients, speaking in emotional terms is akin to speaking a foreign language. A typical exchange might be:

DOCTOR: "How do you feel?"
PATIENT: My back hurts.
DOCTOR: I understand your back hurts, but how do you *feel*?
PATIENT: Achy.
DOCTOR: I mean, do you feel sad, or anxious, or angry, or what?
PATIENT (annoyed): My back is killing me! *That's* how I feel!

Physicians, and even the patient himself, are likely to misdiagnose the condition as hypochondriasis, and since the patient doesn't feel depressed, depression may not occur to anyone. Masked depression, however, is merely another face of major depression. Somatic complaints are common in major depression, but in masked depression they occupy center stage. These patients are readily treatable, but frequently mistreated: They respond well to antidepressants, yet too often receive hypnosedatives. Urging these patients to talk psychologically wastes everybody's time; in conjunction with antidepressants, these patients seem to benefit from therapists and relatives reinforcing the patient's adaptive behaviors (e.g., "Mrs. Sheehy, given how you feel, it's wonderful you played bridge today.").

Seasonal affective disorders (SAD), or "the winter blues," refer to those bipolar (and less often unipolar) depressions which invariably occur in the fall and winter; they improve within days of moving from cold to warm climates or from areas with short to long exposures to daylight. SAD seems to be alleviated by artificial, bright, fluorescent light. If these patients develop hypomania or mania, it's usually in the summer. Clinicians should inquire about seasonal patterns of mood with every patient who presents with any type of affective disorder.

Epidemiology

Among outpatients, affective disorders are the most common mental disorders psychiatrists treat, comprising 27.6% of their practice in 1980. Whether this pattern occurs with nonmedical psychotherapists is unknown. A large study at Cornell showed that about a quarter of all hospitalized *and* ambulatory patients had affective disorders, a sliver less than schizophrenia. Among Cornell patients, 12.8%, 2.7%, and 7.1% had major depressive, dysthymic, and bipolar disorders, respectively.

In the general population, affective disorders rank third, not first. The ECA survey (Chapter 1) found a six-month prevalence rate of 6% for affective disorders; this rate for major depression was 3.1%, for dysthymic disorder 3.2%, and for bipolar disorder 0.7%. These findings may contradict two long-held assumptions. First, it appears that major depression is five times as frequent as bipolar disorder, unlike the 10 to 1 ratio traditionally believed. Second, it was generally assumed that dysthymic disorder was far more common than major depression, but the ECA suggests that if anything major depression is more, not less, frequent than dysthymic disorder: They have a similar six-month prevalence rate and the lifetime prevalence for major depression is 5% and for dysthymic disorder only 3%. (See Tables 1-3, 1-4.) In general, the ECA figures for affective disorders are somewhat lower than those of other surveys.

Affective disorders in general strike twice as many women than men; this ratio varies depending on the disorder. Ninety percent of "atypical depressions" occur in women. Major depression and dysthymic disorder afflict two or three times more women than men. Bipolar disorder is nonsexist. During a lifetime, roughly 20% of women and 10% of men will suffer a major depressive episode; about a third of these patients will be hospitalized. Middle- and upper-class patients have more affective disorders. Urbanites have twice the rate of depression as "ruralites." Whites have slightly more affective disorders than blacks, but the difference is not statistically significant. Jews have slightly more affective disorders than gentiles.

It appears that each successive generation during this century has had an increased rate of depression and an earlier age of onset (Klerman et al., 1985). Simultaneously, the rate of suicide, especially among youth, has also escalated with each generation. For instance, since the 1950s, the suicide rate for 15- to 24-year-olds has tripled, with suicide replacing homicide as the second leading cause of death among youth. (These increased rates of depression and suicide are genuine and not methological artifacts.) Why there's more depression and suicide is unknown. Nevertheless, despite the fact that suicide is still most prevalent among the elderly, more than ever today's clinician must be alert to teenage suicide.

The prevalence of affective disorders varies widely from culture to culture, being as low as 1% among the Amish. Depression is virtually unheard of in Kenya and Rwanda, but frequent in Ghana and Nigeria where depressed patients complain of "worms crawling all over the head." (Suicide is rare in Africa.) Post-war Japan saw its suicide rate plummet while its rate of antisocial behavior soared.

Etiology and Pathogenesis

Some affective disorders arise for no apparent reason; others are triggered by a precipitant. Unless the precipitant is blatantly obvious, clinicians should be cautious about attributing a depression to it. If clinicians look hard enough, they can always find a stressor to "explain" a depression. (Review your past week, and you will surely discover some stressor to "account" for why you should be depressed.) Stress is the way of the world, and therefore, the path toward depression must involve more than stress.

With or without environmental stressors, major depressions present with similar symptoms.[3] The reason they present the same is because no matter how a depression begins, at some point a *final common pathway* is reached, in which biogenic amines change, thereby producing biological signs of depression. This final common pathway may arise from many biological or psychosocial causes: a genetic vulnerability, a "depressogenic" medication, an early loss, a lack of positive reinforcement, etc.

Biomedical Factors

Biochemical theories. The most noted biochemical theory of affective disorders is the *catecholamine hypothesis*, which posits that a functional underactivity of norepinephrine (NE) causes depression, whereas a functional overactivity of NE causes mania. However popular this theory, it is, at best, incomplete: For example, it does not account for why it takes 10–14 days for a patient's depression to lift on antidepressants, even though her NE returns to normal within 24 hours. Other mechanisms must be operative. The *biogenic amine permissive hypothesis* holds that a functional underactivity of serotonin (SE) must exist for any affective disorder — unipolar or bipolar — to exist, but whether the patient is high or low depends on the level of NE. The *adrenergic-cholinergic imbalance hypothesis* maintains that the ratio (in the brain) of acetycholine to catecholamines (e.g., NE, dopamine) is high in depression and low in mania. (See Table 4-1.) The *electrolyte-membrane potential disturbance theory* asserts that depression partly derives from an accumulation of intracellular sodium, and since lithium replaces intracellular sodium, this hypothesis may explain lithium's antidepressant action.

---

[3]Hirschfeld et al. (1985) compared "situational" (i.e., triggered by an environmental event) with "nonsituational" major depressions. Although situational depressives were younger, had fewer depressive episodes, and fewer hospitalizations, both groups had the same overall clinical pictures, types and amounts of stress, premorbid social supports, and family psychopathology.

Genetic theories. Twin studies of bipolar disorder show an average concordance rate of 72% for MZ twins and 14% for DZ twins. For major depression, typical concordance rates are 40% for MZ twins and 11% for DZ twins. These findings suggest that nongenetic factors play a larger role in major depression than in bipolar disorder.

Depression runs in families, but the risk of depression to first-degree relatives (e.g., children) is even greater when a patient with major depression also has a panic disorder. (In contrast, if the depressed patient has a generalized anxiety disorder instead of a panic disorder, the increased risk is minimal.) These relatives are also at greater risk for panic disorder, phobia, and alcoholism (Weissman et al., 1985), which suggests these disorders belong to the same "genetic cluster" or "depressive spectrum."

Winokur (1979) has divided depressions into "pure depressive illness" and "depressive spectrum disease" (DSD). The latter has a high prevalence of alcoholism and antisocial personality disorder in males and a correspondingly high prevalence of early-onset unipolar depression in females. His studies showed that 50% of first-degree relatives of depressed women develop some DSD. Among the relatives who did, the women were almost always depressed, whereas only half of the men were depressed, while a quarter were alcoholic and another quarter sociopathic.

Medical etiologies. Before diagnosing any affective disorder, clinicians should determine if it is secondary to a medical condition. Most often it's congestive heart failure, and when it's mild and not grossly apparent (e.g., labored breathing), patients complain of fatigue, insomnia, anorexia, and slowed thinking; they will move slowly and say they're afraid of dying!

Other diseases that present as depression are myxedema (hypothyroidism), Cushing's syndrome (hyperadrenocorticism), hyperparathyroidism (or any condition producing hypercalcemia, such as sarcoidosis, multiple myeloma, or cancer). Occult carcinoma of the pancreas can mimic depression. Malnutrition can produce, and result from, depression; so too with chronic physical disabilities. (Depressions have been attributed to viruses, but then again, so has everything else.) Propranolol, reserpine, alpha-methyldopa, clonidine, thiazide diuretics, and hypnosedatives may cause depression. Steroids (e.g., Prednisone) can trigger mania or depression; L-Dopa and antidepressants can precipitate mania.

Psychosocial Theories

Despite the variety of psychosocial theories of depression, their differences often rest more in language than content. Most of these theories involve loss and self-esteem. Many types of losses can trigger depression. Besides the obvious — deaths, separations — depression may occur after the removal of a bodily organ or on the anniversary of a personally significant loss. A manifestly good development may bring on a depression: After winning a Pulitzer Prize, a once-obscure writer is suddenly inundated with "admirers"—groupies, "money-management types," the cocktail set, publishers—all wanting a "piece" of him. Unable to meet "everyone's" expectations, dissatisfied with his own inability to write another "masterpiece," and missing his old friends, he becomes depressed. Loss can also trigger mania.

Psychoanalytic theories. Freud proposed that an *early severe loss* or trauma during childhood causes a vulnerability to depression. Although subsequent research has tended to support this hypothesis, it has raised doubts about how much and how frequently early loss contributes *specifically* to depression. Brown (1961) showed that the loss of a parent during childhood occurred in 51% of adult depressives and in 16% of controls. In contrast, Roy (1985) demonstrated that early parental separation and loss accounted for relatively few additional cases, that ages five to eleven were most crucial, and curiously, that loss of a father was slightly more psychonoxious than losing a mother.

In *Mourning and Melancholia* (1917), Freud observed that the normal mourner accepts his positive and negative feelings about the deceased, whereas the melancholic cannot tolerate or consciously acknowledge any negative feelings toward the deceased; his *ambivalence toward the lost object* induces guilt and depression. Mourning is a reaction to a realistic loss, but melancholia may be a reaction to an imagined, or an unconsciously exaggerated, loss.

A controversial, yet widely-touted, hypothesis, is that depression results from "retroflexed anger"—that is, the patient turns his rage against a lost object onto himself. Today, hundreds of therapists will hear a similar story: A patient's fiancé suddenly breaks their engagement, but rather than getting angry at the fiancé, the patient becomes depressed and says things like, "This proves I'm unworthy." The concept of retroflexed anger neatly dovetails with the inverse relation between suicide and homicide; it may also account for the low self-esteem of the depressed, for why some believe they deserve punishment, and for why many are terrified of expressing and experiencing anger. On the other hand, the more depressed patients express fury, the more depressed they become—it's "proof" they're terrible people—and the more likely they are to commit suicide. Retroflexed anger may be germane to some depressions, as either a contributor or a consequence; it may be more prominent in people who normally blame themselves for everything.

Ego psychologists claimed that many depressed patients were "mourning" more for their *loss of self-esteem* than for the loss of the object itself. Whether the object is a job or a lover, when patients believe their self-esteem is an extension of that lost object, then depression becomes increasingly likely. Later, ego psychologists stressed that depression arose from a discrepancy between the patient's actual and idealized self-esteem.

Behavioral theories. Many behaviorists view depression as a product of *learned helplessness*—that is, the patient experiences himself as continually trying and failing. With constant losses of positive reinforcements, the person becomes discouraged, gives up (which further reduces rewards), and becomes depressed.

Cognitive theories. The cognitive theory of depression emphasizes the patient's conscious thoughts. Depressed patients display the "cognitive triad"—a negative view of oneself, the world, and one's future; they think of themselves as inadequate, their world as unrewarding, their future as hopeless. Cognitive theory claims that these attitudes distort the patient's perceptions of reality and cause depression; other studies suggest the cognitive triad is a consequence of depression.

Differential Diagnosis

Dysthymic disorder, in contrast to *major depression*, persists for at least two years, is less severe, and includes euthymic intervals. Whenever a major depression is in partial remission for over two years, dysthymic disorder must be considered. Major depression and dysthymic disorder may coexist; so too with bipolar and cyclothymic disorders. Table 11-4 distinguishes major depression from *bipolar depression*. Unlike dysthymic disorders, *"atypical depressions"* show extreme reactivity to environmental events, rejection sensitivity, emotional lability, "reverse biological signs of depressions," an episodic course, periodic incapacitation, and "neurotic symptoms," such as panic and phobia. Dysthymic disorder differs from *normal mood fluctuations*, which are less severe, frequent, dysfunctional, and persistent; moreover, normal mood fluctuations rarely produce the cluster of symptoms associated with depression.

Uncomplicated bereavement may present with a full picture of depression, except for morbid preoccupations, convictions of worthlessness, prolonged and substantial social and occupational impairments, and psychomotor retardation or agitation. During normal bereavement, mourners episodically fantasize about their own death, berate themselves for not visiting or saving the deceased, or feel guilty that the wrong person died. But when bereavement evolves into major depression, the patient can think of nothing but his loss, himself, or his depression. Normal mourners acknowledge the deceased's unfavorable traits; depressives idealize the departed and repress his faults. Bereavement with symptoms of depression may be delayed, but it emerges within two or three months of a person's death; after three months, the normal mourner has moments of grief, but gradually returns to his usual activities and can sustain thoughts about matters unrelated to the death. In contrast, depression persists for more than three months, may get more (instead of less) severe over time, presents with numerous biological signs of depression, and prevents the patient from getting back into the "swing of things."

Manic episodes should be distinguished from *organic affective syndromes* due to neurological disorders (e.g., multiple sclerosis) or drugs (e.g., amphetamines, steroids). Since manic episodes continue for at least a week, patients with one-to-three-day "highs" or erratic mood swings are more likely to have *"atypical depressions,"* *borderline* or *histrionic personality disorders, adjustment disorders*, or *no mental disorder*.

Since *schizophrenia* and affective disorders can display psychotic, catatonic, and dysphoric features, the most likely diagnosis is the one which presents first, occurs in first-degree relatives, shows the characteristic natural history, and meets *DSM-III's* criteria. Psychosis in depression and mania is usually briefer and less bizarre than in schizophrenia. When schizophrenia cannot be distinguished from mania or depression, diagnose *schizoaffective disorder*. (See Chapter 10.)

Masked depressions differ from *somatoform disorders* in that the latter are without biological signs of depression, pervasive anhedonia, or the episodic course of most major depressions. Pseudodementia and *dementia* are discussed in Chapter 7. *Obsessive compulsive disorders* and *substance misuse* may present with dysphoria, but major depression should only be concurrently diagnosed if all *DSM-III* criteria exist.

Management and Treatment

The management and treatment of affective disorders employs one or more of the following interventions: (a) suicide prevention, (b) biotherapies, (c) psychotherapies, and (d) family involvement. These interventions tend to be used in this sequence; for example, preventing suicide precedes psychotherapy. These interventions are interrelated; for example, suicide prevention often entails family involvement. Each of these interventions serves a different purpose; for example, biotherapies rectify symptoms by correcting biochemical abnormalities, psychotherapies address issues arising from and contributing to the disorder, and family involvement may be used to support the patient or to remedy a pathogenic family system.

Regardless of the intervention, working with affectively disturbed patients is ultimately rewarding since most patients recover, but in the short run it may frustrate the most experienced of therapists and evoke considerable countertransference. Depressed patients frequently present with marked dependency, which they themselves disdain but expect others to meet; however, when this occurs, they get furious. Relatives may respond with pity, which patients will overtly reject, yet feel they deserve. This dynamic of dependency strivings, anger over deprivation, anticipated rejection, and "entitled pity" leads clinicians to feel guilty, helpless, angry, and drained—feelings therapists should keep in check. While clinicians often feel that nothing they do is ever enough, they should be careful not to run the patient's life. Therapists should avoid overpromising; they should dispense hope, not saccharine. Especially during the more impaired or serious periods of the disorder, therapists should be warm, "real," and accepting. To quote Sederer (1986, p. 27):

> The therapist must be able to bear the patient's pain with him; extra time may be needed for this affect to emerge, especially in view of the depressed patient's psychomotor retardation. . . . The depressed patient feels unworthy of and unable to reciprocate to excessive warmth and tends to withdraw and feel worse when this is offered. Excessive humor on the part of the therapist denies the patient his grief and is devaluing.

Suicide Prevention

The clinician's first priority is to prevent *suicide*, which in most cases entails breaking the patient's "inertia cycle." When they finally seek professional help, most suicidal patients have been mired in painful unproductive ruminations, which intensify their helplessness. One way to avert suicide and to stop this inertia is to hospitalize the patient. This key decision may depend less on the patient's actual suicide potential and more on his network's supportiveness. It's crucial to immediately involve the patient's family or close friends, not only to determine how well they can care for the patient, but also to teach them how to be extensions of the treatment team—how to mobilize the patient, what warning signs to look for, what to do with medications, what to discuss (and not discuss) with the patient, etc.

Interrupting the inertia cycle is the start to treatment, not its end, and a good place to start is to assign the patient household chores. No matter how mundane this sounds, the patient feels that "at last" something is happening, that he is a part of it, and that he is now "giving" instead of just "getting." Outpatients should have follow-up appointments within days, not weeks. Until the first appointment, the therapist can have the patient telephone him, if only for three minutes a day. Since a 10-day supply of antidepressants ingested all at once can be lethal, only a few days' worth of pills should be prescribed.

As to an ethical question, the author believes that the patient's so-called "right to suicide" is largely academic. Patients who really wish to kill themselves avoid detection. Only the ambivalent about suicide seek help. The clinician's job is to prevent these patients, at least temporarily, from impulsively ending their life, to afford them a chance to explore their ambivalence, and to help them consider alternatives.

Biological Treatments

The biological treatment of affective disorders involves virtually every biotherapy psychiatrists use, primarily tricyclic antidepressants (TCAs), monoamine-oxidase inhibitors (MAOIs), lithium, and electroconvulsive therapy

(ECT). The names, doses, and side effects of these medications are outlined in Appendices D and E, while their applications are discussed below. (By the way, patients should be told that none of these medications causes physical or psychological dependency.)

Tricyclic antidepressants. Considering patients with *all* types of major depression, 78% improve with ECT, 70% with TCAs, and 23% with placebo. Of the seven well-controlled studies comparing ECT and TCAs, four showed no difference and three favored ECT. Nonetheless, because ECT is more inconvenient to administer and ominous to laymen, TCAs are usually the first biological treatment for major depression.

In general, patients who benefit from TCAs have *biological signs* of depression, while those without biological signs, do not. It doesn't matter whether the depression has been environmentally triggered, whether it is "understandable," whether it presents as a major depression or a dysthymic disorder, or whether the patient expects TCAs to work. What does matter is the presence of biological signs, since this means the final common biochemical pathway has already been reached and is, therefore, amenable to a biological treatment.

For TCAs to work, the patient must be on the *proper dose* for the *proper duration.* For a typical TCA like imipramine, this proper adult dose is usually 150 to 300 mg/day (half this amount for the elderly). Moreover, the patient's mood doesn't lift until he's been on a full dose for at least 10–14 days; some patients require four to six weeks. Patients (and relatives) should be told, "Don't give up because you don't feel 'undepressed' in a day or so. Valium acts right away, but TCAs don't; they take two to six weeks."

Most patients on TCAs show some improvement before two weeks. After three to four days, insomnia abates. By five to seven days, appetite returns. The patient's diurnal mood variation fades around eight days, and by ten days libido revives and anhedonia, hopelessness, and helplessness recede. Dysthymia, excessive guilt, and suicidal ruminations are, unfortunately, the last to go away, around two weeks.

Tricyclic antidepressants are usually begun in escalating doses of 25 mg each night until 150 mg is reached. (Women, but not men, may get a one to two day faster response if also given 25 micrograms of thyroid for the first two weeks only.) Which TCA to prescribe depends on whether one previously helped a close biological relative and on which particular side effects will least bother the patient. If, after two weeks of being on 150 mg/day of imipramine, the patient shows no improvement, gradually boost the dose to 300 mg/day. If the patient still hasn't fully recovered in another four weeks, see if the patient's serum level of TCAs is within the "therapeutic window"; if above or below it, the drug will be ineffective.

As with any psychoactive agent, patients placed on TCAs should be warned that (a) TCAs potentiate alcohol, so that "one drink will feel like two drinks"; (b) "at first, drive briefly in a safe place, since your reflexes might be just a tad off"; (c) "be extra-cautious around machinery, such as a sewing machine, and in crossing streets"; and

(d) "if you feel lightheaded or dizzy, put your head down, wait 30 seconds, get up slowly, call your doctor, and hold your next dose until you reach him."

Patients should remain on TCAs until they have been symptom-free for at least 16–20 weeks. Mild symptoms are just as predictive of relapse as major symptoms, so that even when major symptoms have disappeared, the presence of minor symptoms indicates that the disorder has not run its full course (Prien & Kupfer, 1986). TCAs should be prescribed for longer periods in patients with more frequent depressive episodes, longer depressive cycles, and an older age of onset. If depression is severe and frequent enough, prophylactic, long-term TCA therapy may be indicated, given that such treatment is safer and more effective than lithium or placebo. TCAs should always be discontinued slowly – 25 mg/day; they should never be stopped abruptly: If they are, in two to four days, the patient may have insomnia, nightmares, or nausea.

Despite their overall effectiveness, TCAs do not completely eliminate symptoms in 25% of patients with major depressions. If the patient has not begun to improve after four weeks, and if the diagnosis, dose, and serum level have all been rechecked, another biotherapy should be added to, or replace, the TCA. These biotherapeutic options include: (a) another TCA which affects another biogenic-amine system, (b) MAOIs, (c) lithium, (d) ECT, (e) "second generation antidepressants" (e.g., trazodone), and (f) antipsychotics. For example, studies tend to favor ECT for *psychotic* depression, antipsychotics (with or without TCAs) for *agitated* depression, and MAOIs for major depression with "*atypical*" features, especially panic. Since lithium appears to potentiate the antidepressant effects of TCAs, adding 900 to 1200 mg/day of lithium can reverse a previously unresponsive depression. Supplemental low-dose benzodiazepines may initially alleviate anxiety and insomnia.

Monoamine-oxidase inhibitors. MAOIs are the drug of choice for treating "atypical depression," especially with panic attacks. In the treatment of major depression, MAOIs and TCAs are equally effective, but MAOIs are rarely chosen first. That's because if patients on MAOIs ingest tyramine-containing foods (e.g., herring, beer, cheese, yogurt) or sympathomimetic drugs (e.g., cocaine, amphetamines, hay-fever pills) they can develop a "hypertensive crisis" – soaring blood pressure, splitting headache, chest pain, fever, and vomiting. However gruesome this sounds, the actual dangers of hypertensive crisis are minimal: Few patients develop them, and most who slip up on their diet have relatively minor symptoms. (Contrary to some sources, MAOIs *and* TCAs may be used simultaneously.) MAOIs, however, should not be prescribed for patients who are likely to consistently abuse their diet.

Lithium. Lithium is a salt, much like table salt, except that lithium replaces sodium. Trace amounts of lithium are in the water supply, a tidbit which impresses some patients to reason "it's okay to take lithium because it is a natural substance and not a drug." Being a natural substance, lithium cannot be patented (although its brand names can), which is one reason it took so long for lithium to finally appear (1971) on the American market. Yet through

1984, lithium has saved $6.5 billion[4]; imagine, therefore, the emotional savings from lithium.

Lithium is best for preventing mania, and as effective as TCAs for preventing bipolar depressions. Acute bipolar depressions are treated equally well by lithium and TCAs, whereas acute mania responds best initially to antipsychotics, and once the mania begins to subside, lithium should be substituted.

Following the first manic or depressive episode, if there's no other episode for six months, lithium should be stopped. How long a patient stays on lithium depends on how effective it has been for the patient and on the number, severity, and frequency of prior episodes; "rapid cyclers," who have at least two manic or depressive episodes a year, should be on lithium for longer periods than "slow cyclers," who may have a manic or a depressive episode every several years.

Overall, 75% to 80% of bipolar patients substantially improve on lithium, and so a patient may still have bipolar disorder without responding to lithium. ("Normals," which invariably means college students, become jumpy and irritable on lithium. It only seems to benefit patients with some mental disorders.)

In treating an acute manic episode, antipsychotics start reducing symptoms in 30 minutes, whereas lithium often takes 10 days. It usually takes about four days for antipsychotics to end the patient's excitement and psychotic disorganization, and about a week to quell grandiosity, hostility, and restlessness. Lithium takes an additional week to do the same. In the very infrequent circumstance in which large doses of antipsychotics cannot contain a life-threatening emergency (e.g., starvation, driven suicidal behavior), one to three ECTs will do so.

As soon as the patient's mania subsides, lithium should replace antipsychotics, especially for ongoing therapy. (To expedite treatment, lithium is often started along with antipsychotics.) Lithium doesn't cause tardive dyskinesia; it's also more effective in treating hostility, uncooperativeness, suspiciousness, and poor judgment.

After a careful medical evaluation, including tests for electrolytes, thyroid, and kidney function, lithium can be started in 300-mg doses thrice daily. The amount is elevated until the patient develops either side effects—most often finger tremor[5] or nausea—or reaches a serum lithium level of 1.0 to 1.6 meq/L. When lithium is used for prevention, serum levels should fall between 0.6 to 1.2 meq/L. Ideally, blood samples for serum lithium should be drawn 12 hours after the last dose, but before the morning dose. Always treat the patient, not his serum level. Even the best

---

[4]In contrast, from 1948 to 1985, the total federal investment for research into mental and addictive disorders was $3 billion! (National Academy of Sciences' Institute of Medicine, 1984)

[5]Nurses and activities therapists are often the first to detect this fine tremor; they'll see the patient spilling coffee, writing sloppily, or missing piano keys.

laboratories make mistakes. Many a salt-deficient patient will have a serum lithium inside a therapeutic range, yet still be delirious. Normal salt intake will suffice; extra salt is unnecessary.[6] Acutely manic patients usually require 900 to 2400 mg/day of lithium; prophylactic doses are usually 600 to 1800 mg/day.

A common problem, especially with "rapid cyclers," is mania or depression occurring in a lithium-treated patient. When this happens, first check the patient's serum lithium to see if he's actually taking the drug. Bipolar patients often stop lithium because they miss their highs — can you blame them? Second, check the patient's thyroid, since hypothyroidism mimics depression and may result from prolonged lithium therapy. Third, if the patient becomes depressed, add a TCA or a MAOI. Although usually helpful, giving TCAs to a depressed bipolar patient may increase the rapidity of cyclic mood changes or "switch" the patient to mania in a day or two. Fourth, if none of the above works, or if the patient cannot tolerate lithium's side effects, use the anticonvulsant carbamazepine (Tegretal), which helps 40% of lithium-refractory patients.

Electroconvulsive therapy. Historically, ECT was frightening: Patients would receive over 20 treatments for just about any condition; they'd convulse wildly, fracture spines, lose memories, and be dazed silly. Those days are gone. Today ECT is a safe and effective treatment for severe depressions (and sometimes, for life-threatening mania). Usually six to eight treatments, one every other day, are given. Fractures and wild convulsions no longer occur; memory loss and confusion are either nonexistent or minimal and short-lived. Nobody knows why ECT helps, but it may work by massively discharging or releasing all neurotransmitters. (It does not scare patients into getting better, since sham-ECT doesn't work.)

Before getting the actual ECT, the patient sequentially receives (a) atropine to dry oral secretions and to avert irregular heart rhythms, (b) an intravenous, short-acting anesthesia (e.g., pentathol) to spare the patient any discomfort, (c) a temporary muscle paralyzer (e.g., succinylcholine) to prevent fractures, and (d) oxygen. Then, in the more traditional "bilateral ECT," the psychiatrist places an electrode on the right and left forehead; in "unilateral ECT," an electrode is placed on the front and the back right (nondominant) side of the head. For 0.1 to 0.5 seconds the lowest possible voltage (70 to 130 V) to produce a seizure is applied. Two to three seconds later, the patient contracts all his muscles for 10–12 seconds. This "tonic phase" is immediately followed by a "clonic phase," 30–50 seconds of convulsions, which, because of the muscle paralyzer, appear as a slight tremor of the eyelids or fingers. Five minutes later the patient awakes from the anesthesia, alert and without pain. The patient doesn't remember the shock or complain of discomfort. The entire procedure, from anesthesia to waking-up, takes 15 minutes.

---

[6]Bipolar patients are especially prone to being salt-deficient: They may be too depressed or too manic to eat. Bipolar patients tend to be middle-aged, and thus more likely to be taking diuretics or steroids, following low-sodium diets for cardiac or weight problems, or having impaired kidney function. Since lithium replaces sodium within the cell, a serum lithium may not accurately reflect *intracellular* lithium, which is what counts.

First-time observers of ECT invariably describe it as "underwhelming." Patients too are surprised they don't feel anything, and why should they? — brain-tissue is free of pain fibers. A survey of patients who received ECT revealed that only half found going to the dentist more upsetting than getting ECT. The mortality rate from ECT is lower than for tonsillectomy, the former ranging from 0.008% to 0.05%. Indeed, the most dangerous aspect of ECT is not ECT *per se*, but the anesthesia. The main side effects of ECT are short-term memory loss and confusion; these may not occur or may be minimal. These problems, which are greatly minimized by unilateral ECT, disappear completely within two weeks of the final treatment. ECT does not cause any permanent brain damage or memory loss.

Psychotherapies

The psychotherapy of affective disorders can help patients to (a) learn the "facts" about their disorder, (b) feel less alone, (c) cope better with their disorder, (d) identify and avert situations likely to rekindle another episode, (e) abort episodes that have just begun by early symptom recognition, (f) view themselves and their world more rationally and constructively, (g) improve interpersonal relations, and (h) address the problems which plague the depressed patient.

Which of these goals are pursued depends primarily on the patient's current mental state. If he is amid an acute manic or depressive episode, psychotherapy should stress support more than insight, since he lacks the attention span, abstract thinking, and emotional perspective to use insight appropriately. For example, a man with major depression who "suddenly discovers" his sexual feelings toward his daughter will not apply this realization to understand his marital problem, but to "prove his depravity." Patients with melancholia or psychotic depression are especially unable to profit from insight, and if anything, will use it for self-flagellation. On the other hand, insight-oriented psychotherapies are more likely to benefit patients with dysthymic disorders or those who are in between major affective episodes. Among the more commonly mentioned of these therapies are the following:

Interpersonal psychotherapy (ITP). This therapy assumes that affective disorders are illnesses, that symptoms should be treated biologically, and that patients are victims and not causes of their illness. It treats symptoms biologically. ITP seeks to improve the patient's social and interpersonal functioning, but not to make enduring personality change. Specific problem areas (e.g., grief, role transitions, losses, interpersonal deficits and disputes) are identified and addressed. Instead of concentrating on intrapsychic material, ITP focuses on interpersonal matters, both inside and outside of therapy. Two controlled studies of acutely depressed patients showed the use of ITP and a TCA yielded superior results than either treatment alone. After eight months of ITP, patients displayed better social functioning, but had the same relapse rate. The conduct of ITP has been detailed in a manual (Klerman et al., 1979).

Short-term psychotherapy. Malan (1979) and Sifneos (1979) are the most-cited developers of those short-term psychotherapies, which are specific for depression, are based on psychoanalytic principles, and insist on a specific focus for treatment. Both methods require psychologically-minded, highly motivated patients with above-average intelligence and at least one meaningful relationship. Although these requirements exclude most depressed patients, surely there are some patients who qualify. Malan's treatment lasts 20–40 weeks, Sifneos', 12–15 weeks. Malan emphasizes early parent-child relationships; he believes depressed patients need to express forbidden feelings about loved ones. Sifneos stresses oedipal feelings; unlike Malan, he tries to avoid pregenital regression. Well-controlled studies of these treatments have not been conducted.

Whereas these short-term psychodynamic treatments provoke anxiety, others suppress anxiety: They afford problem-solving, reality testing, and emotional support. Since loss plays a role in many depressions, short-term psychotherapies are well-suited to study the incipient losses of the therapist or therapy as a model of the patient's loss in the "real" world.

Behavior therapies. These approaches assume that depressed patients lack positive reinforcement and, therefore, would benefit from being taught to identify the relationships between events and feelings, to maximize praise from oneself and others, to avoid self-punishment, to set realistic goals, and to improve social skills. The efficacy of these therapies remains unclear.

Cognitive therapy (CT). This treatment has been used most successfully for mild to moderate depression. Because CT focuses on more accessible conscious and preconscious, instead of less accessible unconscious, material, it can be used by many more depressed patients than can traditional psychoanalytic treatments. The actual technique of CT is summarized in Chapter 5, and its use for depression is best detailed by Beck et al. (1979).

The more accessible focus of CT also lends itself to scientific investigation. Comparing the standard 12-week, 20-session course of CT with standard pharmacotherapy for patients with unipolar, nonpsychotic depressions, some researchers found CT and pharmacotherapy to be equally effective, others found CT only useful as an adjunct to medications, and still others found CT plus TCAs surpassed either treatment alone.

Group therapy. It may help depressed patients to avoid excessively dwelling on their miseries to others, to develop more engaging ways of discussing personal problems, and to elicit positive feedback.

On the other hand, patients with psychomotor retardation, slowed thinking, and poor concentration are overwhelmed by a group and often berate themselves for not being "good" members. Although patients with dysthymic disorder and interpersonal difficulties are likely to benefit from a group, those who are unlikely to do so (a) have had a previous bad experience in a group, (b) would have nobody in the group with whom they could identify, and (c) would not develop an affinity to the group as a whole.

Family Involvement

The importance of involving family members cannot be overemphasized. Like therapists, family members often feel their advice and support are ignored, but unlike therapists, family members *live* with their depressed relative, and doing so can drain the most loving and resilient of loved ones. Besides the adverse consequences of depression already mentioned (p. 186), research shows that 12–36 months following their discharge, depressed inpatients had nine times the normal divorce rate seen in the general population. This same study revealed that 54% of depressed inpatients had spouses with a psychiatric disorder (Merikangas, 1984). When bipolar patients on lithium decompensate, it's invariably because they feel coerced into doing something which entails the family (Lieberman & Strauss, 1984). Thus, problems within the family result from and contribute to affective disorders.

There are three general therapeutic reasons for involving relatives: (a) to support the patient, (b) to support the family, and (c) to treat the family. During acute affective episodes, therapists should employ family members as extensions of the treatment. Relatives should be told the "facts" about affective disorders—their symptoms, natural history, genetic risks, prognosis, and treatment. They should be counseled on how to respond to the patient's disorder. They should be cautioned about getting sucked into the patient's pessimistic views, as well as warned about the limits of what they can do to alleviate their loved one's misery. By helping the family help the patient, the therapist helps support the family.

Citing confidentiality, some depressed patients seek to prevent any family involvement. Although confidentiality is usually respected, when a patient's *judgment is impaired*, maintaining confidentiality may be senseless and harmful. Some depressed patients exclude relatives so that the relatives "won't be contaminated by me"; others "use" confidentiality to deny they are ill and need help; others invoke confidentiality to avoid intimacy. In each case, the therapist must assess what information should be shared with the family and what should remain private. That a patient has sexual fantasies about aardvarks is nobody's business; that he's contemplating suicide or selling the family business is!

Outside of acute affective episodes, there are times when it is best to examine the family's or couple's role in causing or aggravating the patient's depression. This possibility is especially important to consider with female patients, since they tend to assume full responsibility for the problem, which is actually the entire family's. As a result, they seek individual treatment, when couple or family therapy is more approperiate.

Family treatment is also of special use for depressed teenagers, because they often come from families with a low tolerance for individuation and anger. The kid will rebel but succumb in despair. One parent frequently abuses substances while the other is chronically depressed. A common pattern is for the parents to be furious with each other, yet bait their child by being "injustice collectors" and "grave-diggers"—that is, resurrecting past misdeeds and using them as accusations. Therapists should help the adolescent distinguish his problems from his parents' while addressing the depression and substance abuse that usually afflict other family members.

Finally, in the ultimate tragedy—suicide—clinicians should talk with the family to afford comfort, to prevent others from committing impulsive suicides, to minimize the self-blame of relatives, which might require pointing out to them that suicide is a hostile act because it hurts everyone, and finally, to help the therapist learn from any mistakes he might have made.

CHAPTER 12

Anxiety Disorders

ALTHOUGH EVERYBODY experiences anxiety, only some are impaired by it. Indeed, a certain measure of anxiety stimulates functioning and creativity. As a symptom, anxiety has internal and external components: Internally, anxiety is a subjective experience of tension, apprehension, worry, and uneasiness. Externally, the somatic signs of anxiety consist of autonomic hyperactivity (e.g., tachycardia, flushing, sweating) and motor hyperactivity (e.g., agitation, hyperventilation, scanning). In *DSM-III* the core characteristic of anxiety disorders is the experience, or the avoidance, of anxiety. Anxiety is experienced in panic, generalized anxiety, and post-traumatic stress disorders; anxiety is avoided in phobic and obsessive compulsive disorders. Although this classification derives from recent research, its fundamental divisions originated with Freud over 80 years ago.

In 1894 Freud described a syndrome of "anxiety neurosis," which encompassed two general patterns of anxiety: The first, which he called "chronic anxiety," consisted of generalized or "free-floating" anxiety. The second, which he called "anxiety attacks," would "erupt suddenly into consciousness without being called forth by any train of thought" (Freud, 1894, p.80). In *DSM-III,* Freud's chronic anxiety corresponds to generalized anxiety disorder (GAD), whereas his anxiety attacks correspond to panic disorder.

GAD and panic disorder differ in other key ways: Panic disorder runs in families; GAD does not. The ratio of MZ to DZ twins for GAD is 1:1, while for panic disorder it's 5:1. The life course and prognosis of GAD are more varied than for panic disorder. There is no specific drug treatment for GAD, but there is for panic disorder.

203

Anxiety disorders are the most prevalent mental disorders in the general population (excluding tobacco use and psychosexual disorders). The ECA survey found the six-month prevalence rate for anxiety disorder to be 8.3%, while the lifetime prevalence was between 10% and 15%. In contrast, anxiety disorders account for less than 4% of the diagnoses in psychiatric practice. The most common of the anxiety disorders are phobic disorders, their six-month prevalence rate being 7.0%. Table 12-1 summarizes the epidemiology of the most frequent anxiety disorders.

That relatively few people with anxiety disorders seek treatment is unfortunate, since treatment is usually effective, and without it less than a quarter of these patients fully recover. In general, the earlier in life patients receive treatment, the better their long-term outcome. Thus, early detection matters.

The Causes of Anxiety

Psychodynamic theory. At first, Freud postulated that pathological anxiety resulted from a failure to repress painful memories, impulses, or thoughts. When the psychic energy used for this repression is particularly intense, the repressed material breaks into consciousness in a disguised form. For instance,

TABLE 12-1
Epidemiology of *DSM-III* Anxiety Disorders*

	LIFETIME PREVALENCE IN PERCENT			
PARAMETER	AGORAPHOBIA†	SIMPLE PHOBIA†	PANIC DISORDER	OBSESSIVE COMPULSIVE DISORDER
TOTAL	4.9	2.5	1.4	2.5
SEX				
Male	1.5	3.9	0.9	2.0
Female	6.0	9.0	2.0	3.0
RACE				
Black	4.4	8.0	1.3	2.5
Nonblack	3.7	6.2	1.3	2.6
EDUCATION				
College graduate	2.2	4.5	1.1	2.0
Other	4.4	7.2	1.5	2.6
LOCATION				
Central city	4.6	6.6	1.7	1.5
Suburbs	4.3	7.6	0.8	2.4
Small town/rural	3.7	6.3	2.1	1.7

*This table synthesizes information from Robins et al. (1984), Blazer et al. (1985), Liebowitz et al. (1985), and Goodwin & Guze (1984).

†These columns indicate the prevalence of phobic *disorders*, which disable, as opposed to phobic *symptoms*, which although more common, are usually not disabling. See text.

after "discovering" she was sexually molested as a child, a woman was flooded not with sexual thoughts, but with anxiety, difficulty breathing, hyperventilation, and other symptoms of a panic attack. Later, Freud introduced the concept of "signal anxiety," whose experience enables the person to avoid dangerous thoughts, impulses, etc., through repression, phobic avoidance, compulsions, etc.

Behavioral theories. In Pavlov's classic experiment, a dog would salivate on repeated simultaneous exposure to food and the sound of a bell. When Pavlov removed the food, the dog had become conditioned to salivate on hearing the bell alone. Watson, Skinner, and most behaviorists view conditioning as essential in perpetuating and intensifying anxiety. Kandel (1983) photographed the actual changes in nerve cells produced by psychosocial conditioning (see p. 61).

Although many assume that psychic anxiety causes and conditions somatic anxiety, William James (1893) proposed the opposite—that is, subjectively experienced anxiety is a conditioned response to physical signals of anxiety, such as tachycardia and rapid breathing. Under stress and at rest, anxious subjects have a higher rate of these bodily signals than do controls. Some evidence suggests that patients who report higher levels of psychic anxiety do so not because they have greater physiologic arousal, but because they are more sensitive to perceiving physiologic arousal.

Biological theories. Whereas James, in what came to be known as the James-Lange theory, claimed that peripheral symptoms provoked central anxiety, Cannon (1932) argued that anxiety originated in the brain, which in turn produced peripheral symptoms. In Cannon's view, anxiety and panic are not consequences but causes of tachycardia, sweating, rapid respiration, etc. Yet if anxiety and panic tend to go from the brain to the body (and not vice versa), where and how does this occur in the brain?

During the late 1970s, two major discoveries began to address these questions. The first advance (Redmond, 1979) involved the locus coeruleus (LC), a dense cluster of neurons, which produces 70% of the brain's norepinephrine. When the LC is stimulated electrically or by the drug yohimbine, anxiety increases; when the LC is inhibited by drugs called "beta-adrenergic blockers" (e.g., clonidine, propranolol), anxiety diminishes. In addition, benzodiazepines and TCAs slow the LC's firing and reduce anxiety.

The second major advance (Skolnick & Paul, 1983) was the discovery of benzodiazepine (BZ) receptors in the brain. These receptors are coupled functionally (if not structurally) to a "supramolecular receptor complex," which involves chloride ions and the "inhibitor" neurotransmitter, GABA. Benzodiazepines (e.g., diazepam) appear to work by augmenting the antianxiety action of this GABA-stimulated chloride system.

How do these two biological systems relate? Nobody knows; no relationships are obvious. Many investigators suspect they pertain to different clinical syndromes — the very ones Freud, and then *DSM-III*, has characterized — the LC to panic disorder and the BZ receptor to GAD. When stimulated, the LC produces the symptoms and intense somatic signs characteristic of panic anxiety, which, like the LC itself, is inhibited by TCAs and clonidine. In contrast, the BZ receptors may play a role in GAD and do not appear to be affected by TCAs.

GENERALIZED ANXIETY DISORDER

Very little is known about generalized anxiety disorder (GAD), including whether it is common or rare. Also unknown are GAD's sex ratio, natural history, etiology, predisposing factors, or epidemiology. Not suprisingly, some experts believe that GAD is not a specific disorder, but merely a residual category for the anxiety disorders. Yet in a study of 108 highly anxious patients, those with anticipatory anxiety had phobic or panic disorders, whereas those without anticipatory anxiety were characterized by chronic worry and apprehensive expectation in multiple life situations (Barlow et al., 1986). These findings suggest that GAD is a valid clinical disorder.

Clinical Presentation

These patients are chronic worry-warts. During a majority of their days, they are tense, highly distractible, irritable, restless, and so "on edge" they're often fatigued and mildly depressed. (Unrelenting anxiety is, by itself, very exhausting.) The patient's anxiety is diffuse, unfocused, free-floating, and ongoing; it may, or may not, be accompanied by prominent physical complaints: sweating, dizziness, clammy hands, tachycardia. When somatic symptoms dominate, patients will consult numerous medical specialists, chiropractors, physiotherapists, or nutritionists, which may lead them to fad diets and substance abuse. GAD also impairs social and occupational functioning.

To diagnose GAD, *DSM-III* requires three out of four groups of symptoms: *motor tension, autonomic hyperactivity, apprehensive expectation*, and *hypervigilance or scanning*. To exclude acute anxiety reactions, *DSM-III-R* plans to expand the minimum duration of anxiety from one to six months. The *DSM-III* criteria for GAD are listed in Table 12-2.

Differential Diagnosis

Many *physiologic conditions* resemble GAD. These include (a) *medical disorders*, such as *cardiac arrhythmias, hyperthyroidism, thyrotoxicosis, pheochromocytoma, Cushing's disease, Addison's disease, hyperventilation,*

TABLE 12-2
DSM-III Criteria for Generalized Anxiety Disorder*

A. Generalized, persistent anxiety is manifested by symptoms from three of the following four categories:

   (1) *motor tension*: shakiness, jitteriness, jumpiness, trembling, tension, muscle aches, fatigability, inability to relax, eyelid twitch, furrowed brow, strained face, fidgeting, restlessness, easy startle

   (2) *autonomic hyperactivity*: sweating, heart pounding or racing, cold clammy hands, dry mouth, dizziness, light-headedness, paresthesias (tingling in hands or feet), upset stomach, hot and cold spells, frequent urination, diarrhea, discomfort in the pit of the stomach, lump in the throat, flushing, pallor, high resting pulse and respiration rate

   (3) *apprehensive expectation*: anxiety, worry, fear, rumination, and anticipation of misfortune to self or others

   (4) *vigilance and scanning*: hyperalertness resulting in distractability, difficulty in concentrating, insomnia, feeling "on edge," irritability, impatience

B. The anxious mood has been continuous for at least one month.

C. Not due to another mental disorder, such as a Depressive Disorder or Schizophrenia.

D. At least 18 years of age.

*DSM-III, p. 233.

and *hypocalcemia*; (b) *alcohol and hypnosedative withdrawal*; and (c) *drug intoxications* from *amphetamines, cocaine, nasal decongestants, yohimbine*, and most often, *caffeine*. Symptoms of caffeine intoxication — nervousness, irritability, agitation, headache, rapid heart rate, tremulousness, and occasional muscle twitches, can result from ingesting over 250 mg of caffeine a day. Caffeine's effects can persist for *seven* hours. Table 12-3 lists the sources and their amounts of caffeine.

   Panic disorder may be confused with GAD, since chronic anxiety often occurs between panic attacks; yet unlike GAD, panic disorder has distinct episodes of intense anxiety. In *phobic disorder* the patient's anxiety is specific for the phobic stimulus, whereas in GAD it's unfocused and continual. The somatic complaints of GAD may resemble *hypochondriasis*, but the hypochondriac more gravely exaggerates the danger of his symptoms.

   Anxiety frequently accompanies *schizophrenia* and severe *major depressive episodes*; when it does, GAD should not be diagnosed. On the other hand, many outpatients present with mild depression and anxiety, which poses a problem in differential diagnosis. Symptoms most suggestive of an anxiety disorder are panic attacks, phobias, derealization, reactive depression, compulsions, temper outbursts, and chest pain; depression is a more likely diag-

TABLE 12-3
Sources of Caffeine*

SOURCE	AMOUNT OF CAFFEINE (mgs.)
Beverages	
Brewed coffee	100–150 per cup
Instant coffee	86–99 per cup
Tea	60–75 per cup
Decaffeinated coffee	2–4 per cup
Cola drinks	40–60 per glass
Mountain Dew and Mellow Yellow	51 per glass
Dr. Pepper	42 per glass
Regular Sunkist Orange	42 per glass
7-Up, Sprite, Fresca, Diet Sunkist Orange, Fanta Orange, Hires Root Beer, Caffeine-free colas	0 per glass
Prescription medications	
Cafergot	100 per tablet
Darvon compound	32 per capsule
Fiornal	40 per tablet
Migral	50 per tablet
Over-the-counter drugs	
Stimulants:	
No-doz	100 per tablet
Vivarin	200 per tablet
Pain relievers:	
Anacin, aspirin compound, Bromo-Seltzer, Cope, Easy-Mens, Empirin compound, Midol, Vanquish	32 per tablet
Excedrin	60 per tablet
Pre-Mens	66 per tablet
Cold pills	30 per capsule

*Modified from Maxmen, J. S. (1986a). *A good night's sleep: A step-by-step program for overcoming insomnia and other sleep problems.* New York: Warner, p. 74.

nosis with persistently depressed mood, early morning awakening, suicidal ideation, psychomotor retardation, anhedonia, and pessimism.

Management and Treatment

Because little is known about specific treatments for GAD, what follows is a synopsis of therapies for the symptom of anxiety. It should be stressed that *all* approaches eventually involve confronting the patient with his anxiety.

Biotherapies. Although the proper use of medication in treating anxiety is controversial, several points are generally agreed on: (a) Benzodiazepines (BZ) are preferred over all other hypnosedatives (e.g., barbiturates) because they are rarely lethal, cause fewer side effects, produce less tolerance, and create less drug dependency. (Their abuse potential is discussed on pp. 129–130.) (b) BZ should not be prescribed for mild anxiety. (c) They can be used safely and effectively to quell episodic agitation or severe apprehension that occur by themselves or along with another disorder, such as major depression. (d) BZ can also be used to treat chronic severe anxiety (as in a GAD), as long as habituation is avoided.

Psychotherapies. Insight-oriented psychotherapies will explore the *unconscious* and symbolic meanings of the patient's anxiety and clarify its defensive and "signal" functions. All psychotherapy seeks to identify the stressors producing the anxiety, offer better means of handling stress, and eliminate dietary or physical sources of anxiety. In cognitive therapy, the patient identifies the precise stresses, events, or circumstances that trigger *conscious* dysphoric "automatic thoughts" and then develops more rational ways of thinking and feeling in response to the same stressors.

Behavior therapy. Muscle relaxation, meditation, biofeedback, and autogenic training are frequently employed either by themselves or as supplements to the previously mentioned therapies.

PANIC DISORDER

"Worse than anything at Auschwitz" is how a concentration-camp survivor described her panic attacks. Suddenly and without reason, panic attacks engulf the victim with a sense of imminent doom, death, or destruction. Since most victims have never heard of panic attacks, they dread they're going mad and won't tell loved ones or physicians about them. Panic attacks may be the most terrifying of all psychiatric symptoms.

Clinical Presentation

Panic disorder frequently evolves in three stages: (a) *panic attack*, (b) *anticipatory anxiety*, and (c) *agoraphobia*. Many patients with panic attacks have the subsequent stages, but some do not, and there's no way of predicting which will in advance. Different stages may dominate at different periods. Some long-term agoraphobics forget that panic attacks gave rise to their phobia. The *DSM-III* criteria for panic disorder (Table 12-4) don't include the second and third stages, but *DSM-III-R* will. Later it will be shown how each stage benefits from a different treatment (Klein, 1964).

TABLE 12-4
DSM-III* Criteria for Panic Disorder

A. At least three panic attacks within a three-week period in circumstances other than during marked physical exertion or in a life-threatening situation. The attacks are not precipitated only by exposure to a circumscribed phobic stimulus.

B. Panic attacks are manifested by discrete periods of apprehension or fear, and at least four of the following symptoms appear during each attack:

   (1) dyspnea
   (2) palpitations
   (3) chest pain or discomfort
   (4) choking or smothering sensations
   (5) dizziness, vertigo, or unsteady feelings
   (6) feelings of unreality
   (7) paresthesias (tingling in hands or feet)
   (8) hot and cold flashes
   (9) sweating
   (10) faintness
   (11) trembling or shaking
   (12) fear of dying, going crazy, or doing something uncontrolled during an attack

C. Not due to a physical disorder or another mental disorder, such as Major Depression, Somatization Disorder, or Schizophrenia.

D. The disorder is not associated with Agoraphobia.

DSM-III, pp. 231–232.

The essential feature of panic disorder is a history of *panic attack*. These attacks usually affect women and strike outside the victim's home — most often in a store, sometimes on the street. The woman feels she's in a life-threatening situation from which she must escape — immediately. She might fear an imminent stroke, heart attack, or nuclear explosion. Very often she can't pinpoint what she fears, but knows it's horrendous. Her imagination takes over: She might die right on the spot, go berserk, or be killed, butchered, or maimed. Her heart pounds so, it could bust or burst through her chest. She may scream or look blank, even though she's frozen in fear and unable to move. The woman from Auschwitz, now quite elderly, says she's terrified of falling and clutching onto strangers. Another woman described her arms turning to stone and people appearing miles away. Most patients will gasp for air, hyperventilate, develop paresthesias, or feel dizzy and light-headed. They will race outside and only then will their breathing slow and their attack subside. Most attacks last three to ten minutes, and never more than 30 minutes.

Many patients shrug off the first attack, but in several days, unprovoked attacks recur; these are less intense, but still frightening. Patients begin to dread future attacks. Although the timing of panic attacks is unpredictable, the locations may follow a pattern. A patient may panic in the same bank on three occasions, but not on the fourth or in any other bank. A patient's attacks usually have their own symptom cluster: Some patients have primarily respiratory distress, some worry about going crazy, some fear nuclear death.

In time, instead of returning to their baseline state, most patients develop *anticipatory anxiety* in between panic attacks. This anxiety resembles that seen in GAD, including continued motor tension, autonomic hyperactivity, apprehension, hypervigilance, and initial insomnia. Patients say this anxiety stems from a terror of having future attacks. This anxiety can be mild or severe; it may be the most dominant symptom, thereby misleading clinicians into diagnosing GAD.

Subsequently, some patients—and there's no way of knowing which ones—develop *phobic avoidance*. They may be phobic for situations associated with the initial panic attack, on the mistaken belief that the situation caused the attack. For example, a patient may avoid driving because she thinks driving caused her to panic. More often, patients avoid situations in which they fear being trapped or unable to get help (e.g., busses, elevators, bridges, department stores). When restrictions on travel away from home significantly impair functioning, the diagnosis of *agoraphobia* is merited. The number of blocks a patient ventures away from home is a good simple measure of impairment.

Clinical Course

Panic disorder usually begins during the late teens and twenties, rarely after age 35, but occasionally as late as 60. Initially, there is usually a discrete attack, but chronic anxiety, fatigue, or dizziness may precede it. Most patients originally consult a physician for difficulty breathing or chest discomfort, and less often, for abdominal distress or "irritable colon." In one survey, 70% of the patients had visited more than 10 physicians, 95% had prior psychiatric treatment, and 98% had long trials of hypnosedatives; on average, each patient took over 8,772 doses (without relief).

Over time, the intensity of panic attacks, anticipatory anxiety, and phobic avoidance varies. Spontaneous remissions occur for months, and sometimes, for years. A patient may go five to ten years without an attack, suddenly have three attacks in a month, and then not have another for a decade. In general, five to 20 years after the initial attack, 50% to 60% of patients will be recovered substantially while 20% will remain moderately impaired. Some studies suggest bleaker prognoses.

The earlier patients get treatment, the better the outcome. If panic attacks can be squelched relatively early, anticipatory anxiety and phobia may be averted or minimized. Even if the latter stages occur, early treatment can reduce their incapacitations and complications.

Complications

Substance abuse is a frequent complication because patients discover that alcohol and hypnosedatives will temporarily calm their anticipatory anxiety. Misdiagnosis by physicians may also lead to hypnosedative misuse. Occupational, social, and marital impairments are common, often compounded by the patient's hiding her attacks and by others not knowing that panic disorder exists.

Depression may affect up to 50% of all patients with panic disorder. These depressions are usually mild, two-thirds last under three months, and most are associated with a precipitating stress, such as a divorce. Yet a third of patients with panic disorder have had a major depression years *before* having their first panic attack. This suggests that for some patients, depression is not a complication of panic disorder, but a second disorder.

Epidemiology

Panic disorder afflicts 1% to 2% of the population, two to three times more women than men, and is most prevalent between the ages of 16 and 40. During pregnancy, the frequency of panic attacks appears to decline sharply. Severe separation anxiety or sudden object loss during childhood may predispose to panic disorder.

Mitral valve prolapse (MVP) is found in 40% to 50% of patients with panic disorder or agoraphobia, whereas MVP occurs in 4% to 10% of the general population. In MVP a heart valve doesn't close properly and produces a murmur or "systolic click." MVP is usually asymptomatic, but it may cause fatigue, shortness of breath, palpitations, and chest pain. Although why MVP and panic frequently coexist is unknown, it's worth noting that MVP, by itself, is associated with autonomic hyperactivity, anxiety, and elevated catecholamines.

Etiology

Panic disorder runs in families. About 20% of these patients' first-degree relatives have panic disorder, in comparison to about 4% in the general population. Given an MZ to DZ ratio of 5:1 for panic disorder, genetics seem to play a major role in this familial transmission. (Knowing this, parents with panic disorder can spare their children considerable grief by ensuring that their kids know about the disorder and obtain early treatment.)

The initial panic attack, though not triggered by a specific stressor, usually occurs during an unusually stressful period, such as during a serious illness or after a divorce. First attacks frequently happen in patients with thyroid disorders, during the immediate postpartum period, and after taking marijuana, cocaine, or amphetamines. Caffeine produces panic attacks in 71% of patients with panic disorder and stopping caffeine reduces their frequency and intensity.

Lactic acid, the stuff causing stiff muscles from exercise, plays some, currently unknown, role in panic disorder. Intravenous infusions of sodium lactate trigger panic attacks in those with panic disorder, but not in controls. Yet if the patients with panic disorder receive a tricyclic antidepressant (TCA) prior to being infused with lactate, they will not develop an attack. This finding is noteworthy, given that TCAs block panic attacks.

Differential Diagnosis

All of the *medical conditions* which simulate GAD can mimic panic disorder. (See pp. 206–207.) When other mental disorders, especially *schizophrenia, somatization disorder*, and *borderline personality disorder* produce panic symptoms, panic disorder should not be diagnosed.

Differentiating *depression* from panic disorder can be tough. For starters, *mild depression* is a frequent complication of panic disorder, whereas *major depression* may exist independently and either precede or coexist with panic disorder. Don't panic, but panic attacks are also a common feature of "atypical depression." Thus, if depression and panic attacks occur concomitantly, the more likely diagnosis is depression.

Differenting *generalized anxiety disorder* from panic disorder may be complicated because anticipatory anxiety may be the dominant symptom of panic disorder; the patient may even have forgotten she ever had panic attacks. A history of repeated discrete attacks points to panic disorder.

Although *phobic disorders* may produce anticipatory anxiety, the "pure" phobic does not have spontaneous anxiety attacks. The phobic can specify the phobic stimulus and knows she will become anxious when exposed to it. In contrast, panic attacks erupt spontaneously and unpredictably, with the patient having trouble identifying the panic stimulus. For instance, in the *social phobia* of stage fright, the patient knows that being on a stage triggers anxiety, whereas panic attacks can't be predicted.

Management and Treatment

From the start, the clinician should help the patient and her family have reasonable expectations of treatment and of the patient. It should be pointed out that panic disorder is not a figment of the patient's imagination, but a genuine illness, with biological components, which often causes severe impairments. The patient and family should be told that panic disorder has a fluctuating course, and so the patient should not feel that she, or the treatment, has failed if some symptoms persist or recur. They should know that improving the patient's ability to function and to travel are key goals of treatment. The therapist should carefully describe the three stages of panic disorder, make sure the patient knows which ones she's experiencing, and explain that each stage requires a different treatment.

Panic attacks. TCAs, especially imipramine (IMI), prevent 95% of all panic attacks. Although TCAs are antidepressants, nondepressed patients with panic attacks respond equally well to TCAs. For patients who've recently developed panic attacks, TCAs are usually sufficient, but if the patient has gone on to having anticipatory anxiety or agoraphobia, additional treatments are needed. When taking IMI, some patients claim they haven't improved, because they are still having anticipatory anxiety, which does not respond to IMI.

Because patients with panic disorder are particularly worried by physical symptoms, IMI is introduced at a slower rate and lower dose than with depression. Typically, 25 mg of IMI is started at bedtime and increased every three days. The average effective dose is 200 mg/day, but some patients respond to 50 mg/day. If the patient is bothered by IMI's side effects, desipramine may be substituted. If the patient completely recovers, IMI is tapered after six months. However, if the patient's panic attacks have not *completely* stopped after two weeks of therapeutic levels of IMI, monoamine oxidase inhibitors (MAOIs) or the benzodiazepine, alprazolam, can be prescribed. Although MAOIs and TCAs are equally effective in preventing panic attacks, TCAs are used first because of their greater safety. The only place MAOIs have been more effective than IMI is in blocking panic attacks which arise from "atypical depression" (Klein et al., 1980).

Anticipatory anxiety. When the fear of having panic attacks continues for months and years, the anxiety which develops in anticipation of these attacks becomes entrenched and resistant to treatment. Although it may seem redundant to the therapist, repeatedly telling the patient that she won't get panic attacks while on IMI goes a long way toward quelling anticipatory anxiety. Muscle relaxation also helps. Although TCAs do not touch anticipatory anxiety, some patients remain on TCAs simply to feel secure from future panic attacks. Diazepam-like drugs will reduce anticipatory anxiety, but because of their habituation potential, their use should be temporary. Propranolol, a beta-adrenergic blocker, is particularly effective against somatic signs of anxiety.

Agoraphobia. As discussed below, any treatment that eventually exposes the patient to the phobic stimulus is likely to work, whereas any treatment which never exposes the patient to the stimulus is likely to fail. Systematic desensitization is frequently recommended, but any psychotherapy which gets the patient to gradually confront the feared situation is helpful. TCAs and MAOIs may also help.

PHOBIC DISORDERS

A phobia is an irrational dread of, and compelling desire to avoid, a specific object, situation, or activity. By definition, the person knows his phobia is "crazy," unreasonable, or excessive. Unlike panic attacks, phobias are always anticipated and never happen spontaneously. (Patients with both panic attacks and phobias are diagnosed as having panic disorder.)

The *original phobia* is usually followed by mild to severe *anticipatory anxiety*, although, if the phobic stimulus is avoided, some patients will be anxiety-free. The patient's degree of anticipatory anxiety depends primarily on her confidence that she can avoid the phobic situation. Patients who are phobic to unusual things, such as snakes, are generally calm in other circumstances; those who dread things which might suddenly and unexpectedly appear, such as pigeons, tend to be chronically anxious, unless they're in a safe haven (e.g., home).

Avoidant behaviors often occur. A fish-phobic not only is uncomfortable around fish, but before visiting new friends phones ahead to make sure they won't serve herring and don't have goldfish. If the fish can't be hidden or trashed, the fish-phobic won't visit.

On occasion, virtually everyone, especially children, is bugged by some phobia — mice, snakes, etc. Phobic *symptoms* become phobic *disorders* when they cause undue distress and impair functioning. Roughly 20% of patients with phobic symptoms develop phobic disorders.

Many phobias remit quickly without therapy, but if they hang on for over a year, they're unlikely to remit spontaneously. Most childhood phobias vanish within a year; treatment hastens their disappearance. The prognosis is worse in adults: In five years, 50% of patients will improve, but only 5% will be symptom-free.

One medical dictionary lists 275 types of phobia; *DSM-III* lists three (see Table 12-5): *Agoraphobia* originally meant "fear of the marketplace," but now refers to fears of being alone, of leaving home, or of being unable to escape from public places (e.g., shops, streets). The most severe of the phobic disorders, agoraphobia accounts for 60% of phobic disorders in clinical practice. *Social phobia* is when the person is terrified of being scrutinized and judged, as in "stage fright"; social phobias comprise 10% of phobic disorders. *Simple phobia* is an irrational fear and avoidance of specific objects or situations

TABLE 12-5
DSM-III* Criteria for Phobic Disorders

I. AGORAPHOBIA

A. The individual has marked fear of and thus avoids being alone or in public places from which escape might be difficult or help not available in case of sudden incapacitation, e.g., crowds, bridges, public transportation.

B. There is increasing constriction of normal activities until the fears or avoidance behavior dominate the individual's life.

C. Not due to a major depressive episode, Obsessive Compulsive Disorder, Paranoid Personality Disorder, or Schizophrenia.

II. SOCIAL PHOBIA

A. A persistent, irrational fear of, and compelling desire to avoid, a situation in which the individual is exposed to possible scrutiny by others and fears that he or she may act in a way that will be humiliating or embarrassing.

B. Significant distress because of the disturbance and recognition by the individual that his or her fear is excessive or unreasonable.

C. Not due to another mental disorder, such as Major Depression or Avoidant Personality Disorder.

III. SIMPLE PHOBIA

A. A persistent, irrational fear of, and compelling desire to avoid, an object or a situation other than being alone, or in public places away from home (Agoraphobia), or of humiliation or embarrassment in certain social situations (Social Phobia). Phobic objects are often animals, and phobic situations frequently involve heights or closed spaces.

B. Significant distress from the disturbance and recognition by the individual that his or her fear is excessive or unreasonable.

C. Not due to another mental disorder, such as Schizophrenia or Obsessive Compulsive Disorder.

*DSM-III: Agoraphobia (p. 227), Social Phobia (p. 228), Simple Phobia (pp. 229–230).

not covered by agoraphobia or social phobia. Simple phobias are usually to animals (e.g., insects), things (e.g., hypodermic needles), or places (e.g., heights, closed spaces). Whereas social phobias are normally to a few stimuli, simple phobias are usually to one object. In comparison to social phobias, simple phobias begin earlier in life, rarely incapacitate, and have better prognoses.

Among the phobias, simple phobias are most common in the population, but agoraphobias are most common in the office.

Clinical Presentation

Agoraphobia. The public places or open spaces typically feared by these patients include driving a car, crossing bridges, being in tunnels, walking through crowds, or shopping. Exposure to the phobic stimulus often triggers intense somatic anxiety. Some phobic patients dread going berserk in public — screaming without reason, propositioning strangers, gaffawing nonstop, disrobing, or masturbating. Agoraphobia mushrooms: Fears of taking a bus may escalate to fears of going anywhere by any means. Because agoraphobics often become terrified of leaving safe places (e.g., home), of being without a familiar object (e.g., a cane), or of traveling alone, they become highly dependent on others. Unless treated early, patients may increasingly restrict their activities and only venture outside with a trusted companion.

When agoraphobia is not a sequela of panic attacks, it usually arises during the early twenties, even though it may begin at any age. Many patients delay getting treatment for a decade or more. Over time, symptoms typically fluctuate from mild to severe. Spontaneous remissions occur, but uncommonly. Superimposed strong emotions, such as rage or dread, will temporarily alleviate some phobias. Without early treatment or a spontaneous remission, patients tend to get worse over time.

Complications are frequent. If the patient is home-bound, depression is common. Alcohol and hypnosedative abuse may result from the patient medicating her anticipatory anxiety, or from a physician incorrectly treating the patient's depression or anxiety. Many agoraphobics develop compulsions: They may not leave home without repeatedly checking if the oven is on or if the door is locked. Marital and sexual problems may precede or follow agoraphobia.

Social phobia. These patients have an irrational fear of being scrutinized, judged, or humiliated in public. It may be a dread of embarrassing oneself while speaking in public, eating in restaurants, or using public lavatories. Social phobics tend to blush and twitch, whereas agoraphobics become dizzy, faint, short of breath, weak in the limbs, and have ringing or buzzing in their ears (Liebowitz et al., 1985).

With a mean age of onset of 19, social phobias usually begin before agoraphobia. Without early therapy, social phobia has an unremitting, chronic course. At some point, a third to a half will have depressive symptoms, a majority will stop work or school, 60% will abuse alcohol or drugs, and about half will avoid all social interaction outside the immediate family. Although many social phobias do not significantly interfere with work, the fear of taking trips or of speaking in public can block career advancement.

Simple phobia. The most common, benign, and circumscribed of the phobias, these usually start in childhood or early adolescence and cease within five years in 50% of patients. Most simple phobias are single and specific—to an animal (e.g., cats), an animal product (e.g., tunafish), a situation in nature (e.g., dirt, thunderstorms, darkness), or an instrument with sexual or aggressive associations (e.g, knives, pins). Because complications and impairments from simple phobias are minimal, patients rarely seek therapy.

Epidemiology

Epidemiologic surveys of phobias can yield very different results because what qualifies as a phobia can vary considerably. Is somebody phobic if she's queasy around snakes? Does one count phobias that appear with other disorders? In the general population, the prevalence of phobic *symptoms* is 19% to 44%, whereas for phobic *disorders* it's 5% to 15%.

Although women have two to three times more agoraphobia and simple phobia than men (Table 12-1), social phobias affect the sexes equally. Adults who are phobic and nonphobic have the same rates (4%) of phobias during childhood. Separation anxiety during childhood and sudden loss of a loved one predispose to agoraphobia.

Etiology and Pathogenesis

As a general proposition, it can be said that unknown biological or psychosocial mechanisms cause phobic patients to acquire an ingrained and unconscious stimulus-response association, which generates fear on subsequent exposure to the phobic stimulus. However, why some objects are feared and not others and why some phobias vanish while others intensify are unknown. The standard (tautological) explanations are that the phobic object is "chosen" because it has enormous symbolic importance to the individual, that patients are unaware of its unconscious meaning, and that repression and displacement are the chief defense mechanisms that cause phobias. For example, a woman who as a child was usually punished by being locked in her bedroom may become claustrophobic when fired by her boss. Yet if she has forgotten (or repressed) those childhood banishments, she will be unaware of being conditioned to associate punishment with being locked in a room, and will be puzzled by her current claustrophobia.

Agoraphobia runs in families; most social and simple phobias do not. Nevertheless, some studies show that children specifically phobic to insects and animals are likely to have mothers with similar phobias. This suggests that imitation, indoctrination, or identification may transmit phobias in some cases. Genetic factors seem to play a minimal role in the pathogenesis of phobia.

Differential Diagnosis

A phobic disorder should *only* be diagnosed when the patient does *not* have another mental or personality disorder. *Schizophrenia* may produce social withdrawal resembling agoraphobia and social phobia, but schizophrenics have many more symptoms and avoid situations because of a delusion, whereas phobics know their phobia is absurd. *Paranoid disorders* can lead to avoidant behavior, but unlike the phobic, the paranoid sees nothing irrational about his behavior. Because many patients with *depressive disorders* feel worthless, gradually restrict their activities, and become reclusive, they may appear agoraphobic. Pervasive symptoms, biological signs of depression, and excessive guilt and shame point to depression. Phobias are common in "*atypical depression*," in which case the diagnosis is "atypical depression" and not a phobic disorder.

Patients with *dementia* may withdrawal to "think clearly," but this phobic-like avoidance is not associated with a specific feared stimulus; MSE testing will eliminate any remaining diagnostic confusion. *Obsessive compulsive disorder* may also produce phobic-like behavior, as when a patient avoids dirt. Yet, whereas the feared object leads the obsessive to perform rituals or to block out intrusive thoughts, it primarily induces anxiety in the phobic patient. Phobias commonly occur in patients with *borderline, paranoid*, and *avoidant personality disorders*.

Normal fears of public speaking should be distinguished from social phobia, as should normal fears of bugs or snakes from simple phobia. In these cases, the border between "normal" and pathological depends on the degree of distress and disability the phobia generates.

Management and Treatment

> One can hardly master a phobia if one waits till the patient lets the analysis influence him to give it up . . . one succeeds only when one can induce them by the influence of the analysis to . . . go [about alone] . . . and to struggle with their anxiety while they make the attempt. — Sigmund Freud (1919)

Essential for treating phobias is the patient's having a prolonged, uninterrupted exposure to the feared object or situation. This applies to all treatments, including psychoanalytic psychotherapy, behavior therapy, hypnosis, or medication. Historically, the preferred treatment for phobias was primarily behavior therapy, supplemented by supportive individual, family, and group therapy, whenever appropriate. More recently, however, evidence suggests that supportive psychotherapy is just as effective as behavior therapy, as long as the patient encounters the feared situation. It's further recognized that eliminating phobias by "superficial" behavioral or pharmacologic means rarely, if ever, leads to "symptom substitution."

Biotherapies. Most studies show little use for TCAs and MAOIs in phobic patients without panic attacks. Because beta-adrenergic blockers (e.g., propranolol) diminish somatic (but not psychic) anxiety, they may be useful for some social phobias, such as stage fright, in which somatic anxiety is paramount. Hypnosedatives can be used temporarily to reduce anticipatory anxiety, but their long-term use risks habituation.

Behavior Therapies. Live exposure to the phobic stimulus — the essential therapeutic intervention — may be performed in three ways. First is *flooding*, in which the patient is directly confronted with the phobic stimulus for sessions lasting from 30 minutes to eight hours. Flooding may also involve bombarding the patient with the feared stimulus. The author cured a man of his pillow phobia by having him sit for two 45-minute sessions in a hospital bedroom stuffed with 127 pillows. Second is a *graduated exposure*, in which the patient initially confronts the phobic object for a brief time (e.g., 30 seconds to one minute), and then gradually escalates the duration of exposure to over 60 uninterrupted minutes. Marks et al. (1983) have shown that there is only a nominally added benefit to therapist-aided exposure over the patient doing it by himself as homework. The third approach is *systematic desensitization*, usually with *muscle relaxation*, as described in Chapter 5.

Because patients with chronic phobia exhibit marked dependency needs, many would seem to benefit from *assertiveness training*, which would include modeling, role playing, behavior rehearsal, and *in vivo* homework assignments.

Psychotherapies. Individual psychotherapy can supplement behavior therapy by encouraging patients to enter the phobic situation, by addressing any secondary gain that might perpetuate their avoidant behaviors, and by exploring the symbolic meaning of the phobic object. Group psychotherapy may help patients redevelop social skills, foster assertiveness, reduce or spread dependency behaviors, and decrease loneliness. For some patients and their families, self-help groups for phobics are invaluable.

OBSESSIVE COMPULSIVE DISORDER

Being "obsessive" or "compulsive" is not the same as having *obsessions* or performing *compulsions*. The distinction between "si*ve*" and "si*on*" is more than two letters; it's the difference between a personality *style* with many adaptive features and a mental *disorder* that's often incapacitating.

Obsessions are persistent, disturbing, intrusive thoughts or impulses which the patient finds illogical, but irresistible. Unlike delusions, patients consider obsessions absurd, actively resist them, and are ambivalent about them. *Compulsions* are obsessions expressed in action. Obsessions and compulsions are methods for reducing anxiety. True obsessions and compulsions are the essential traits of obsessive compulsive disorder (OCD), a relatively uncommon disorder diagnosed in under 5% of psychiatric patients.

Clinical Presentation

DSM-III's diagnostic criteria for OCD (Table 12-6) illustrate the many ways obsessions and compulsions can present. Obsessions may appear as *ideas*— words, rhymes, or melodies that annoyingly interrupt normal thought and are often considered obscene or blasphemous by the patient; they may be *images*, which are usually violent or disgusting (e.g, children burning, rape); they may be *ruminations*—persistent, unproductive, inconclusive thinking that interferes with getting anything accomplished. Esoteric and unanswerable religious or philosophical questions will be dwelt on; doubt becomes paralyzing; decisions are never reached. The patient may also dread his obsessional

TABLE 12-6
DSM-III Criteria for Obsessive Compulsive Disorder*

A. Either obsessions or compulsions:

Obsessions: recurrent, persistent ideas, thoughts, images, or impulses that are ego-dystonic, i.e., they are not experienced as voluntarily produced, but rather as thoughts that invade consciousness and are experienced as senseless or repugnant. Attempts are made to ignore or suppress them.

Compulsions: Repetitive and seemingly purposeful behaviors that are performed according to certain rules or in a stereotyped fashion. The behavior is not an end in itself, but is designed to produce or prevent some future event or situation. However, either the activity is not connected in a realistic way with what it is designed to produce or prevent, or may be clearly excessive. The act is performed with a sense of subjective compulsion coupled with a desire to resist the compulsion (at least initially). The individual generally recognizes the senselessness of the behavior (this may not be true for young children) and does not derive pleasure from carrying out the activity, although it provides a release of tension.

B. The obsessions or compulsions are a significant source of distress to the individual or interfere with social or role functioning.

C. Not due to another mental disorder, such as Tourette's Disorder, Schizophrenia, Major Depression, or Organic Mental Disorder.

*DSM-III, p. 235.

impulses to hurt himself or others. Also common are *"magical ideas"* — that is, thought = deed (e.g., "Thinking badly of my father caused him to die.")

These obsessions readily produce *compulsions* — that is, obsessive rituals. Counting, cleaning, checking, and avoidance rituals are most common. A patient cannot leave his home without counting the first 10 brown cars that pass his door. Dinner can't be served until the patient washes his hands four times. Doors are locked five times; ovens closed six more. Pathological meticulousness drives everyone nuts. If cucumber slices are not exactly one-eighth of an inch thick, they're thrown away. Pencils must all face north, or no work proceeds.

Clinical Course

OCD usually arises in the early twenties, if not earlier, with the first psychiatric contact being around age 27, and the first hospitalization (if any), during the thirties. Although it tends to begin gradually, OCD may erupt suddenly after a severe psychosocial stressor. Over the long haul, symptoms may remit completely, fluctuate, or get worse. Whereas 5% to 10% of patients will be markedly incapacitated at some point, 60% to 80% will be asymptomatic or markedly improved one to five years after the initial diagnosis. The patient's outcome is not related to the content of his obsessions. Instead, patients with milder symptoms, briefer duration of symptoms, and higher premorbid functioning have better prognoses.

Complications

Depression is the most frequent complication for these patients, followed by a failure to marry and an inability to sustain interpersonal relations. Although going mad, being totally incapacitated, or permanently incarcerated are all common fears of the obsessional, these fears rarely materialize. Despite much suicidal thinking, less than 1% of these patients commit suicide.

Epidemiology

The lifetime prevalence of OCD in the general population is 2.5% (Table 12-1). The sexes are equally affected. OCD is more common among the higher educated, higher socioeconomic groups, and those with higher IQ scores — three interrelated factors.

Etiology and Pathogenesis

Psychologically, obsessions and compulsions arise in three phases: (a) an internally perceived dangerous impulse, (b) the threat of what would occur if this impulse is acted upon, and (c) the defenses to avert the threat. The most commonly used defenses are repression, reaction-formation, isolation, and undoing.

Psychopathology in general and obsessions in particular run in the families of obsessionals. Given that concordance rates for OCD are 80% and 50% among MZ and DZ twins, respectively, some genetic transmission may be involved.

Differential Diagnosis

Normal obsessions and compulsions are not resisted or considered ridiculous by the person having them. Avoiding sidewalk cracks and other compulsions are common during childhood, but kids don't mind them; they do mind OCD. Adults may feel their obsessive brooding, ruminations, and preoccupations are annoying and excessive, yet they usually think they're meaningful; not being fully ego-dystonic, these are not the true obsessions of OCD. Similarly, the obsessive and compulsive traits in *compulsive personality disorder* are ego-syntonic, whereas they are ego-dystonic in OCD; moreover, patients with compulsive personality disorder do not have true obsessions or compulsions. Neither are so-called *"compulsive" gambling, eating, and sexual behavior* true compulsions; the person enjoys doing them.

OCD should not be diagnosed when obsessions and compulsions arise in other disorders, especially *schizophrenic, affective, Tourette's*, and *organic disorders*. Schizophrenic delusions may resemble obsessions, but are usually ego-syntonic. Because *major depression* is often accompanied by ruminative, guilt-ridden, and self-critical obsessions, and since major depression and OCD both have episodic courses, differentiating the two can be difficult. In general, the diagnosis of OCD should be reserved for when a OCD clearly precedes a major depression.

Management and Treatment

Few patients with OCD enter treatment, and of the treatments that are available, none is impressive. Even the most optimistic of psychoanalytic writers are unenthusiastic about insight-oriented therapy. Similarly, biotherapies are equally unimpressive, with the possible exception of chlorimipramine, an experimental TCA with a specific antiobsessional effect. Yet even here, although chlorimipramine is helpful for alleviating compulsive rituals and coexisting depression, its beneficial actions cease when the drug is stopped.

At present, *in vivo* exposure, also known as "exposure therapy," is considered the most effective treatment for OCD. One to 30 sessions maintain improvement for an average of at least three years. Whereas relaxation exercises afford little benefit, self-exposure homework is critical to the treatment's success. Relatives operating as cotherapists can greatly facilitate this homework (Marks, 1981).

POST-TRAUMATIC STRESS DISORDER

Post-traumatic stress disorder (PTS) occurs after a severe and unusual stressor: a massive fire, hurricane, holocaust, rape, mugging, military combat, or terrorist bombing. The stressful events are usually more than "normal" bereavement, chronic illness, business losses, divorce, etc.

Hours or months following the stressor, the patient wavers between the two main stages of PTS: denial and intrusion. In the *denial* phase, "psychic numbing" dominates: The patient minimizes the significance of the stress, forgets it happened, feels detached from others, loses interest in life, displays constricted affect, daydreams, and abuses drugs or alcohol. After days or months, this denial blends into the *intrusion* phase: The patient is hyper-vigilant, "on edge," and flooded by intrusive images (e.g., illusions, hypno-gogic hallucinations, true hallucinations, nightmares, mental images). He can-not sleep or concentrate. He ruminates about the stressor, cries "without reason," shows emotional lability, and develops somatic anxiety. He fears going "crazy." The patient compulsively relives the stressful event and is often unable to think about anything else. In *DSM-III's* criteria for PTS (Table 12-7), the denial phase is generally covered in criterion C, and the intrusive phase in B and D.

Normal and pathological responses to traumatic events are usually, but not always, easy to distinguish. (See Figure 12-1.) Normal responders react with sadness or anxiety and find it harder to acknowledge their guilt, rage, or shame. They may undergo periods of denial and intrusion, which during the first two World Wars were called "shell-shock" and not considered patho-logical.

PTS disorder has two subtypes: acute and delayed (or chronic). The acute form arises within six months of the stressor and lasts for less than six months; the delayed form emerges at least six months past the trauma and continues for over six months. The delayed subtype has a worse prognosis. A study of 26 Vietnam and 10 World War II veterans with delayed PTS showed that *all* of them had an additional psychiatric disorder during their life—most often alcoholism and depression. PTS arose first in all but four of these cases. Two-thirds of these patients had family members with a psychiatric disorder, usual-ly substance abuse or an anxiety disorder. In both subtypes, encountering a circumstance similar to the original stressor often aggravates or rekindles symptoms. The intensity and duration of symptoms are usually less severe if the trauma is caused by nature (e.g., hurricane) than people (e.g., rape, torture).

TABLE 12-7
DSM-III Criteria for Post-traumatic Stress Disorder*

A. Existence of a recognizable stressor that would evoke significant symptoms of distress in almost everyone.

B. Reexperiencing of the trauma as evidenced by at least one of the following:

(1) recurrent and intrusive recollections of the event
(2) recurrent dreams of the event
(3) sudden acting or feeling as if the traumatic event were reoccurring, because of an association with an environmental or ideational stimulus

C. Numbing of responsiveness to or reduced involvement with the external world, beginning some time after the trauma, as shown by at least one of the following:

(1) markedly diminished interest in one or more significant activities
(2) feeling of detachment or estrangement from others
(3) constricted affect

D. At least two of the following symptoms that were not present before the trauma:

(1) hyperalertness or exaggerated startle response
(2) sleep disturbance
(3) guilt about surviving when others have not, or about behavior required for survival
(4) memory impairment or trouble concentrating
(5) avoidance of activities that arouse recollections of the traumatic event
(6) intensification of symptoms by exposure to events that symbolize or resemble the traumatic event

*DSM-III, p. 238.

After spending four years in a Korean POW camp, an ex-marine returned to his Indiana home. That was April. He felt fine until December, when seeing the first snow unleashed memories of being a POW. He broke into hot and cold flashes, arose screaming from nightmares (of cats with oriental eyes), stared blankly at food, stuttered, and was unable to study. Images of being yelled at, beaten, bleeding, and freezing in the snowy camp flooded his mind, despite all efforts to stop them. Four weeks of twice weekly psychotherapy uncovered considerable (irrational) bitterness at his fellow marines for not preventing his capture, and rage at his family and government for not being more sympathetic to his plight as a POW. After some family counseling, his delayed PTS ended.

PTS may go undiagnosed because (a) the patient doesn't report the initial trauma or the subsequent symptoms, (b) substance abuse masks the symptoms, or (c) his traumatic visual imagery is misattributed to schizophrenia, LSD intoxication or flashbacks, temporal lobe epilepsy, or a dissociative disorder. On the other hand, when PTS is, or may be, used to justify financial

FIGURE 12-1
Sequential Responses to Trauma*

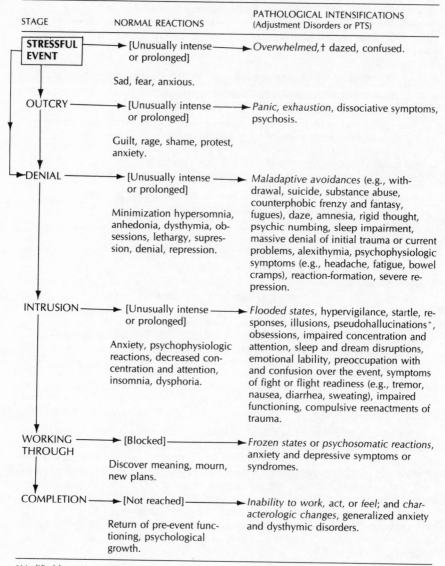

STAGE	NORMAL REACTIONS	PATHOLOGICAL INTENSIFICATIONS (Adjustment Disorders or PTS)
STRESSFUL EVENT	[Unusually intense or prolonged]	*Overwhelmed,†* dazed, confused.
	Sad, fear, anxious.	
OUTCRY	[Unusually intense or prolonged]	*Panic, exhaustion,* dissociative symptoms, psychosis.
	Guilt, rage, shame, protest, anxiety.	
DENIAL	[Unusually intense or prolonged]	*Maladaptive avoidances* (e.g., withdrawal, suicide, substance abuse, counterphobic frenzy and fantasy, fugues), daze, amnesia, rigid thought, psychic numbing, sleep impairment, massive denial of initial trauma or current problems, alexithymia, psychophysiologic symptoms (e.g., headache, fatigue, bowel cramps), reaction-formation, severe repression.
	Minimization hypersomnia, anhedonia, dysthymia, obsessions, lethargy, supression, denial, repression.	
INTRUSION	[Unusually intense or prolonged]	*Flooded states,* hypervigilance, startle, responses, illusions, pseudohallucinations+, obsessions, impaired concentration and attention, sleep and dream disruptions, emotional lability, preoccupation with and confusion over the event, symptoms of fight or flight readiness (e.g., tremor, nausea, diarrhea, sweating), impaired functioning, compulsive reenactments of trauma.
	Anxiety, psychophysiologic reactions, decreased concentration and attention, insomnia, dysphoria.	
WORKING THROUGH	[Blocked]	*Frozen states* or *psychosomatic reactions,* anxiety and depressive symptoms or syndromes.
	Discover meaning, mourn, new plans.	
COMPLETION	[Not reached]	*Inability to work, act,* or *feel;* and *characterologic changes,* generalized anxiety and dysthymic disorders.
	Return of pre-event functioning, psychological growth.	

*Modified from: Horowitz, M. J. (1985). Disasters and psychological responses to stress. *Psychiatric Annals,* 15, 161–167.

†Main features are italicized.

+Pseudohallucinations are fantasized reactions, in which people intensely experience something as real, despite intellectually knowing otherwise. These may be the "felt presence" of a dead granddad or an "out of body" experience.

compensation, malingering might be the diagnosis. Differentiating PTS from malingering can be difficult, partly because the patient may no longer be able to distinguish what's "for real" from what's fabricated. Nevertheless, deliberate malingerers rarely present with the specific diagnostic criteria in *DSM-III*, but rather display their own version of what they (or television) consider madness.

The usual treatment for PTS entails five to 16 weeks of psychotherapy, during which the therapist (in sequence) (a) gets a history from the patient, (b) gives the patient a realistic appraisal of the event and the patient's reactions to it, (c) identifies themes which the patient is still resisting, (d) interprets the patient's pathological defenses, (e) encourages active confrontation of feared topics and harsh memories, (f) begins discussing termination, (g) clarifies remaining conflicts or issues, (h) summarizes the gains in therapy, (i) alerts the patient to future concerns, and like this chapter (j) bids goodbye (Horowitz, 1985).

CHAPTER 13

Somatoform Disorders

DOCTOR: It's all in your head.
PATIENT: But it's *not* in my head; it's in my stomach.

What the doctor considers reassurance the patient considers an accusation. The doctor says nothing is *physically* wrong with the patient, but the patient hears that *nothing* is wrong. Yet there *is* something wrong: The patient's stomach hurts. Even when psychological factors produce the pain, for the patient that pain is just as real and just as miserable. When the physician ignores this, the patient feels accused of being a fake or crazy.

Patients with psychogenic physical symptoms frustrate professionals, because they don't have "real" illnesses, don't respond to conventional medical treatments, shop around for doctors, are stubbornly unpsychological, and dwell on physical complaints. The professional claims the patient's physical problems are psychogenic, and because the patient disagrees, he is, in essence, rejecting the professional's expertise.

Consequently, these patients receive lousy care. Not knowing what else to do and succumbing to the patients' demands for medication, physicians often prescribe drugs, expecting them not to work. These medications are frequently hypnosedatives and patients become addicted. (At least now they have a "real" problem!) These patients receive countless tests, procedures, and operations— mostly useless. In comparison to controls, these patients have three times the weight of body organs removed surgically (Cohen et al., 1953). Sensing, often correctly, that doctors consider them "crocks," these patients distrust doctors and don't follow their advice. Yet they also feel helplessly dependent on doctors, glom onto them, and further alienate them. These patients are in a "no-win situation": They distrust the very doctors they must rely on.

Fortunately, in recent years imprecise labeling and name-calling have been replaced by a relatively valid and helpful system for diagnosis. Also, there are now genuinely effective treatments for many of these conditions.

In *DSM-III, somatoform disorders* are mental disorders in which patients have physical symptoms for which there are no demonstrable organic findings or known physiological mechanisms; there must also be positive evidence, or at least a strong presumption, that the symptoms are related to psychological factors. This conception insists that the diagnosis of somatoform disorder requires more than merely the *absence* of a reasonable physical explanation, but the *presence* of psychological evidence, such as a definite temporal and causal relationship between the occurrence of a psychosocial stress and the emergence of a somatic symptom. This definition underscores that somatoform disorders have no *known* organic basis, *not* that they have no physical basis. These underlying physiologic mechanisms may yet to be discovered, or the diagnostic technology to detect already known ones is lacking.

For example, a 40-year-old lawyer had seven years of episodic, unexpected "orgastic feelings running up and down my legs." After two normal EEGs and three psychotherapies "to resolve psychosexual conflicts," a fine metal electrode was painlessly inserted into his thalamus and revealed that he'd been having sensory seizures. Anticonvulsant medications cured his "psychosexual conflicts."

Somatoform disorders differ from three other psychiatric conditions which generate symptoms resembling physical illness. In *malingering* and *factitious disorders*, patients deliberately make and fake symptoms, whereas in somatoform disorders symptoms are produced involuntarily. In *psychological factors affecting physical condition*, often called "psychosomatic disorders," emotional factors trigger, aggravate, or exacerbate a clearly existing medical condition through a known pathophysiologic mechanism, whereas in most somatoform disorders there is no identifiable organic disease nor any known pathophysiologic mechanism to account for the patient's symptoms.

DSM-III describes four major somatoform disorders: (a) conversion disorder, (b) psychogenic pain disorder, (c) somatization disorder, and (d) hypochondriasis.

CONVERSION DISORDER

Clinical Presentation

The cardinal feature of a conversion disorder is an involuntary loss, or alteration, of a function, which, although resembling a physical disorder, appears to arise from psychological mechanisms. Conversion disorders usually consist of a single neurological symptom (e.g., blindness, paralysis). Also common are tunnel vision, seizures, coordination disturbances, akinesia, dyskinesia, anosmia (no smell), anesthesia, and paresthesias. A single, non-neurological, symptom may arise, such as pseudocyesis (i.e., false pregnancy). By *DSM-III* criteria (Table 13-1), if pain is the only symptom, the diagnosis is psychogenic pain disorder; if the only disturbance is psychosexual, a psychosexual disorder is diagnosed.

The strong psychological evidence required for the diagnosis can assume various forms. The conversion symptom may have symbolic meaning to the patient: For example, pseudocyesis may represent a fear of, and wish for, pregnancy. "Psychogenic vomiting" may symbolize revulsion or disgust. Conversion symptoms may arise from unconscious identification. For instance, a writer developed a limp after his "Great American Novel" was rejected. Why a limp? It snowed on the day he learned of the rejection, which unlocked a repressed childhood trauma of watching a truck turn over on snow and crush his mother's leg. "Glove anesthesia," in which sensation is felt to stop evenly at the wrist, is neurologically impossible (unless one's wrist is slashed!), but

TABLE 13-1
DSM-III Criteria for Conversion Disorder*

A. The predominant disturbance is a loss of or alteration in physical functioning suggesting a physical disorder.

B. Psychological factors are judged to be etiologically involved in the symptom, as evidenced by one of the following:

   (1) there is a temporal relationship between an environmental stimulus that is apparently related to a psychological conflict or need and the initiation or exacerbation of the symptom
   (2) the symptom enables the individual to avoid some activity that is noxious to him or her
   (3) the symptom enables the individual to get support from the environment that otherwise might not be forthcoming.

C. It has been determined that the symptom is *not* under voluntary control.

D. The symptom cannot, after appropriate investigation, be explained by a known physical disorder or pathophysiological mechanism.

E. The symptom is not limited to pain or to a disturbance in sexual functioning.

F. Not due to Somatization Disorder or Schizophrenia.

---

*DSM-III, p. 247.

it conforms to the patient's conception of the nervous system. (Remember Frankenstein?)

Soon after the swine-flu vaccine was found to produce Guillain-Barré syndrome, an ascending paralysis *arising* from the feet, the author saw three cases of "Guillain-Barré" in the emergency room: These patients had a "paralysis," but they misread the newspapers: Their "paralysis" spread *downward*!

Although these patients are often said to have histrionic personalities, many do not. They are also known for displaying "la belle indifference"—a nonchalance to their impairment, which has the paradoxical effect of making the impairment more noticeable. This trait, however, occurs in many other patients and is of little diagnostic value.

Conversion symptoms may begin at any age, but usually during adolescence and early adulthood. An acute psychosocial stressor generally triggers the symptom, which will arise suddenly, last for several days or weeks, and then stop abruptly. Conversion symptoms can persist for months or years. When this occurs, organic pathology must be reevaluated, since many of these patients turn out to have neurological disease. Long-term conversion symptoms may cause disuse atrophy and muscle contractures. "Psychological contractures" also occur: Patients become so mired in the sick role that after a conversion symptom disappears, work and social functioning may remain impaired.

Epidemiology

Conversion disorder presents far less today than during Freud's time; back then it mainly afflicted women. Today, it appears mostly around battlefronts and in military hospitals; its sex distribution is now equal. Globus hystericus (i.e., a discomfort in swallowing) is more common in female globi. Conversion symptoms are reported to be twice as prevalent among blacks as among whites, and more common in lower socioeconomic classes.

Etiology and Pathogenesis

Conversion symptom affords the patient either *primary gain*—that is, it *protects* him from experiencing a painful underlying affect—or *secondary gain*—that is, it *gratifies* him by enabling him to receive concern and support from others. For example, a nurse, who cared for her dying father, became "blind" immediately after his death. The psychological evidence for a conversion disorder was the temporal relation between the death and the symptom's onset. The primary gain from this "blindness" was that it prevented her from seeing her father dead; the secondary gain was the added sympathy she would receive. Moreover, because she interpreted her father's death as a profoundly personal/professional failure, her "blindness" unconsciously relieved her of guilt (primary gain) and protected her from others' blame (secondary gain).

Clinicians should be careful in deciding what constitutes psychological evidence. Because environmental stressors occur all the time, only those of obviously substantial effect on the patient should qualify. Furthermore, if clinicians want to find something, almost anything can have unconscious significance. Consider psychogenic vomiting: If the reader tries he surely can find something in his psyche to explain why he has psychogenic vomiting.

Differential Diagnosis

Conversion disorder typically involves one, usually neurological symptom, whereas other *somatoform disorders* present with many symptoms in numerous organ systems. Patients with conversion disorders minimize their problems; those with other somatoform disorders dramatize them. Conversion disorders arise suddenly, whereas *somatization disorder* and *hypochondriasis* emerge gradually. Unlike conversion disorders, there is no loss of function in hypochondriasis.

Physical disorders, especially those with vague, episodic, and hard-to-document symptoms, must be considered, such as *multiple sclerosis* and *systemic lupus erythematosus*. Since it is common for neurological disorders to be uncovered a full decade after symptoms first present, *all* patients with a long-standing conversion symptom should be evaluated *repeatedly* for an underlying organic condition.

Management and Treatment

Because many conversion symptoms spontaneously disappear within a few weeks to months of their onset, early treatment may be unnecessary. Once conversion symptoms become entrenched, however, they're tough to treat. Among 1,000 patients at the Columbia Psychoanalytic Center—half treated by psychoanalysis and half by psychoanalytic psychotherapy—11% had conversion symptoms at the start of treatment and 7% at the end of treatment (Weber et al., 1967). Hardly impressive! Even the quick results ascribed to hypnosis are deceptive, since conversion symptoms usually return within months (Ochitill, 1982).

PSYCHOGENIC PAIN DISORDER

Eighty percent of all patients who consult physicians do so for pain-related problems. Low back pain alone disables 7 million Americans and prompts more than 8 million doctor visits a year. In 1980, disability payments for chronic pain were $10 billion. What percent of these patients have a psychogenic pain disorder is unknown.

Not all patients with psychogenic pain have a psychogenic pain *disorder*. For instance, among patients hospitalized to a three-week program for chronic pain, 32% had a major depression, 41% abused alcohol, and over half had their disorder before their chronic pain developed (Katon et al., 1985). In *DSM-III*, psychogenic pain disorder is not diagnosed if the pain is due to another mental disorder.

Clinical Presentation

Psychogenic pain disorder is characterized by a predominant complaint of pain whose existence or severity cannot be medically explained and appears to have been produced to a significant extent by psychological factors. Table 13-2 lists *DSM-III*'s criteria for psychogenic pain disorder. The following case is typical.

Carol, a 45-year-old high school teacher, was standing outside her classroom when three students began taunting her with lewd remarks. When she objected, one picked her up, wheeled her around, and threw her to the ground, breaking her left arm and causing numerous facial contusions. The next day Carol developed sharp pains radiating up her neck and both arms, across her chest, and toward her pelvis. After a month, her arm and face mended, but her radiating pains continued, even though no medical explanation could account for this pain. Although medically approved to return to work and eager to do so—she needed the money—Carol's pain kept her home. She then sued the school for not protecting its teachers. Carol frequently expressed her rage about these students, not just for hurting her, but especially because of their sexual innuendos.

On psychiatric examination, Carol wore a neck brace and made sure one noticed how slowly she sat down. While her flitting forefinger pointed to every radiating pain in her body, she said, "The pain just zaps you like shock waves. It attacks your entire body. If I touch anything, it triggers another shooting pain." (She missed the pun.) Initially, she denied any psychiatric problems, but later admitted that for months before her injury, her boyfriend had been "trying real hard to get me into the sack, and when I refused he'd always call me a prude." However, since her pains developed, "He's been a prince: He's stopped pushing me sexually and been very considerate."

Carol's case raises three questions: First, is there sufficient physical evidence to explain her pain. No. Second, is she faking the pain? Probably not. As with many of these patients, possible compensation suggests malingering, but the apparent gen-

TABLE 13-2
DSM-III* Criteria for Psychogenic Pain Disorder

A. Severe and prolonged pain is the predominant disturbance.

B. The pain presented as a symptom is inconsistent with the anatomic distribution of the nervous system; after extensive evaluation, no organic pathology or pathophysiological mechanism can be found to account for the pain; or, when there is some related organic pathology, the complaint of pain is grossly in excess of what would be expected from the physical findings.

C. Psychological factors are judged to be etiologically involved in the pain, as evidenced by at least one of the following:

   (1) a temporal relationship between an environmental stimulus that is apparently related to a psychological conflict or need and the initiation or exacerbation of the pain
   (2) the pain's enabling the individual to avoid some activity that is noxious to him or her
   (3) the pain's enabling the individual to get support from the environment that otherwise might not be forthcoming

D. Not due to another mental disorder.

DSM-III, p. 249.

uineness of her pain and her eagerness to return to work suggest otherwise. Third, is there psychological evidence to account for her pain? Yes. Her pain affords the secondary gain of cooling her "oversexed" boyfriend while eliciting his support and affection. There is also temporal and psychodynamic evidence: When she was having sexual conflicts with her boyfriend, the students' sexual insults especially hit below the belt, just where her pains were shooting. Therefore, the most likely diagnosis was psychogenic pain disorder. With the treatment described below, her pain gradually disappeared in three months and she returned to school.

Psychogenic pain disorder may arise anytime in life, most often during adolescence and young adulthood. Symptoms are usually initiated by an acute stressor, erupt suddenly, intensify over the next several days or weeks, and subside when the acute stressor is gone. Less often, (presumably because of secondary gain), the pain persists long after the acute stressor, waxes and wanes for months or years, worsens under stress, and may continue forever. These patients "doctor-shop," become dysthymic, abuse analgesics, receive unnecessary surgery and tests, get stuck in the sick role, restrict social and occupational functioning — some are bed-ridden for years — and develop secondary muscle spasms and pins-and-needles sensations around painful areas.

Epidemiology

In the absence of proper epidemiologic study, it appears that psychogenic pain disorder primarily afflicts women and is common in clinical practice. However, surveys might find that after other causes of psychogenic pain (e.g., major depression) are eliminated, psychogenic pain disorders may be less frequent.

Etiology and Pathogenesis

In Katon et al.'s (1985) study of hospitalized patients with all types of chronic pain, about 60% had a first-degree relative with chronic pain, 38% with alcohol misuse, and 30% with an affective disorder. These figures may be high, but, as many others believe, they suggest a link — psychological or biological — between chronic pain, alcoholism, and depression. That patients with chronic pain dramatically improve with antidepressants fuels the old speculation that chronic pain is a "depressive-equivalent." These patients may repress intense affects and conflicts, or their cognition or perception of internal feeling states may be greatly distorted. Given that pain runs in families, identification may also play an etiological role for some patients.

Differential Diagnosis

The *dramatic presentation of organic pain* may appear excessive, but this alone does not qualify as a psychogenic pain disorder. Dramatic presentations may reflect a person's normal or cultural style of communicating. To qualify as a psychogenic pain disorder, pain must be prolonged, severe, and relate etiologically to psychological factors. Patients with psychogenic pain disorder may, or may not, have genuine organic disease, but unlike those with "tension headaches," there is no known psychophysiologic mechanism to account for the pain. If a patient's pain is produced by *another mental disorder*, psychogenic pain disorder is not diagnosed.

Management and Treatment

Acute pain management. Among the worst mistakes professionals make is giving *insufficient* narcotics to hospitalized medical or surgical patients in acute pain. Marks and Sachar (1973) found that inadequate doses of narcotics caused moderate to severe distress in 73% of these patients. Studies have replicated this finding, even after staff received lectures on the subject (Perry, 1984). The main reasons (rationalizations) doctors and nurses give for underusing narcotics is a fear of "addicting" and "overdosing" patients, even though both are rare with such patients. Another common excuse is that "patients don't really hurt *that* much." Since nobody can know how much pain another person feels, it's never clear how patients are supposed to *prove* the extent of their pain. Professionals often point to the patient's *demanding* narcotics as evidence of his being "manipulative." Nonsense. Patients might just want narcotics because they're in pain! And even if the doctor or nurse is "manipulated," that's hardly a calamity, for one hopes the professional's ego will survive.

Next to underusing narcotics, the next biggest error is to dispense them "as needed" instead of on a regular schedule (e.g., every four or six hours). When given "as needed" (or p.r.n.), the drug invariably arrives late (like everything else in a normal hospital) and the patient may become conditioned to associate complaining of pain with getting a drug-induced euphoria. Thus, for hospitalized medical/surgical patients in acute pain, narcotics should be given freely and on a regular schedule, *without* the patient having to ask (or beg) for them.

Chronic pain management. There are few studies of psychogenic pain disorder *per se*, but many of chronic pain in general. Research demonstrates that patients having all kinds of chronic pain clearly benefit from antidepressants, behavior therapy, and supportive group therapy. Individual psychotherapy seems less useful. These treatments are effective (or ineffective) whether or not the patient's pain has a physical basis.

Blumer and Heilbronn (1984) reported that of 1,000 patients with chronic pain, only 11% did not improve with TCAs; of those who did, 52% displayed "moderate improvement" and 37% showed "solid improvement." Women were helped more than men. In contrast, benzodiazepines and ECT afforded little benefit. Thus, any patient with chronic pain deserves a trial on tricyclic antidepressants.

Pain clinics employ a multidisciplinary team to provide antidepressants, behavior therapy, and group psychotherapy. In a typical program, Fordyce et al. (1973) treated 36 patients whose pain lasted an average of seven years and who did not improve from conventional medical treatments. Patients were hospitalized one to three months and continued as outpatients for another three weeks. The program's aims and methods were: (a) To decrease the patient's use of medication, drugs were given at regular intervals and not "on demand"; over time, drugs were tapered. (b) To diminish pain behavior, the staff praised patients for conducting nonpain-related activities; when patients exhibited pain-related behavior (e.g., not going to movies on account of pain), staff ignored the patient. (c) To increase functioning, patients were rewarded for participating in a tailored program of gradually increasing physical activity. Rest would be contingent on performing activity, not on complaining of pain. (d) To maintain the patient's gains after discharge, the staff trained relatives to reinforce nonpain, instead of pain, behaviors.

At discharge, there was a 50% increase in time spent sitting, standing, walking, and exercising; most patients were taking little or no medication. At other pain centers, 60% to 80% of patients have shown similar gains in functional activity, decreased medication, and improved quality of life for at least three to five years. These improvements occurred regardless of whether patients were still in pain. What's more, most patients not only *talked* less about pain, they *experienced* less pain (Ochitill, 1982).

Group therapy for inpatients hasn't been systematically studied, but with outpatients it reduces their perception of pain and their use of medication; dysthymia is alleviated and employment increases. These groups provide support, ventilation, education about pain mechanisms, relaxation techniques to reduce the experience of pain, and reinforcement of nonpain behaviors.

SOMATIZATION DISORDER

Clinical Presentation

Somatization disorder — also named "Briquet's syndrome" after the French physician who first described it in 1859 — is a chronic condition featuring multiple, unexplained, somatic symptoms in numerous organ systems. Vomiting, aphonia (inability to produce sounds), painful limbs, muscle weakness, dizziness, painful menstruation, burning sensation in sex organs, paralyses, and conversion symptoms are common.

DSM-III lists 37 symptoms from which women must have 14 and men 12 to qualify for somatization disorder. (*DSM-III-R* may change this number to 13 for both sexes.) Table 13-3 lists *DSM-III*'s criteria for somatization disorder and gives a *rough* idea of how frequently each symptom occurs. Because remembering 37 symptoms is not easy, for clinical convenience Othmer and DeSouza (1985) found that any two out of seven specific symptoms predicted the correct diagnosis of somatization disorder in 80% to 90% of cases; they incorporated this finding into the screening test outlined on Table 13-4.

Everyone has physical symptoms, but they mostly ignore them. Not so for patients with somatization disorder. For every ache and pain they will see a doctor, want a complete workup, and expect a prescription. (Any patient who enters a doctor's office schlepping three dozen medications has a somatization disorder till proven otherwise.) These patients don't just present symptoms, the dramatize them: "I'm puking like a volcano." "I almost fainted in front of a subway." "I'm breathing so hard, I'm going to suffocate." Hyperbole is their norm: Headaches aren't headaches, they're "the worst headaches ever." Their histories are vague; it's never clear when their symptoms began, why they seek help now, and what they want. On repeated tellings, symptoms "change": One day a backache is dull, the next day it's sharp; one day it began 12 months ago, on the next visit it started a month ago. Symptoms never end; as soon as the clinician thinks he's heard them all, another pops up. These

TABLE 13-3
***DSM-III* Criteria for Somatization Disorder* and the Frequency of Complaints†**

A. A history of physical symptoms of several years' duration beginning before the age of 30.

B. Complaints of at least 14 symptoms for women and 12 for men, from the 37 symptoms listed below. To count a symptom as present the individual must report that the symptom caused him or her to take medicine (other than aspirin), alter his or her life pattern, or see a physician. The symptoms, in the judgment of the clinician, are not adequately explained by physical disorder or physical injury, and are not side effects of medication, drugs or alcohol. The clinician need not be convinced that the symptom was actually present, e.g., that the individual actually vomited throughout her entire pregnancy; report of the symptom by the individual is sufficient.

1. *Sickly*: Believes that he or she has been sickly for a good part of his or her life [44] +.

Conversion or pseudoneurological symptoms:

2. difficulty swallowing [49]	3. loss of voice (aphonia) [32]
4. deafness [8]	5. double vision [53]
6. blurred vision [71]	7. blindness [21]
8. fainting [50] or loss of consciousness [30]	9. memory loss [29]
	10. seizures or convulsions [19]
11. trouble walking [62]	12. paralysis [21]
13. urinary retention [8] or difficulty urinating [23]	14. MUSCLE WEAKNESS [84]

Gastrointestinal symptoms:

15. ABDOMINAL PAIN [77]	16. NAUSEA [77]
17. vomiting spells (other than during pregnancy) [35]	18. bloating (gassy) [64]
19. intolerance (e.g., gets sick) of a variety of foods [50]	20. diarrhea [40]

(continued)

histrionics should not mislead clinicians into underestimating their genuine discomfort.

Somatization disorder usually arises during adolescence, but always before age 30. Its course is fluctuating, lifelong, and exacerbated by environmental stressors—a fact deemed irrelevant or accusatory by the patient. Hardly a year passes without intense discomfort and medical treatment. Frequent complications are substance abuse, excessive laboratory tests and surgery, work and social impairment, chronic demoralization, dysthymia, anxiety, marital problems, and divorce. The disorder is important to diagnosis if only to reduce these complications. These patients commonly attempt suicide, but rarely commit it.

TABLE 13-3
(Continued)

Female reproductive symptoms: Judged by the individual as occurring more frequently or severely than in most women:

21. painful menstruation [68]
23. excessive bleeding [50]
24. menstrual irregularity [56]

22. severe vomiting throughout pregnancy [30] or causing hospitalization during pregnancy.

Psychosexual symptoms: For the major part of the individual's life after opportunities for sexual activity:

25. sexual indifference [67]
27. pain during intercourse [65]

26. lack of pleasure during intercourse [23]

Pain:

28. BACK [84]
30. extremities [67]

32. pain on urination [44]

29. joints [74]
31. genital area (other than during intercourse) [30]

33. other pain (other than headaches) [36]

Cardiopulmonary symptoms:

34. Shortness of breath [74]
36. CHEST PAIN [80]

35. Palpitations [72]
37. DIZZINESS [88]

---

*Modified from *DSM-III*, pp. 243–244; the same symptoms are listed as in *DSM-III*, but their order has been slightly rearranged.

†Data pooled from DeSouza, C., & Othmer, E. (1984). Somatization disorder and Briquet's syndrome: An assessment of their diagnostic concordance. *Archives of General Psychiatry, 41*, 334–336; Perley, M., & Guze, S. B. (1962). Hysteria—the stability and usefulness of clinical criteria. *New England Journal of Medicine, 266*, 421–426.

+Figures in brackets are percent of patients with somatization disorder that have the symptom. The most frequently occurring symptoms are capitalized.

Epidemiology

Somatization disorders occur almost exclusively in women. Beyond this, epidemiologic data for this disorder are sketchy and inconsistent. The ECA found its prevalence in the general population to be 0.1%. *DSM-III* says it affects 1% of the general female population. Its frequency among general psychiatric patients is reported to range from 1.1% to 6.0%, whereas among medical/surgical patients referred for psychiatric consultation, it may be as high as 14%. It occurs more among blacks, lower socioeconomic groups, and less formally educated people—three interrelated groups.

TABLE 13-4
Screening Test for Somatization Disorder*

MNEMONIC	SYMPTOM	ORGAN SYSTEM
S omatization	Shortness of Breath	Respiratory
D isorder	Dysmenorrhea	Female Reproductive
B esets	Burning in sex organs	Psychosexual
L adies	Lump in throat	Pseudoneurological
A nd	Amnesia	Pseudoneurological
V exes	Vomiting	Gastrointestinal
P hysicians	Painful extremities	Skeletal muscle

Questions used to assess the presence of the seven symptoms of the screening test for somatization disorder:

S. Have you ever had trouble breathing?
D. Have you ever had frequent trouble with menstrual cramps?
B. Have you ever had burning sensations in your sexual organs, mouth, or rectum?
L. Have you ever had difficulties swallowing or had an uncomfortable lump in your throat that stayed with you for at least an hour?
A. Have you ever found that you could not remember what you had been doing for hours or days at a time? (If yes) Did this happen even though you had not been drinking or taking drugs?
V. Have you ever had trouble from frequent vomiting?
P. Have you ever had frequent pain in your fingers or toes?

If any two of the above seven questions are answered affirmatively, this *screening* test is positive; a positive test simply means the patient *might* have a somatization disorder. To confirm the diagnosis, the patient should meet *DSM-III*'s criteria for somatization disorder (Table 13-2).

*This table is adapted from Othmer, E., & DeSouza, C. (1985). A screening test for somatization disorder (hysteria). *American Journal of Psychiatry, 142*, 1146–1149.

Etiology and Pathogenesis

About 20% of first-degree female relatives of these patients will have a somatization disorder—that's roughly 20 times the normal frequency for women in the general population. Somatization disorder appears to be genetically linked to antisocial personality disorder and alcoholism.

Family studies reveal a high prevalence of antisocial personality disorder and alcoholism among the *male* relatives of somatization patients. Conversely, there's an increased prevalence of somatization disorder among the *female* relatives of convicted male felons. Many delinquent girls develop somatization disorder as adults, and adult female felons have an increased prevalence of medical contacts (Goodwin & Guze, 1984).

Somatization is often considered a defense mechanism, in which the patient unconsciously avoids painful affects by experiencing physical discomfort. Supposedly, in somatization disorder the central defense mechanism is somatization, and the painful affect, depression. Indeed, alexithymia has been especially associated with somatization disorder. However, not only does alexithymia commonly occur in other disorders, but a recent linguistic analysis of the affect and thought of patients with depression and somatization disorders revealed the latter were not defending against depressive feelings, but were more troubled by confused and negative self-identities (Oxman et al., 1985).

Differential Diagnosis

Hypochondriasis and somatization disorder share many features, including an early and gradual onset. Yet in somatization disorder patients focus on *symptoms* of disease, whereas in hypochondriasis they are preoccupied with a *fear* of disease. Hypochondriasis may appear in somatization disorder, but not as the dominant symptom.

Dysthymic and *generalized anxiety disorders* are not diagnosed in patients with somatization disorder, since the latter often present with anxiety and dysthymia. On the other hand, *major depression, schizophrenia* and *panic disorder* may be diagnosed concurrently with somatization disorder if both conditions distinctly exist; such dual diagnoses, however, are unusual. Somatic delusions are common in major depression and schizophrenia; their presence rules out somatoform disorder. *Masked depression* mimics somatization disorder and hypochondriasis, but has biological signs of depression, more distinct and episodic periods of illness, and more impaired social functioning. In panic disorder, chest pain, difficulty breathing, and other somatic fears arise and subside abruptly, whereas in somatization disorder physical complaints ebb, flow, and linger.

Management and Treatment

Since most of these patients are leery of psychiatry, they rely on nonpsychiatric, especially primary-care, physicians. The doctor can greatly help these patients if he remembers to do the following: (a) Repeatedly check his annoyance with these patients. Since somatization disorders are chronic, lifelong conditions, being angry at patients for complaining about symptoms is akin to being angry at diabetics for having uncooperative blood sugars. (b) The prime goal of treatment is not to eliminate the physical complaints, but to improve her functioning. (c) The physician should avoid raising false hopes or promises, such as, "You're going to feel completely better." (d) Protect the patient from needless laboratory tests, medical treatments, and surgical interventions.

(e) Relate to the patient "as she is": Try changing her personality and the only change will be one less patient. (f) Offer positive reinforcement for "noncomplaining behaviors," ignore complaining behaviors, and teach the family do likewise.

More specifically, on her first visit to the doctor, a patient with somatization disorder should receive a thorough history and physical. Assuming this examination is "negative," the doctor should tell her, "I'm pleased there is nothing *seriously* wrong with you, but I know you're experiencing considerable discomfort. So I want to follow you carefully and see you in a week." An appointment is made whether or not the patient has symptoms; the patient doesn't "*have*" to get sick to see the doctor. Next week, the doctor conducts a briefer exam, repeats the same message, and schedules another appointment. Each week, the doctor devotes his full attention to the patient for 15 minutes. He tells her how marvelously she's doing despite her symptoms, lauds her planned trip to Arizona, restates that she doesn't have cancer and that nothing else is seriously wrong. Eventually, the patient not only *complains* less about symptoms, but actually *experiences* fewer symptoms.

HYPOCHONDRIASIS

Clinical Presentation

Hypochondriasis is an overwhelming, persistent, preoccupation with physical symptoms based on unrealistically ominous interpretations of physical signs or sensations. (The Greeks believed the seat of these troubles was the *hypochondrion*, the area between the rib cage and the navel.) Hypochondriacs usually have a physical disease, but what distinguishes them is their unrealistic and dire interpretation of it. The somatization patient *worries* about symptoms, whereas the hypochondriac *fears* them. The somatization patient who coughs complains that it hurts; the hypochondriac who coughs thinks he has lung cancer. To the hypochondriac, a skipped heart beat is a heart attack, a headache, a brain tumor. Hypochondriacs usually present with many symptoms in many organ systems, but they may have with a single preoccupation, as does the "cardiac neurotic." *DSM-III*'s criteria for hypochondriasis are listed in Table 13-5.

Hypochondriasis affects the sexes equally, usually begins during youth, but often arises in men during their thirties and in women during their forties. Its severity fluctuates over time and it rarely stops completely or permanently. Hypochondriasis may, or may not, impair occupational and social functioning; it almost always strains them. Needless operations and tests occur.

TABLE 13-5
DSM-III **Criteria for Hypochondriasis***

A. The predominant disturbance is an unrealistic interpretation of physical signs or sensations as abnormal, leading to preoccupation with the fear or belief of having a serious disease.

B. Thorough physical examination does not support the diagnosis of any physical disorder that can account for the physical signs or sensations or for the individual's unrealistic interpretation of them.

C. The unrealistic fear or belief of having a disease persists despite medical reassurance and causes impairment in social or occupational functioning.

D. Not due to other mental disorder such as Schizophrenia, Affective Disorder, or Somatization Disorder.

*DSM-III, p. 251

Etiology and Pathogenesis

Little is known about hypochondriasis' etiology, but it probably arises for a number of reasons: For some patients, secondary gain is crucial; for others it may be a defense against low self-esteem or a fear of being defective; for still others, introjection may be paramount — they "prefer" punishing themselves over being angry at others. Given the higher incidence of painful injuries and diseases among close relatives of hypochondriacs, identification may be a key influence on some patients.

Differential Diagnosis

Of prime concern is *true organic disease*, since, like everybody else, hypochondriacs get sick. A friend of the author's, a woman in her early thirties with hypochondriasis, was unmercifully teased by friends until she had breast cancer and died. Commonly overlooked illnesses are those which are in their early stages, affect numerous organ systems (e.g., lupus), or present with elusive symptoms (e.g., multiple sclerosis). Hypochondriasis is diagnosed in the presence of true organic illness, if the patient exaggerates the danger of the illness or is unduly preoccupied with it.

Somatic delusions are common in *schizophrenia* and *major depression with psychotic features*, but in hypochondriasis, the patient will entertain the possibility that another interpretation of his symptoms might be valid. Hypochondriasis should not be diagnosed in psychotic patients. Somatic concerns also occur in *dysthymic, major depressive, somatization, obsessive compul-*

sive, and *panic disorders*, but a dread or misinterpretation of disease is not their central feature.

Management and Treatment

Investigations on treating hypochondriasis are few, and rarely controlled. Although hypnosedatives diminish somatic symptoms in anxious patients and TCAs diminish somatic complaints in depression, most clinicians find that neither drug lessens hypochondriasis.

In Kellner's (1982a) literature review, the beneficial interventions for hypochondriasis were *repeatedly* (a) giving the facts about the patient's difficulties, (b) clarifying the difference between pain and the *experience* of pain, (c) describing how emotions affect the *perception* of physical sensations (e.g., "real" pain is experienced as more painful when a person is anxious than when he's calm), (d) demonstrating how selective attention and suggestion contribute to overestimating a symptom's seriousness, (e) stressing that "life can go on" despite physical symptoms, (f) conveying acceptance of the patient and empathy for his hypochondriasis, and (g) applying the approach described on pp. 241–242 for treating somatization disorder. Several studies indicate that these strategies yield complete or vast improvement in roughly 75% of hypochondriacs for six months to three years, and for over three years in a third of the patients. In view of the generally unfavorable prognosis of this condition, these results are striking. Even if these findings reflect nothing more than a more invested physician, if that works, it's nothing to sneeze at.

CHAPTER 14

Dissociative Disorders

How COME DISSOCIATIVE disorders, although uncommon, are of such uncommon interest? *Sybil, The Three Faces of Eve, The Boston Strangler*, and (if brainwashed) Patty Hearst fascinate many because they are very ordinary individuals who have made an extraordinary transformation. And if these people can become completely different people, then couldn't we? If such strangeness can lurk beneath them, why not within us?

Dissociative states refer to the "splitting off" from conscious awareness of some ordinarily familiar information, emotion, or mental function. In other words, selected mental contents are removed, or dissociated, from conscious experience, but continue to produce motor or sensory effects. In a dissociative state the person may appear unconscious and focus selectively on the environment (e.g., sleepwalking, trance), act bizarrely (e.g., running "amok," going "berserk"), lose his identity and wander away from home (e.g., fugue), lose memory without wandering away from home (e.g., amnesia), assume an alien identity (e.g., multiple personality, witchcraft, possession), or be brainwashed.

Some dissociative states are not pathological, and to some extent, some are highly adaptive. We all forget things. We all switch states of consciousness, from meditating to sleeping to working to daydreaming; to do so, sets of memory and attitudes must also switch. Dissociation also may occur in crystal gazing, intense prayer, "mass hysteria," religious revivals and healing ceremonies (e.g., Holy Spirit possession, glossolalia ["speaking in tongues"]), and hypnosis.

Most dissociative states are set off by a psychosocial trigger, arise suddenly, and end abruptly. During normal intervals, people are partly or totally amnestic for their dissociative episodes. For example, in *posthypnotic suggestion*, the hypnotist may instruct a hypnotized subject, "After you awake, when I scratch my head, you'll sing 'God Save the Queen,' but not remember that I told you to." Ten minutes after the subject awakens, the hypnotist scratches and the subject wails "God Save the Queen." Ask why he's singing and he may confess he doesn't know or he may confabulate: "I thought people would like the music."

DSM-III defines dissociative disorders as conditions whose "essential feature is a sudden, temporary alteration in the normally integrative functions of consciousness, identity, or motor behavior" (p. 253). The type of alteration dictates the type of dissociative disorder: In *psychogenic amnesia*, consciousness is altered and significant personal events forgotten. In *psychogenic fugue*, identity and motor behavior are altered; the patient unexpectedly travels far from home, assumes a new identity, and forgets his old one. In *multiple personality*, numerous identities arise. In *depersonalization disorder*, the patient feels that part of his identity—namely, his own reality—is lost. Table 14-1 presents *DSM-III*'s criteria for these disorders. There's also a residual category, *atypical dissociative disorder*, which covers "brainwashing" and thought reform, and what *DSM-III-R* will call a *trance/possession disorder*.[1]

Clinical Presentations

Psychogenic amnesia. These patients are suddenly unable to remember significant personal information, which is far in excess of ordinary forgetfulness. Patients know they've forgotten something, but don't know what, nor do they seem to care. Feeling perplexed, disoriented, and purposeless, they're often picked up by police for being lost or for wandering aimlessly. During their amnesia, patients are able to perform relatively simple tasks (e.g., taking a bus), and less often, more complicated ones (e.g., shopping, cooking).

Most often the patient's amnesia is *localized* to several hours during and after a highly disturbing event, but it may be *generalized* for an entire life. Although most amnesias are total, they may be *selective* for only some events, usually the most traumatic. Rare is *continuous* amnesia, wherein patients forget everything from the time of the stress until the present.

An example of localized amnesia is the case of a photojournalist in Vietnam who, confused and bewildered, strolled into the office of Army intelligence. He had no recollection of the past three days, but his camera did. It showed photographs of a

---

[1]*Sleepwalking* (or somnambulism) is another dissociative state, but in *DSM-III-R* is grouped with sleep disorders.

TABLE 14-1
DSM-III* Criteria for Dissociative Disorders

PSYCHOGENIC AMNESIA

A. Sudden inability to recall important personal information that is too extensive to be explained by ordinary forgetfulness.

B. The disturbance is not due to an Organic Mental Disorder (e.g., blackouts during Alcohol Intoxication).

PSYCHOGENIC FUGUE

A. Sudden unexpected travel away from one's home or customary place of work, with inability to recall one's past.

B. Assumption of a new identity (partial or complete).

C. The disturbance is not due to an Organic Mental Disorder.

MULTIPLE PERSONALITY

A. The existence within the individual of two or more distinct personalities, each of which is dominant at a particular time.

B. The personality that is dominant at any particular time determines the individual's behavior.

C. Each individual personality is complex and integrated with its own unique behavior patterns and social relationships.

DEPERSONALIZATION DISORDER

A. One or more episodes of depersonalization sufficient to produce significant impairment in social or occupational functioning.

B. The symptom is not due to any other disorder, such as Schizophrenia, Affective Disorder, Organic Mental Disorder, Anxiety Disorder, or epilepsy.

DSM-III, pp. 255, 257, 259, and 260, respectively.

Buddhist monk immolating himself. Like most psychogenic amnesias, his completely cleared within 24 hours of being discovered.

Psychogenic fugue. These patients unexpectedly flee from home or their customary locale, forget their previous identity, and adopt a new one. During a fugue, patients usually behave with sufficient skill to go unnoticed by most casual observers. Fugues typically are precipitated by an acute stressor and consist of a several-day excursion with minimal social contact. Some are more elaborate, lasting weeks to months: Patients may establish a new residence, fashion a new (and often more gregarious) identity, have a full social calendar, and appear no different from any other new arrival in town. Patients have traveled thousands of miles and passed numerous customs officials without detection. A rare few are violent. Afterwards, patients can't remember what transpired during the fugue.

Multiple personality. These patients have two or more distinct personalities, each dominant at a particular moment. Each personality is a complex, integrated being with its own name, memories, behavioral traits, emotional characteristics, social relations, employment histories, mental and physical disorders, and psychological test responses. Even rates of cerebral blood flow and evoked electrical potentials differ between the personalities. Needing to eat for three personalities, one patient ate nine meals a day! The average number of personalities is eight to 13 but 50 have been reported. Sybil had 16 personalities, and Eve, 22 faces.

Transitions from one personality to another are usually sudden, follow a stressor, and catch most observers off-guard. They're spooky to watch, since the "new" person seems to have taken over the patient's body and soul. Dress, speech, gait, and facial expressions may change so much the person goes unrecognized.

The original (or primary) personality is usually unaware of the other (or secondary) personalities, but most secondary personalities are aware of the primary personality. The secondary personalities generally have some inkling of the others; they converse with each other, protect each other, or one may act while others watch. Secondary personalities are often extreme caricatures of the original personality. A shy, conventional primary personality may have secondary personalities as a whore, drag queen, devil, and social worker. Secondary personalities may have a different sex, race, or age from the original personality.

Clinicians are frequently unaware that they're treating a multiple personality, since these patients are tough to detect. One psychiatrist reported seven years passed before realizing his patient had multiple personality. Few enter treatment complaining of a multiple personality, and if they come at all, it's usually for depression. These patients may reveal themselves through memory lapses, time distortions ("lost weekends"), using "we" rather than "I" in conversations, being charged for items they don't remember buying (imagine the VISA bills!), and finding friends who act like strangers and strangers who act like friends. If asked to write their thoughts freely for a half-hour, another personality may emerge. Another personality breaks through half the time in psychotherapy (Harvard, 1985).

Multiple personality, with the proliferation of new personalities, often continues for life, making this condition the worst of the dissociative disorders. These patients are frequently depressed, abuse substances, mutilate themselves, attempt suicide, and have psychotic episodes, tension headaches, phobias, conversion symptoms, and hypochondriasis.

Depersonalization disorder. Depersonalization is a common perceptual distortion in which the person experiences his body, or parts of it, as either not being attached to him, not belonging to him, or having changed size or distance. The person may feel anesthetized or made of wood; a sense of unreality or self-estrangement may confound him. Although the person doesn't feel, and indeed fears, that he's not in full control, gross reality testing is *not* impaired.

Because temporary depersonalization frequently occurs during normal and psychopathologic states, depersonalization *disorder* is only diagnosed in the absence of another mental disorder, or when its prevalence and intensity significantly interfere with social or occupational functioning. Over time, its severity fluctuates and hypochondriasis is frequent. Nevertheless, the disorder rarely produces lasting impairment.

Atypical dissociative disorder. This category of disorders that don't fit anyplace else includes brainwashing. Three myths about brainwashing abound: (a) that it doesn't exist; (b) that it's no different than education, advertising, and psychotherapy; and (c) that it's an irresistible method that robs people of their beliefs and personalities. Instead, "brainwashing" can be defined as a "comprehensive, systematic, and total program using psychological techniques, to stress *confession* and then *reeducation* in order to change fundamental beliefs. During confession, the subject admits to past errors and renounces past affiliations; during reeducation, the subject is refashioned to conform to the idealized image of the brainwasher" (Lifton, 1963).

Epidemiology

Dissociative disorders are rare, although psychogenic amnesia and fugue are common during war and natural disasters. Away from battle, adolescent and young adult women have slightly more dissociative disorders. In psychiatric populations, multiple personality is reputed to affect four times as many women as men, but if prison populations were included, the sex differential would narrow. Except for psychogenic fugue's variable age of onset, dissociative disorders rarely begin after the age of 40 and almost never originate among the elderly.

Etiology and Pathogenesis

Because dissociative states induced by organic factors are classified under organic mental disorders, by definition dissociative disorders are produced psychosocially. Most often, the immediate precipitating factor is an imminent threat of injury or death, the performance of a guilt-provoking act (e.g., an affair), or a serious auto accident. Meditation and hypnosis can also induce a dissociative disorder. Heavy substance abuse predisposes patients to psychogenic fugue and depersonalization disorder.

Psychoanalytic theory suggests that dissociative states protect the individual from experiencing painful sexual or aggressive impulses. With amnesia, one forgets what's painful; with fugue, one runs away from it; with multiple personality, one displaces it onto a new identity; with depersonalization, one abandons it.

Virtually all multiple personalities were physically or sexually abused as children. Sybil's mother tortured her as a child, while Billy Milligan's father frequently raped him from the ages of nine to 16 and threatened to kill him if he told anybody. These children have been cannon fodder in custody fights, raised as the opposite sex, had their genitals squeezed in a vice, and kidnapped by parents. Dissociation defends against these traumas: It isolates their horror, sections off the child's negative self-images, and permits a modicum of self-control. By compartmentalizing his emotions, the child says, in effect, "I can't deny this is happening, but I can deny that it's happening to me" (Harvard, 1985).

Differential Diagnosis

Organic mental disorders may simulate psychogenic amnesia, except in OMDs memory loss is more recent than remote and usually unrelated to a specific stressor; most OMDs arise slowly, rarely improve, and are accompanied by other organic signs, such as confusion, disorientation, attention deficits, and clouding of consciousness. Unlike those with psychogenic fugue, most organic patients who wander off are unable to perform complex, purposeful tasks.

Substance-induced intoxications can produce *alcoholic "blackouts,"* an amnesia for events occurring while intoxicated. In "blackouts," the history of drinking and the lack of a complete recovery exclude psychogenic amnesia. In *alcohol amnestic disorder*, five-minute (not immediate) memory is lost. *"Dissociative" anesthetics*, primarily phencyclidine (PCP), frequently cause depersonalization, but a drug history and urine screen are sufficiently diagnostic.

In *postconcussion amnesia*, patients generally have a retrograde memory loss for the period before the head trauma, whereas in psychogenic amnesia there's generally an anterograde memory loss for the period since the precipitating stress. Hypnosis and amytal interview can usually retrieve lost memories in psychogenic amnesia, but not in concussion. In dissociative amnesias, memory loss tends to be global and total; after concussion, it tends to be spotty and patchy. Patients with concussive amnesia do not form new identities. In psychogenic amnesia patients retain prior skills, have little difficulty conducting current tasks, and apparently benefit from secondary gain; patients with postconcussion amnesia lose some prior skills, have problems coping with present tasks, and do not appear to acquire secondary gain (Ludwig, 1985).

Temporal lobe epilepsy may cause sudden memory loss and flight, but unlike psychogenic fugue, patients can't perform complex tasks or form a new identity; they're often dysphoric, there's no precipitating stress, and there's an abnormal EEG.

Malingering must always be considered, especially if there's obvious secondary gain. Attorneys are seeing many more claims of multiple personality by criminals. "Hey judge, it's not *me* who slaughtered the guy, it's that *other* personality." Kiersch (1962) found that of 32 cases of alleged amnesia who were standing trial, 21 subsequently confessed to lying about their memory loss. Patients with dissociative conditions usually recover during hypnosis and amytal interviews, but malingerers do not.

Descriptively and psychodynamically, multiple personality often resembles *borderline personality disorder*. Emotional lability, low self-esteem, impulsivity, substance abuse, chronic boredom, identity confusion, temper tantrums, manipulative interpersonal relations, and suicide attempts characterize both disorders. In fact, in one investigation, 70% of multiple personalities were also diagnosed as borderline. Observing the patient's abrupt personality changes settles the diagnosis.

Distinguishing among dissociative disorders is usually easy. When a person forgets *and* travels to another locale, the diagnosis is psychogenic fugue; when she "merely" forgets, it's psychogenic amnesia. Patients with psychogenic amnesia look more befuddled, rarely conduct complex tasks, and are more readily spotted by lay observers. Awareness of one's original identity is absent in psychogenic amnesia and fugue, but present in multiple personality.

Management and Treatment

The literature on treating dissociative disorders is scant, devoid of controlled studies, mainly anecdotal, and summarized forthwith:

Psychogenic Amnesia and Fugue. Because of their relatively acute onset, brief duration, and high rate of spontaneous recovery, this sequence of interventions is recommended: (a) *Evaluate* the patient, allowing a few days for a spontaneous remission. If the patient does not fully recover, (b) provide *discussion, support, and persuasion*: Encourage her to talk freely of recent events, periodically suggest avenues for exploration, and gently persuade her to keep after lost memories. If these methods are not sufficient, (c) employ an *associative anamnesis* by having the patient free associate to events surrounding the amnesia. (d) *Hypnotize* the patient; amnestic patients are extremely good subjects. Instruct them to give a running commentary of known past incidents, which usually leads to abreaction. Once these emotions calm, the patient is told to keep talking, and then, to wake up. When awake, the patient is surprised to be recounting past events, and her amnesia ends. If it doesn't, (e) administer a *barbiturate-stimulant interview*,[2] and then gently prod the patient to review events around the forgotten period. The closer in time to the onset of the amnesia, the more effective the interview. (f) If the patient's memory still hasn't returned, reconsider *organic causes*, and if none are found, (g) gather a more exhaustive *psychological history* with antennae atuned to possible secondary gain (Coombs & Ludwig, 1982).

Multiple Personality. Originally, these patients fascinate, but they soon overwhelm and exasperate the therapist. Patients resist recalling traumatic events. As soon as psychotherapy with the primary personality gets going, a secondary personality takes over, and then another, and another, and another; many are hostile, seductive, and manipulative; some will bait the primary personality, try blocking alliances with the therapist, or act out by drug-taking and wrist-slashing.

Treatment can have one of two goals: *Fusion*—that is, the slow reintegration of the personalities into one. The therapist helps each personality recognize it's missing something as a dissociated part of a fully integrated person. If fusion flops by accelerating dissociation or going no place, the other goal is *detente*—that is, a slowly forged truce between the personalities. Fusion takes longer than detente, yet both require years. With either strategy, the therapist must avoid favoring certain personalities, since the others are then more likely to sabotage treatment.

Hypnosis may engage certain personalities, but it should not be introduced too early, since the patient may experience it as an emotional assault. *Group therapy* often backfires, because members consider the patient a fraud. An intriguing approach is "internal group therapy," in which the therapist "moderates" a discussion between the patient's personalities and facilitates the quiescent ones to speak via hypnosis. *Videotaping* early in treatment may help personalities get acquainted. *Family counseling* should be considered. Unless one of the personalities has another mental disorder (e.g., major depression), *medications* have no particular use.

---

[2]Detre and Jarecki (1971) detail how to conduct these interviews (pp. 656–662).

CHAPTER 15

Eating Disorders

In 1689, Dr. Richard Morton described a self-starving 18-year-old female who looked like a "skeleton only clad with skin." He called her condition "nervous consumption"; in 1874, Sir William Gull called it *"anorexia nervosa."* It's characterized by an irrational dread of becoming fat, a zealous pursuit of thinness, massive weight loss, and a disturbed body image. *Bulimia*, which wasn't recognized until the 1950s, is characterized by binge-eating and self-induced vomiting. Unlike anorexia nervosa, bulimia usually afflicts normal, or slightly overweight, individuals.

By creating a separate chapter for these eating disorders, this text departs from *DSM-III*, which places them under "disorders usually first evident in infancy, childhood or adolescence." Eating disorders merit their own chapter because their frequency is rapidly escalating. For example, in Monroe County, New York, the incidence of anorexia nervosa among women aged 15–24 jumped a walloping 400% between 1960–1969 and 1970–1976; similar increases have been reported in Zurich and London. These dramatic increases are genuine and not merely caused by greater awareness. Anorexia nervosa is also *lethal*, with its mortality rate averaging 5%, but often reported around 10%, and in one study as high as 19% (Hsu, 1980; Norman, 1984). The combined prevalence of anorexia nervosa and bulimia remains small — only 0.1% of the general population — yet among college women it ranges between 3% and 13%.

Although this chapter discusses anorexia nervosa and bulimia, *DSM-III* describes two other eating disorders: *Pica*, in which children persistently ingest nonnutritive substances (e.g., lead paint chips, hair, dirt). (Pica is the latin word for "magpie," a bird and renown scavenger.) The other, *rumination disorder of infancy* or merycism, is a rare, and sometimes fatal, disorder of repeated regurgitation. *Obesity* isn't a *DSM-III* mental disorder because it lacks a consistent psychological pattern. *DSM-III* suggests that when psychological forces promote obesity, they should be indicated as "psychological factors affecting physical condition" (Chapter 20).

ANOREXIA NERVOSA

Clinical Presentation

The essential features of anorexia nervosa are a dread of being fat and a compulsion to be thin, substantial weight loss, refusing to maintain a healthy weight despite being skinny or emaciated, distorted internal and external perceptions of one's body as fat, and in women, amenorrhea. Table 15-1 lists *DSM-III*'s criteria for anorexia nervosa.

No clinician forgets his first hospitalized anorectic. The patient looks dead, or close to it. Cachectic, pale, puffy, and wrinkled, this wizened bag of bones prances down the hallway with unrelenting cheerfulness that exhausts onlookers who are riveted in disbelief. Ask why she's skinny, and she'll say she's fat. Ask why she's running and dieting, and she'll say it's to look beautiful. The anorectic is childlike in her logic, appearance, and emotions.

In a typical case, a teenager or woman in her early twenties starts dieting for being mildly overweight; this may occur after a stressor (e.g., puberty, a broken romance, a family divorce) or for no apparent reason. After shedding a few pounds, she virtually stops eating, initially because she's disgusted by food, and later because her appetite's gone. (Hence, *anorexia* nervosa is

TABLE 15-1
DSM-III Criteria for Anorexia Nervosa*

A. Intense fear of becoming obese, which does not diminish as weight loss progresses.

B. Disturbance of body image, e.g., claiming to "feel fat" even when emaciated.

C. Weight loss of at least 25% of original body weight or, if under 18 years of age, weight loss from original body weight plus projected weight gain expected from growth charts may be combined to make the 25%.†

D. Refusal to maintain body weight over a minimal normal weight for age and height.

E. No known physical illness that would account for the weight loss.

DSM-III, p. 69.

†*DSM-III-R* may lower this figure from 25% to 15%; it may also require the absence of at least three consecutive menstrual periods—in women, preferably.

a misnomer, since true anorexia doesn't occur until late in the disorder.) She becomes preoccupied with food, memorizing calories and preparing meals for everyone but herself. She may hide food, steal it, or play with it. To lose weight, she exercises frenetically, goes on fad diets, abstains from carbo-hydrates and fats, takes laxatives and diuretics, gorges food (i.e., bulimic episodes), and induces vomiting. In time, "Twiggy" resembles a concentration-camp victim.

At first, she's energetic, enthusiastic, and pert, but then depressive symptoms set in, especially dysthymia, insomnia (or hypersomnia), social withdrawal, and decreased libido. She's usually perfectionistic and often hypochondriacal. She'll have stomach pains, (unintentional) vomiting, nausea, constipation, cold intolerance, headaches, frequent urination, low blood pressure, and diminished secondary sex characteristics. As teenagers, they shy away from boys and fear sex. Male anorectics get hemorrhoids.

Clinical Course and Complications

Although anorexia nervosa may stop within 12 months, it usually persists for years, punctuated by remissions and exacerbations. *Nutritionally*, patients usually recover in two to three years, but even then about half continue to have menstrual problems, sexual and social maladjustment, massive weight fluctuations, or disturbed appetite, while two-thirds continue to fret over their weight and body image. Follow-up studies vary considerably, but on average, 70% of patients return to a normal weight, 20% are skinny, and under 10% are overweight. In terms of their overall prognosis, 40% are completely recovered, 30% are considerably improved, 20% are unimproved or severely impaired, and 5% to 10% prematurely die, usually by starvation, electrolyte imbalance (from vomiting or purging), or suicide (Hsu, 1980; Norman, 1984). A few patients develop osteoporosis leading to pathological fractures, and so complaints of bone or back pain should be investigated.

How anorexia begins has little bearing on its course or outcome. Instead, predictors of a favorable outcome include a good premorbid level of functioning, more educa-tion, early age of onset, less weight loss, less denial of illness, overactivity, greater psychosexual maturity, and feeling hunger when hospitalized. Indicators of a poor prognosis are the opposite of the above, plus perinatal complications, bingeing, self-induced vomiting, and purging, longer duration of illness, longer delay in initially ob-taining treatment, severe dysthymia and obsessions, and greater exaggeration of body width.

Epidemiology

The typical anorectic is a white, teenage girl from the middle and upper classes, who will attend college. Given that 95% of anorectics are female, the diagnosis should be made extra cautiously in males. People who can't eat because of poverty rarely can't eat because of eating disorders. Although it appears that eating disorders rarely affect blacks, controlled surveys have yet to confirm this assumption. Dance and modeling students have a higher incidence of anorexia nervosa, but only *after* they become students. All in all, the prevalence of anorexia nervosa in the general population is between 0.37% and 1.60%.

Etiology and Pathogenesis

Psychologically, anorectics share two cardinal features: the dread of not being in control and the distorted perception of one's own body. Before becoming ill the typical anorectic is a "model child"; afterwards, everything's a power struggle. Superficially strong and defiant, she's devoid of self-confidence, paralyzed with helplessness, and terrified by her lack of self-control. To compensate, everything is absolute and nothing is relative. The anorectic reacts to gaining a pound with the same distress that the reader might have if he gained 50 pounds overnight. When frantic parents fight with her about eating, they merely feed the patient's stubbornness, since to her, the issue isn't health or even love, but control. (To parents, however, the issue is rejection: "By rejecting my food, she rejects me.")

Struggles over control are inflamed by the patient's internal and external misperceptions of her own body. She minimizes internal stimuli: In comparison to normals, she feels less hunger after not eating and feels less exhaustion after exercizing. Externally, she sees her body differently from the way others see it. Precise measuring shows that anorectics greatly overestimate their width, yet correctly estimate their height, the height and width of female models, and the size of physical objects. Genuinely perceiving her scrawny body as chubby or fat, the anorectic doesn't think she's making herself sick, but merely trying to be attractively thin.

Psychosocial Theories

Psychodynamic. Early psychoanalysts felt these patients' core conflict was a fear of oral impregnation, while later analysts blamed domineering mothers for preventing the anorectic from completing the two chief psychosocial tasks of adolescence — individuating and separating. Both theories are clearly products of their era, but even so, they both point to genuine phenomena: Anorectics fear sex; they also demand independence while clinging to their mothers. Yet with these, as with most, etiological theories of anorexia nervosa, what's purported to be a cause of the disorder is probably a consequence of it.

Family. Many papers describe the anorectic's father as ineffective, her mother as overbearing, and both parents as intrusive. The family system is out of whack, and the parents are acting screwy. But how would any "normal" parents behave watching their daughter starve herself to death?

When anorectics are hospitalized, clinicians are often struck by how parents will hover over their daughter and be within an inch of exploding. But once again, is this cause or effect? Amdur et al. (1969) showed it was effect, because the parents' behavior reflected their daughter's condition. For the first six weeks of hospitalization, when patients were at their worst, staff rated parents as unfeeling, intellectualizing, and rigid; during the last six weeks, when patients were recovering, staff rated parents as appropriately emotional, flexible, and supportive of autonomy. This study does not address the original cause of anorexia nervosa; instead, it suggests that once the disorder has arisen, family psychopathology is more a reaction to the patient's difficulties than a cause of them. Such reactions surely aggravate matters and merit treatment.

Social. Given that anorexia nervosa is a disorder of the middle and upper classes, it may allow perfectly behaved adolescents a way to rebel by exaggerating the inordinate value these classes place on thinness, beauty, "proper" behavior, diets, nutrition, exercise, health clubs, etc. The poor share these values, but can't afford them. It's no fat chance that American society's ideal female body image has slimmed in direct parallel to the growth in anorexia nervosa.

Biological Theories

A major debate in recent biological research has been whether or not eating disorders are variants of depression. The affirmative side points to the high frequency of depression in anorectics (41%) and bulimics (24%), their positive responses to antidepressants, the neuroendocrine similarities between eating and affective disorders, and the higher prevalence of affective disorders in close relatives of anorectics and especially bulimics. The negative side points out that eating and depressive disorders are more different than alike. Although the question remains open, anorexia nervosa might be a heterogeneous disorder, with some cases having, and other cases not having, a biological link to depression.

Genetic. Anorexia nervosa is more prevalent among the first-degree female relatives of anorectic patients. For instance, 6.6% of sisters of anorectics have the disorder. The prevalence of depression and alcoholism, but not schizophrenia, appears greater among family members. Winokur, March, and Mendels (1980) reported affective disorders in 22% of relatives of anorectics, compared to 10% of controls.

Biochemical and Anatomical. As measuring techniques improve and attention to these disorders increase, neuroendocrine abnormalities in the hypothalamic-pituitary and gonadotropin-ovarian axes keep popping up. Most, but not all, authorities view these changes more as consequences than causes. Similarly, CT scans of anorectics show them to have enlarged third and lateral ventricles in the brain, but this too might be nothing more than a consequence of malnutrition (Datlof et al., 1986).

Differential Diagnosis

Anorexia nervosa is easy to distinguish from other disorders, primarily *schizophrenia* and *depression*, in which massive weight loss is prominent. Besides lacking the common symptoms seen in these disorders, anorectics and bulimics misjudge their body image, misperceive internal body cues, binge and purge, and display hyperactivity, inordinate cheerfulness, a zealous pre-occupation with food, and a dread of obesity. These distinctions also apply for *malnutrition* and *starvation* (e.g., *tuberculosis, Crohn's disease, ulcerative colitis, extreme poverty*), as well as various *neurological diseases*, such as *epilepsy* and *brain tumors*. Differentiating anorexia from *bulimia* may be difficult and is discussed under bulimia.

Management and Treatment

The legacy of Karen Carpenter, the young pop singer who died from anorexia nervosa, should remind clinicians that the first goal in treatment is always to (a) keep the patient alive. Beyond this, the goals are to (b) establish adequate nutrition, (c) correct abnormal eating habits, (d) supplant family overinvolvement with more appropriate intrafamilial relationships, and (e) enhance self-control, identity, and autonomy.

Behavior therapy. If the patient's weight is *medically precarious*, hospitalization is mandatory. Bargaining by the patient—"Please, I beg! I promise to gain weight"—means zilch. If matters have so deteriorated that the patient is in danger of losing her life, professionals must take charge. Family members can't. Once the patient is hospitalized, treatment follows the same principles set down in 1874 by the very Sir William Gull who named the disorder: "Patients should be fed at regular intervals and surrounded by persons who would have moral control over them; relatives and friends being generally the worst attendants."

More specifically, first behavior therapy is used to prevent starvation, restore nutritional balance, and increase weight. Programs vary, but in essence, the patient is told that she must gain at least a half pound each day above her highest recent weight. How she does so is her business. There's no fuss, no special diets, no exercise restrictions. If she wants a dietician's advice, that's okay. She's weighed every morning in the nude, since these patients are pros at sneaking extra pounds in the heels of shoes, hems of nighties, etc. If she doesn't gain her half pound, in some programs she's tube fed, in others, she's confined to bed all day. If she does gain a half pound, she does whatever she wants. This program is continued until the patient reaches a medically safe weight, usually within 10% of the norm.

Nurses play a critical role during this phase. Besides implementing this regimen, nurses should tell the patient to notify them as soon as she's tempted to stuff her face, and they will stop her from doing so. This is a potent message: It shows they understand her dread of becoming fat; this allies them *with* her, not *against* her, thereby undercutting the rebellious aspect of overeating and circumventing the power struggles that occurred within the family. (Just knowing the nurses are *available* is usually enough for the patient to stop herself.) Although never insisted on, it helps if nurses eat with the patient so to monitor her negativism and anorexia, while encouraging healthy eating habits and good nutrition. Nurses must prevent parents from cajoling the patient on how to eat.

Family therapy. Early on, parents should not have any responsibility for the patient's care. This diffuses family tension, permits autonomy for the patient, and gracefully lets the parents off the hook. In some programs, either a week after admission or once the patient begins to gain weight, informal lunches with the entire family are held to evaluate family interactions at mealtime, to reduce intrafamily power struggles, and to promote more helpful behavior around the table. These family therapy lunches are continued after discharge to establish more balanced intrafamilial relationships.

Psychotherapy. Psychoanalysis is contraindicated, at least until the patient's physical health has been stable for years. On the other hand, once the patient is out of medical danger, in *individual psychoanalytic psychotherapy* the patient can learn to abandon her self-destructive stabs at autonomy and to find more enduring self-worth and self-control from within. *Group therapy* helps patients reestablish lost social skills and assists patients in viewing themselves as "somebody other than an eating freak." Many locales offer self-help groups for patients with eating disorders.

One caveat: Anytime a therapist says, "The patient's making progress in therapy, even though she's losing weight," the patient's in trouble. This statement is the psychiatric equivalent of "The operation was a success, but the patient died." Psychotherapies are no substitute for proper nutrition and weight.

Medication. Between 40% and 60% of patients benefit from tricyclic antidepressants; nonresponders may improve with the serotonin antagonist, cyproheptadine (Periactin). Yet employ these medications with caution, since malnourished patients are especially sensitive to drugs.

BULIMIA

Clinical Presentation

Binge-eating is the central feature of bulimia. Also diagnostic are that bulimics view their bingeing as pathological, dread their inability to control their eating, and become unhappy and self-depreciating after bingeing. Although self-induced vomiting occurs in 88% of patients, it is not a diagnostic requirement. In contrast to anorexia nervosa, severe weight loss and amenorrhea are uncommon in bulimia. *DSM-III*'s criteria for bulimia are listed in Table 15-2.

Eating binges last a few minutes to two hours; on average, they're an hour. Bulimics may binge once or twice a month, or over ten times a day. Dysphoria usually precedes a binge, and is relieved by it. Patients usually give more than one reason for bingeing: feeling anxious or tense (83%), craving certain foods (70%), feeling unhappy (67%), "can't control appetite" (59%), hunger (31%), insomnia (22%).[1] Bulimics are more likely to binge as the day goes on. While gorging themselves, most patients aren't aware of hunger and don't stop even when satisfied. They don't chew, they gobble, preferably foods high in calories and easy to devour. On a typical binge they'll "pig-out" on three pounds of chocolate, popcorn for an army, and four pints of ice cream. Many bulimics spend over $100 a day on food; some steal food. To avoid detection, most binge in private.

Bingeing usually stops when the patient is discovered, falls asleep, develops stomach pain, or induces vomiting. By diminishing abdominal cramps and distention, this self-induced vomiting permits further binges. Besides wishing to lose weight, bulimics continue to binge in order to delay the inevitable postbinge dysphoria. This dysphoria is often described as guilt (87%), "feeling too full" (64%), worried (53%), still hungry (22%). A minority feel "relaxed" (23%) or "satisfied" (15%). In therapy, bulimics describe their bingeing as "disgusting," but irresistible. After having a normal meal—on average a twice-a-week event—they fear bingeing again or gaining weight.

These patients are preoccupied with their appearance, body image, and sexual attraction, as well as how others, men especially, perceive and respond to them. By using various techniques—binge-eating (100%), fasting (92%), exercise (91%), vomiting (88%), spitting out food (65%), laxatives (61%), diet pills (50%), diuretics (34%), saunas (12%)—bulimics can readily add or shed ten pounds a day. Rarely are bulimics skinny; 5% are overweight. (Prior

---

[1]The percentages given in this section are mostly from Mitchell et al.'s (1985) study of 257 bulimics.

TABLE 15-2
DSM-III* Criteria for Bulimia

A. Recurrent episodes of binge eating (rapid consumption of a large amount of food in a discrete period of time, usually less than two hours).

B. At least three of the following:
   (1) consumption of high-caloric, easily ingested food during a binge.
   (2) inconspicuous eating during a binge
   (3) termination of such eating episodes by abdominal pain, sleep, social interruption, or self-induced vomiting
   (4) repeated attempts to lose weight by severely restrictive diets, self-induced vomiting, or use of cathartics or diuretics
   (5) frequent weight fluctuations greater than ten pounds due to alternating binges and fasts

C. Awareness that the eating pattern is abnormal and fear of not being able to stop eating voluntarily.

D. Depressed mood and self-deprecating thoughts following eating binges.†

E. The bulimic episodes are not due to Anorexia Nervosa or any known physical disorder.

DSM-III, pp. 70–71.
†*DSM-III-R* may eliminate criterion D and list these symptoms as associated features.

to their bulimia, 14% were underweight, 56% were overweight.) About a third will have abused drugs and alcohol and about a fifth received treatment for it. A minority will steal, mutilate themselves, or attempt suicide. To look thin and sexually attractive — a redundancy to the bulimic — and to alleviate sadness, they'll go on clothes-buying sprees. Many are promiscuous, but a minority is afraid to hold hands.

During rapid weight gain, their hands, feet, and ankles often swell from a "refeeding edema." These patients endure weakness (84%), abdominal bloating (75%), stomach pain (63%), sore throats (54%), painful swellings of salivary and parotid glands called "puffy cheeks" (50%), dental caries (37%), finger calluses (27%), headaches, and dizziness. Menstrual irregularities are common, but sustained amenorrhea is not.

Clinical Course and Complications

Like anorexia nervosa, bulimia usually arises during the teens or early twenties, and rarely after 30. Bulimia is a chronic disorder, with fluctuating intensity and alternating periods of bingeing and normal eating. Less often normal eating doesn't occur; the patient cycles between periods of bingeing and fasting. Anecdotally, bulimics generally improve or completely recover. Death, usually from hypokalemia, is rare.

Electrolyte imbalance and dehydration are common in underweight bulimics who vomit after bingeing. Patients report problems with intimate or interpersonal relations (70%), family (61%), finances (because of food purchasing) (53%), and work (50%).

Epidemiology

Like the anorectic, the prototypic bulimic is a white, adolescent girl from the middle and upper classes, who will attend university. Ninety percent of bulimics are female, and only three cases of bulimia have been reported in blacks. In Mitchell et al.'s (1985) survey of 257 bulimics, 88% were from social classes I through III; two patients were Native Americans, the rest were white.

The prevalence of bulimia varies enormously depending on the population. Although the prevalence is less than 0.5% in the general population, in a survey of 500 college students, 4.4% had eating disorders; 86% of these had bulimia while only 14% had anorexia nervosa (Strangler & Printz, 1980). Other surveys of high school and college students indicate that 8% to 19% of women and 5% of men have bulimia, and that 5% of women and 1% of men will seek treatment. Binge-eating is reported by 68% to 79% of university women (Halmi et al., 1981).

Although eating disorders are clearly on the rise, their frequency is often inflated in popular press, such as "at least one-half of the women on campuses today suffer from some kind of eating disorder" (Squire, 1983). Professionals have also been guilty of overestimating their prevalence. A common mistake is to equate binge-eating with an eating disorder. The difference can be substantial. Hart and Ollendick (1985) found binge-eating among 41% of working women and 69% of female university students, but the full bulimic syndrome was seen in only 1% of working, and 5% of college, women.

Etiology and Pathogenesis

Very little is known about the causes of bulimia. Traditional psychodynamic theories postulated that bingeing gratified sexual and aggressive wishes and that vomiting was a symbolic "purging of the bad self" or "rejection of love." Descriptive and biological psychiatrists have noted a relationship between bulimia and depression. About a quarter of bulimics have moderate to severe depression; a majority improve on drugs normally used for depression (e.g., TCAs, MAOIs); first-degree relatives of bulimics have a higher frequency of depression (and substance abuse); and neuroendocrine abnormalities (e.g., abnormal DST) found in depression also occur in bulimia.

Bulimic families appear enmeshed but disengaged. In comparing 105 bulimic with 86 control families, Johnson and Flach (1985) found the former set high expectations but discouraged these by placing little emphasis on their daughter's intellectual, cultural, or recreational activities. Despite the fact that the overall structure and rules of bulimic families resembled those in normal families, the bulimic families were more disorganized, showing little ability to solve problems, manage crises, or get things done. Their disorganization and lack of concern for the patient's activities correlated with the severity of the patient's symptoms.

Differential Diagnosis

Few people make a habit of bingeing and vomiting, except for bulimics and 40% to 50% of anorectics. Consequently, distinguishing these disorders is the only common diagnostic difficulty. First the official view: *DSM-III* claims they are two separate disorders. Anorectics are skinny, whereas bulimics are mildly overweight or underweight. In anorexia, weight fluctuations are more dramatic and life-threatening. Bulimics are more likely to have depressive symptoms. Except for food, most anorectics are "well-behaved"; most bulimics are not. Anorectics "defend" their eating habits, bulimics consider bingeing a compulsion, and self-induced vomiting a curse.

Now the alternative view: Bingeing anorectics (the bulimic subtype) are more akin to normal-weight bulimics than to anorectics who don't binge (the restrictive subtype). In comparison to "restrictive" anorectics, normal-weight bulimics and "bulimic" anorectics perceive more family conflict and are more impulsive, outgoing, sexually active, and emotionally disturbed; they may be more prone to depression and have twice as many affectively disturbed relatives.

Management and Treatment

Medication. Bulimia, or at least bingeing, seems highly responsive to TCAs (Pope et al., 1983) and MAOIs (Walsh et al., 1984). About 30% of the patients on TCAs and 50% of the patients on MAOIs recovered completely; the remainder of the patients reduced bingeing episodes by over 50%. Because of this slight edge, MAOIs might be the preferred drug *except* in those patients who will not, or cannot, follow a tryamine-free diet.

Group therapy. The apparently fine results from medication are matched by controlled studies of group therapy. At the end of a 10-week outpatient program with 30 minutes of individual psychotherapy and 90 minutes of group therapy per week, 93% of patients stopped their bingeing and vomiting completely; control subjects did not improve. On two-year follow-up, 71%

no longer binged and vomited, while the rest only did so about three times a year (Lacey, 1983).

Another controlled investigation, which examined patients whose treatment was limited to a nine-week "psychoeducational group," yielded equally impressive results, suggesting that group, not individual, therapy is the critical ingredient. The first phase of the group emphasized education, self-monitoring, and identifying environmental precipitants. The second phase focused on setting short-term goals, such as eating regular meals and not bingeing for a day; the importance of small successes and the avoidance of extreme measures were stressed. During the third phase, patients were trained to be more assertive, to apply progressive relaxation instead of bingeing or vomiting, and, with cognitive therapy, to correct their tendencies to minimize successes, to maximize failures, and to lose perspective (Connors et al., 1984).

From the above, it seems that medication and group therapy are helpful, but many questions remain: Which patients improve more with a particular treatment? Are group proponents right in claiming that whereas medications reduce bingeing and vomiting, groups *also* improve assertiveness and mood? Does medication *and* group work better than either treatment alone? Since some of the patients who improved on medications were unresponsive to talking therapies, should drugs only be used on these patients? Given that studies of TCAs, MAOIs, and group therapies have all yielded good results, will the same happen with family and individual treatments? Stay tuned.

CHAPTER 16

Psychosexual Disorders

WHAT CAN YOU SAY when 40% of medical students still believe there are two kinds of orgasm—clitoral and vaginal? What can you say when 15% believe that masturbation causes mental illness? Or that 18% believe "impotence in men over 70 is nearly universal"? (Lief, 1979). One thing you can say is no wonder there are so many sexual problems. Another thing you can say is that doctors know precious little about sexual problems (although medical schools are rectifying this), and that other health professionals may not be all that more aware. Many students might feel they know about sex, and therefore, have no need to study it. Yet students know about depression and still have a need to study it. Some students avoid learning about sexual problems, fearing that "somebody might wonder why I'm reading about this stuff." Yet, when students read about depression, do people wonder why?

Sex, however, is not depression (though it can be depressing). Sex plays a uniquely pervasive role in people's lives; it influences how we think, feel, dress, flirt, play, mate, and love. Maybe that's one reason the ECA found that psychosexual disorders will affect one in four adults, making them the second most frequent mental disorders in America (Table 1-4).

In *DSM-III*, psychosexual disorders are sexual problems which are not caused by physical factors or by other mental disorders.[1] It lists four classes of, and 22 specific, psychosexual disorders (Appendix A). *Gender identity disorders* involve a person's discomfort with his or her anatomic sex and

[1]*DSM-III-R* plans to rename this class "gender and sexual disorders" for two reasons. Gender identity disorders are not disturbances in "sexual" functioning. "Psychosexual" will be expanded to "sexual," because whereas in *DSM-III* organic sexual dysfunctions were not included under psychosexual disorders, they will be in *DSM-III-R*.

265

behavioral patterns associated with the other sex, mainly transsexualism. *Paraphilias* are persistent patterns of sexual arousal in response to atypical and bizarre stimuli that interfere with reciprocal affectionate sex (e.g., transvestism). *Psychosexual dysfunctions* are inhibitions in sexual desire or the psychophysiologic changes that characterize the sexual response cycle (e.g., premature ejaculation). Finally, there is the residual category of *other psychosexual disorders*, chiefly ego-dystonic homosexuality.

At the outset, some basic terms and concepts need clarification. A person's *anatomic sex* is his or her biologic sex as determined by whether he has XY, or she has XX, chromosomes. *Gender identity* is the individual's *internal* feelings as to whether he or she is a male or a female. *Gender role* refers to whether a person wishes to be seen by others (or by oneself) as a male or as a female; gender role involves the person's *external* appearance and behavior, including sexual behavior. *Sexual orientation* describes a person's preference for partners of the same (homosexual) or opposite (heterosexual) sex.

GENDER IDENTITY DISORDERS

These disorders involve a disturbance in the person's sense of being a man or a woman — that is, a conflict between one's anatomical sex and one's gender identity. If a male, the patient will say, "I'm a woman trapped in a man's body." People with gender identity disorders strongly and genuinely wish to belong to the opposite sex. By definition, this desire must not be the product of psychosis or of congenital sexual anomalies, such as a hermaphrodite who has testicular and ovarian tissues.

Gender identity disorders are rare. Even transsexualism, the most frequent disorder in this category, has a prevalence among men that varies from 1 in 40,000 to 1 in 100,000; among women, prevalence varies from 1 in 100,000 to 1 in 400,000.

Transsexualism

Transsexualism is a persistent (over two years) feeling of severe discomfort with one's anatomical sex, accompanied by a strong wish to be rid of one's genitals and to live as the opposite sex. (Don't confuse trans*vest*ism with trans*sex*ualism; the former changes his vest, the latter, his sex.) The patient's parents usually recollect that as a child he wanted to be a she — even as early as three years old. This cross-gender identification confounds relatives and patients alike. While growing up, most transsexuals are scorned and victimized by relatives, peers, doctors, and ministers. This abuse leads to high rates of attempted suicide, antisocial behavior, and self-mutilation (frequently of the genitals).

A parent's quiet evening was suddenly interrupted by shrieks from their six-year-old son's bedroom. They raced to the room to find the walls splattered with blood and with their child writhing in pain. Next to their son was a rope—one end attached to a doorknob, the other to his penis and testicles. Having tied the rope to his genitals and to the doorknob, he slammed the door shut in a deliberate auto-castration. This tragedy is the extreme, but the intensity of the unhappiness generating it, frequent.

As adults, many transsexuals try to live as if they belonged to the opposite sex. Many pull it off (so to speak), without coworkers and friends knowing she is a he (or vice versa). Sexual intimacy is restricted; a majority of transsexuals don't marry, and when they do the marriages usually fail. Drugs and talk therapies do not alter the transsexual's cross-gender identification. (Psychotherapy can alleviate emotional problems arising from transsexualism.) Once the transsexual clearly decides to switch sexes, professionals should not oppose it. The transsexual no more chooses a gender identity of the opposite sex than the reader chooses a gender identity of his or her own sex. If the clinician has moral qualms about supporting the transsexual's change, he should excuse himself from the case.

A majority of transsexuals wish to change their sex permanently. In America, two to eight times more men than women go to sex reassignment clinics. To qualify for a surgical sex transformation, most centers require the patient to live as the opposite sex for at least two years, during which they demonstrate good social and occupational functioning, continue enduring friendships, and are free of major psychopathology. Meanwhile, after obtaining a thorough medical and psychiatric evaluation, they receive estrogen or testosterone. The surgical transformation is more successful for the male, than the female, transsexual. The man's genitals are amputated, an artificial vagina is constructed from existing fascial planes, and the urethra is moved to its feminine location. Bladder infections are the most common post-operative physical complication. Although many sexual, personal, and occupational problems persist after sex reassignment, virtually all transsexuals never regret having the surgery.

PARAPHILIAS

Derived from the Greek meaning "along side of" and "love," a paraphilia is the involuntary and repeated necessity for unusual or bizarre imagery, acts, or objects to obtain sexual excitement. Paraphilias involve either (a) nonhuman objects, (b) real or simulated suffering or humiliation, or (c) sexual activity with nonconsenting partners. The patient's imagery or actions must produce sexual excitement, orgasm, or relief from nonerotic tension. (*DSM-III-R* will probably require paraphilias to last at least six consecutive months.) Paraphiliac disorders are rare and of unknown etiology; they usually occur in men.

Whether a paraphilia is "normal" or pathological depends on the degree of harm it causes and whether it is the person's preferred or sole way of obtaining sexual gratification. Although some people enjoy their paraphilias, others feel guilty, develop psychosexual dysfunctions, or end up behind bars.

Few paraphilics seek treatment, but if so, it's usually to extricate themselves from secondary legal or marital difficulties. Therapy tries to (a) diminish sexual arousal from the paraphilia, (b) increase "normal" heterosexual arousal, (c) teach appropriate assertiveness and social skills, since many of these patients have trouble simply talking to the opposite sex, (d) provide sex education, and (e) correct psychosexual dysfunctions. Transvestism is discussed below, while the other common paraphilias are sketched on Table 16-1.

Transvestism

Transvestites are heterosexual men who persistently, and at least initially, derive erotic pleasure by dressing as women. Usually beginning during his childhood or adolescence, the transvestite first experiments in private (often with masturbation), and then increases the frequency and number of worn items. He may join a transvestite subculture. In time, cross-dressing may no longer be erotic, but merely relieve anxiety. When not cross-dressing, transvestites look like regular guys. Although heterosexual, their sexual experiences involve few women, and may include an occasional man. Some transvestites claim that during childhood they were punished and humiliated by mothers or sisters into wearing female attire.

Interfering with this cross-dressing frustrates transvestites, and is a useful diagnostic clue. Transvestites differ from *transsexuals* in that the former have male gender identities and do not wish to get rid of their genitals, while the latter have female gender identities and don't receive sexual excitement by wearing women's clothes. When transvestism evolves into transsexualism, transsexualism becomes the diagnosis. When *cross-dressing solely to relieve anxiety* occurs, without sexual pleasure, transvestism is not the diagnosis. When *male homosexuals* dress as ladies—for a goof, for masquerade, or for attracting another man—there's no erotic sensation. Neither are *female impersonators* sexually aroused by cross-dressing. *Fetishism* is diagnosed when objects other than clothes stimulate sexual excitement.

PSYCHOSEXUAL DYSFUNCTIONS

Psychosexual dysfunctions are disturbances in the human sexual response cycle (Table 16-2). The seven specific psychosexual dysfunctions defined in *DSM-III* are outlined in Table 16-3. In describing a psychosexual dysfunc-

TABLE 16-1
The Paraphilias

Exhibitionism is achieving sexual excitement by compulsively and repetitively exposing one's genitals to an unsuspecting stranger, with no attempt at further sexual activity with the stranger. Masturbation may occur, but more often erections can't be obtained. Exhibitionism, which typically begins in the mid-twenties, tends to occur in shy, married, heterosexual males.

Fetishism is when the preferred way of obtaining sexual arousal is by using nonliving objects (fetishes), which are not limited to female clothes used for cross-dressing (transvestism) or to devices solely designed for sexual stimulation (e.g., vibrators). Most fetishes involve clothes, such as women's undergarments.

Pedophilia is when the preferred way of being sexually excited involves fantasies or acts of engaging in sexual activity with prepubertal children. Often sexually abused as children, these patients usually turn (on) to pedophilia in midlife during a setback in marriage or in another close relationship. Most pedophiliacs are male heterosexuals with low self-esteem, who enjoy a sense of mastery and safety when fondling children. Pedophilia is usually a chronic disorder with frequent relapses, which is resistant to therapy.

Sexual masochism involves preferring sexual arousal from being humiliated, bound, whipped, beaten, or made to suffer in some other way. Masochistic fantasies often arise during childhood, but are not acted on until early adulthood. Normals engage in some sexual masochism, but whether it is pathological depends on the extent of the harm. Unintentional suicides have resulted from sexual masochism.

Sexual sadism involves obtaining sexual pleasure by the real or simulated repeated infliction of a psychological or physical pain onto a nonconsenting partner. It may also involve a consenting partner if it's the sadist's preferred way of experiencing sexual arousal, or if the bodily harm to the partner is extensive, permanent, or potentially fatal. Mild, consensual, "benignly kinky" sadism is not a mental disorder. Although sexual sadism may lead to murder and rape, few rapists are sexual sadists.

Voyeurism is the repeated observation of unsuspecting people who are naked, disrobing, or engaged in sexual activity. "Peeping Toms" are more erotically stimulated by watching than by other sexual acts. They don't wish sex with the observed, and would be frightened if it were offered. They prefer to masturbate while observing or to fantasize about the observed woman feeling helpless, mortified, or terrorized if she knew Tom was observing her. Voyeurists, lewd phone callers, and politicians are discouraged by bored responses; only excited ones encourage them.

Zoophilia is the repeated and preferred use of animals for sexual excitement. This may entail sexual intercourse, licking, fondling, etc. Occasional sexual activity with farm or domestic animals is not zoophilia.

Atypical paraphilia is a residual category for being sexually stimulated by smearing feces (*coprophilia*), rubbing against strangers (*frotteurism*), self-administering enemas (*klismaphilia*), lying in filth (*mysophilia*), having sex with a corpse (*necrophilia*), making lewd phone calls (*telephone scatologia*), and a golden oldie, urinating on others (*urophobia*).

269

TABLE 16-2
The Human Sexual Response Cycle

NUMBER	PHASE	KEY FEATURES
I.	Appetitive	Fantasies about sexual activity and the desire (i.e., libido) to have it.
II.	Excitement	Subjective sense of sexual pleasure with accompanying physiologic changes in the male leading to erection, and in the female leading to vasocongestion, vaginal lubrication, and swelling of the external genitalia. Mediated by the parasympathetic nervous system, this phase includes the "excitement" and "plateau" stages described by Masters and Johnson (1970), and the "vascular" stage described by Kaplan (1974).
III.	Orgasm	The peaking of sexual pleasure and the release of sexual tension. This phase is mediated by the sympathetic nervous system and called the "muscular" stage by Kaplan. During it, males sense an inevitable ejaculation, which is followed by a single, intense muscular contraction which emits semen. In a more variable response, females contract the outer third of their vagina.
IV.	Resolution	There is a generalized and muscular relaxation, during which males are physiologically refractory to further erection or orgasm, whereas women can respond immediately to additional stimuli. (There are no *DSM-III* disorders arising from this final phase.)

tion, the clinician should indicate if it's *primary* or *secondary* (without and with previously normal functioning); if it's *generalized* or *situational* (with a particular partner); or if it's *conjoint* or *solitary* (with or without [as in masturbation] another partner.) The clinician should also mention its frequency, setting, duration, degree of sexual impairment, level of subjective distress, and effects on other areas of functioning (e.g., social, occupational).

Most psychosexual dysfunctions arise during young adulthood or with first sexual encounters. The overall clinical course is highly varied; it may be brief, recurrent, smoldering, or permanent. Patients usually delay seeking treatment for three to 12 years *and* after several years of a sustained sexual relationship. Dysfunctions also arise later in life: Inhibited sexual desire and excitement (especially in males) is common during middle adulthood, while the elderly are increasingly presenting with a variety of sexual dysfunctions.

Some dysfunctions are associated with specific psychiatric traits: Women, especially with histrionic personalities, are more likely to have inhibited sexual desire and inhibited orgasm. Compulsive men are prone to inhibited sexual desire and excitement. Anxiety predisposes to premature ejaculation.

A patient's dysfunction will involve one or more etiological factors. These may be (a) *intrapsychic*, such as "performance anxiety," guilt, low self-esteem, denial, and undue self-monitoring; (b) *interpersonal*, such as fear of abandonment, power struggles, lack of trust, failure to explicitly inform partners about one's particular sexual needs and specific pleasures, a "sex manual mentality," or displaced anger; (c) *cultural*, such as sexual myths, insufficient or incorrect information, and negative attitudes about sex learned from parents, religion, or society; (d) *medical*, such as drugs, alcohol, and illness; or (e) *mental disorders*, such as depression and obsessive compulsive disorder.

TABLE 16-3
***DSM-III*'s Psychosexual Dysfunctions**

Inhibited sexual desire is a phase I disorder with a pervasive and persistent lack of sexual interest (or libido). It is often accompanied by other sexual dysfunctions.

Inhibited sexual excitement is a phase II disorder, in which, prior to the sexual act being concluded, there is a partial or complete failure to attain or maintain either an erection (i.e., impotence), or the lubrication-swelling response until completion of the sexual act (i.e., frigidity).

Inhibited female and male orgasm are two phase III disorders in which there is a recurrent and persistent inhibition of the orgasm after "sufficient" sexual excitement. Inhibited sexual excitement may be concomitant dysfunction.

Premature ejaculation is a phase III disorder, in which ejaculation occurs before the man wishes because of a recurrent and persistent absence of reasonable voluntary control of ejaculation. The clinician must determine what's "reasonable control," depending on the patient's age, novelty of the sexual partner, and the frequency and duration of coitus.

Functional dyspareunia is when intercourse is associated with recurrent and persistent genital pain, usually in women, but sometimes in men. The dysfunction should only be diagnosed when lubrication is adequate and there is no functional vaginismus.

Functional vaginismus is a history of recurrent and persistent involuntary muscular spasm of the outer third of the vagina which makes penetration difficult, painful, or impossible.

The most common failure in treating psychosexual dysfunctions is misdiagnosis of a medical illness, another mental disorder, or a drug effect. No matter how obviously emotional problems are affecting the patient, no psychosexual dysfunction should be treated until *after* the patient has a complete medical workup, preferably by a physician well-versed in the medical causes of sexual dysfunction.

Modern sex therapies are short-term and experiential, aim for symptomatic relief, focus on the here-and-now sexual interactions of a couple, and combine treatments, such as education, couples psychotherapy, vibrators, homework assignments, desensitization, the squeeze and stop-start techniques, and sensate focusing.[2] Using modern sex therapies, Masters and Johnson (1970) report an 80% overall success rate, with 5% of patients having a recurrence of symptoms within a five-year period. In general, male dysfunctions respond best, with success rates highest for (in declining efficacy) premature ejaculation, retarded ejaculation, secondary impotence, and primary impotence. Treatment is reputed to reverse vaginismus 100% of the time, with less success for generalized unresponsiveness and inhibited orgasm among women.

EGO-DYSTONIC HOMOSEXUALITY

> Homosexualty is assuredly no advantage, but it is nothing to be ashamed of, no vice, no degradation, it cannot be classified as an illness; we consider it to be a variation of the sexual functions produced by a certain arrest of sexual development.
> —Sigmund Freud (1935/1951) Letter to an American Mother

Homosexuality is a persistent preferential erotic attraction for members of the same sex. Its cause is as mysterious as the cause of heterosexuality. Seduction by the same sex no more produces homosexuality than seduction by the opposite sex produces heterosexuality. Homosexuals no more "choose" to become homosexual than heterosexuals "choose" to become heterosexual. A typical story is in Dr. Henry D. Messer's (1979) article "The Homosexual as Physician":

> Like many homosexual men I know, I seem to have always been that way.
> I cannot recall any time in my life when I was attracted to the opposite sex more

---

[2]The squeeze and stop-start (actually start-stop) techniques are mainly for premature ejaculation. Clients start concentrating on arousal while the penis is stimulated, and then stop stimulation just before ejaculatory inevitability. With stop-start, control quietly returns; with the squeeze, the partner squeezes the penis below the corona until the erection slumps, after which stimulation is resumed. Sensate focusing teaches partners to enjoy sexual activity that is not intended to lead to intercourse.

than to the same sex. . . . Because I had been so strongly indoctrinated with the "sex is dirty" idea, especially *abnormal* sex, I attempted to completely give up any type of overt sexual activity during college. I believe that it was better to be miserable and do without sex than to be found out and get into trouble. (pp. 117–118)

Sexual orientation is a relative matter. The Kinsey Scale of sexual orientation goes from 0 (exclusively heterosexual) to 6 (exclusively homosexual). Using this scale as a reference point, Kinsey et al. (1948, 1953) reported that 5% of men and 2% of women are exclusively homosexual (i.e., 6), whereas 50% of men and 72% of women are exclusively heterosexual (i.e., 0). Therefore, 44% of men and 26% of women fall in between. Kinsey's stats also show that 37% of males and 20% of females have homosexual experiences after adolescence, and that 25% of males and 10% of females have had as many, or more, homosexual than heterosexual encounters. Over half the population will have homosexual *fantasies*. The prevalence of homosexuality appears to be constant throughout history.

In defining homosexuality, the clinician should distinguish between sexual behavior, fantasies, and arousal. Homosexuals commonly experiment with heterosexual relations; some marry "to become straight," to deny their homosexuality, to please parents/society, or have companionship, and especially, to raise children. Crime rates, including child molestation, are no higher among homosexuals.

Homosexuality is *not* a mental disorder; it does not meet *DSM-III*'s requirement that a mental disorder's distress or disability must *not be "limited to a conflict between an individual and society . . . "* (p. 6). Homosexuality is only considered a mental disorder when the person persistently and intensely dislikes his own homosexuality. *DSM-III* calls this "ego-dystonic homosexuality" (EDH), and defines its essential features as: (a) heterosexual arousal that is persistently weak or absent, (b) homosexual arousal that significantly interferes with desired heterosexual relations, and (c) homosexual arousal that is a chronic, unwanted source of inner distress. Patients with EDH will cite one or more of these essential features as causing them continual guilt, dysthymia, anxiety, shame, and loneliness.

EDH originates when a person first becomes acutely aware of his homosexual impulses; for men, that's usually in adolescence, for women, the twenties. But whereas most homosexuals pass through several years of turmoil over their homosexuality before coming to accept it, those with EDH have yet to accept it, despite years of concern, heterosexual experimentation, and homosexual encounters. It is rare for patients with EDH to spontaneously increase their heterosexual arousal or decrease their homosexual arousal; even with treatment, it's highly debatable if they do so on any permanent basis.

Patients with EDH must be distingushed from *ego-syntonic homosexuals* (ESH). ESH may seek treatment for problems related to their homosexuality, such as parental rejections after "coming out," a lover dying from AIDS, or a hypochondriacal dread of AIDS. ESH also want treatment for the same reasons heterosexuals do: the death of a parent, a romantic disaster, to get out of a professional rut, etc. But unlike heterosexuals, homosexuals of all kinds are more likely to attribute these problems to their sexual orientation. In true EDH the patient has had a persistent and intense dislike of his homosexuality, whereas in ESH, homosexuality is being used as a temporary scapegoat. Statements like "Life would be easier if I were straight," do not qualify as EDH, nor do episodically uncomfortable episodic homosexual impulses or acts. Patients with *inhibited sexual desire and excitement* may fear they're "latent homosexuals," without realizing that occasional homosexual *urges* are experienced by 50% of men and 24% of women. *Homosexual panic* starts and stops quickly, usually occurs with heterosexuals, and is rare in EDH.

Psychosocial, behavior, and drug therapies usually fail to permanently change the sexual orientation of ego-syntonic homosexuals. On the other hand, a shift in sexual orientation is reported to occur in 20% to 50% of highly motivated EDH patients (Marmor, 1971); to what extent these changes are genuine and enduring is questionable. Thus, *before* any such change is attempted, therapist and patient alike should be very clear on the reasons for wanting a change in sexual orientation.

CHAPTER 17

Factitious Disorders

FACTITIOUS DISORDERS ARE rare conditions in which patients feign physical or psychological symptoms with the sole intent of being a patient. Their "symptoms" so closely resemble known illnesses that they trick doctors into hospitalizing them, conducting numerous tests, and performing unnecessary surgeries. Little is known about these patients, because when they're finally detected, they flee the hospital and are lost to follow-up. They will repeat their charade at many hospitals.

The patient creates symptoms *intentionally*, in the sense of feeling that he controls their production. Clinicians infer this intentional quality from the adeptness at simulating illness. Although the patient intentionally generates symptoms, he's driven to do so. His fakery is compulsive; he can't refrain from subjecting himself to procedures, which he knows are dangerous and needless. His illness-feigning behavior is deliberate and purposeful, but his motivations for producing it are not; for reasons beyond his control, he is impelled to be a patient.

Factitious disorders lie in the middle of a continuum between the outright fakery of physical symptoms (malingering) and their unconscious production (somatoform disorders). Unlike patients with factitious disorders, *malingerers* fabricate symptoms for reasons other than being a patient, such as draft evasion, drugs, disability payments, or missing classes. The malingerer's behavior *and* motivations are conscious, deliberate, and easily understandable. Unlike patients with factitious disorders, those with somatoform disorders are not consciously faking illness.

DSM-III divides factitious disorders into those with *psychological symptoms* and those with *chronic physical symptoms*. In the former, symptoms can't be explained by another mental disorder, but are often superimposed on one. In the latter, the patient's physical "symptoms" result in multiple hospitalizations. Table 17-1 lists *DSM-III* criteria for these two factitious disorders.

Clinical Presentation

With Physical Symptoms. Asher (1951) coined the name "Munchausen syndrome" to portray patients who travel from hospital to hospital, dramatically presenting plausible histories and receiving surgery. Their stories are so elaborate that Asher named their condition after Baron Karl Friedrich Hieronymus Freiherr von Munchhausen (1720–1797), a German cavalry officer and raconteur. *DSM-III* equates Munchausen syndrome with chronic factitious disorder with physical symptoms.

These patients' "symptoms" are limited only by their creativity and medical knowledge; many work in hospitals as nurses or technicians; some study medical texts and speak medicaleze. Most will dramatically enter an emer-

---

TABLE 17-1
***DSM-III* Criteria for Factitious Disorders**

CHRONIC FACTITIOUS DISORDER WITH PHYSICAL SYMPTOMS*

A. Plausible presentation of physical symptoms that are apparently under the individual's voluntary control to such a degree that there are multiple hospitalizations.

B. The individual's goal is apparently to assume the "patient" role and is not otherwise understandable in light of the individual's environmental circumstances (as in the case of Malingering).

FACTITIOUS DISORDER WITH PSYCHOLOGICAL SYMPTOMS†

A. The production of psychological symptoms is apparently under the individual's voluntary control.

B. The symptoms produced are not explained by any other mental disorder (although they may be superimposed on one).

C. The individual's goal is apparently to assume the "patient" role and is not otherwise understandable in light of the individual's environmental circumstances (as is the case in Malingering).

---

*DSM-III, p. 290.
†DSM-III, p. 287.

gency room with a classical description of a disease (e.g., crushing chest pain, sudden loss of breath, convulsions). Once hospitalized, they may insist on narcotics or tell staff which lab tests and procedures to perform.

Their *pièce de resistance* is feigning objective physical signs and abnormal laboratory findings. One patient "raised" his rectal temperature by relaxing and contracting his anal sphincter. Another swallowed blood, strolled into the ER, and puked. Patients will spit saliva into urine samples to elevate urinary amylase, or they may prick a finger and squeeze a little blood into their urine to "develop" hematuria. Self-injecting insulin will produce hypoglycemia. Fecal bacteria will somehow find their way into urine. Patients have swallowed nails, fish hooks, and paint. By self-inducing disease, some of these patients become genuinely sick, although death is rare.

These patients often spin intriguing yarns ("pseudologia fantastica")—false accounts of famous parents, financial wizardry, or show-biz exploits; they might be still another bastard descendant of Aaron Burr or claim a surgical scar came from battlefield heroics. For all the patient's "accomplishments" or "notoriety," the staff may begin to wonder why he has so few visitors, phone calls, or friends. Further clues to the diagnosis are the patient's extensive travel, self-mutilation, la belle indifference to pain and painful procedures, drug abuse (in 50% of cases), ever-changing medical complaints, and substantial evidence of prior treatment, such as venous cutdown scars, signs of recent cardioversion, or a "gridiron abdomen" from multiple operations (Sussman & Hyler, 1985).

When the staff becomes suspicious, the patient becomes increasingly strident and may present new evidence of illness. Any suggestion of a psych consult is angrily rejected. If confronted with his contradictory stories or inconsistent findings, the patient, instead of recanting or displaying embarrassment, will question the staff's competence or threaten litigation. Once these ploys fail, the patient will sign out of the hospital against medical advice or leave surreptitiously. A few days later he may pop up at another hospital, recycling the same saga.

Factitious disorder usually begins during early adulthood, but can start during childhood. Although initially the patient may receive medical care for a real illness, he then develops a pattern of repeated ambulatory treatments and hospitalizations. The prognosis worsens as the patient escalates from (a) giving a fictitious history, (b) to simulating signs of illness, (c) to inducing pathological states.

With Psychological Symptoms. These patients will fake several, usually psychotic-like, symptoms, which laymen would take as a mental illness, but professionals would realize are inconsistent with any known psychiatric disorder. A patient may complain of hallucinations, erratic memory loss, itchy feet, facial twitches, and episodic blindness — a symptom cluster that, although inventive, doesn't exist. These patients may take psychedelics or amphetamines to mimic a psychosis. They're also highly suggestible: If told that hallucinating patients don't sleep, these patients don't sleep. When observed, their symptoms get worse. Some are negativistic and refuse to answer questions. Many have a (genuine) borderline personality disorder.

Others, especially prisoners, may have Ganser syndrome, whose chief symptom is *vorbeireden* — that is, giving approximate answers, near misses, or talking past the point. They appear to understand questions, but to deliberately give false answers: Ask when Santa comes, and they'll say Halloween; ask them to substract 7 from 100, and they'll respond, "92, 84, 76" etc. *Vorbeireden*, however, is found in other disorders.

Epidemiology

Factitious disorder is rare, but its true prevalence is unknown: The rate may be underestimated because patients don't stay around to be counted, or, since patients move from hospital to hospital, the same patient may be reported many times. One patient had over 420 documented hospitalizations. Epidemiologic figures from university populations may be inflated, since these patients are drawn to these facilities. This might account for why Pope et al. (1982) found 6.4% of patients admitted to a psychosis-research service to have factitious disorders with psychological symptoms. Males may have more factitious disorders than females, but nobody really knows.

Etiology and Pathogenesis

What causes factitious disorders is unknown, but they probably develop from a confluence of factors, which vary depending on the patient. Given their self-destructiveness, masochistic or suicidal impulses may feed on a love-hate relationship with health-care professionals. These patients often suffer from childhood deprivation, neglect, and abuse, which may steer them into dependent roles in which they expect health professionals to make up for lost parenting. This might account for factitious disorder "by proxy," a rare phenomenon of a parent inducing symptoms in his child in order to live vicariously through the child as he receives the parental affection of doctors and nurses. Some Munchausen patients identify with health-care professionals, while enjoying a sense of mastery and control from learning about illness, coping with pain, and outwitting physicians.

Differential Diagnosis

The main reason for identifying factitious disorder is to spare the patient from potentially harmful medical procedures and operations. Thus, the chief diagnostic problem is to distinguish factitious disorder from *true organic illness*. Factitious disorders should be entertained when patients stage their history as high drama, exhibit pseudologia fantastica, disrupt a ward and break hospital rules, argue continuously with staff, show off medical jargon and knowledge, demand narcotics, "advertise" signs of numerous prior medical treatments and surgeries, give contradictory histories, develop frequent or inexplicable medical complications, present new symptoms after every negative workup, and become hostile when questioned about their medical history or personal background.

As discussed previously, factitious disorder should be distinguished from *somatoform disorder* and *malingering*. *Antisocial personality disorder* may be misdiagnosed on account of these patients' pseudologia fantastica, impostership, lying, drug abuse, and few close relations. Sociopaths, however, avoid painful tests and hospitals; Munchausen patients "attract" them. Some *schizophrenics* self-induce physical symptoms, but secondarily to a specific delusion or command hallucination.

Diagnosing factitious disorder with psychological symptoms is especially difficult, because most psychological symptoms can't be objectively verified. Whenever symptoms don't fit the pattern of a *known mental disorder*, factitious disorder merits consideration. Factitious disorder with psychological symptoms *and* another mental disorder can both be diagnosed, as long as the factitious symptoms are produced without an ulterior motive (as in malingering).

MANAGEMENT AND TREATMENT

Wilhelm Kaiser claimed the only requirement for successful therapy is that two people be in a room. And since patients with factitious disorders don't stay in the room, the only thing that's clear about treating them is that nothing is known to work. Failed treatments include hypnosis, medications (of all kinds), ECT, insulin coma, and lobotomy. Several authors advocate psychotherapy, but have too few treatment cases to establish its efficacy. Even when physicians gently confront these patients with their true diagnosis, patients still react with hostility and reject any offer of help.

The physician's frustration has led to some far-out "therapeutic" suggestions: (a) Tatoo the patient's diagnosis on his belly to alert the next physician; (b) establish a central registry of these patients; (c) imprison patients for nonpayment of hospital bills; (d) tell patients about Munchausen syndrome with the hope they will inadvertently tip off future caregivers by showing off their use of the term; and (e) encourage the adoption of "pseudo-factitious" behaviors (e.g., such as drawing abdominal scars with indelible ink), which are less dangerous yet still satisfy the individual's perverse need to be a patient (Jefferson & Ochitill, 1982).

Despite the absence of any clearly effective treatment, experts generally recommend that, once the diagnosis of factitious disorder is established, physicians should: (a) Be careful not to overlook genuine medical disease. (b) Keep the patient in the hospital — for once out, always out — so as to involve him in extended psychiatric treatment. (c) Avoid power struggles and public humiliations. (d) Be ever-alert to the behaviors and dynamics (including splitting) commonly associated with borderline personality disorder. (e) Don't get bent out of shape because the patient outsmarts them. The disorder is the patient's, not the staff's.

CHAPTER 18

Impulse Disorders

ON OCCASION, EVERYONE is impulsive, many like to gamble, and plenty thrill to a blaze. But unlike these normal behaviors, disorders of impulse control have three essential characteristics: (a) The person *can't resist* an impulse or drive to do something that he knows will be harmful to himself or others. (b) He experiences increasing *tension* before performing the act. Patients often describe this tension as "pressure," "restlessness," "anxiety," or "discomfort." (c) The patient feels enormous *relief*, gratification, or satisfaction when committing the act. As a result, while acting on the impulse is momentarily ego-syntonic, later on he might feel guilt, self-reproach, or regret. The patient may, or may not, be aware of the impulse, and the deed may, or may not, be premeditated. Patients with impulse disorders tend to portray themselves as weak souls who readily cave into temptation or get overwhelmed by external forces. In a way, they're right, in that pathological impulsivity stems less from deliberate intent and more from an irresistible urge to discharge tension.

DSM-III groups impulse disorders in a residual category called "Disorders of Impulse Control Not Elsewhere Classified," because impulse disturbances also occur in bulimia, mania, substance abuse, paraphilias, borderline and antisocial personality disorders. *DSM-III*'s residual category lists five specific impulse disorders: pathological gambling, kleptomania, pyromania, intermittent explosive disorder, and isolated explosive disorder. (*DSM-III-R* may add *trichotillomania*—the failure to resist impulses to pull out one's own hair, resulting in noticeable hair loss.) This chapter will highlight pathological gambling as a prototypic impulse disorder; the other impulse disorders are briefly described.

281

PATHOLOGICAL GAMBLING

Distinguishing "social" from pathological gambling is akin to differentiating the social drinker from the alcoholic. Social gambling, like social drinking, is done for pleasure, with friends, and feels optional. Pathological gambling, like alcoholism, is done because the person can't stop, excludes friends, and feels obligatory. In most respects, pathological gambling, like alcoholism, is an *addiction*.

Clinical Presentation

The gambling "addict" feels unable to resist gambling, despite knowing that he'll lose and can't afford it. As one explained, "I've placed hundreds of bets not caring whether I win or lose. Why? Because I love the action. I'm drawn to the excitement. When I bet, I feel good and important. My orgasm is gambling."

Like other addictions, pathological gambling encourages further gambling, which goes on to disrupt and damage every aspect of a person's life. Gambling debts take precedence over grocery bills. Forgery, fraud, arrests, tax evasion, excessive borrowing, stealing from friends, defaulting on loans, juggling financial obligations, lying, and forgetting who's owed what—it's all part of the disorder. Obligations to family and friends are replaced by obligations to loan sharks and pawn brokers. Even when the patient is not gambling, he's preoccupied with gambling. Everything he does is a result of gambling. Like a child, he will sneak away from home to borrow money or to place a bet. Some compulsive gamblers develop a perverse thrill or pride in the creativity of their reasons for why their debts aren't being paid and why their "big winnings" aren't paying off. Short of violence, anything will be done for money. As a "big game" approaches, the pathological gambler reaches an intolerable level of tension, which only the game relieves. Winning or losing has no effect on his gambling; he gambles only as long as people will let him. Table 18-1 presents *DSM-III*'s criteria for pathological gambling; the characteristics listed in B highlight the disorder's chief problems.

The compulsive gambler turns every nongambling situation into a gamble. "When a normal person," explains a pathological gambler, "is driving with a quarter tank of gas on a highway and spots a sign saying the next gas station is 50 miles away, he'll stop for gas. The gambler won't. He'll make a bet with himself that he can reach the next station without stopping for gas. This is a typical 'mind bet,' and when I'm not making a real bet, I'm making a mind bet."

TABLE 18-1
DSM-III **Criteria for Pathological Gambling***

A. The individual is chronically and progressively unable to resist impulses to gamble.

B. Gambling compromises, disrupts, or damages family, personal, and vocational pursuits, as indicated by at least three of the following:

(1) arrest for forgery, fraud, embezzlement, or income tax evasion due to attempts to obtain money for gambling
(2) default on debts or other financial responsibilities
(3) disrupted family or spouse relationship due to gambling
(4) borrowing of money from illegal sources (loan sharks)
(5) inability to account for loss of money or to produce evidence of winning money, if this is claimed
(6) loss of work due to absenteeism in order to pursue gambling activity
(7) necessity for another person to provide money to relieve a desperate financial situation

C. The gambling is not due to Antisocial Personality Disorder.

*DSM-III, pp. 292–293.

Gambling, or talk of gambling, dominates conversation; it's as if every social skill has atrophied, except for gambling or talking about gambling. Damon Runyon's characters might be fiction, but his descriptions of the gambler's mentality are not. For instance, a Runyon character says that whenever Feet Samuels — so-named because his feet are always at 90° angles — stands at a corner, gamblers will bet on which way Feet Samuels will go. In *Guys and Dolls*, Nathan Detroit calls Sky Masterson "the highest player of them all. . . . Another time he was sick and would not take penicillin because he bet his fever would go to a 104."

Generalizations surely, but impulsive gamblers tend to be "big talkers" and "big spenders." Normally overconfident, self-centered, abrasive, energetic, and jovial, their moods reflect their earnings: On winning, they're temporarily elated; on losing, they're moody and anxious.

Clinical Course and Complications

While a teenager, the future pathological gambler bets socially; his gambling usually becomes serious in early adulthood, often after some modest winnings and during some stressful period. Gamblers Anonymous (see below) describes four phases in the deterioration of the pathological gambler. First is the *winning phase*, in which the person gambles occasionally, fantasizes about winning, escalates his bets, and wins big. Next comes the *losing phase* — he gambles alone, skips work, lies, borrows heavily, doesn't pay debts, and returns the next day to win back losses ("chasing"). Third is the *desperation phase*, during which he is filled with remorse and his reputation suffers: He becomes separated from family and friends, gets fired, blames others, panics, and steals. Last is the *hopeless phase*, in which he feels utterly futile, gets arrested and divorced, drinks heavily and abuses drugs, becomes demoralized and depressed, and on hitting "rock bottom," contemplates or attempts suicide. Pathological gambling is a chronic disorder that waxes and wanes.

Pathological gambling is not limited to gambling, but impairs most aspects of an individual's life. Lost jobs, broken marriages, stealing, imprisonment, financial ruin and attempted suicide are common. While stressing the many similarities between pathological gambling and alcoholism, a "reformed" gambler aptly points to a big difference: "If you're an alcoholic with $1,000, you'll drink $50-worth of booze and fall asleep; when you awake, you've still got $950. If you're a druggie and shoot up $400-worth, you'll drift off and still awake with $600. But if you're a gambler, you'll blow all $1,000 and end up with *nothing*!

Epidemiology

Although the precise prevalence of pathological gamblers is unknown, with the growth of legalized gambling in the United States their numbers have climbed from 4 million in 1976 to 12 million in 1980 (Ginsberg, 1985). A parallel pattern has occurred in Great Britain, suggesting that legalized gambling may promote pathological gambling.[1]

More men than women are purported to be pathological gamblers, but since it's traditionally more acceptable for men to gamble, the number of female "closet gamblers" may be underestimated. Gambling affects all social classes, and if anything, is greater among the wealthy than among the poor.

Etiology and Pathogenesis

Little is known about the etiology of pathological gambling, except psychosocial factors are generally blamed. The typical impulsive gambler comes from a family in which social gambling is at least condoned, or in which a parent of the same sex is a compulsive gambler or alcoholic. Disturbed childhoods, broken homes, financial difficulties, and materialism characterize the gambler's upbringing. Fenichel (1945) speculated that gambling and masturbation were psychological equivalents in that both involve a buildup of tension, which is heightened by anticipation, and discharged by repetitive action.

---

[1]Nearly two-thirds of Americans patronize legalized gambling: casinos, horse racing, dog racing, church bingo, state-run lotteries, etc. Their promotors don't call it "gambling," but run ads imploring listeners to, "Get where the action is!" a most telling phrase given the pathological gambler's thirst for excitement.

Differential Diagnosis

When a patient's chief complaint is *"depression,"* pathological gambling may be readily overlooked. If seeking treatment during the desperation or hopeless phases, the gambler may be so ashamed of his "moral weakness of gambling" that he avoids the topic, complaining instead of hopelessness, helplessness, suicidal thoughts, insomnia, and other depressive symptoms. Since clinicians rarely ask depressed patients if they gamble excessively, the disorder can elude diagnosis. Unlike people with *antisocial personality disorder*, most pathological gamblers have good work records prior to their serious gambling, and they steal solely to pay debts or to have money for gambling.

Pathological gambling may be confused with *manic* or *hypomanic episodes*, since (a) mania often leads to outrageous betting, (b) both conditions involve poor judgment and little foresight, and (c) euphoria usually follows a gambler's winning streak. The presence of other manic behaviors, however, easily rules out pathological gambling. As previously discussed, pathological gambling should be distinguished from *social gambling*.

Management and Treatment

Many gamblers will enter treatment simply to get relatives off their back; once things cool down, gambling resumes. If they remain in treatment, four particular attitudes frequently undermine therapy: (a) lack of money is seen as *the* problem, (b) an instant or miraculous cure is expected, (c) life without gambling is inconceivable, and (d) repaying debts is desirable, but impossible (Custer, 1979). Denying these attitudes during treatment, especially near the beginning, raises doubts about the authenticity of the patient's commitment to change. Since these patients are often bright and have a gift of gab, place little stock in what they *say* and far more in what they *do*. Treatment should be judged on the duration of gambling-free intervals, on debts being paid, and on developing interests other than gambling.

The last goal is often overlooked, but crucial since substitute excitements and pleasures must eventually replace gambling; hence, vocational counseling and recreational therapy may be an invaluable adjunct to therapy. Meeting periodically with relatives is also important, as much for the relative as for the gambler. Clinicians should remind themselves and loved ones that pathological gambling is a *chronic* disorder, in which lapses are expected and do not necessarily mean that therapy is a bust.

If the gambler is on trial for problems secondary to his gambling, such as tax eva-sion, the best sentence might involve an extended probation *contingent* on the patient's participating fully in therapy, repaying all debts on schedule, not gambling, being regularly employed, and periodically showing financial accountability. Imprisonment is only useful when the gambler doesn't fulfill this program.

Founded in 1957, Gamblers Anonymous (GA) is modeled after Alcoholics Anony-mous, claims 12,000 members, and affiliates with Gamanon, which is for relatives of gamblers and similar to Alanon. (Contact: GA's National Service Office, P.O. Box 17173, Los Angeles, California, 90017, 213-386-8789.) Only 5% to 8% of gamblers who join GA stop gambling, but if GA is combined with comprehensive inpatient care, half who complete the program refrain from gambling for a year, and a third do so for several years (Kellner, 1982b). Given the similarities between gambling and alco-holism and between GA and AA, if a GA chapter isn't available, attending AA is a good substitute.

KLEPTOMANIA

Kleptomania is the recurrent failure to resist impulses to steal objects that are not for immediate use or for economic gain. The kleptomaniac has enough money to buy the object, and once possessing it, she—kleptomania being more common among women—has no use for it; she's likely to give it away, return it, or forget it. Unlike other thieves or shoplifters, the kleptomaniac experiences mounting tension before stealing and a gratifying relief of ten-sion afterwards. The kleptomaniac steals by herself, spontaneously, and without compatriots. She steals to alleviate tension, and when that tension becomes unbearable, she's more concerned with discharging anxiety than with taking precautions. Kleptomaniacs make lousy thieves: Their bounty isn't worth much and they're frequently caught. Contrary to myth, kleptomaniacs do *not* want to be caught: What they do want is the thrill of discharging that tension.

Kleptomania seems to wax and wane over time and often "burns out" with age. Four percent of apprehended shoplifters are kleptomaniacs. Kleptomania should not be diagnosed in the presence of *mania, schizophrenia, antisocial personality disorder, or conduct disorders*—all conditions which may lead to compulsive stealing.

Since there are no published series of cases—were they stolen?—little is known about the disorder's causes and cures. Some speculate that compulsive buying and stealing provide similar pleasures, while others draw analogies between the bulimic's bingeing and the kleptomaniac's stealing. These observations suggest that treatment should substitute the kleptomaniac's tension-gratification cycle with a more socially acceptable tension-gratification cycle. Because anecdotal reports indicate that these patients steal more often during stressful periods and are plagued by unsatisfying rela-tionships, insight-oriented family or group therapy sounds reasonable. Until more is known, the treatment principles presented for pathological gambling would apply for treating kleptomania.

PYROMANIA

Pyromania is the recurrent failure to resist setting fires, along with an intense fascination with igniting and watching them. Setting fires is gratifying because it discharges mounting tension. The pyromaniac thrills at seeing flames leap up and destroy things. By definition, the pyromaniac does not set fires for any other reason (e.g., greed, revenge, politics).

Case studies show that as children most future pyromaniacs are fascinated by fires, fire engines, firemen, and any firefighting equipment. They pull many a false alarm and relish the sight of firefighters rushing to the scene; orchestrating this whole to-do may afford the child an enormous sense of power, control, and mastery, which he probably lacks in other areas of life. Incendiary habits usually begin when a parent remarries or the child thinks a parent has been unfaithful; the link between parents, fidelity, sex, and power may contribute to the pyromaniac's erotic pleasure, and sometimes masturbation, in watching a blaze; firesetting can also serve as revenge against such disloyal parents. This might partly account for why, after setting a fire, they rarely feel remorse or regret, despite fully knowing that they've destroyed property, maimed victims, or murdered. Even planning arson, which they do way in advance, brings pleasure.

Pyromaniacs are drawn to any huge fire (which is the first place police look to nab a firesetter). Since most pyromaniacs come to psychiatrists via the courts, the literature about them is skewed. Nevertheless, pyromania is a rare disorder, affecting males 90% of the time. Pyromaniacs often have mild mental retardation, learning disabilities, hyperkinesis, heavy drinking, poor impulse control in other areas (e.g., temper tantrums, recklessness), and enuresis during childhood—facts which all suggest some neurophysiologic component to pyromania.

Urinating on a fire one has set is allegedly pathognomonic for pyromania. Shades of Gulliver. Pyromania in children differs from *normal childhood fascination with fires*, in that the latter is less frequent, pernicious, and all-consuming. Although patients with *antisocial personality disorders* set fires, their reasons are not limited to being gratified by the fire. *Deliberate sabotage*, as "paid torches," political terrorism, and good old-fashioned revenge, must be ruled out. *Schizophrenics* set fires, but in response to delusions or hallucinations. Unlike pyromaniacs, *demented* patients set fires, although by accident, and always without planning or without realizing the consequences of the act.

There being no controlled studies assessing treatment, anecdotal reports indicate that most child pyromaniacs recover fully, whereas adult pyromaniacs do not. With their mildly low intelligence and ingrained impulsiveness, few pyromaniacs benefit from insight-oriented psychotherapy. Behavior therapies might be more useful by substituting pathological with healthy gratifications and by improving social skills. Given the pervasive impulsivity of pyromaniacs, lithium and carbamazepine have been tried, but with mixed results. Perhaps the most useful intervention is to insure they don't drink.

INTERMITTENT EXPLOSIVE DISORDER

This very rare disorder is characterized by discrete episodes of violence with little or no provocation. The outbursts, which start and stop abruptly, usually last several minutes but may persist for several hours. The person suddenly breaks windows, throws chairs, and so on. The "seizures" or "spells" may be immediately preceded by a rapid mood change, flushing, tachycardia, or altered sensorium (e.g., confusion, amnesia). Patients will then describe an "irresistible impulse that comes over them" to smash everything in sight. Afterwards, most will assume responsibility for the act and express genuine remorse.

This disorder primarily affects men, and usually arises during their twenties or thirties. The prototypic patient grew up in a broken home where he was physically abused by an alcoholic parent; he was either hyperkinetic or had encephalitis or perinatal or head trauma; as an adult, he's muscular, concerned with his masculine identity, and in jail.

These patients have been labeled "explosive characters," "epileptoid personalities," and in *DSM-III-R*, "organic personality syndrome, explosive type." That's because they frequently display soft neurological signs, and because their "attacks" are often triggered by alcohol, sedatives, premenstrual tension, bright lights, and loud noises — the same stimuli that trigger epileptic seizures. Despite this, their EEGs are invariably normal.

There is no clearly effective treatment, although some patients have been helped by anticonvulsant medications (e.g., carbamazepine), beta-blockers (e.g., propranolol, metaprolol), lithium, phenothiazines, and antidepressants. Hypnosedatives may worsen the condition. Group therapy is claimed to be more useful than individual therapy.

ISOLATED EXPLOSIVE DISORDER

The sweet boy down the block, who wouldn't harm a fly, who's never seen a shrink, who's always helped old ladies cross the street, and who one day climbs a tower, takes out a Winchester, slaughters 20 people, and commits suicide: He's got an isolated explosive disorder. His reasons are vague and not those of a political terrorist in the usual sense. The disorder usually occurs in men between the ages of 20 and 50, and is a single event in a life that, unlike this chapter, ends with a bang.

CHAPTER 19

Adjustment Disorders

ADJUSTMENT DISORDERS are a large part of clinical practice and often the most rewarding conditions to treat. When *DSM-III* was pretested, clinicians diagnosed adjustment disorder in about 10% of adults and 32% of adolescents. Adjustment disorders can be disruptive and distressing, yet with time and treatment they resolve; in fact, many patients emerge healthier and wiser.

Adjustment disorders are the most benign of the mental disorders, but more severe than "normal" problems in living (e.g., uncomplicated bereavement, marital problems). Thus, adjustment disorders *are* psychopathology, and their diagnosis critical: When adjustment disorders are dismissed as normal problems in living, clinicians risk underestimating the seriousness of the patient's difficulties, such as truancy, financial disaster, and suicidal intent. On the other hand, when adjustment disorders are misdiagnosed as more ominous conditions, the patient may receive inappropriate medication, psychotherapy, and hospitalization.

Clinical Presentation

Adjustment disorders, according to *DSM-III*, are maladaptive reactions to psychosocial stressors occurring within the past three months; they are self-limiting (less than six months in *DSM-III-R*), have happened previously, and are not due to another mental disorder (Table 19-1). In other words, these are relatively benign, transient, but maladaptive, situational reactions.

To qualify as a maladaptive reaction, it must impair functioning, or it must be stronger or last longer than a "normal" person's response to the same stressor. These reactions constitute patterns of behaviors, not single events. On watching his house burn down, a frightened man starts smashing his

289

TABLE 19-1
DSM-III **Criteria for Adjustment Disorder***

A. A maladaptive reaction to an identifiable psychosocial stressor that occurs within three months of the onset of the stressor.

B. The maladaptive nature of the reaction is indicated by either of the following:

(1) impairment in social or occupational functioning
(2) symptoms that are in excess of a normal and expectable reaction to the stressor

C. The disturbance is not merely one instance of a pattern of overreaction to stress or an exacerbation of one of the mental disorders previously described.

D. It is assumed that the disturbance will eventually remit after the stressor ceases or, if the stressor persists, when a new level of adaptation is achieved.

E. The disturbance does not meet the criteria for any of the specific disorders listed previously or for Uncomplicated Bereavement.

DSM-III, pp. 300–301.

neighbors' windows. His reaction, although excessive, is limited to this outburst; subsequently, he experiences nothing besides the expected sadness and frustration. This man does *not* have an adjustment disorder.

Steve Walsh did. Extremely bright and bored by school, at 16 Steve began to skip classes and to peddle marijuana and cocaine. School officials and the police dragged in Steve, who dragged in his parents, who were finding Steve to be a drag. While upstairs in his room one evening, Steve overheard one of his parents' many screaming matches. Steve says that his mother yelled at her husband, "My psychiatrist says I need tranquilizers because you're such a bastard," to which his father replied, "At least I didn't breed that delinquent bastard son of yours." Although Mrs. Walsh tried hushing her husband so Steve wouldn't hear, it was too late. Stunned at first, Steve turned up his stereo earphones to blast and empty his mind. At three in the morning, Steve quietly emerged, grabbed his mother's barbiturates, fled Dayton, drove to Cleveland, and began selling the barbiturates on the street. Steve hated living on the street, but had no place to go. He felt unloved and unwanted; Steve wanted his parents, but refused to call them. Five days later his father tracked him down, scooped him up, and returned him to Dayton on the condition that the entire family would get therapy. Steve desperately wanted to get away from home and attend a challenging private school. The parents agreed, partly for Steve's sake, but also because they wanted to improve their relationship without Steve's acting-up constantly (and "conveniently") distracting them. The plan worked.

Adjustment disorders present with *generalized* symptoms (e.g., disruptions of mood or conduct), as opposed to *specific* ones (e.g., hallucinations, delusions, phobias, and panic attacks). Depression and anxiety are the most frequent mood disturbances. Except for suicide attempts, depressive symptoms are more common in adults (87%) than adolescents (64%), whereas conduct (or behavioral) problems are more prevalent in adolescents (77%) than adults (25%). Suicidal thoughts are more often reported by adults (36% versus 29%), but among those having these thoughts, adolescents (86%) attempt suicide more than adults (47%). Conduct problems among adolescents include truancy, drinking, temper outbursts, vandalism, school suspension, persistent lying, repeated arrests.

The stressor can be just about anything: It may be acute or chronic, single or multiple, affect individuals or groups; it may be associated with a specific event or a developmental stage. The stressor's impact varies according to its duration, timing, context, and meaning, and so the severity of any particular stressor depends on the particular individual. (Indicate the severity of the stressor on Axis IV.) For adults, the most common stressors are marital problems (25%), separation or divorce (23%), moving (17%), finances (14%), and work (9%). For adolescents they are school problems (60%), parental rejection (27%), substance abuse (26%), parental separation or divorce (25%), boyfriend-girlfriend problems (20%), and parental marital problems (18%). Death of a loved one affected a mere 3% of the adults and 11.5% of the adolescents (Andreasen & Wasek, 1980).

As seen in *DSM-III*'s criterion D, the diagnosis of an adjustment disorder requires an assumption, or a reasonable prediction, that the patient's condition will remit or that the patient will attain a new (higher or lower) level of adaptation. This "guestimate" considers not just the stressor, but the patient — his track record in dealing with similar stressors, his highest previous level of adaptive functioning, etc.

Clinical Course

Whereas the *DSM-III* label of "*adjustment* disorder" stresses adaptation, not cure, the corresponding *DSM-II* label of "*transient* situational reaction" stressed full recovery. Indeed, in most cases, once the precipitating stressor disappears, so does the adjustment disorder. In a study of 2,078 male Navy enlistees hospitalized for transient situational reactions, the average inpatient stay was two weeks, with 90% returning to full active duty. Those who didn't return were young and had fewer occupational skills (Looney & Gunderson, 1978).

In nearly every respect, adults fare better than adolescents. Adjustment disorders in adolescents are more severe, last longer, require more treatment, and have worse outcomes. Three to five-year follow-ups revealed 59% to 71% of adults functioning well, but only 44% of adolescents doing so. Among those doing poorly in both groups, although suicide was rare (2% to 4%), affective, antisocial personality, and substance use disorders were common.

Overall, the most reliable predictors of poor outcome were the chronicity of the adjustment disorder, being younger, the frequency of misconduct symptoms, and the number of stressors. Depressive symptoms did *not* predict outcome (Andreasen & Hoenk, 1982).

Epidemiology

Although adjustment disorders are common, because they're a new diagnostic category, few epidemiologic studies have been conducted. Adjustment disorders have been diagnosed in 5% of inpatients, 20% of outpatients, and three times as often in adolescents than in adults. However, clinicians may overdiagnose adjustment disorders because of their benign connotations. Their prevalence among various sexes, races, and classes is unknown.

Etiology and Pathogenesis

When *normal* responses to stress are intensified, prolonged, or blocked, they produce either (the milder) adjustment disorders or (the more severe) post-traumatic stress disorders. Responses to stress—normal or pathological—evolve in stages, as previously described. (See Figures 4-3 & 12-1.) A common adjustment disorder which follows this sequence is the classic "midlife crisis." In *crisis theory*, Caplan (1964) proposed that people may emerge from a crisis better off than before; they may develop greater maturity, ego-strength, wisdom, or self-confidence.

It's unknown why some patients react to a stressor with an adjustment disorder, some with a post-traumatic stress disorder, and some with no difficulties at all. Only a few clues exist: *DSM-III* claims that organic and personality disorders predispose patients to developing adjustment reactions. Except for having alcoholic fathers, no other family traits are associated with adjustment disorders.

Differential Diagnosis

Adjustment disorders should not be diagnosed until "normal *problems in living*" and other mental disorders have been ruled out. *DSM-III* calls these normal problems in living "Conditions Not Attributable to a Mental Disorder That Are a Focus of Attention or Treatment," and they're outlined in Appendix F. Adjustment disorders differ from these conditions either by impairing functioning or by exceeding the normally expected reactions to such a stressor. These distinctions are relative and require clinical judgment.

Unlike *post-traumatic stress disorders* (PTS), adjustment disorders must occur within three months of the stressor. The stressors producing adjustment disorders are "typical" (e.g., marital problems, retirement), whereas those generating PTS are unusual, often beyond normal human experience, catastrophic, frequently affecting multitudes (e.g., "Jonestown," plane crash, earthquake). Adjustment disorders are briefer and less severe than PTS.

When a psychosocial stress exacerbates a medical illness, instead of calling it an adjustment reaction, the preferred diagnosis is *psychological factors affecting physical condition*. If a stressor aggravates a *personality disorder*, an adjustment disorder is diagnosed only when a new symptom appears that is not central to the personality disorder. For example, after her last child leaves home for college, a mother with a histrionic personality disorder becomes uncharacteristically withdrawn.

Management and Treatment

The main controversy over treating adjustment disorders is whether to treat them at all. Although most patients recover fully with therapy, a substantial number do not. The arguments against treatment are that because (by definition) adjustment disorders are time-limited, treating them wastes the patient's time, money, and effort. The patient may be harmed by interfering with the, at least in theory, natural recovery process. Additional problems might be generated: The patient may become a "therapy addict"; he may be unable to cope with a newly discovered set of difficulties—how much he hates his father, how little he loves his wife—or if therapy is a bust, he may leave it more discouraged than ever.

The arguments for therapy are that because no clinician can really know in advance whether a patient will fully recover, if nothing else treatment can minimize adverse consequences, such as preventing patients from making dumb, spur-of-the-moment, irreversible decisions. Therapy could also hasten recovery, stop the patient from blowing matters out of proportion, and enable him to avert similar crises in the future.

Experts generally believe that treatment should derive from Caplan's (1964) crisis intervention model. Accordingly, the primary goal of treatment is to have the patient return to baseline; the secondary goal, or possibility, is to capitalize on the emotional turmoil of the crisis to change some long-standing maladaptive patterns into more useful and self-satisfying ones. In this model, treatment is brief, time-limited, and focused exclusively on problems linked to the stressor. (About half the patients who enter brief psychotherapy for adjustment disorders finish in four weeks.)

The most frequently used treatment is *individual psychotherapy*. It identifies the stressor, examines how it affects the patient, and discusses how the patient should deal with it. *Family therapy* is the second most widely used treatment. When the family plays a major role in the adjustment disorder, family treatment can follow the same principles of crisis intervention. *Medications* might be used temporarily, as long as there is a clear target symptom (e.g., insomnia, depression) that impairs functioning or slows recovery.

CHAPTER 20

Psychological Factors
Affecting Physical Condition

The sorrow which has no vent in tears may make other organs weep.
— Henry Maudsley

UNTIL THE 1970s, psychiatrists generally held that *certain* medical illnesses could *only* arise if particular psychological (and biological) events occurred. When these events contributed to pathologically altered tissues or organs, the resultant diseases were called "psychosomatic" (e.g., ulcers); when they disrupted pathophysiologic processes (without causing obvious tissue damage), the resultant illnesses were called "psychophysiologic" (e.g., migraine).[1] By implication, other diseases were neither psychosomatic nor psychophysiologic. These concepts, however, have all been revised. *Whether* psychosocial factors affect disease is no longer questioned: They *do*. But instead of only *some* illnesses being psychosomatic, today, they *all* are. The key questions now are *how* and to *what degree* psychosocial factors influence disease.

Therefore, in a deliberate effort to reflect these new outlooks, instead of simply calling this section "psychosomatic illnesses," *DSM-III* uses "Psychological Factors Affecting Physical Condition" (PFAPC). What's the difference? A diagnosis of psychosomatic illness would focus on the *resultant* illness, whereas a diagnosis of PFAPC focuses on the *causation* of illness. A

---

[1]For literary convenience this chapter interchanges "illness" and "disease," despite the distinction drawn on pp. 5–6.

diagnosis of psychosomatic illness implies that some illnesses are not psychosomatic, whereas a diagnosis of PFAPC may apply to any illness.

Clinicians should diagnose PFAPC when psychological factors have substantially launched, aggravated, or perpetuated a medical disease (e.g., diabetes) or symptom (e.g., vomiting). To apply this label, there should be a clear *temporal* relationship between the environmental stressor and the medical ailment. Yet it's up to the professional to judge whether these forces were sufficiently influential to merit the diagnosis of PFAPC. The diagnosis, by the way, can be used whether or not the patient is aware of the stressor. Sometimes how stressors affect illness is abundantly clear: A man's wife dies, and within months his health deteriorates. Sometimes the relationship between stressor and illness is minor or inconsequential. Sometimes it's unclear: When an elderly woman finds it harder to walk and becomes increasingly depressed over a six-month period, did the depression cause the impairment or vice versa? Such chicken-and-egg problems are often difficult to unscramble.

Unlike somatoform disorders, PFAPC must have demonstrable organic pathology (e.g., ulcerative colitis) or a known pathophysiologic process (e.g., "tension headaches"). In fact, the diagnosis of PFAPC requires the absence of a somatoform disorder. PFAPC is listed on Axis I, the physical condition on Axis III.

Environmental Factors Affecting Illness

The chief purpose of diagnosing PFAPC is to focus attention on the environmental factors influencing the patient's medical condition. But at a more basic level, how does this occur? Assuming there's a link between a woman losing her job and her developing pneumonia, how does an environmental stress change lung tissue? Moreover, why pneumonia? Why not a heart attack, or a stroke, or insomnia? Although numerous mechanisms have been postulated to answer these questions, every psychosomatic theory assumes that psychosocial factors interact with a biological predisposition to yield a disease. At this juncture, concepts diverge.

Psychological Factors

From the 1930s through the 1950s, a belief popularized by Alexander (1950) was that specific *unconscious conflicts* produced seven psychosomatic illnesses — essential hypertension, asthma, neurodermatitis, peptic ulcer, ulcerative colitis, rheumatoid arthritis, and thyrotoxicosis. Known as the "holy seven," these diseases could only arise if the patient had (a) the particular unresolved emotional conflict associated with the disease, (b) a biological vulnerability to the specific disease, and (c) the needed psychosocial trigger to bring on the disease. For example, when a person driven by infantile desires to be cared for (or fed) had these wishes stymied, he might develop an ulcer. This theory fell into disrepute in part because most of the evidence was gathered retrospectively instead of prospectively, and in part because psychoanalytic treatment aimed at resolving these conflicts did not improve the patient's disease. It also became clear that psychosomatic processes were not limited to the holy seven.

Dunbar (1946) advanced the view that specific *personality profiles* produced specific diseases. She suggested, for instance, that patients with myocardial infarctions are workaholics, whose heart attacks would follow a severe work-related stress. This approach led to studies of the Type A personality of heart disease, which is hard-driving, preoccupied with achievement, impatient, time-pressured, and aggressively competitive. Type As have roughly twice as many heart attacks as those without these traits — that is, Type B personalities. In post-heart-attack patients, a combined program of group and behavior therapies seems to reduce Type A traits and decrease their rate of subsequent coronaries in half.

Instead of the psychosocial culprit being a specific conflict or personality, it may be that a *stress of any type* activates a person's biological susceptibility to a specific disease. For instance, Riley (1975) exposed two sets of mice to the Bittner virus, which causes breast cancers. Mice in the first set were then placed in a high-stress crowded environment, the second in a stress-free environment. After 400 days, cancers developed in 92% of the first set and only 7% of the second. It's a hypothesis only, but stress may have lowered adrenal steroids, which diminished T cells, which decreased the body's immunologic resistance, which increased the mice's susceptibility to cancer. In humans, Holmes and Rahe (1967) showed the frequency and magnitude of life changes directly correlated with the onset and severity of illness. Most striking is that relatives of the recently deceased die at a rate of seven times that of the general population (Rees & Lutkins, 1967).

Instead of psychological factors producing physical conditions, maybe it's just the reverse? Maybe basic *physiologic events* give rise to ingrained personality traits. For instance, hypothetically a newborn with gastric hypersecretion requires more feedings to diminish cramps and grows up with greater needs for attention and conflicts over dependence. Another possibility is that the same gene may predispose an individual to both a particular physical ailment *and* a particular personality trait.

Sociocultural Factors

Sociocultural forces also shape how people experience, understand, and deal with illness. Zborowski's (1952) classic study in medical sociology demonstrated how ethnic factors can influence a patient's reaction to pain. In a hospital survey, he showed that Jewish and Italian patients tended to respond emotionally and would exaggerate the experience of pain, "old Americans" were likely to be stoic and objective, and the Irish were inclined to deny or to minimize pain. Whereas the Italians primarily wanted relief from pain, the Jews were more concerned with the pain's meaning and future consequences. Zborowski's findings do not mean that all patients with the same ethnicity react these ways, but do imply that ethnic factors influence how people perceive and cope with illness.

People have aches and pains everyday, but they don't run to the doctor every time — well, most don't. Whether they do depends on the severity of the symptom. But even how people perceive a symptom's severity is influenced by socioeconomic class. To illustrate: When Koos (1954) asked people if they believed blood in the urine merited consulting a physician, four times more upper-class (87%) than lower-class (19%) patients answered affirmatively. This finding was irrespective of whether subjects could afford the physician, take time from work, etc.

Responses to Physical Illness

The stages that people generally pass through in response to a major stressor have already been outlined (Figures 4-3, 12-1), but when the stressor is a medical illness, these same stages tend to present in the following ways:

1. Denial, and less often, outcry come first. If the patient learns he has cancer, he may respond with emotional outbursts or may act as if nothing is wrong. For example, on being told she had breast cancer needing immediate surgery, a woman innocently asked her doctor if he could do her spring-cleaning. These patients often feel emotionally numbed, describing themselves as in a state of "shock" or "disbelief."

2. Intrusion follows, with the patient struggling to face the reality of his condition. One moment he knows his life has changed, the next moment he "reverses the clock" by pretending his illness never existed or disappeared. A middle-aged man who was blinded in a car accident wanted to learn braille in the morning, but later in the day he tried walking out of the hospital as if he were sighted. Emotionally, this phase is dominated by anger, anxiety, and frustration.

3. *Working-through* begins when the person has emotionally accepted the existence and seriousness of the illness and starts focusing on, "What do I do now?" Although true progress has been made by accepting his illness, he should still be expected to undergo episodes of despair, apathy, and dysphoria.

4. *Completion*, the final stage, involves the integration of his present medical problems with his prior skills, knowledge, and attitudes. The chief aim is to get on with life. For example, after a hysterectomy and a period of

demoralization, a stockbroker did what she had always done to get through a crisis — work.

Being familiar with these stages has three major therapeutic implications: First, a clinician is unlikely to become overly concerned if a patient initially denies the seriousness of an illness. This denial is natural, not pathological. Second, when a doctor tells a patient he has cancer (or any severe illness), if the doctor divulges too much information too soon, the patient will be too overwhelmed to incorporate it, much less retain it. Details should be presented day-by-day, not all at once; briefly reviewing the salient facts each day also helps. Thus, in telling a patient he has cancer, the key question is not *if* to tell the patient, but *when* and *how*.

Third, considering these stages allows for more effective *anticipatory guidance* — that is, telling patients what to expect in advance of a major procedure. For example, when surgical patients are told what difficulties to expect after an operation, they develop fewer post-operative problems, have fewer drug side effects, and are discharged sooner. Yet giving patients all this anticipatory guidance assumes they are psychologically equipped at that moment to hear it. Patients in the outcry and denial stage can assimilate little, if any, new information; those in the intrusion stage can do so a bit better, and those in later stages are well-equipped. Thus, although *what* anticipatory guidance is given is critical, so too is *when* it is given.

Evaluating Psychosocial Factors

Although many psychosocial factors can affect or result from a physical condition, in the "real" world it's impractical for health professionals to ask patients about every one of them. Because time is limited, the most salient psychosocial facts for clinicians to learn are those which most enable them to improve the patient's present condition. Although the specific information required to do so depends on the individual, the seven questions on Table 20-1 are a good place to start, because their answers will address almost any germane psychosocial problem affecting the patient. All the answers don't have to be obtained at the first visit, but eventually most should be ascertained.

Treatment Caveats

Clinicians should be cautious about misapplying and overestimating psychosocial information. Although many professionals and laymen surely deny emotional factors, others act as if "everything" is psychology and that cure is "nothing" but "mind over matter." Much harm has been done by well-intended friends and doctors telling a patient with an incurable illness that

TABLE 20-1
The Medical Psychosocial Data Base

1. Does the patient understand his illness, its prognosis, and treatment?

   Can he describe his illness to a physician unfamiliar with his case? Can he name his illness and his medication?

2. Does the patient fear that his illness may be fatal or that it is worse than he's been told?

   Does the patient feel the doctors have been lying to him or not telling the "whole story"?

3. How has (or may) the patient's illness affected or altered his life, including his family, job, and income?

   Do people think he's not doing enough to help himself? Will his illness require different living or working conditions? How will he pay for treatment and does he worry about this?

4. Has the patient had any major "entrance" or "exist" events during the course of, or just prior to, his illness?

   An "entrance event" may be a new child, job, or boyfriend. An "exit event" may be a death, a broken romance, or moving abroad.

5. What has been the patient's prior experiences with illness, medical care, hospitals, and health care professionals?

   How does the patient habitually deal with illness? Does he deny? Overreact? Withdraw? Have his coping strategies been adaptive or maladaptive? Does the patient's dominant personality style as a patient tend to be suspicious, dependent, or what? Does he delay in seeking help? Has he been maltreated? Was there a specific quality or trait about a previous doctor or nurse which comforted or alienated the patient?

6. What have been the experiences of the patient's close relatives with illness, medical care, and health professionals?

   Have these experiences influenced the patient's feelings about his current condition and treatment? For instance, a patient was terrified of having a routine tonsillectomy, because his parents were both hospitalized at different times for different problems and both died.

7. Who in the patient's social network is likely to encourage the patient to cooperate with treatment?

   Who does the patient trust more? Who does the patient turn to in a crisis? Who will be available? Who visits the patient? Who telephones?

"all he has to do is develop a positive attitude and he will conquer his disease." Most patients experience such advice as an accusation, since by not adopting a positive attitude they are by implication perpetuating their own disease.

It would be reasonable to assume, for instance, that the mental outlook of recently diagnosed cancer patients would greater affect their subsequent clinical course. Yet a study of 7,000 adults found that people who lacked social and community ties have two to three times the cancer-rate of those with such ties, but that once cancer strikes it is biological and not psychosocial factors that determine the patient's outcome (Cassileth et al., 1985).

That's why clinicians should be very careful about "interpreting" or "psychologizing" a patient's medical illness. Most patients resent it, especially when some authority figure/expert claims that a patient "enjoys" his symptoms; such "insights" are insulting and wrong. They belong to that genre of accusation always addressed to others, but rarely to oneself. It reflects what the chronically sick and disabled come to know as the "arrogance of the healthy," that presumption that good health is the natural order and is to be taken for granted. When people ramble on about their symptoms yet "do nothing about them," this probably means they feel compelled to talk about their symptoms and fear treatment: It does not mean they "enjoy"their symptoms. Nobody "enjoys" symptoms.

CHAPTER 21

Personality Disorders

"PERSONALITY" OR "CHARACTER" *traits* are ingrained, enduring patterns of behaving, feeling, perceiving, and thinking, which are prominent in many contexts. Personality is the psychological equivalent of physical appearance: A person grows up with both, and although he can adjust each, they remain essentially the same and affect the rest of his life. As Heraclitus observed, "A man's fate is his character." Personality features may, or may not, be adaptive. Compulsiveness in a student is adaptive when it promotes orderly study habits, but it's maladaptive when the student spends hours sharpening pencils instead of studying. Personality traits become personality *disorders* when they (a) become inflexible and maladaptive, and (b) significantly impair social and occupational functioning or cause substantial subjective distress.

In *DSM-III*, personality traits and disorders are listed on Axis II while mental disorders are indicated on Axis I. This separation distinguishes a patient's current and more florid mental disorder from his ongoing, baseline personality; this should result in more *realistic* treatment goals. Since Axis I mental disorders are more responsive to treatment than Axis II personality disorders, a realistic treatment goal may be to remedy the former but not the latter. For instance, it may be unrealistic to expect a dependent personality who develops a major depression to be rid of both during a brief hospitalization.

Kahana and Bibring (1964) showed how identifying a medical patient's personality type may alter how clinicians relate to patients. For example, when a doctor pats Mr. Moscowitz on the shoulder and says, "Don't worry, everything will be fine," a dependent patient will be greatly relieved; do the same with a paranoid patient and he'll draw away and think, "How does he know I'll be okay? Why's he being so chummy? How dare he touch me!" Paranoid patients feel safer with doctors who keep their distance. Thus, for all practical purposes, in most medical settings clinicians should

302

not attempt to change the patient's personality, but rather should adjust their own behavior to fit the patient's personality type.

Understanding a patient's personality traits can guide psychotherapy, medication use, family involvement, nurses' monitoring, etc. To illustrate: During group therapy, Mrs. Grant suddenly asked to see her hospital chart. If Mrs. Grant were a paranoid personality, the group therapist could be fairly sure she wanted to uncover malicious information about her. However, Mrs. Grant is not paranoid; she has an avoidant personality, and as such, the therapist can reasonably guess she wanted to know whether the therapist liked her—a proposition he raised for the group's consideration. Another illustration: If during a highly stressful period a patient asked for a seven-day supply of sleeping pills, all things being equal, a patient with a borderline personality would be far more likely to abuse the pills than would a schizoid personality. If a psychiatric nurse has to leave patients in the care of another patient, she would much prefer a compulsive personality to a sociopath.

This chapter will summarize the 11 personality disorders listed in *DSM-III*. In general, personality disorders first become apparent during adolescence or earlier, persist through life, and become less obvious by middle or old age. Most personality disturbances are sustained, but some are frequently episodic (e.g., "writer's block"). Personality disorders should only be diagnosed when they cause lifelong problems, and not just discrete periods of dysfunction. Except for schizotypal, borderline, and antisocial personalities, hospitalizations are rare.

In a retrospective chart review, 36% of 2,462 psychiatric patients had a personality disorder. Borderline personality disorder was diagnosed most (12% of total); next (at 10%) was *DSM-III*'s residual category of "mixed, atypical, or other personality disorder." Each of the other personality disorders were diagnosed in under 3% of patients. Substance abuse disorders were the most common Axis I diagnosis found among those with personality disorders (Koenigsberg et al., 1985).

DSM-III divides personality disorders into three clusters: The first consists of paranoid, schizoid, and schizotypal personality disorders; it's characterized by odd or eccentric behavior. The second includes histrionic, narcissistic, antisocial, and borderline personality disorders; it's characterized by dramatic, overemotional, and erratic behavior. The third consists of avoidant, dependent, compulsive, and passive-aggressive personality disorders; it's characterized by highly anxious and fearful affects.

PARANOID PERSONALITY DISORDER

The essential features of a parnoid personality disorder (PPD) are (a) pervasive and unwarranted suspiciousness and mistrust of people, (b) hypersensitivity, and (c) a restricted affect; none of these should stem from another mental disorder, such as schizophrenia or paranoid disorder. Table 21-1 lists the *DSM-III* criteria for PPD.

"Paranoids have enemies" mainly because they're paranoid. Paranoid people are very unpleasant, always blaming and suspicious of others. Suspicions may be justified and adaptive, but when contradictory evidence is presented, most people abandon them. Paranoids do not, but rather view this as further proof the person intends to harm them. The paranoid's world is hostile, devious, and dark, filled with persecutory forces, for which the paranoid must be eter-

TABLE 21-1
DSM-III Criteria for Paranoid Personality Disorder*

The following are characteristic of the individual's current and long-term functioning, are not limited to episodes of illness, and cause either significant impairment in social or occupational functioning or subjective distress.

A. Pervasive, unwarranted suspiciousness and mistrust of people as indicated by at least three of the following:

   (1) expectation of trickery or harm
   (2) hypervigilance, manifested by continual scanning of the environment for signs of threat, or taking unneeded precautions
   (3) guardedness or secretiveness
   (4) avoidance of accepting blame when warranted
   (5) questioning the loyalty of others
   (6) intense, narrowly focused searching for confirmation of bias, with loss of appreciation of total context
   (7) overconcern with hidden motives and special meanings
   (8) pathological jealousy

B. Hypersensitivity as indicated by at least two of the following:

   (1) tendency to be easily slighted and quick to take offense
   (2) exaggeration of difficulties, e.g., "making mountains out of molehills"
   (3) readiness to counterattack when any threat is perceived
   (4) inability to relax

C. Restricted affectivity as indicated by at least two of the following:

   (1) appearance of being "cold" and unemotional
   (2) pride taken in always being objective, rational, and unemotional
   (3) lack of a true sense of humor
   (4) absence of passive, soft, tender, and sentimental feelings

D. Not due to another mental disorder such as Schizophrenia or a Paranoid Disorder.

DSM-III, p. 309.

nally vigilant. On entering a restaurant, he will scan the room to ensure no enemies are present, and then sit with his back to the wall so that nobody can sneak behind him. Highly secretive, he may hide behind dark glasses. Paranoids bristle at the slightest contradiction or criticism, distrust people's loyalty, and misconstrue what they say. When a coworker congratulated a paranoid man on plans to buy a home, the paranoid snapped, "It's mine! You can't have it!" Paranoids may be ambitious and bright, yet stubborn and defensive. They're quick to argue and find fault. They'll seize an alleged injustice, overblow its significance, and distort the facts to fit their suspiciousness.

A paranoid English professor discovered that a classroom he had reserved was occupied by another faculty member. The professor became enraged, citing it as "this draconian administration's efforts to drive me from the university." The next day, after learning the university press would not publish his definitive study of Iago, he launched a $3 million lawsuit against the university. Four months later, the university threatened not to renew his contract. He dropped the suit, but then instigated student protests against the university for "stiffling academic freedom."

People keep their distance from paranoids, which merely confirms the paranoid's general distrust. Paranoids are pathologically jealous, tense, rigid, unwilling to compromise, moralistic, always detecting ill-intent and special messages, litigious, humorless, coldly objective, overly rational, haughty, and distant. That's why "paranoids have enemies," few friends, and fewer, if any intimate relationships. They have contempt for the weakness in others; they disdain the sickly, defective, and imperfect—that is, everybody but themselves. They think in hierarchies: who's superior to whom; who controls whom. With their egocentricity and exaggerated self-importance, they make a great show of self-sufficiency. They're drawn to politics, history, science, and technology; to them, the arts are for sissies. As unpleasant as the paranoid can be, remember his is a terribly uncomfortable existence.

PPD is more common in men than women. Social relations and job advancement are often severely impaired. Unlike paranoid disorders and paranoid schizophrenia, paranoid personalities are *not* psychotic. Psychotic disorders, however, may be superimposed on a PPD.

In treatment, the therapist's main task is to minimize the patient's distrust of the therapist and of therapy. It often takes months before the patient feels at all relaxed in treatment. Clinicians should be respectful, but avoid intimacy, which paranoids experience as invasive. Deep psychological interpretations are verboten, since paranoids are already leery of shrinks because they read people's minds and trick them. Insight to a therapist is "mind-fucking" to a paranoid. In the office, clinicians should *not* sit between the patient and the door; the paranoid feels far less threatened if nobody "blocks" his exitway. What's an office to a therapist is an observation chamber to a paranoid. When the clinician errs, he should admit the mistake, apologize, and get on with it; overapologizing fosters distrust. Nor should clinicians ask paranoids to trust them, since to the paranoid that's like a Nazi guard asking a Dachau inmate to trust him. Being straightforward and "professional" is the most reassuring approach.

SCHIZOID PERSONALITY DISORDER

The central features of a schizoid personality disorder (SDPD) are detached social relations, restricted expression of emotion, a striking lack of warmth and tenderness, and an apparent indifference to others' praise, criticism, feelings, and concerns. Unlike schizotypal personalities (see below), schizoid patients do *not* exhibit eccentricities of speech, behavior, or thinking. Table 21-2 lists *DSM-III*'s criteria for SDPD.

Patients with schizoid personalities are "in a fog," absentminded, loners, detached from others, self-involved, "not-connected." What appears as aloofness is actually profound shyness. Often dull and humorless, they will disavow feelings of anger or interests in sex; they prefer solitary activities and daydreaming to friendships. Dating is painful, marriage rare. Although SDPD greatly impedes social relationships and professional advancement, these patients can excel if permitted nominal interpersonal contact. The prevalence of SDPD is unknown, though schizoid individuals may be common on skid row.

SDPD resembles *avoidant personality disorder*, since both display prominant social isolation. Yet whereas the avoidant personality wants friends, the schizoid doesn't; whereas the avoidant is alone because he's hypersensitive to slights, the schizoid has no interest in personal involvement. Once considered a prodromal phase of *schizophrenia*, SDPD and schizophrenia are unrelated (see below). Few schizoid patients become psychotic.

Treatment is difficult, and a therapist must be willing to endure long silences. It usually entails long-term, supportive individual and/or group psychotherapy; assertiveness training may be added. However, the efficacy of these treatments is unknown. Whatever the treatment, therapists should avoid depth interpretations and forced interactions, since the patient is likely to flee.

SCHIZOTYPAL PERSONALITY DISORDER

In *DSM-III* (p. 312), the essential features of a schizotypal personality disorder (STPD) "are various oddities of thought, perception, and behavior that are not severe enough to meet the criteria for Schizophrenia." These patients have few friends because they are very strange. They live in The Twilight Zone, filled with weird thoughts, ideas of reference, paranoid ideation, telepathy, and "magical thinking" — e.g., "If I think hard enough, I can make the wind blow"; "My teeth itch." Their speech is hard to follow, although without

TABLE 21-2
DSM-III* Criteria for Schizoid Personality Disorder

The following are characteristic of the individual's current and long-term functioning, are not limited to episodes of illness, and cause either significant impairment in social or occupational functioning or subjective distress.

A. Emotional coldness and aloofness, and absence of warm, tender feelings for others.

B. Indifference to praise or criticism or to the feelings of others.

C. Close friendships with no more than one or two persons, including family members.

D. No eccentricities of speech, behavior, or thought characteristic of Schizotypal Personality Disorder.

E. Not due to a psychotic disorder such as Schizophrenia or Paranoid Disorder.

F. If under 18, does not meet the criteria for Schizoid Disorder of Childhood or Adolescence.

DSM-III, p. 311.

loose associations or incoherence. Their affect is flat or inappropriate. Sloppy, unkempt, giggling for no reason, and often talking to themselves, they are hypersensitive to criticism and dreadfully anxious around people, especially if more than three are together. *DSM-III-R* may indicate that perceptual disturbances are less common than indicated in *DSM-III*. Table 21-3 lists the *DSM-III* criteria for STPD.

Unlike schizoid personalities, schizotypal personalities are more likely to (a) display bizarre and peculiar traits; (b) develop fanatic, eccentric, or racist beliefs, (c) become dysthymic and anxious, (d) have an accompanying borderline personality disorder, (e) become psychotic under stress, (f) evolve into schizophrenia, and (g) run in families (Baron et al., 1985). Unlike STPD, patients with *schizophrenia, residual type* would have previously displayed a florid schizophrenic psychosis. If schizophrenia develops in a schizotypal patient, the schizotypal diagnosis is dropped. Indeed, schizophrenia should always be suspected in schizotypal patients under 35.

Psychotherapy of the schizotypal patient is similar to that of the schizoid patient, except that reality testing and antipsychotic medications are more likely to be needed to quell brief psychotic episodes.

HISTRIONIC PERSONALITY DISORDER

More than anything else, patients with histrionic personality disorder (HPD) are overly emotional and demand attention. These patients present the worst of female stereotypes: vain, vapid, and vague; they are impres-

TABLE 21-3
DSM-III Criteria for Schizotypal Personality Disorder*

The following are characteristic of the individual's current and long-term functioning, are not limited to episodes of illness, and cause either significant impairment in social or occupational functioning or subjective distress.

A. At least four of the following:

(1) magical thinking, e.g., superstitiousness, clairvoyance, telepathy, "6th sense," "others can feel my feelings" (in children and adolescents, bizarre fantasies or preoccupations)
(2) ideas of reference
(3) social isolation, e.g., no close friends or confidants, social contacts limited to essential everyday tasks
(4) recurrent illusions, sensing the presence of a force or person not actually present (e.g., "I felt as if my dead mother were in the room with me"), depersonalization, or derealization not associated with panic attacks
(5) odd speech (without loosening of associations or incoherence), e.g., speech that is digressive, vague, overelaborate, circumstantial, metaphorical
(6) inadequate rapport in face-to-face interaction due to constricted or inappropriate affect, e.g., aloof, cold
(7) suspiciousness or paranoid ideation
(8) undue social anxiety or hypersensitivity to real or imagined criticism

B. Does not meet the criteria for Schizophrenia.

*DSM-III, pp. 312–313.

---

sionistic, illogical, superficial, demanding, inconsiderate, self-indulgent, and preoccupied with their looks. Their suicidal threats and gestures are frequent, manipulative, and except by accident, rarely fatal. Table 21-4 lists *DSM-III*'s criteria for HPD.

Histrionic personalities are "actresses," but always on stage. Since role-playing, exaggeration, and hyperbole are their norm, others find it hard to gauge when they're "genuinely" upset. Bette Davis' Margo Channing in "All About Eve" is the prototypic histrionic personality: Margo is pure charm, but if her every whim isn't granted she starts throwing dishes. Minor stresses are major catastrophes. Margo's director/boyfriend glances at a female, and she stomps out of rehearsal. These patients often have relatively brief periods of demoralization, dissatisfaction, depression, and somatization, but always react to psychosocial stressors (no matter how trivial).

Sustaining concentration comes hard to the hysteric, so even though she may be highly knowledgeable in how to do things, she will be grossly deficient in factual knowledge. These limitations significantly impair occupational and social functioning, while leading hysterics away from scientific or technical matters. They do best in the arts. Their stormy interpersonal relations, apparent shallowness, and roller-coaster moods frequently interfere with close relationships.

HPD is diagnosed far more often in women, and in effeminate and homosexual men. Hysterics commonly have somatic complaints, somatization disorder, and a coexisting borderline personality disorder. Under severe stress, these patients may become psychotic, but they quickly reconstitute. HPD runs in families, presumably by psychosocial means.

Treatment is usually long-term, individual psychoanalytic psychotherapy. It focuses on how the patient's histrionic behavior interferes with interpersonal relations and career advancement. Psychotherapy may help the patient think more systematically, describe things more precisely, express emotions that are proportionate to the event, and learn how her behavior affects others.

If one talks about personality *styles* rather than *disorders*, "hysterics" and "compulsives" are cognitive opposites. Hysterics think in impressions, compulsives in facts. If Holly Go-Lightly, the Hysteric, and Carl Compulsive describe a person they recently met, Holly would exclaim, "He's just a darling, and such thrilling eyes. He must've murdered somebody. Either that or he's a poet. Did you see how he looked straight through me? I loved it." Carl

---

TABLE 21-4
DSM-III* Criteria for Histrionic Personality Disorder

The following are characteristic of the individual's current and long-term functioning, are not limited to episodes of illness, and cause either significant impairment in social or occupational functioning or subjective distress.

A. Behavior that is overly dramatic, reactive, and intensely expressed, as indicated by at least three of the following:

   (1) self-dramatization, e.g., exaggerated expression of emotions
   (2) incessant drawing of attention to oneself
   (3) overreaction to minor events
   (4) irrational, angry outbursts or tantrums

B. Characteristic disturbances in interpersonal relationships as indicated by at least two of the following:

   (1) perceived by others as shallow and lacking genuineness, even if superficially warm and charming
   (2) egocentric, self-indulgent, and inconsiderate of others
   (3) vain and demanding
   (4) dependent, helpless, constantly seeking reassurance
   (5) prone to manipulative suicidal threats, gestures, or attempts

*DSM-III, p. 315.

would say, "He's about five-feet, eleven-inches tall, weighs 160 pounds, has black hair, bushy eyebrows, a Southern accent. . . . " Compulsives present exhaustive, and ultimately boring, details; hysterics make global comments, lacking specificity and focus. Compulsives are too mired in detail to make hunches, whereas hysterics base their decisions on hunches; they eschew logic and information. Most people invoke hunches as temporary hypotheses, but hysterics use them as final conclusions (Shapiro, 1965). Because they so complement each other, it's not uncommon for compulsive professionals to marry histrionic artists.

COMPULSIVE PERSONALITY DISORDER

In *DSM-III*, the essential features of compulsive personality disorder (CPD) are (a) a restricted ability to express warm and tender emotions, (b) a perfectionism that interferes with the ability to grasp "the big picture," (c) an insistence that others submit to his way of doing things, (d) an excessive devotion to work and productivity to the exclusion of pleasure, and (e) indecisiveness. Table 21-5 lists *DSM-III*'s criteria for CPD.

Wilhelm Reich (1949) called these patients "living machines." The compulsive is highly productive, but never enjoys what he produces. Everything is a chore; nothing is effortless. Every decision demands exhaustive analysis. Everything must be right and nothing must be left to chance. He won't make hunches, since hunches may be wrong. He's a perfectionist: Wines *must* be chilled not 55 or 65, but exactly 60 minutes or a meal is ruined. Cleanliness is Godliness. The compulsive excels at concentrating, but he never stops concentrating (Shapiro, 1965). He can't skim a page; he must scrutinize every word. His focus is sharp, yet narrow; he sees the parts, but never the whole.

The compulsive is interpersonally obtuse. He bores and annoys: He subjects people to endless irrelevant details, refuses to make decisions, is moralistic and hypocritically self-righteous, insists on conformity (from others), and never gets to the point. Harold, a compulsive accountant spent eight years obsessing over whether to leave his wife and three kids for his mistress-secretary. "I stay only for the kids," he'd insist, but in truth, he never saw them. Repeatedly calculating the pros and cons—even devising a mathematical formula—Harold would ask a friend for advice, promptly reject it, criticize the friend for not helping him enough, and cap it off by complaining his friend doesn't donate enough money to the synagogue. Like most people with CPD, Harold considered himself an intellectual, while others considered him rigid.

CPD is diagnosed more often in men and in the oldest sibling. Although the precise prevalence is unknown, CPD is probably common. At some point in their lives, a majority—72% in one study—develop an obsessive compulsive disorder, with true

TABLE 21-5
DSM-III **Criteria for Compulsive Personality Disorder***

At least four of the following are characteristic of the individual's current and long-term functioning, are not limited to episodes of illness, and cause either significant impairment in social or occupational functioning or subjective distress.

(1) restricted ability to express warm and tender emotions, e.g., the individual is unduly conventional, serious and formal, stingy

(2) perfectionism that interferes with the ability to grasp "the big picture," e.g., preoccupation with trivial details, rules, order, organization, schedules, and lists

(3) insistence that others submit to his or her way of doing things, and lack of awareness of the feelings elicited by this behavior, e.g., a husband stubbornly insists his wife complete errands for him regardless of her plans

(4) excessive devotion to work and productivity to the exclusion of pleasure and the value of interpersonal relationships

(5) indecisiveness: decision-making is either avoided, postponed, or protracted, perhaps because of an inordinate fear of making a mistake, e.g., the individual cannot get assignments done on time because of ruminating about priorities

*DSM-III, pp. 327–328.

obsessions (i.e., persistently intrusive unwanted thoughts) and compulsions (e.g., checking, counting). Other frequent complications are major depression, dysthymia, and hypochondriasis.

Laymen call these patients "tight-assed"; psychoanalysts call them "anal characters," because theoretically they have arrested at the anal stage of psychosexual development. The "anal character" is known for having problems with control, authority figures, autonomy, shame, and self-doubt. CPD runs in families, but it's unclear how much this results from the emotionally constipated, anger-supressing families which often rear these patients, and how much from heredity, as suggested by several twin and adoption studies.

Compulsives are tough to treat, largely because their obsessiveness paralyzes therapy. Though bright, they invoke insight not to change, but to avoid change. Psychology is abstract, but compulsives are concrete. They swamp therapists in detail. Simply ask a compulsive if he's reviewed the want-ads and he critiques everyone in the paper. If interrupted, he becomes angry; if allowed to continue, 10 minutes later he blames the therapist for wasting time. Consequently, therapy should focus on the here-and-now and stress feelings instead of thoughts. Progress should be measured in changed behavior, not insight. Group therapy may help those with serious interpersonal problems, while chlorimipramine, a tricyclic antidepressant, has been very effective in some cases.

NARCISSISTIC PERSONALITY DISORDER

Narcissus was the mythological Greek youth who fell so in love with his own reflection that he pined away and died. Several (million) years later, amid considerable psychoanalytic debate over the definition, etiology, and treatment of narcissism, *DSM-III* became the first *DSM* to include a diagnostic entity centering on narcissism—namely, the narcissistic personality disorder (NPD), whose essential features are (a) grandiose self-importance, (b) preoccupation with fantasies of unlimited success, (c) driven desire for attention and admiration, (d) intolerance to criticism, and (e) disturbed, self-centered interpersonal relations. Table 21-6 lists *DSM-III*'s criteria for NPD.

These patients' *grandiosity* manifests as an exaggerated sense of self-importance or uniqueness. Others call them "conceited." They greatly overestimate not only their accomplishments and abilities, but their failures as well. For example, at age 30, Isaac once described himself as "the greatest young actor in America." When he failed to land a part in a major motion picture, he insisted that "everyone in Hollywood will think I'm washed up."

Fantasies of fame substitute for actual achievements. Everyone daydreams, but true narcissists are preoccupied with brilliance, wealth, ideal love, beauty,

TABLE 21-6
DSM-III Criteria for Narcissistic Personality Disorder*

The following are characteristic of the individual's current and long-term functioning, are not limited to episodes of illness, and cause either significant impairment in social or occupational functioning or subjective distress.

A. Grandiose sense of self-importance or uniqueness, e.g., exaggeration of achievements and talents, focus on the special nature of one's problems.

B. Preoccupation with fantasies of unlimited success, power, brilliance, beauty, or ideal love.

C. Exhibitionism: the person requires constant attention and admiration.

D. Cool indifference or marked feelings of rage, inferiority, shame, humiliation, or emptiness in response to criticism, indifference of others, or defeat.

E. At least two of the following characteristic of disturbances in interpersonal relationships:

    (1) entitlement: expectation of special favors without assuming reciprocal responsibilities, e.g., surprise and anger that people will not do what is wanted

    (2) interpersonal exploitativeness: taking advantage of others to indulge own desires or for self-aggrandizement; disregard for the personal integrity and rights of others

    (3) relationships that characteristically alternate between the extremes of overidealization and devaluation

    (4) lack of empathy: inability to recognize how others feel, e.g., unable to appreciate the distress of someone who is seriously ill.

DSM-III, p. 317.

copping an Oscar (or two), or whatever. In real life, most people enjoy reaching these goals, but narcissists don't. Their ambition is driven, their pursuit of excellence is a burden, their accomplishments don't satisfy. Isaac will audition in front of a mirror, but not at an audition. He only takes roles if his agent gets him one; even then, he loves the applause, but hates the acting.

The narcissistic personality craves *attention* and universal admiration. Appearance is more important than substance. Being seen with the "right" people is more important than liking them. Narcissists are preoccupied with their physical image, not merely to look attractive, but to appear godlike. Isaac's home is a museum studded with photographs of Issac, mostly in the nude.

Intolerance to criticism arises from their low self-esteem. When their grandiosity is doubted, they respond with "narcissistic rage": cool disdain, anger, humiliation, extreme boredom, pessimism, negativism, and shame. Depressed moods result when they're rejected, neglected, or frustrated. When Isaac missed a key while playing the piano, he blamed the piano tuner for not doing his job correctly. At a party, Isaac was regaling his audience with showbiz stories, but when another actor joined in, Isaac became stone silent.

Interpersonally selfish, narcissists act with a sense of "entitlement," as if they're masters, and everyone else servants. Arriving an hour late on the set, Isaac doesn't apologize ("Why should I? I rushed like hell to get there; if anything, they should thank me.") They are not mean *per se*, but so oblivious to others' concerns and feelings that they continually exploit relationships. Because they don't consciously intend to hurt, they're baffled why after they do hurt somebody that somebody becomes furious with them. Isaac repeatedly told a woman how much he loved her, yet when she discovered he'd been seeing a "chickee-babe" on the sly, Isaac was genuinely unable to comprehend why she felt betrayed and outraged. This self-centeredness is a major feature of "Don Juan personalities," narcissists who assume that every woman has the "hots" for them. In sexual relationships, narcissists don't care if their partner is satisfied, only themselves. A girlfriend described sex with Isaac as "watching somebody masturbate." Later, when she developed pelvic inflammatory disease, Isaac's sincere belief was that the only reason she got the disease "was to deliberately spite me." In the narcissist's world, everything relates to him and nothing occurs independently of him.

Narcissistic and *histrionic personalities* are both self-centered, but the narcissist is more grandiose, egotistical, arrogant, vigorous, and selfish, whereas the hysteric is more overdramatic, flighty, and apprehensive. *Manics* are grandiose, but episodically and often psychotically, whereas the narcissist's grandiosity is continual and nonpsychotic. Few patients with NPD become psychotic, and when they do, it's briefly.

Although NPD's prevalence and sex ratio are unknown, it's been attributed more often to men. Wilheim Reich (1949) described the "phallic-narcissistic character" whose "penis is not in the service of love but is an instrument of aggression and vengeance" (p. 203). He contended that many phallic-narcissists were aviators, soldiers, athletes, and engineers. Indeed, some narcissism creates many a business tycoon, surgeon, trial lawyer, politician, movie producer, actor, and orchestra conductor. Great accomplishments require great egos.

Patients with NPD infrequently seek treatment ("Why should I? There's nothing wrong with me."). But when they do, it's usually because their being depressed or medically ill threatens their grandiosity. Long-term psychoanalytic psychotherapy is usually recommended, even though its chance of inducing major change is low. With their invincibility exposed, narcissists will project their resentment onto the therapist, and will alternate between idealizing and devaluing him. How a therapist should respond has been a major controversy in psychoanalysis. One school, led by Kernberg (1975), views the patient's use of idealization and devaluation as a defense and recommends it should be interpreted in the classical psychoanalytic manner. In contrast, Kohut (1971) and his school of self psychology contend that initially the therapist should support the patient's idealization and grandiosity, and only later gently point out the patient's realistic limits. Both schools agree on the end: The patient should acquire a more realistic view of himself and the world. Where the schools differ is on the means: Kernberg punctures the patient's defenses; Kohut cushions the blow.

ANTISOCIAL PERSONALITY DISORDER

In *DSM-III*, the essential features of antisocial personality disorder (ASPD) are: (a) continuous and chronic antisocial behavior which violates the rights of others, (b) onset prior to age 15, (c) persistence into adulthood, and (d) several years of poor job performance. Table 21-7 lists *DSM-III*'s criteria for ASPD. This condition is also called "sociopathy."

Clinical Presentation

Although many sociopaths are charming and resourceful, they're without enduring or intimate relationships. Friendships, even with fellow crooks, are opportunistic alliances to be broken whenever it's convenient. With radar for people's vulnerabilities, sociopaths can readily manipulate, exploit, control, deceive, and intimidate others. Unlike other criminals, sociopaths enjoy "making suckers" of people. Their sexual relations are thrilling conquests, and nothing more — and that includes marriage.

Emotionally shallow, they seem incapable of shame, guilt, loyalty, love, or any persistently sincere emotion; although quick to anger, they don't even sustain hatred. One moment, they'll proclaim how deeply they feel about someone, and momentarily, they might believe themselves. These feelings are at most fleeting. Expressions of guilt and remorse don't affect future conduct.

Like addicts crave heroin, sociopaths crave stimulation. Excitement alone medicates their allergies to boredom, depression, and frustration. They can't

TABLE 21-7
DSM-III* Criteria for Antisocial Personality Disorder

A. Current age at least 18.

B. Onset before age 15 as indicated by a history of three or more of the following before that age:

    (1) truancy (positive if it amounted to at least five days per year for at least two years, not including the last year of school)

    (2) expulsion or suspension from school for misbehavior

    (3) delinquency (arrested or referred to juvenile court because of behavior)

    (4) running away from home overnight at least twice while living in parental or parental surrogate home

    (5) persistent lying

    (6) repeated sexual intercourse in a causal relationship

    (7) repeated drunkenness or substance abuse

    (8) thefts

    (9) vandalism

    (10) school grades markedly below expectations in relation to estimated or known IQ (may have resulted in repeating a year)

    (11) chronic violations of rules at home and/or at school (other than truancy)

    (12) initiation of fights

C. At least four of the following manifestations of the disorder since age 18:

    (1) inability to sustain consistent work behavior, as indicated by any of the following: (a) too frequent job changes (e.g., three or more jobs in five years not accounted for by nature of job or economic or seasonal fluctuation), (b) significant unemployment (e.g., six months or more in five years when expected to work), (c) serious absenteeism from work (e.g., average three days or more of lateness or absence per month), (d) walking off several jobs without other jobs in sight (Note: similar behavior in an academic setting during the last few years of school may substitute for this criterion in individuals who by reason of their age or circumstances have not had an opportunity to demonstrate occupational adjustment)

    (2) lack of ability to function as a responsible parent as evidenced by one or more of the following: (a) child's malnutrition, (b) child's illness resulting from lack of minimal hygiene standards, (c) failure to obtain medical care for a seriously ill child, (d) child's dependence on neighbors or nonresident relatives for food or shelter, (e) failure to arrange for a caretaker for a child under six when parent is away from home, (f) repeated squandering, on personal items, of money required for household necessities

    (3) failure to accept social norms with respect to lawful behavior, as indicated by any of the following: repeated thefts, illegal occupation (pimping, prostitution, fencing, selling drugs), multiple arrests, a felony conviction

    (4) inability to maintain enduring attachment to a sexual partner as indicated by two or more divorces and/or separations (whether legally married or not), desertion of spouse, promiscuity (ten or more sexual partners within one year)

(continued)

TABLE 21-7
(Continued)

---

(5) irritability and aggressiveness as indicated by repeated physical fights or assault (not required by one's job or to defend someone or oneself), including spouse or child beating

(6) failure to honor financial obligations, as indicated by repeated defaulting on debts, failure to provide child support, failure to support other dependents on a regular basis

(7) failure to plan ahead, or impulsivity, as indicated by traveling from place to place without a prearranged job or clear goal for the period of travel or clear idea about when the travel would terminate, or lack of a fixed address for a month or more

(8) disregard for the truth as indicated by repeated lying, use of aliases, "conning" others for personal profit

(9) recklessness, as indicated by driving while intoxicated or recurrent speeding

D. A pattern of continuous antisocial behavior in which the rights of others are violated, with no intervening period of at least five years without antisocial behavior between age 15 and the present time (except when the individual was bedridden or confined in a hospital or penal institution).

E. Antisocial behavior is not due to either Severe Mental Retardation, Schizophrenia or manic episodes.

DSM-III, pp. 320–321.

hold a job; it will be too dull. Sociopaths are always on the move, "making deals," bumming around, picking fights, raping people, or killing them.

In the classic text on antisocial personalities, *The Mask of Sanity*, Cleckley (1950) observed that underlying their various traits is a basic cognitive deficiency: the ability to appreciate the passage of time. Sociopaths live solely in the present; the past is a dim memory and the future a fiction. Unconcerned with the consequences of their actions and unable to learn from experience, the threat of punishment affords little restraint. Rewards must come now, not later; gratification cannot be delayed. Sociopaths are said to have "superego lacunae," that is, they are virtually without conscience. Expediency, immediate pleasure, and "stimulus hunger" override all other restraints.

Clinical Course

Antisocial personalities have "always" been up to "no good"; they are not "good kids" who simply "fell into a bad crowd." *DSM-III* stresses that ASPD begins before age 15. In boys, it emerges during early childhood, in girls around puberty.

As children, sociopaths habitually lie, steal, skip school, and defy authority. They're restless and irritable; many are hyperactive. They conceal feelings and talk to parents only when they want something. Exploiting parental affection, using sibs, running away from home, delighting in forbidden acts, and hanging around with older delinquents are common.

A mother describes her delinquent son: "He's always been different from my others, as if he's possessed. What kind of five-year-old steals from his mother's purse? Once I caught him hammering a squirrel to death, and when I yelled at him to stop, he just smiled. He enjoyed taunting me."

As adolescents, sociopaths abuse substances, gamble heavily, and display unusually early or aggressive sexual behavior. They mock rules, cut class, cause fights, and get expelled; their grades plummet. They're "pathological liars"; they lie without reason. Sociopaths delight in terrorizing others. A delinquent youth pulled out a pistol, aimed it at his teacher's head, and demanded he undress. When the teacher was nude, the youth nudged the teacher's testicles with his gun, and fired. The gun wasn't loaded. Only the youth laughed.

By age 30, their promiscuity, fighting, criminality, and vagrancy tend to diminish. They "burn out." Their existence becomes marginal. Some end up on skid row, some are chronic substance abusers, some die by violence; 30% to 80% are in prison. Many subsist from one low-paying job to another, and from one town to another. Only 2% of cases with full-blown ASPD remit after age 21.

Alcoholism and depression are the mental disorders most often affecting sociopaths, and thus, the most common reasons they seek treatment. Sociopaths often have conversion symptoms, especially when stressed or arrested. Many delinquent teenage girls develop somatization disorder as adults. Most sociopaths have low-to-normal IQs; a few have significant mental deficiency (IQ < 70).

Complications

ASPD markedly impairs social and occupational functioning. Plagued by infidelity, jealousy, and child abuse, their marriages usually end in separation and divorce. Sociopaths tend to marry young, beat their wives, and marry other sociopaths. Besides getting murdered, they have unusually high rates of venereal disease, out-of-wedlock pregnancies, injuries from fights and accidents, substance dependence, and gun wounds—which all lead to their shorter life expectancies. Suicidal threats and gestures are common; completed suicides are rare.

Epidemiology

In the general population, ASPD affects 3% of men and under 1% of women. Among psychiatric populations, ASPD affects 3% to 15% of men, and 1% to 3% of women. In many prisons, 75% of the inmates may have ASPD. ASPD is more prevalent in lower socioeconomic groups and among urban dwellers.

Etiology and Pathogenesis

One should distinguish the "habitual" criminal (i.e., ASPD) from the "occasional" criminal. Habitual antisocial behavior stems from genetic *and* psychosocial factors, whereas occasional antisocial behavior seems to arise more from psychosocial causes. This is a big generalization, but in large measure "habitual" criminals are born and "occasional" criminals are made. This section only discusses the "habituals."

Psychosocial Factors

Sociological. Poverty contributes to ASPD, but it's hardly the sole cause. In a study of Philadelphia inner-city youth, 35% of males under 18 had at least one contact with the police, but only 6% caused half of all delinquencies and two-thirds of all violent crimes. (These data confirm the difference between "habitual" and "occasional" criminals.) While nobody endorses poverty as a lifestyle, these data suggest that despite substantial economic deprivation the vast majority of the poor do *not* become sociopaths.

Additional evidence demonstrates that factors other than poverty must be involved. First, ASPD arises in middle and upper socioeconomic groups. Second, ASPD is becoming more prevalent worldwide, even where there's increasing wealth. Third, the childhood behaviors of adult sociopaths are remarkably similar regardless of economic class. Fourth, these childhood antisocial behaviors emerge so early, it's improbable that sociological factors are a primary cause.

Familial. Sociopaths generally grow up amid considerable parental discord (e.g., desertion, separation, divorce, custody fights) and familial disruption (e.g., early deaths, frequent moves, brutal discipline). The most convincing prospective evidence for environmental influences came from the Gluecks (1959). They showed the best predictor of serious delinquency in a person 18 and over was being reared, before the age of six, by a mother (or mother surrogate) who did not provide consistent affection and discipline. When compared with socioeconomically matched controls, the childhoods of sociopaths had considerably more maternal neglect, indifference, and alcoholism, but similar amounts of paternal conflicts, serious illness, and parental death.

Although generally confirming the Gluecks' findings, Rutter (1981) also observed that having emotionally inconsistent parents, those who unpredictably pop in and out, is far more likely to produce a sociopath than having parents who "simply" die or disappear. It should be noted, however, that many sociopaths are reared in stable families, with loving parents and normal siblings. Obviously, ASPD has multiple etiologies.

Biomedical Factors

Whereas the Gluecks pointed to mothers, Robins (1966) found the best predictor of ASPD was having a sociopathic or alcoholic father. Curious about this finding was that the children grew up to become delinquents whether or not the father reared them. Was the father's absence or inconsistency the culprit? Or was sociopathy being inherited from these fathers? The evidence is inconclusive.

Studies of male felons, most having ASPD, revealed that 20% of their first-degree male relatives were sociopaths and 33% were alcoholics. Among female felons, half being "habitual" criminals, a third of their male relatives were sociopaths and half were alcoholics. Although most research demonstrates higher concordance rates for ASPD among identical (36%), than among familial (12%), twins, these different rates are not as eye-popping as those with other mental disorders. Adopted-away research suggests that genetic factors play some etiological role, but that environmental factors are also important.

Differential Diagnosis

ASPD should be diagnosed *unless* the antisocial behavior stems from *severe mental retardation, schizophrenia, or mania*. Severe mental retardation and schizophrenia preempt ASPD because it's hard to know which of these three is producing the antisocial conduct. Mania is easy to differentiate because its antisocial behavior is episodic, time-limited, and doesn't occur during childhood. Sociopaths often abuse drugs and alcohol, but a *substance use disorder* should only be diagnosed when the patient meets the full *DSM-III* criteria for it.

Management and Treatment

No psychotherapy has been found to help sociopaths. ASPD is ego-syntonic, sociopaths have no desire to change, consider insights excuses, have no concept of the future, resent all authorities, including therapists, view the patient role as pitiful, detest being in a position of inferiority, deem therapy a joke and therapists as objects to be conned, threatened, seduced, or used.

Judges are as stuck as psychotherapists. They know that "rehabilitation" does not help the "hard-core criminal" and that sentencing sociopaths to psychotherapy wastes everybody's time. Sociopaths made to enlist in the army can't tolerate the discipline, go AWOL, and are dishonorably discharged. So what can be done? Not much. But consider the following:

1. *Prevention* is the most important intervention mental and medical health professionals can make. Early detection of antisocial behavior in children and young teenagers should be treated promptly before it gets out of hand.

2. *Family counseling* is critical. Therapists may not do much for sociopaths, but they may help his family. Manipulated so often, family members swing from hate to guilt, never knowing what to feel. Because they are so close to the problem, commonsense guidelines by an objective outsider/professional can help them place matters into perspective.

3. Since antisocial acts increase during intoxication, *treat substance misuse.*

4. Whenever possible, *counseling should be independent of punishment and parole.* If the sociopath knows the therapist exerts no influence on his sentence, the sociopath is a bit more likely to use treatment constructively. Studies in the treatment of rapists and child molesters lend credence to this notion.

BORDERLINE PERSONALITY DISORDER

In *DSM-III*, borderline personality disorder (BPD) presents with at least five of the following: (a) impulsivity, (b) unstable and intense interpersonal relations, (c) inappropriate or intense anger, (d) identity confusion, (e) affective instability, (f) problems being alone, (g) physically self-destructive acts, and (h) chronic feelings of emptiness and boredom. Table 21-8 lists *DSM-III*'s criteria for BPD.

At first, the term "borderline" referred to patients who straddled the border between neurosis and psychosis. The diagnosis of "borderline schizophrenia," used widely until the mid-1970s, assumed that borderline disorders were a type of "latent schizophrenia." Although the diagnosis is still controversial, most authorities now believe that borderline conditions are personality disorders. What nobody disputes is that borderlines *look much better than they are*, a fact which continually deceives professionals as well as laymen.

Clinical Presentation

Feeling chronically bored and empty, borderlines desperately seek stimulation: They might gamble, sexually act-up, abuse drugs, overdose, instigate brawls, or attempt suicide. Many slash their wrists or douse lit cigarettes on their arms, not to kill or hurt themselves, but to *feel* something. ("I feel so dead, cutting myself is the only way I know I'm alive.") Their moods are always reactive, intense, and brief; trivial problems mushroom into calamities.

The borderline's interpersonal relations swing between suffocating dependency and mindless self-assertion. She hates being alone, and leaches onto others. She will call a recently-made friend every day about a "disaster" needing immediate attention. Initially, the friend may be flattered by the borderline's "idealization" of him, yet he soon finds himself sucked into a

TABLE 21-8
DSM-III Criteria for Borderline Personality Disorder*

The following are characteristic of the individual's current and long-term functioning, are not limited to episodes of illness, and cause either significant impairment in social or occupational functioning or subjective distress.

A. At least five of the following are required:

    (1) impulsivity or unpredictability in at least two areas that are potentially self-damaging, e.g., spending, sex, gambling, substance use, shoplifting, overeating, physically self-damaging acts

    (2) a pattern of unstable and intense interpersonal relationships, e.g., marked shifts of attitude, idealization, devaluation, manipulation (consistently using others for one's own ends)

    (3) inappropriate, intense anger or lack of control of anger, e.g., frequent displays of temper, constant anger

    (4) identity disturbance manifested by uncertainty about several issues relating to identity, such as self-image, gender identity, long-term goals or career choice, friendship patterns, values, and loyalties, e.g., "Who am I?", "I feel like I am my sister when I am good"

    (5) affective instability: marked shifts from normal mood to depression, irritability, or anxiety, usually lasting a few hours and only rarely more than a few days, with a return to normal mood

    (6) intolerance of being alone, e.g., frantic efforts to avoid being alone, depressed when alone

    (7) physically self-damaging acts, e.g., suicidal gestures, self-mutilation, recurrent accidents or physical fights

    (8) chronic feelings of emptiness or boredom

B. If under 18, does not meet the criteria for Identity Disorder.

*_DSM-III_, pp. 322–323.

gooey, all-consuming relationship. When he tries to cool things, the borderline denigrates him ("devaluation") with a vengeance: She'll pour ink on his couch, demand money and accuse the friend of "being miserly," call him at 3 a.m. to complain he's a "bastard," etc. The borderline's digs contain just enough truth to fester under the friend's skin, which eventually leads the friend to apologize.

Borderlines paint people in black and white, never gray, first idealizing people and then devaluing them. The borderline's relationships, platonic and romantic, are all-or-nothing. She's in love with love, not people: Anything less than total love is hate; anything less than total commitment is rejection ("rejection sensitivity").

She expects — nay demands — that others do for her what she can't do for herself. Chronically sad and demoralized, she adopts friends, not because she likes them, but because she expects them to rid her of unhappiness. When they don't, she dumps them, finds another savior, and repeats the cycle. Unable to figure out who or what she is ("identity diffusion"), she gloms onto others so as to acquire an identity by osmosis. A 25-year-old borderline said she dresses like the rock star Madonna, "to express my individuality." While she's convinced nobody ever does enough for her, others find her exhausting and draining—an "empty gas tank" in need of constant refueling.

Borderlines are notorious for *splitting*—that is, they view people as "all good" or "all bad"—and then get others to act out these roles. Everywhere borderlines go, they set people against each other, create havoc, and walk away without anybody realizing until later that the "innocent" borderline caused the chaos.

Mary Rae, an inpatient with BPD, superficially slashed her wrist, squeezed the blood, and showed it dripping to her psychiatrist. As anyone would have predicted, he cancelled her weekend pass. This infuriated Mary Rae. She then "confided" in nurse Peter:

> You're the only person who understands me. My doctor, and everyone else here, hates me. . . . When I cut my wrist I realized I should tell my doctor. So I did, and right away. I *thought* that was the right thing to do. So what does Dr. Jerk-ass do? He locks me up. I don't get it: Staff says we're supposed to be open with them. Well, I was! From now on, I keep everything to myself. I wasn't suicidal—I would hardly tell people if I were. Peter, if only *you* would have been here. Then I could have gone to you and never cut myself at all. As it is, I'm stuck here all weekend: Just thinking about it makes me suicidal. Can't you help me?

Flattered that Mary Rae confided in him, Peter campaigns to restore her weekend pass. He doesn't realize that Mary Rae has similarly "confided" in five other staff members, each thinking they have a "unique and confidential relationship" with her, which must be kept secret. The unit's staff soon splits between those who feel Mary Rae has been victimized for "being honest," and those who think she's a manipulator and should be shipped to a state hospital. Very quickly, both sides cease squabbling about Mary Rae, but attack each other as insensitive or naive. Meanwhile, as an innocent bystander, Mary Rae fiddles while the staff burns.

Borderline patients may have many "neurotic" symptoms—panic attacks, phobias, anxiety, somatic complaints, conversion symptoms, dysthymia. Under stress, some become *briefly* psychotic. Highly characteristic of borderlines is their giving sane answers on structured psychological tests (e.g., WAIS), but bizarre, psychotic responses on unstructured tests (e.g., Rorschach).

BPD has a chronic, fluctuating course. Although it does *not* lead to schizophrenia, it significantly impairs social and occupational functioning. A five-year follow-up showed they function at about the same, poor level. Those with higher premorbid levels of functioning have better prognoses.

Epidemiology

Twice as many women as men are borderline. Using strict diagnostic criteria, 1.6% to 4% of the general population has BPD; with broader criteria, Kernberg estimates the prevalence may be as high as 15%. Borderlines have lower marital rates than the general population.

Etiology and Pathogenesis

Kernberg (1975) hypothesizes that borderlines have a "constitutional" inability to regulate affects, which predisposes them to psychological disorganization under specific adverse conditions during childhood. He claims that splitting arises because the child's early experience does not permit her to form an image of a mother who can tolerate intense, negative feelings toward herself. Subsequently, the child is unable to synthesize the favorable and unfavorable aspects of her mother, and later, of herself. Without these integrations the child habitually dissociates good from bad, and can't conceive of, much less tolerate, their coexistence. When reality confronts the borderline with this coexistence, she wards off her anxiety by "splitting." She even applies these all-or-nothing caricatures to her health, feeling "perfect" one day, "dying" the next.

BPD runs in families. When compared to controls, first-degree relatives of borderlines have 10 times the rate of BPD, and three times the rate of alcoholism. These relatives of borderlines also have higher rates of affective disorders, but normal rates of schizophrenia and bipolar disease. While the mode of this familial transmission is unclear, most investigations have focused on psychosocial determinants.

Mahler et al. (1975) proposed that borderline conditions stem from a disturbance in the "rapprochement subphase of the separation-individuation" process—from 18–36 months. During this period, the child, having experimented with separating self from mother, tries returning to mother for approval and emotional "refueling." These mothers, however, have had their own difficulties with separation, and so they resent the child's "clinging," as if to say, "Before you wanted me, now you don't. So get lost!" These mothers experience their child's attempts at autonomy as abandonments (e.g., "How dare you leave me!"). As the child grows up, she replays these dependence-independence conflicts with others.

Along similar lines, Masterson (1976) contends that the essence of the borderline's dilemma is a conflict between a desire for autonomy and a fear of parental abandonment. He claims these mothers reward their child's regressive behaviors and discourage their individuation.

Strip aside everything borderlines do and say, and what remains is an underlying dread, or perhaps a conviction, of being *bad*; or as a patient remarked, "Underneath madness lies badness." Borderlines may disown this badness by projecting it onto others ("projective identification"), act-up to escape feeling this badness, employ reaction-formation, as when romanticizing ideal love (e.g., Blanche DuBois), or behave self-destructively. Similar defenses are used by borderlines who feel they are *nothing* inside, mere shells of humanity, scarecrows masquerading as people.

Differential Diagnosis

Known as the "disorder which doesn't specialize," BPD presents with such variegated symptomatology that it appears in many patients' list of differential diagnoses. BPD may coexist with *schizotypal, histrionic, narcissistic*, and *antisocial personality disorders*, but what usually distinguishes BPD are chronic feelings of emptiness, self-mutilation, transitory psychoses, manipulative suicide attempts, intensely demanding relationships, and superficial intactness.

The sadness common to borderlines is short-lived and highly reactive. Still, *major depression* and *dysthymic disorder* may coexist with BPD or be confused with it. *Cyclothymic disorder*, like BPD, has roller-coaster mood swings, but borderlines don't have true hypomanic periods.

Management and Treatment

Long-term, psychoanalytic psychotherapy is the preferred treatment for BPD, even though no well-controlled studies demonstrate its efficacy. In one approach the therapist's initial task is to foster the patient's trust in treatment so that exploration of unconscious wishes and fantasies may follow. Another approach stresses reality testing, provides structure, and avoids overstimulating "depth interpretations," which induce psychological disorganization.

Drug treatment usually involves MAOIs alleviating dysphoria in rejection-sensitive borderlines, and low doses of antipsychotics for squelching brief reactive psychoses.

AVOIDANT PERSONALITY DISORDER

The essential features of avoidant personality disorder (APD) are extreme social discomfort because of a pervasive fear of being judged negatively. More specifically, *DSM-III* lists these characteristics: (a) hypersensitivity to potential rejection, humiliation, or shame, (b) only entering relationships in which uncritical acceptance is virtually guaranteed, (c) social withdrawal, (d) a desire for affection and acceptance, and (e) low self-esteem. Table 21-9 presents *DSM-III*'s criteria for APD.

Both schizoid and avoidant personalities are loners, but whereas the schizoid person doesn't want friends, the avoidant person does. The latter want affection, but not as much as they fear rejection. Because they dread the slightest disapproval and will misconstrue people's comments as derogatory, they have few, if any, friends. Angry and upset by their own inability to relate, they'll try to prevent rejection by ingratiating themselves to others. Although social phobia commonly arises in APD, the two disorders should not be confused: Social phobias are to *specific* situations (e.g., public speaking), whereas APD pervades all social relations. Most avoidant children and teens can't avoid becoming avoidant adults.

Little is known about the disorder. Supposedly, it's common. Its prognosis and etiology are unknown. Usually recommended is long-term *psychoanalytic psychotherapy*. Confrontation is initially avoided to prevent the avoidant personality from avoiding treatment. *Assertiveness training* or *group therapy* may also help, but only as long as the patient's sensitivity to slights is respected

TABLE 21-9
DSM-III Criteria for Avoidant Personality Disorder*

The following are characteristic of the individual's current and long-term functioning, are not limited to episodes of illness, and cause either significant impairment in social or occupational functioning or subjective distress.

A. Hypersensitivity to rejection, e.g., apprehensively alert to signs of social derogation, interprets innocuous events as ridicule.

B. Unwillingness to enter into relationships unless given unusually strong guarantees of uncritical acceptance.

C. Social withdrawal, e.g., distances self from close personal attachments, engages in peripheral social and vocational roles.

D. Desire for affection and acceptance.

E. Low self-esteem, e.g., devalues self-achievements and is overly dismayed by personal shortcomings.

F. If under 18, does not meet the criteria for Avoidant Disorder of Childhood or Adolescence.

*DSM-III, p. 324.

and the patient can feel some control over how his hypersensitivity is discussed.

DEPENDENT PERSONALITY DISORDER

In *DSM-III*, the essential features of dependent personality disorder (DPD) are (a) passively allowing others to assume responsibility for major areas in one's life, because (b) she lacks self-confidence or the ability to function independently, (c) she then subordinates her needs to those of others, (d) becomes dependent on them, and (d) avoids any chance of being self-reliant. Table 21-10 lists the *DSM-III* criteria for DPD.

Everybody has dependent traits and wishes. What distinguishes the dependent personality is that her dependency is total, pervading all areas of her life; she dreads autonomy. The dependent individual may be productive, but only if supervised. She's likely to call herself "inept" or "stupid." When pressed to name her redeeming qualities, she will reluctantly confess to being a good companion, loyal, and kind.

Ethel is prototypic. She refers to herself as "man's best friend." Her man is Mitch, a husband who schedules her days, tells her what foods to eat, picks her doctors, chooses her clothes, and selects her friends. Explains Ethel: "He likes to think, and I don't. Why should I decide things, when he'll do it for me?" This arrangement pleased both for years until Mitch announced he was going to China for three weeks on business. Ethel was frantic and sought treatment. Like most dependent personalities, she wanted help not for dependency, but for losing it.

Historically, DPD was known as "passive-dependent" personality, and dependent personalities were known as "oral characters." This label referred

TABLE 21-10
DSM-III Criteria for Dependent Personality Disorder*

The following are characteristic of the individual's current and long-term functioning, are not limited to episodes of illness, and cause either significant impairment in social or occupational functioning or subjective distress.

A. Passively allows others to assume responsibility for major areas of life because of inability to function independently (e.g., lets spouse decide what kind of job he or she should have).

B. Subordinates own needs to those of persons on whom he or she depends in order to avoid any possibility of having to rely on self, e.g., tolerates abusive spouse.

C. Lacks self-confidence, e.g., sees self as helpless, stupid.

*DSM-III, pp. 325–326.

to their most striking clinical feature — the insistence on being "fed" or taken care of; it also suggests the etiology of overindulged or frustrated wishes during the oral stage of psychosexual development. (More recently, the role of maternal deprivation during the oral stage has been stressed.) "Oral" features include a constant demand for attention, passivity, dependency, a fear of autonomy, a lack of perseverance, dread of decision-making, suggestibility, and "oral behaviors" (e.g., smoking, drinking, thumb-sucking). Oral traits are common in "normals," but even more so in psychiatric patients.

The 1963 Midtown Manhattan survey showed that 2.5% of the residents had passive-dependent personalities. DPD is more prevalent in women and in the youngest sibling. Prolonged physical illness during childhood may predispose to DPD. *Histrionic, schizotypal, narcissistic,* and *avoidant personality disorders* often coexist with DPD, and *dysthymic disorder* and *major depression* are frequent complications. Although dependent traits are common in *agoraphobia*, the agoraphobic will *actively* insist that others assume responsibility, whereas the dependent personality *passively* abdicates control to others.

More insightful patients may benefit from *psychoanalytic psychotherapy*. Often addressed in this sequence are the patient's (a) low self-esteem and its origins; (b) fears of harming others by seeking autonomy; (c) dependency on the therapist; and (d) the experience of termination as it relates to dependency. Less psychologically-minded patients may benefit from supportive *group therapy* or *assertiveness training*.

PASSIVE-AGGRESSIVE PERSONALITY DISORDER

In *DSM-III*, passive-aggressive personality disorder (PAPD) is a habitual indirect resistance to demands for adequate social or occupational performance, which the person could do, but doesn't, resulting in pervasively impaired functioning. These patients resent and oppose reasonable and appropriate requests; but instead of doing so actively, openly, and directly, they do so passively and indirectly. They express covert aggression by dawdling, procrastinating, feigning stupidity, "forgetting," etc. Examples of passive-aggressiveness include the secretary who mistypes letters knowing it will embarrass her boss; people who always arrive 30 minutes late for meetings; the patient who awakes his therapist by calling him early Sunday morning about a trivial matter and says, "I'm sorry, but you did say I could at *any* time." Table 21-11 lists *DSM-III*'s criteria for PAPD.

In a PAPD, passive-aggressive behaviors occur in a variety of contexts and relationships — most often at work between bosses and underlings, but also in personal settings between equals. These patients are dependent, unambitious, and pessimistic; they lack confidence and are oblivious to their passive-aggressiveness. The severity of these traits varies throughout life, yet these patients rarely commit suicide. Because PAPD aggravates the effects of other

TABLE 21-11
DSM-III* Criteria for Passive-Aggressive Personality Disorder

The following are characteristic of the individual's current and long-term functioning, and are not limited to episodes of illness.

A. Resistance to demands for adequate performance in both occupational and social functioning.

B. Resistance expressed indirectly through at least two of the following:

   (1) procrastination
   (2) dawdling
   (3) stubbornness
   (4) intentional inefficiency
   (5) "forgetfulness"

C. As a consequence of A and B, pervasive and long-standing social and occupational ineffectiveness (including in roles of housewife or student), e.g., intentional inefficiency that has prevented job promotion.

D. Persistence of the behavior pattern even under circumstances in which more self-assertive and effective behavior is possible.

E. Does not meet the criteria of any other Personality Disorder, and if under age 18, does not meet the criteria for Oppositional Disorder.

DSM-III, p. 329.

mental disorders, patients with PAPD are often hospitalized, especially for depression and alcoholism.

About 1% of the general population has PADP. The disorder's sex ratio, family patterns, and etiology are unknown. The differential diagnosis of PAPD includes *dependent, avoidant,* and *compulsive personality disorders.*

There being no better treatment available, *supportive psychotherapy* is the treatment of choice, even though it's fraught with difficulty. These patients will refuse to acknowledge, much less discuss, their dependency. Instead, they'll act out their resentment by coming late, not paying their bill, prematurely stopping treatment, obsessing about irrelevancies that clearly annoy the therapist, or attempting suicide. Clinicians should treat their suicide gestures as expressions of covert hostility, instead of consequences of loss or depression. *Group therapy* can diffuse the patient's dependency if it's too consuming for one therapist to handle. All psychotherapies should encourage these patients to take responsibility for their behavior. "I know it's your 'civil liberty' to blast your radio at the office, but if everyone objects, what's going to happen to your job?" In other words, therapy keeps focusing on why the problem belongs to the patient and nobody else.

Appendices

APPENDIX A

DSM-III Classification: Axes I and II Categories and Codes*

*American Psychiatric Association (1980). *Diagnostic and statistical manual of mental disorders* (3rd ed.). Washington, DC: American Psychiatric Press, pp. 15–19.

All official DSM-III codes and terms are included in ICD-9-CM. However, in order to differentiate those DSM-III categories that use the same ICD-9-CM codes, unofficial non-ICD-9-CM codes are provided in parentheses for use when greater specificity is necessary.

The long dashes indicate the need for a fifth-digit subtype or other qualifying term.

DISORDERS USUALLY FIRST EVIDENT IN INFANCY, CHILD-HOOD OR ADOLESCENCE
Mental retardation
(Code in fifth digit: 1 = with other be-havioral symptoms [requiring attention or treatment and that are not part of another disorder], 0 = without other behavioral symptoms.)
317.0(x) Mild mental retardation, _____
318.0(x) Moderate mental retarda-tion, _____
318.1(x) Severe mental retarda-tion, _____
318.2(x) Profound mental retarda-tion, _____
319.0(x) Unspecified mental retarda-tion, ——

Attention deficit disorder
314.01 with hyperactivity
314.00 without hyperactivity
314.80 residual type

Conduct disorder
312.00 undersocialized, aggressive
312.10 undersocialized, nonaggressive
312.23 socialized, aggressive
312.21 socialized, nonaggressive
312.90 atypical

Anxiety disorders of childhood or adolescence
309.21 Separation anxiety disorder
313.21 Avoidant disorder of childhood or adolescence
313.00 Overanxious disorder

Other disorders of infancy, childhood or adolescence
313.89 Reactive attachment disorder of infancy
313.22 Schizoid disorder of childhood or adolescence

313.23 Elective mutism
313.81 Oppositional disorder
313.82 Identity disorder

Eating disorders
307.10 Anorexia nervosa
307.51 Bulimia
307.52 Pica
307.53 Rumination disorder of infancy
307.50 Atypical eating disorder

Stereotyped movement disorders
307.21 Transient tic disorder
307.22 Chronic motor tic disorder
307.23 Tourette's disorder
307.20 Atypical tic disorder
307.30 Atypical stereotyped movement disorder

Other disorders with physical manifestations
307.00 Stuttering
307.60 Functional enuresis
307.70 Functional encopresis
307.46 Sleepwalking disorder
307.46 Sleep terror disorder (307.49)

Pervasive developmental disorders
Code in fifth digit: 0 = full syndrome present, 1 = residual state.
299.0x Infantile autism, _____
299.9x Childhood onset pervasive developmental disorder, _____

299.8x Atypical, ——

Specific developmental disorders
Note: These are coded on Axis II.
315.00 Developmental reading disorder
315.10 Developmental arithmetic disorder
315.31 Developmental language disorder
315.39 Developmental articula-tion disorder
315.50 Mixed specific develop-mental disorder
315.90 Atypical specific develop-mental disorder

ORGANIC MENTAL DISORDERS
Section 1. Organic mental disorders whose etiology or pathophysiological process is listed below (taken from the mental disorders section of ICD-9-CM).

Dementias arising in the senium and presenium

Primary degenerative dementia, senile onset,
290.30 with delirium
290.20 with delusions
290.21 with depression
290.00 uncomplicated
Code in fifth digit:
1 = with delirium, 2 = with delusions, 3 = with depression, 0 = uncomplicated.
290.1x Primary degenerative dementia, presenile onset, _____
290.4x Multi-infarct dementia, _____

Substance-induced

Alcohol
303.00 intoxication
291.40 idiosyncratic intoxication
291.80 withdrawal
291.00 withdrawal delirium
291.30 hallucinosis
291.10 amnestic disorder
Code severity of dementia in fifth digit:
1 = mild, 2 = moderate, 3 = severe, 0 = unspecified.
291.2x Dementia associated with alcoholism, _____

Barbiturate or similarly acting sedative or hypnotic
305.40 intoxication (327.00)
292.00 withdrawal (327.01)
292.00 withdrawal delirium (327.02)
292.83 amnestic disorder (327.04)

Opioid
305.50 intoxication (327.10)
292.00 withdrawal (327.11)

Cocaine
305.60 intoxication (327.20)

Amphetamine or similarly acting sympathomimetic
305.70 intoxication (327.30)
292.81 delirium (327.32)

292.11 delusional disorder (327.35)
292.00 withdrawal (327.31)

Phencyclidine (PCP) or similarly acting arylcyclohexylamine
305.90 intoxication (327.40)
292.81 delirium (327.42)
292.90 mixed organic mental disorder (327.49)

Hallucinogen
305.30 hallucinosis (327.56)
292.11 delusional disorder (327.55)
292.84 affective disorder (327.57)

Cannabis
305.20 intoxication (327.60)
292.11 delusional disorder (327.65)

Tobacco
292.00 withdrawal (327.71)

Caffeine
305.90 intoxication (327.80)

Other or unspecified substance
305.90 intoxication (327.90)
292.00 withdrawal (327.91)
292.81 delirium (327.92)
292.82 dementia (327.93)
292.83 amnestic disorder (327.94)
292.11 delusional disorder (327.95)
292.12 hallucinosis (327.96)
292.84 affective disorder (327.97)
292.89 personality disorder (327.98)
292.90 atypical or mixed organic mental disorder (327.99)

Section 2. Organic brain syndromes whose etiology or pathophysiological process is either noted as an additional diagnosis from outside the mental disorders section of ICD-9-CM or is unknown.

293.00 Delirium
294.10 Dementia
294.00 Amnestic syndrome
293.81 Organic delusional syndrome
293.82 Organic hallucinosis
293.83 Organic affective syndrome
310.10 Organic personality syndrome
294.80 Atypical or mixed organic brain syndrome

SUBSTANCE USE DISORDERS

Code in fifth digit: 1 = continuous, 2 = episodic, 3 = in remission, 0 = unspecified.

305.0x Alcohol abuse, _____
303.9x Alcohol dependence (Alcoholism), _____
305.4x Barbiturate or similarly acting sedative or hypnotic abuse,
304.1x Barbiturate or similarly acting sedative or hypnotic dependence, _____
305.5x Opioid abuse, _____
304.0x Opioid dependence, _____
305.6x Cocaine abuse, _____
305.7x Amphetamine or similarly acting sympathomimetic abuse, _____
304.4x Amphetamine or similarly acting sympathomimetic dependence, _____
305.9x Phencyclidine (PCP) or similarly acting arylcyclohexylamine abuse, _____ (328.4x)
305.3x Hallucinogen abuse, _____
305.2x Cannabis abuse, _____
304.3x Cannabis dependence, _____
305.1x Tobacco dependence, _____
305.9x Other, mixed or unspecified substance abuse, _____
304.6x Other specified substance dependence, _____
304.9x Unspecified substance dependence, _____
304.7x Dependence on combination of opioid and other non-alcoholic substance, _____
304.8x Dependence on combination of substances, excluding opioids and alcohol, _____

SCHIZOPHRENIC DISORDERS

Code in fifth digit: 1 = subchronic, 2 = chronic, 3 = subchronic with acute exacerbation, 4 = chronic with acute exacerbation, 5 = in remission, 0 = unspecified.

Schizophrenia,
295.1x disorganized, _____
295.2x catatonic, _____
295.3x paranoid, _____
295.9x undifferentiated, _____
295.6x residual, _____

PARANOID DISORDERS

297.10 Paranoia
297.30 Shared paranoid disorder
298.30 Acute paranoid disorder
297.90 Atypical paranoid disorder

PSYCHOTIC DISORDERS NOT ELSEWHERE CLASSIFIED

295.40 Schizophreniform disorder
298.80 Brief reactive psychosis
295.70 Schizoaffective disorder
298.90 Atypical psychosis

NEUROTIC DISORDERS: These are included in Affective, Anxiety, Somatoform, Dissociative, and Psychosexual Disorders. In order to facilitate the identification of the categories that in DSM-II were grouped together in the class of Neuroses, the DSM-II terms are included separately in parentheses after the corresponding categories. These DSM-II terms are included in ICD-9-CM and therefore are acceptable as alternatives to the recommended DSM-III terms that precede them.

AFFECTIVE DISORDERS
Major affective disorders

Code major depressive episode in fifth digit: 6 = in remission, 4 = with psychotic features (the unofficial non-ICD-9-CM fifth digit 7 may be used instead to indicate that the psychotic features are mood-incongruent), 3 = with melancholia, 2 = without melancholia, 0 = unspecified.

Code manic or mixed episode in fifth digit: 6 = in remission, 4 = with psychotic features (the unofficial non-ICD-9-CM fifth digit 7 may be used instead to indicate that the psychotic features are mood-incongruent), 2 = without psychotic features, 0 = unspecified.

Bipolar disorder,
296.6x mixed, _____
296.4x manic, _____
296.5x depressed, _____

Major depression,
296.2x single episode, _____
296.3x recurrent, _____

Other specific affective disorders
301.13   Cyclothymic disorder
300.40   Dysthymic disorder
         (or Depressive neurosis)

Atypical affective disorders
296.70   Atypical bipolar disorder
296.82   Atypical depression

ANXIETY DISORDERS

         Phobic disorders (or Phobic
         neuroses)
300.21   Agoraphobia with panic attacks
300.22   Agoraphobia without panic
         attacks
300.23   Social phobia
300.29   Simple phobia

         Anxiety states (or Anxiety
         neuroses)
300.01   Panic disorder
300.02   Generalized anxiety disorder
300.30   Obsessive compulsive disorder
         (or Obsessive compulsive
         neurosis)

         Post-traumatic stress disorder
308.30   acute
309.81   chronic or delayed

300.00   Atypical anxiety disorder

SOMATOFORM DISORDERS
300.81   Somatization disorder
300.11   Conversion disorder
         (or Hysterical neurosis, con-
         version type)
307.80   Psychogenic pain disorder
300.70   Hypochondriasis
         (or Hypochondriacal neurosis)
300.70   Atypical somatoform disorder
         (300.71)

**DISSOCIATIVE DISORDERS
(OR HYSTERICAL NEUROSES,
DISSOCIATIVE TYPE)**
300.12   Psychogenic amnesia
300.13   Psychogenic fugue
300.14   Multiple personality
300.60   Depersonalization disorder
         (or Depersonalization neurosis)
300.15   Atypical dissociative disorder

**PSYCHOSEXUAL DISORDERS
Gender identity disorders**
Indicate sexual history in the fifth digit
of Transsexualism code: 1 = asexual,
2 = homosexual, 3 = heterosexual,
0 = unspecified.

302.5x   Transsexualism, _____
302.60   Gender identity disorder of
         childhood
302.85   Atypical gender identity dis-
         order

Paraphilias
302.81   Fetishism
302.30   Transvestism
302.10   Zoophilia
302.20   Pedophilia
302.40   Exhibitionism
302.82   Voyeurism
302.83   Sexual masochism
302.84   Sexual sadism
302.90   Atypical paraphilia

Psychosexual dysfunctions
302.71   Inhibited sexual desire
302.72   Inhibited sexual excitement
302.73   Inhibited female orgasm
302.74   Inhibited male orgasm
302.75   Premature ejaculation
302.76   Functional dyspareunia
306.51   Functional vaginismus
302.70   Atypical psychosexual dysfunc-
         tion

Other psychosexual disorders
302.00   Ego-dystonic homosexuality
302.89   Psychosexual disorder not
         elsewhere classified

FACTITIOUS DISORDERS
300.16   Factitious disorder with
         psychological symptoms
301.51   Chronic factitious disorder
         with physical symptoms
300.19   Atypical factitious disorder
         with physical symptoms

**DISORDERS OF IMPULSE CONTROL
NOT ELSEWHERE CLASSIFIED**
312.31   Pathological gambling
312.32   Kleptomania
312.33   Pyromania
312.34   Intermittent explosive disorder
312.35   Isolated explosive disorder
312.39   Atypical impulse control dis-
         order

ADJUSTMENT DISORDER

309.00 with depressed mood
309.24 with anxious mood
309.28 with mixed emotional features
309.30 with disturbance of conduct
309.40 with mixed disturbance of
        emotions and conduct
309.23 with work (or academic)
        inhibition
309.83 with withdrawal
309.90 with atypical features

PSYCHOLOGICAL FACTORS
AFFECTING PHYSICAL CONDITION

Specify physical condition on Axis III.
316.00 Psychological factors affecting
        physical condition

PERSONALITY DISORDERS
Note: These are coded on Axis II.
301.00 Paranoid
301.20 Schizoid
301.22 Schizotypal
301.50 Histrionic
301.81 Narcissistic
301.70 Antisocial
301.83 Borderline
301.82 Avoidant
301.60 Dependent
301.40 Compulsive
301.84 Passive-Aggressive
301.89 Atypical, mixed or other
        personality disorder

V CODES FOR CONDITIONS NOT ATTRIBUTABLE TO A MENTAL DISORDER THAT ARE A FOCUS OF ATTENTION OR TREATMENT

V65.20 Malingering
V62.89 Borderline intellectual
        functioning (V62.88)
V71.01 Adult antisocial behavior
V71.02 Childhood or adolescent
        antisocial behavior
V62.30 Academic problem
V62.20 Occupational problem
V62.82 Uncomplicated bereavement
V15.81 Noncompliance with medical
        treatment
V62.89 Phase of life problem or other
        life circumstance problem
V61.10 Marital problem
V61.20 Parent-child problem
V61.80 Other specified family circum-
        stances
V62.81 Other interpersonal problem

ADDITIONAL CODES

300.90 Unspecified mental disorder
        (nonpsychotic)
V71.09 No diagnosis or condition on
        Axis I
799.90 Diagnosis or condition deferred
        on Axis I

V71.09 No diagnosis on Axis II
799.90 Diagnosis deferred on
        Axis II

APPENDIX B

Medical-Psychiatric History Form

Instructions: Please complete this form and return it to your therapist at your next appointment. By doing so, you will provide important diagnostic information while freeing-up time with your therapist for other matters. If you are unsure about a question or are unable to answer it, don't worry about it: Simply place a question mark ("?") next to it and move on. Everything you indicate will be held in the strictest confidence.

PATIENT DATA

Name _____ Today's Date _____

Street Address _____

City _____ State _____ Zip _____

Telephone <home> _____ <work> _____

Business Street Address _____

City _____ State _____ Zip _____

Occupation _____ Age _____ Birth Date _____

Person to contact in case of emergency: Name _____

Relation _____ Telephone _____

City _____ State _____ Zip _____

MEDICAL HISTORY

Your Physician's Name _____

Street Address _____ City _____

State _____ Zip _____ Telephone ( ) _____

Are you allergic to any drugs? yes ( ) no ( ). If so, to which ones:

_____

Do you have any other allergies? yes ( ) no ( ). If so, to what:

_____

Are you pregnant? yes ( ) no ( ). Do you smoke? yes ( ) no ( ).

When was your last EKG? _____ Was it normal? yes ( ) no ( ).

When did your physician last examine you? _____

Have you been treated for any of the following:

AIDS, or Acquired immune deficiency syndrome ( )
Alcohol abuse ( ), alcoholism ( )
Anemia ( )
Asthma ( ), hay fever ( )
Diabetes ( )
Drug abuse or addiction ( )
Epilepsy, seizures, or convulsions ( )
Fainting spells, feeling light-headed, or dizziness ( )
Gastrointestinal problems ( )
Glaucoma ( )
Heart murmur or disease ( )
Hepatitis, liver disease, or jaundice ( )
High blood pressure [hypertension] ( )
Kidney disease ( )
Lung disease ( )
Migraine ( )
Rheumatic fever ( )
Stroke ( )
Thyroid problems ( )
Ulcer ( )
Venereal disease ( )
Other ( ) If so, what ? _____

Please list any (prescription or over-the-counter) medication that you are currently taking?

_____

Have you ever had, or are presently taking, any of the following:

anesthesia of any kind—local or general ( )
Anticonvulsants ( ), Dilantin [phenytoin] ( )
Antihistamines of any type ( )
Ativan ( ), Atarax ( ), Tranxene ( ), Serax ( ), Xanax ( )
Aventyl [nortriptyline] ( ), Pertofrane or Norpramin [desipramine] ( )
    Sinequan ( ), Surmontil ( ), Vivactil ( )
barbiturates ( ), Amytal ( ), Nembutal ( ), Phenobarbital ( ), Seconal ( ), Tuinal ( )
Benedryl ( ), Cogentin ( ), Artane ( ), Kemadrin ( ), Symmetrel ( )
Benzedrine or Dexedrine [amphetamine or "speed" or "uppers"] ( )
butyl nitrite ( ), "Rush" ( ), "Locker Room" ( ), glue ( )
caffeine ( ), coffee ( ), cola ( ), tea ( )
chloral hydrate or Noctec ( )
clonidine [Catapres] ( )
cocaine ( ), freebase ( )
codeine ( ), Empirin with codeine ( ), Percodan ( )
Dalmane ( ), Halcion ( ), Restoril ( )
Desyrel ( ), Loxitane ( )

Dexamyl ( )
Doridan ( ), Noludar ( ), Placidyl ( )
Elavil [amitriptyline] ( ), Tofranil [imipramine] ( )
Electroconvulsive therapy, "shock therapy," or ECT ( )
Etrafon ( ), Triavil ( )
Equanil or Miltown [meprobamate] ( )
Haldol ( ), Mellaril ( ), Navane ( ), Prolixin ( ), Stelazine ( ), Thorazine ( ), Trilafon ( )
Inderal [propranolol] ( )
Librium ( ), Librax ( )
Lithium ( ), Lithobid ( ), Eskalith ( )
LSD ( ), mescaline ( ), DMT ( ), "ecstasy" ["XTC," MDMA] ( ), peyote ( ),
    other "psyche
marijuana ( ), hashish ( ), THC ( )
megavitamins of any type ( )
methadone ( ), heroin ( ), morphine ( ), opium ( )
Nardil ( ), Parnate ( )
Over-the-counter medications ( ) _____ _____
PCP ["angel dust"] ( )
Prednisone or any steroid ( )
Quaalude, Sopor, or "Ludes" ( )
Ritalin ( )
Serpasil [reserpine] ( )
sleeping pills of any kind ( )
Talwin ( )
Tegretol [carbamazepine] ( )
thyroid ( ), Cytomel ( )
Tobacco in any form ( )
tryptophan ( )
Valium ( ), diazepam ( )

Please list any other prescription medication you have recently, or are currently, taking:

_____

_____

APPENDIX C

Glossary of Psychopathologic Signs and Symptoms

Affect is the instantaneous, observable expression of emotion. It differs from mood (see below), which is a pervasive, subjectively experienced emotion. As the saying goes, "Affect is to mood as weather is to climate." Moods are symptoms; affects are signs. Commonly described affects are:

Blunted, flat, and *constricted* affects describe (in decreasing order of severity) patients who show almost no emotional lability, appear expressionless, look dulled, and speak in a monotone.

Broad affect is a normal range of affect.

Inappropriate affect is clearly discordant with the content of the patient's speech: A patient giggles while talking about his father's death.

Labile affect shows a range of expression in excess of cultural norms, with repeated, rapid, and abrupt shifts of emotion, as when a patient cries one moment and laughs the next. There are two types of labile affect: With "organic" etiologies, the lability of affect presents as a massive emotional overreaction to external stimuli, which is often part of a catastrophic reaction (see p. 105), and which the interviewer is usually unable to stop. With "functional" etiologies, the lability of affect is an overresponse to internal stimuli, which is less rapid and less extreme.

Alexithymia is a mood (see below) in which the patient has a constricted emotional life, diminished ability to fantasize, and a virtual inability to articulate emotions. Like anhedonia, alexithymia describes the absence of emotion, but in anhedonia emotion seems blocked or stymied, whereas in alexithymia it's as if emotion hardly exists. Patients will complain about anhedonia, but not about alexithymia. (See Anhedonia.)

Ambivalence is having two strongly opposite ideas or feelings at the same time, which renders the individual virtually unable to respond or decide.

Amnesia is a pathological loss of memory. There are two types:

Anterograde amnesia is for events occurring after a significant point in time.

Retrograde amnesia is for events occurring before a significant point in time.

Anhedonia is a mood (see below) in which there is a pervasive inability to perceive and experience pleasure in actions and events that are normally pleasurable or satisfying for the individual or most individuals. Anhedonia often begins with the person's trying to carry out the activity hoping the anticipated pleasure will materialize, but it doesn't and in time the person loses all interest in the activity and tends to avoid it: A football freak ignores the Super Bowl; a devoted father is totally bored by his children; a civil-rights activist no longer cares. (Contrast "anhedonic" with "hedonistic." See Alexithymia.)

Anorexia is a loss of appetite.

Anxiety can refer to a symptom or a syndrome. As a symptom, anxiety is a mood (see below) of inner tension, restlessness, uneasiness, or apprehension. As a syndrome, anxiety combines this (internal) mood with (external) physiologic signs, such as tremor, heart-pounding, hypervigilance, dilated pupils, and agitation. Anxiety is pathological only when it chronically interferes with a person's functioning. Whereas anxiety implies the absence of a consciously recognized, external threat, fear implies that such a threat exists. Anxiety focused on an up-coming event is called *anticipatory anxiety*; unfocused anxiety is called *free-floating anxiety*. (See Craving, Panic attack, Phobia.)

Autistic thinking is thought derived from fantasy: The person defines his environment based on internal fantasies instead of on external realities. Autistic thinking also refers to an individual's being preoccupied with his own private world; social withdrawal into one's inner world usually results.

Blocking is when a person's train of thought abruptly and unexpectedly stops. Blocking may or may not be pathological, depending on the degree.

Catatonia is extreme psychomotor agitation or retardation. Catatonic patients seem driven, even when motionless; some appear frantic, others fanatical. (See Mutism, Posturing, Stereotypy.) Examples include:

Catatonic excitement is extreme overactivity seemingly unrelated to environmental stimuli.

Catatonic negativism is an apparently motiveless and extreme resistance to all instructions or attempts to be moved. Three manifestations of this negativism are (a) *catatonic posturing*, in which a bizarre position is rigidly held for long periods; (b) *catatonic rigidity*, in which the patient resists all efforts to be moved; and (c) "*waxy flexibility*," in which the patient resists having his body moved, but ends up with parts of his body being "molded" into odd positions, as if they were pliable wax.

Cataplexy is a sudden, unexpected, purposeless, generalized, and temporary loss of muscle tone.

Clanging is a type of language in which the sound of a word, instead of its meaning, dictates the course of subsequent associations (e.g., "ding, dong, dell . . . ").

Clouding of consciousness is when the patient is awake and functioning, but has an incomplete or distorted awareness of the environment. It is a higher level of awareness than stupor (see below), in which an awake patient is unaware and unresponsive to the environment.

Circumstantiality is a pattern of speech, which, although filled with detours, irrelevant details, and parenthetical remarks, eventually reaches its point; tangentiality (see below) is when the point isn't reached. Circumstantiality may, or may not be, pathological.

Coma is the most impaired end on a continuum of consciousness. The patient may be totally unresponsive to a (painful) stimulus, such as a pinprick, or he may twitch, but not display any further evidence of awareness. Slightly better on this continuum is stupor (see below), in which the patient may rouse to his name, but his speech is not rational, he shows little awareness of his environment, and he may promptly slip back into a coma.

Compulsions are repeated, stereotyped, overtly senseless, actions or rituals, which are performed to prevent anxiety. Compulsions are obsessions (see below) expressed in behavior. Obsessions are thoughts, compulsions are deeds. Lady Macbeth's hand-washing is a compulsion to wipe clean her obsession with Duncan's blood.

Concrete thinking is the inability to think abstractly, metaphorically, or hypothetically. Ideas and words are usually limited to a single meaning. Figures of speech are taken literally, and nuances of language are missed and not used.

Confabulation is when a patient invents responses, facts, and events to mask an organic impairment.

Craving is a symptom in which the person is consistently preoccupied with, thinks about, or strongly desires an habituating substance or physical activity (e.g., bulimic episodes, gambling, jogging, weight-lifting). Craving only exists when the habituating substance or activity is not in use, and is only relieved when it is. Craving is not necessarily associated with physical distress; it may, or may not, coexist with anxiety (see above), but they are different phenomena.

Déjà vu is a sense of familiarity when confronted by a situation or event which has not been experienced previously. Literally = already seen. Although it usually occurs in nonpathological states, it may be pathological.

Delusions are fixed, blatantly false convictions deduced from incorrect inferences about external reality; they are maintained despite enormous obvious, incontrovertible proof to the contrary, and they are not widely believed in the person's culture or subculture. A false belief that involves an extreme value judgment is a delusion only when it defies credibility. Delusions differ from overvalued ideas (see below), which are unreasonable and persistent beliefs. To various degrees, delusions are systematized or unsystematized. In comparison to *unsystematized* delusions, *systematized* delusions are united by a common theme or event and belong to a complete and relatively well-organized network of beliefs; they develop more insidiously, cause less confusion and impairment, and last longer. (See Folie à deux, Hallucinations, Ideas of reference, Mood-congruent, Mood-incongruent, Paranoia, Schneiderian first-rank symptoms.) Examples:

Bizarre delusions are patently absurd and weird.

Grandiose delusions involve an exaggerated sense of one's own importance, power, ability, or identity. "I am Christ."

Jealousy (delusions of,) involve suspicions about a rival (e.g., business rival), or about one's sex partner being unfaithful. Othello.

Nihilistic delusions involve themes of nonexistence (not "negativity"), either of the patient, others, or the world. "My insides are gone." "At 1:30 p.m., the world will evaporate."

Persecutory delusions are those in which the person is convinced others are trying to harm, cheat, attack, or conspire against him.

Reference (delusions of,) are beliefs that external events or people are sending messages or commands of great personal importance to the patient. These delusions are self-referential. A woman insists that a man on TV was speaking to her specifically and instructing her to buy Ajax. (And she did — 1,280 cans!) (See Ideas of reference.)

Somatic delusions pertain to the patient's body, are not consistent with cultural beliefs or with physiology or medicine. "My intestines are rotting." "My brain is turning black."

Depersonalization is when a person perceives his body as unreal, floating, dead, or changing in size. A person's arm may feel like wood or seem detached from his body. Depersonalization differs from derealization (see below), in which a person perceives his environment as unreal. Both phenomena often occur in nonpathological situations, with or without stress.

Derailment is a gradual or sudden deviation in a patient's train of behavior, speech, or thought onto a very different track. It may be hard to distinguish from flight of ideas and looseness of associations (see below). (See Incoherence.)

Derealization is when a person perceives his environment as unreal. The individual feels removed from the world, as if he is viewing it on a movie screen. (See Depersonalization.)

Disorientation is the inability to correctly identify the current time, place, and person's name.

Distractibility is when a patient's attention is frequently being directed to unimportant or irrelevant external stimuli.

Echolalia is a meaningless, persistent, verbal, repetitions of words or sounds heard by the patient — often with a mocking, mumbling, staccato, or parrot-like tone.

(Greek *echo* = "an echo," and *lalia* = "to babble.") Echolalia is in response to the same stimulus, whereas perseveration (see below) is repeated responses to varied stimuli.

Echopraxia is the repetitive imitation of another person's movements.

Ego-dystonic is a sign, symptom, or experience which the patient finds uncomfortable or doesn't want. For example, obsessions are ego-dystonic.

Ego-syntonic is a sign, symptom, or experience which the patient finds acceptable and consistent with his personality. Many, but not all, delusions, hallucinations, and overvalued ideas are ego-syntonic.

Flight of ideas is accelerated speech with many rapid changes in subject that derive from understandable associations, distracting stimuli, or play on words. In flight of ideas (FOI) the connections linking thoughts are understandable, whereas in looseness of associations (LOA) they are not. Nevertheless, extremely rapid FOI may be indistinguishable from LOA, and when there is a marked cultural gap between patient and interviewer, FOI is often misidentified as LOA. (See Derailment, Incoherence.)

Folie à deux, or "madness for two," is when two closely related persons, usually in the same family, share the same delusions.

Fugue is a sudden, "purposeless," and unexpected flight or wandering away from home or work, during which the person assumes a new identity and has an anterograde amnesia (see above).

Guilt is a painful emotion directed towards oneself, in which the person feels he has violated his own principles or conscience; the individual may feel bad, worthless, or in need of punishment. Whereas guilt is an affective state, conscience is a cognitive state consisting of ideas, beliefs, principles, values, standards, and norms. Both guilt and shame (see below) are emotions, but in shame the person feels embarrassed or ashamed before other people.

Hallucinations are false perceptions in the senses — hearing, seeing, touching, tasting, and smelling — based on no external reality. They differ from illusions (see below) which are false perceptions based on real stimuli. Hallucinations are disorders of perception; delusions (see above) are disorders of thinking. Delusions are always psychotic, hallucinations only sometimes: Some patients know their hallucinations are unreal (e.g., "My mind is playing tricks on me"); those who don't are described as giving a "delusional interpretation" to their hallucinations. Hallucinosis (see below) is a state in which the patient realizes his hallucinations are false. Except for dreams, hallucinations are pathological. *Hypnagogic* and *Hypnopompic* hallucinations are dreams which occur on falling asleep or on waking up, respectively; if unaccompanied by other symptoms, they are merely variants of normal. Pathological hallucinations include:

Auditory hallucinations are false perceptions of sound, usually of a voice or voices.

Gustatory hallucinations are false, usually unpleasant, perceptions of taste. (Metallic tastes may be a side effect of medications or physical illnesses.)

Olfactory hallucinations are false perceptions of smell, such as the patient who kept smelling her, as she said, "Happily dead husband."

Somatic hallucinations are false perceptions of a physical experience inside the body. "I feel an orgasm running in my spleen."

Tactile hallucinations are false perceptions of touch. *Formication*—with an "m"—is a tactile hallucination in which the patient feels that things, often insects, are crawling under his skin; it occurs most during withdrawal from alcohol, cocaine, or hypnosedatives.

Visual hallucinations are false perceptions of sight; they may consist of actual people or flashes of light.

Hallucinosis is when patients hallucinate following cessation or reduction of a substance, usually in a clear (or mildly clouded) consciousness. Most, but not all, hallucinosis is very unpleasant. Knowing these hallucinations are not real, the patient is less likely to act on them than on hallucinations he believes to be genuine.

Hypersomnia is a pattern of excessive sleeping.

Ideas of reference are overvalued ideas in which the patient is virtually, but not totally, convinced that objects, people, or events in his immediate environment have personal significance for him. A man felt whenever a red car parked in front of his home it probably was a well-disguised message from the FBI that he should be on the alert for dope addicts. With a delusion of reference, all doubt would cease. When they occur in a hypervigilent state, ideas of reference are not necessarily pathological: For instance, a man at a "swinger's bar" says, "all the chicks can't keep their eyes off me."

Illogical thinking involves conclusions that contain clear internal contradictions or are blatantly erroneous given the initial premises. A patient refuses to go to the movies because the tickets are green. Illogical thinking may, or may not, lead to a delusion, or result from one. "I am a virgin, and therefore, I am the Virgin Mary."

Illusions are misperceptions of real external stimuli. During delirium tremens, alcoholics will misperceive the hair on their arms as bugs: These are illusions, not hallucinations, since they are based on a real stimulus.

Incoherence is a general term to describe incomprehensible speech arising from any kind of psychopathologic thinking.

Insomnia is difficulty sleeping, either as *initial insomnia*, which is trouble falling asleep; *middle insomnia*, which is waking in the middle of the night and eventually falling back to sleep; *terminal insomnia* (also known as "early morning awakening"), in which the person awakes at night and cannot return to sleep; *paninsomnia* refers to difficulty sleeping throughout the night.

Looseness of associations are speech patterns characterized by leaps from subject to subject without the connections being clear nor the patient being aware of his rapid shifts. "School is nice. I adore earlobes." (See Derailment, Flight of ideas, Incoherence.)

Magical thinking is when a person is convinced that his words, thoughts, feelings, or actions will produce or prevent a specific outcome that defies all laws of cause and effect. Depending on how firmly the magical thinking is held, it may be a delusion, or an overvalued idea, as in this example: "I know this seems odd, but when I move my third finger forward, I can make people walk faster; when I move my finger backward, they walk slower." Children, people in primitive cultures, and patients with obsessive-compulsive and schizophrenic-like disorders use magical thinking.

Mood is a pervasive and subjectively experienced feeling state, as opposed to affect (see above), which is transitory and apparent to others. Unlike affect, mood colors the person's view of the world. (See Alexithymia, Anhedonia.) Mood states include:

Apprehensive mood involves worried expectation or anticipation.

Dysphoria is any unpleasant mood, including irritable, apprehensive, dysthymic moods.

Dysthymia is the mood of depression or pervasive sadness, including a subjective sense of heaviness or feeling "weighted-down," blue, or down-in-the-dumps. The term "dysthymia" implies a mood which is more serious than "run-of-the-mill unhappiness."

Elevated mood is more cheerful than normal for the person, but is not necessarily psychopathological. (See Euphoric mood.)

Euphoric mood is an exaggerated sense of well-being and contentment; it implies psychopathology, when elevated or expansive. (Elevated moods are "vertical"; expansive moods are "horizontal.") An elevated mood: "I feel wonderful, things are great!" An expansive mood: "I can do anything, bat .400, win every game single-handedly, and have all the fans worship me." A euphoric mood may be elevated and expansive: "I'm flying, I'm on cloud 9, I feel like a god, I'm invincible."

Euthymia is a normal range of mood without dysphoria or elation.

Expansive mood refers to a lack of restraint in expressing one's feelings and an overvaluation of one's importance; it is often accompanied by an elevated or euphoric mood. (See Euphoric mood.)

Irritable mood is an inner feeling of tension or nervousness; one feels prickly, easily annoyed, provoked to anger, or frustrated.

Mood-congruent delusions or hallucinations are consistent with the patient's dominant mood. A mood-congruent delusion in depression may be "My body's rotting with cancer"; in mania, it may be "I'm the Second Christ."

Mood-incongruent delusions and hallucinations are those that are inconsistent with the patient's dominant mood. Mood-incongruent delusions may be persecutory (e.g., "The Moral Majority is poisoning my tulips"); or may involve Schneiderian symptoms (see below).

Mutism is not speaking, and a frequent feature of catatonia.

Neologisms are distortions of words or new words that a patient invents for psychological reasons; neologisms may also be standard words given idiosyncratic meanings by the patient. A new or misused word is not a neologism when it arises for cultural or educational reasons (e.g., malapropisms).

Obsessions are unwanted and uncomfortable ideas, thoughts, images, or impulses that persistently invade one's consciousness. Unlike people with delusions or overvalued ideas, those with obsessions know their beliefs are absurd and find them ego-dystonic (See Compulsions.)

Overvalued ideas are unreasonable and persistent beliefs, which are not generally held in the patient's subculture, and are held with less than delusional intensity. "The mob is tapping my phone — well, I think it is." Patients are more likely to act on delusions (see above) than on overvalued ideas. When patients recover from psychosis, they often go from delusions to overvalued ideas to "normality." Overvalued ideas may have a basis in reality, and some are not pathological, such as preoccupations that one's nose is too big, that only diet can cure cancer, or that "having a baby is the only way I will ever be happy." Ideas of reference (see above) are one type of overvalued idea.

Panic attacks are acute, terrifying, unexpected, and "senseless" attacks of anxiety, in which the person suddenly feels overwhelmed by an imminent sense of doom, despair, and destruction. The attacks include physiologic signs of anxiety (see above) and usually end in several minutes.

Paranoia is not a symptom, but a mental disorder characterized by delusions of grandeur and persecution, suspiciousness, jealousy, and resentment.

Paranoid delusion is a delusion of persecution (see above). *DSM-III* recommends avoiding the term "paranoid delusion," since formerly it also meant delusions of grandeur.

Paranoid ideation is an overvalued idea (see above) that one is being persecuted.

Paranoid style is a character style in which people are unduly or excessively guarded, jealous, sullen, rigid, humorless, and hypersensitive to injustices allegedly being done to them. When a paranoid style substantially interferes with functioning, it becomes a *paranoid personality disorder*.

Perseveration is a persistent repetition of speech or movement to varied, usually internal stimuli. It does not include repeated use of stock phrases, such as "you know," or "like." Echolalia (see above) and perseveration are often, but not always, found in organic illness. (See Stereotypy.)

Phobia is undue and irrational anxiety (see above) focused on an avoided object or place.

Posturing is the assumption of relatively fixed bodily positions, usually in catatonia.

Poverty of content of speech, sometimes called "poverty of content," is speech which conveys little information because it is vague, empty, barren, or filled with empty repetitions or obscure phrases.

Poverty of speech is a striking lack of speech, so that replies to questions are unelaborated, brief, or monosyllabic; some questions are not answered at all. Poverty of speech refers to an inadequate quantity, poverty of content of speech (see above) to inadequate quality.

Pressured speech is rapid, virtually nonstop, often loud and emphatic, seemingly driven, and usually hard to interrupt. It typically occurs in mania and in some drug-induced states.

Psychomotor agitation, or simply "agitation," mean repetitive, nonproductive motor activity usually associated with inner feelings of tension—e.g., pacing, being fidgety, constant standing and sitting.

Psychomotor retardation describes slowed movements, reactions, or speech.

Psychosis is a mental state in which the person is unable to distinguish reality from fantasy.

Reality testing is the ability to distinguish reality from fantasy. The failure to test reality—what Lily Tomlin calls "man's collective hunches"—is the hallmark of psychosis.

Schneiderian First-Rank Symptoms (FRS) are specific types of delusions and hallucinations that all involve themes of passivity. In 1939, Kurt Schneider originally claimed that FRS were pathognomonic for schizophrenia, but today FRS are only deemed as highly suggestive of schizophrenia. Patients with neurological disorders that produce pathological impulses or behaviors (e.g., unprovoked fighting, massive weeping) will commonly say, "This behavior isn't me," yet they will readily admit they are responsible for the behavior. In contrast, patients with FRS deny responsibility for the strange behavior, claiming that "others made me do it." Specific FRS are:

Audible thoughts are auditory hallucinations in which the patient hears his own thoughts being spoken aloud by others. A patient says, "I will think about eating, and then I'll hear a man with a French accent repeat my very own words."

Being controlled (delusions of,) are the patient's experience of his actions being completely under the control of external influences. He feels like an automaton and a totally passive observer of his own actions. "Andy and Barbara have placed an electronic bug in my brain which makes me run wild through Central Park. Blame them, not me." These are also called "made acts."

"Made" feelings are delusions in which the patient experiences emotions which he insists are not his own, but have been imposed on him by others.

"Made" impulses are delusions in which the patient believes that powerful drives or urges have been forced upon him which compel him to act. Although he disowns the impulse, he admits that it was he, and not others, who committed the act.

Somatic passivity are somatic hallucinations in which the patient is convinced that an external agent has caused him to be a passive recipient of unwanted bodily sensations.

Thought broadcasting (delusions of,) are beliefs that one's inner thoughts are no longer private, have escaped from one's mind, and have become known to everyone. "Everyone in the hospital knows what I'm thinking." Telepathy is not thought broadcasting, since it is culturally sanctioned, and therefore, not delusional.

Thought insertion (delusions of,) are ego-alien convictions that thoughts have been placed into one's mind, with the person believing his thoughts are not his own.

Thought withdrawal (delusions of,) is a patient's ego-dystonic belief that thoughts are being taken, or stolen, from his mind or brain, and that he has fewer thoughts than before. "I was discussing Rome, when suddenly my whole brain was sucked empty by the Pope's vacuum cleaner."

Voices arguing are auditory hallucinations in which the patient hears two or more people arguing, typically about the patient whom they refer to as a third party.

Voices commenting are auditory hallucinations in which the patient hears people commenting on his actions while they are occurring: "He is standing up! He is walking!"

Shame is an emotion in which the person feels embarrassed or dishonored before others. (See Guilt.)

Stereotypy is an isolated, repetitive, and purposeless movement. It appears most often in catatonic and drug-induced states. (See Catatonia, Perseveration.)

Stupor is a state of foggy consciousness and nonalertness in which the patient may respond to noxious stimuli, but otherwise be oblivious to his environment. (See Coma.)

Tangentiality is a disturbance of communication in which the person "goes off on a tangent," but unlike circumstantiality (see above), does not return to the point. Tangentiality may be viewed as repeated derailments (see above), which continually evade a central theme. It may, or may not be, pathological.

Thought disorder is a very general term to describe pathological thinking. Traditionally, thought disorder was divided into *disorders of thought content* (e.g., overvalued ideas, delusions), and *formal thought disorder*, which are abnormalities in the stream and continuity of thought (e.g., blocking, circumstantiality, flight of ideas). Because the boundaries between the form and content of thought are often unclear, *DSM-III* suggests that both terms be avoided, and that more specific descriptions and terms be used instead.

Vegetative signs are the "biological (or physiologic) signs" of depression, such as insomnia, anorexia, weight loss, diurnal mood variation, constipation, and diminished libido. These signs are called "vegetative," because they primarily involve growth and nutrition; they're also called *"hypothalamic signs,"* since they arise from disturbances involving the hypothalamic-pituitary axis.

Word salad is an apparently random and illogical mixture of words and sounds.

APPENDIX D

Psychiatric Medications: Names and Doses

NAMES		DOSAGE (mg/day)	
Generic	Brand	Inpatient	Outpatient
ANTIPSYCHOTICS			
Phenothiazines			
Acetophenazine	Tindal	60–80	40–60
Chlorpromazine	Thorazine	200–2,000	50–400
Fluphenazine	Prolixin Permitil	2–20	1–10
Fluphenazine enanthate	Prolixin enanthate	25–75*	25–50*
Fluphenazine decanoate	Prolixin decanoate	25–75*	25–50*
Mesoridazine	Serentil	100–400	30–150
Perphenazine	Trilafon	12–64	8–24
Perphenazine with	Etrafon	16/100–24/150	2/10–6/75
Amitriptyline	Triavil	16/100–24/150	2/10–6/75
Promazine	Sparine	100–1,000	50–400
Thioridazine	Mellaril	200–800	50–400
Trifluoperazine	Stelazine	10–40	4–10
Triflupromazine	Vesprin	100–150	30–100
Butyrophenones			
Haloperidol	Haldol	6–40	2–10
Haloperidol decanoate	Haldol decanoate	60–300°	25–150°
Thioxanthenes			
Chlorprothixene	Taractan	75–600	30–75
Thiothixene	Navane	10–60	6–15
Miscellaneous			
Loxapine	Loxitane	60–250	20–125
Molindone	Moban	100–225	15–100
Reserpine	Serpasil	1–5	1–2

NAMES		DOSAGE (mg/day)	
Generic	Brand	Inpatient	Outpatient

MOOD STABILIZERS

Tricyclics			
Amitriptyline	Elavil	150–300	75–150
	Endep		
Amoxapine	Asendin	150–300	100–300
Desipramine	Norpramin	150–300	75–150
	Pertofrane		
Doxepin	Sinequan	150–300	75–150
	Adapin		
Imipramine	Tofranil	150–300	75–150
	Janimine		
	SK-Pramine		
Imipramine pamoate	Tofranil-PM	100–300	75–150
Nortriptyline	Aventyl	75–150	75–100
	Pamelor		
Protriptyline	Vivactil	30–60	15–40
Trimipramine	Surmontil	150–300	75–125
Monoamine-Oxidase Inhibitors (MAOIs)			
Isocarboxazid	Marplan	20–30	10–20
Phenelzine	Nardil	60–90	45–90
Tranylcypromine	Parnate	20–30	20–30
Miscellaneous			
Bupropion	Wellbutrin	375–450	225–375
Carbamazepine	Tegretol	1,000–1,600	400–1,000
Lithium Carbonate	Eskalith	900–2,400	600–1,200
	Lithane		
	Lithobid	1,500–1,800	900–1,200
Lithium citrate	Cibalith-S	900–2,400	600–1,200
Maprotiline	Ludiomil	100–250	75–150
Mianserin	(investigational)	30–120	30–120
Nomifensine	Merital†	150–300	100–200
Trazodone	Desyrel	200–600	150–400
Tryptophan	Tryptophan	3,000–10,000	3,000–10,000

NAMES		SINGLE DOSE (mg)	
Generic	Brand	Daytime Sedation	Nighttime Hypnotic

HYPNOSEDATIVES

Barbiturates			
Amobarbital	Amytal	60–200	100–200
Butabarbital	Butisol	15–40	50–100
Methobarbitol	Mebaral	32–100	—
Pentobarbital	Nembutal	30–40	100–200
Phenobarbital	Luminal	15–30	100–200
Secobarbital	Seconal	—	100–200

NAMES		SINGLE DOSE (mg)	
Generic	Brand	Daytime Sedation	Nighttime Hypnotic
Secobarbital with Amobaribtol	Tuinal	—	50–100
Barbiturate-like			
Chloral hydrate	Noctec	—	500–1,000
Ethchlorvynol	Placidyl	—	500–750
Ethinamate	Valmid	—	500–1,000
Glutethimide	Doriden	—	250–500
Mebrobamate	Equinil	400	—
	Miltown	400	—
Methaqualone	Quāālude	—	150–300
Methyprylon	Noludar	—	200–400
Benzodiazepines (short-acting)			
Alprazolam+	Xanax	0.25–0.50	—
Lorazepam	Ativan	1–4	—
Oxazepam	Serax	10–30	—
Temazepam	Restoril	—	15–30
Triazolam	Halcion	—	0.125–0.50
(long-acting)			
Chlordiazepoxide	Librium	5–25	—
Clorazepate	Tranxene	3.25–22.50	—
Diazepam	Valium	2–10	5–15
Flurazepam	Dalmane	—	15–30
Prazepam	Centrax	10–20	
Miscellaneous			
Propranolol	Inderal	20–40	—

NAMES		DOSAGE (mg/day)	
Generic	Brand	Oral	Intramuscular
ANTIPARKINSONIAN MEDICATION			
Amantadine	Symmetrel	100–300	—
Benztropine	Cogentin	2–6	1–2
Biperidin	Akineton	2–6	1–2
Diphenhydramine	Benedryl	50–100	25–50
Procyclidine	Kemadrin	5–10	—
Trihexyphenidyl	Artane	4–15	—

*Intramuscular dose given every 7–14 days.
°Initial intramuscular dose should be 10–15 times the lowest effective oral dose of haloperidol; injections should be every 3–4 weeks.
†Withdrawn from sale in the United States as of January, 1986.
+The dose of alprazolam for treating depression and for blocking panic attacks averages 2–5 mg/day.

Psychiatric Medications: Side Effects and Their Management

SIDE EFFECT	KEY FACTORS	PRECAUTIONS/TREATMENT
	I. ANTIPSYCHOTICS	

Allergic

SIDE EFFECT	KEY FACTORS	PRECAUTIONS/TREATMENT
1. Agranulocytosis; bone marrow suppression.	Only with phenothiazines and thioxanthenes; most often with chlorpromazine, in elderly women, and during first 12 weeks of treatment.	Stop all antipsychotics; treat symptomatically; monitor temperature for 2 weeks; periodic blood counts do not offer preventive detection.
2. Dermatoses; contact dermatitis.	Most often with chlorpromazine.	Stop drug; may switch to another antipsychotic.
3. Jaundice (cholestatic or hepatocellular)	As with agranulocytosis (#1), except occurs only during first month of treatment.	Stop drug; wait; consider other causes of jaundice.
4. Photosensitivity.	As with dermatoses (#2).	As with dermatoses (#2); avoid sun.

Anticholinergic

SIDE EFFECT	KEY FACTORS	PRECAUTIONS/TREATMENT
5. Blurred vision, for close-up, not distant, vision.	More often with less potent antipsychotics (e.g., chlorpromazine, thioridizine); less often with more potent antipsychotics (e.g., fluphenazine, haloperidol).	No longer bothersome in 1–2 weeks; if symptom persists, give total daily dose at bedtime; lower dose, switch to more potent antipsychotic, or stop all antipsychotics; use cholinergic drugs; reduce or stop antiparkinsonian drugs, or switch to amantadine.

353

SIDE EFFECT	KEY FACTORS	PRECAUTIONS/TREATMENT
6. Confusion; toxic delirium.	Related to dose; elderly and brain-damaged are more vulnerable; more common with low potency antipsychotics.	Physostigmine 1–4 mg IV; stop antiparkinsonian agents (or switch to amantadine); stop or reduce or switch to a higher potency antipsychotic.
7. Dry mouth.	As with blurred vision (#5).	As with blurred vision (#5); prevent secondary fungal infection (thrush).
8. Fecal impaction and constipation.	As with blurred vision (#5); more common in elderly	As with blurred vision (#5); prunes.
9. Glaucoma aggravated.	As above (#5/8).	Stop antipsychotics.
10. Paralytic ileus; abdominal distention.	As above (#5/8).	As with blurred vision (#5); use cholinergics for acute severe distention.
11. Tachycardia.	As with blurred vision (#5)	As with blurred vision (#5).
12. Urinary retention.	As with blurred vision (#5), except that enlarged prostrate increases frequency and severity.	As with blurred vision (#5); use cholinergics for acutely severe retention.
13. Hypotension; dizzy or light-headed on standing.	More often on low potency antipsychotics, higher doses, IM/IV routes, and increasing age.	Stand up slower; tends to disappear in 1–2 weeks, so if mild, wait; switch to high potency antipsychotic; divide doses.
14. Inhibition of ejaculation.	Most often with thioridizine; adrenergic blockade.	Switch from thioridizine (or the offending drug) to another, usually more potent, antipsychotic.
15. Nasal congestion.	Sympathetic depression.	Goes away naturally; if not, try local vasoconstrictors.

Behavioral

16. Oversedation.	More common at first and with less potent antipsychotics; related to dose and to individual tolerance.	Usually disappears in 1–2 weeks; prevent by smaller initial dose, or by using more potent antipsychotics.
17. Impaired motor functioning; "slowed reflexes."	As above, especially at first.	Patient must be careful driving, crossing streets, and working near machinery; prevention and remedies as above (#16).

SIDE EFFECT	KEY FACTORS	PRECAUTIONS/TREATMENT

Central Nervous System (other)

18. "Neuroleptic Malignant Syndrome": fever, muscular rigidity, diminished consciousness, autonomic dysfunction.	Unknown cause; often in patients who have taken antipsychotics before without difficulty; more common with IM/IV route, high potency antipsychotics, males, youth, and in dehydrated/exhausted patients.	Withdrawal of all psychotropic drugs; treat symptomatically: stabilize blood pressure, correct fluid and electrolyte balance, treat hyperthermia.
19. Seizures	Related to dose, drug, prior brain damage, and more sedating antipsychotics.	Reduce dose slowly; might add anticonvulsant.

Endocrine

20. Edema	Increased antidiuretic hormone secretion.	Wait; goes away naturally.
21. False pregnancy test.	?	Use another test.
22. Lactation; swollen breasts.	Hypothalamic effect; more common with low potency antipsychotics.	Stop or change antipsychotic.
23. Menstrual irregularities.	As above (#22).	As above (#22).
24. Weight gain.	Hypothalamic effect with/without overeating; common with chlorpromazine, uncommon with perphenazine.	Switch antipsychotic; diet.

Extrapyramidal

25. Akathisia, "the jitters" motor restlessness.	More common with more potent antipsychotics, women, and the elderly.	Add antiparkinsonian drug, switch to a less potent antipsychotic (especially thioridizine), or stop all antipsychotics.
26. Akinesia, "pseudoparkinsonism," bodily stiffness.	Related to dose, age, genetic predisposition, family history of parkinson's disease; more common with high potency antipsychotics.	As above (#25).
27. Dystonia, fixed, rigid, bizarre posture.	Idiosyncratic; mildly dose related; more frequent in males, youth, and high potency antipsychotics; occurs between 5 hours and 10 days of taking drug.	Treat acute reaction with IV/IM antiparkinsonian; then do as with #25.

SIDE EFFECT	KEY FACTORS	PRECAUTIONS/TREATMENT
28. Dyskinesia, repeated bizarre movements of face, arms, legs, and hips.	Occurs while on drug; more common in females and with high potency antipsychotics.	Treat as with #25.
29. Tardive dyskinesia; as above, except stops during sleep.	Occurs in patients who stop or greatly reduce dose after being on it for 5+ months (average 2 years); related to lifetime total dose; increased risk with age; drug-free holidays lower prevalence.	Stop drug and hope dyskinesia disappears; if not consider "anti-TD" drugs (e.g., deanol), or suppress TD with more antipsychotic; best treatment is prevention: Only use antipsychotics when mandatory.

Miscellaneous

30. Retinitis pigmentosa.	Only with thioridizine, >800 mg/day >2 months.	Keep thioridizine <800 mg/day.

II. MOOD REGULATORS

Allergic

31. Agranulocytosis.	As with #1; TCAs.	As with #1.
32. Jaundice, as with #3.	As with #3; TCAs.	As with #3.

Anticholinergic

33. Blurred vision as in #5.	More often with TCAs than MAOIs; not with lithium; common in elderly.	No longer bothersome in 1–2 weeks; if symptom persists, give total daily dose at bedtime; lower dose; switch to trazodone or to secondary TCAs (e.g., desipramine); cholinergic agents.
34. Confusion; toxic delirium.	Related to dose; elderly and brain-damaged especially often with normal doses of TCAs and MAOI, and during lithium toxicity.	If diagnostic question, give physostigmine 1–4 mg; reduce TCA; stop MAOI, correct lithium toxicity by checking electrolytes, salt intake, renal function, and serum lithium.
35. Dry mouth.	As with blurred vision (#33).	As with blurred vision (#33) prevent secondary fungal infection (thrush).
36. Fecal impaction and constipation.	As with blurred vision (#33).	As with blurred vision (#33).
37. Glaucoma aggravated.	As with blurred vision (#33).	Stop TCAs/MAOIs.

SIDE EFFECT	KEY FACTORS	PRECAUTIONS/TREATMENT
38. Paralytic ileus; abdominal distention.	As with #10.	As with #10.
39. Tachycardia.	As with blurred vision (#33)	As with blurred vision (#33); obtain EKG.
40. Urinary retention.	As with #12.	As with #12.

Autonomic Nervous System (other)

41. Hypotension, as in #13.	TCAs and MAOIs, not lithium; mechanism unclear.	As in #13.
42. Inhibition of ejaculation.	As above (#41); thioridizine; adrenergic blockade.	Reduce dose, switch to another TCA/MAOI.

Behavioral

43. Excitement; restlessness; initial insomnia.	Mainly with MAOIs and protriptyline.	Change drugs.
44. Impaired motor functioning, as in #17.	As in #17; especially common with amitriptyline, doxepin, and trazodone.	As in #17.
45. Oversedation.	More common at first and with drugs listed in #44; related to dose and to individual tolerance.	Usually disappears in 1–2 weeks; prevent by smaller initial increases; switch to secondary TCAs, especially protriptyline.
46. Psychosis aggravated.	Either a TCA-induced "switch phase" into mania or an MAOI-induced psychosis.	If "switch phase," add lithium or stop TCA; if MAOI-induced change MAOIs or add antipsychotic.
47. Suicide.	Patient may have underestimated dangerousness of MAOI or TCA.	Limit quantities; have nurse or relative give drug; ECT?

Central Nervous System (other)

48. Hypertensive crisis: sudden throbbing frontal headache, pallor, sweats, vomiting, chills; chest pain.	MAOIs only; induced by tyramine-foodstuffs, sympathomimetic drugs, and meperidine; combined MAOI+TCA is unlikely to cause hypertensive crisis.	Instruct patient on diet; phentolamine 5 mg IV or chlorpromazine 50 mg IM.
49. Peripheral neuropathy.	Seen with TCAs & MAOIs, and with pyridoxine deficiency.	Stop drugs; give vitamins.

SIDE EFFECT	KEY FACTORS	PRECAUTIONS/TREATMENT
50. Seizures	Related to dose, drug, prior brain damage, and more sedating TCAs.	Reduce dose slowly; might add anticonvulsant.
51. Tremors; twitching; ataxia; poor coordination.	Related to age; may occur on normal doses of TCAs and MAOIs; may occur as lithium toxicity.	Reduce or stop TCA/MAOI; correct lithium toxicity (#34); reduce lithium.
Endocrine		
52. Edema	Imipramine, probably as in #20.	As in #20.
53. Hypothyroidism; sluggishness, "depression."	Secondary to 6+ months of lithium.	Evalute thyroid function; add thyroid replacement.
54. Menstrual irregularities.	Mainly TCAs.	As with #22.
55. Weight gain.	Hypothalamic effect with/without overeating; may result from normalized mood.	Switch drugs; diet.
Miscellaneous		
56. EKG changes.	Bundle-branch block; mainly due to toxicity from TCAs, but also from lithium.	? Reduce dose or stop drug.
57. GI upset.	Lithium toxicity.	Serum lithium; reduce dose.
58. Polyuria.	Lithium toxicity.	Check lithium toxicity (#34).
59. Acute tubular necrosis.	Lithium toxicity.	Stop lithium; treat symptomatically.

APPENDIX F

"Problems in Living"

Mental and medical health professionals see many clients with emotional or behavioral difficulties, which are *not* mental disorders, but "problems in living." (How they differ is discussed in Chapter 1, pp. 5–6). Though mainly a classification of mental disorders, *DSM-III* also catalogs and briefly describes these problems in living under the title of "Conditions Not Attributable To a Mental Disorder That Are a Focus of Attention Or Treatment."[1] For some problems in living, such as uncomplicated bereavement or occupational problems, clients themselves seek help; for other problems in living, such as malingering or adolescent antisocial behavior, people other than clients request professional consultation. Since an individual can have a mental disorder *and* a problem in living yet only want assistance for the latter, if the problem in living is not a manifestation or consequence of the mental disorder, the problem in living should be specified (on Axis I). For instance, an agoraphobic may seek help for academic problems, but not phobia. This appendix names and sketches these *DSM-III* "Conditions. . . . "

Academic problem refers to school or learning difficulties not due to a specific developmental, mental, or medical disorder. Examples include the student with poor study habits or the serious underachiever.

Adult antisocial behavior refers to rule-breaking or law-breaking by those without a mental disorder, such as conduct, antisocial personality, and impulse control disorders. Examples include many, but not all, thieves, mobsters, and dope dealers.

Borderline intellectual functioning refers to those seeking help with problems which substantially arise from having IQs of 71–84. Borderline intellectual functioning

---

[1] *DSM-III*; pp. 331–334.

is easily missed in the presence of another mental disorder, such as schizophrenia or panic disorder, and it may also be hard to distinguish from mental retardation.[2]

Childhood or adolescent antisocial behavior refers to isolated acts of rule-breaking or law-breaking by youth; when it is a pattern, the person may have an antisocial personality disorder.

Malingering refers to the voluntary and deliberate production of false or grossly exaggerated physical or psychological symptoms to achieve a goal; the person wants this goal, and its attainment is understandable in view of the person's circumstances and not just his psychology. Malingering may be evading the draft or playing hooky; it may also serve more respectable ends, such as feigning illness while held by terrorists. Two caveats: First, malingerers do get sick. Second, some malingerers who are ostensibly faking an illness may actually be doing so as a face-saving way to get help with a genuine illness. Malingering should be differentiated from somatoform and factitious disorders, and should be considered if: (a) medicolegal issues may be involved, e.g., workman's compensation, malpractice, "pain and suffering" cases; (b) inconsistent or contradictory information is given in the history; (c) there are marked discrepancies between history and objective findings; (d) the patient does not cooperate with diagnostic evaluation; (e) he adamantly refuses to be hypnotized or to have an amytal interval; (f) he does not comply with treatment; and (g) there is evidence of antisocial personality disorder.

Marital problems are marital problems.

Noncompliance with medical treatment which is not due to a mental disorder but does receive professional attention arises when a patient won't take medication because of religious beliefs, or when someone feels the treatment is worse than the disease. Major differentials are personality disorders with paranoid, passive-aggressive, or masochistic features.

Occupational problems refer to work difficulties that do not result from a mental disorder, such as job dissatisfaction or uncertainty in choosing careers.

Other interpersonal problem refers to interpersonal difficulties outside the family (e.g., lover, friends) which are not categorized elsewhere.

---

[2]Subtypes of mental retardation are defined by IQ scores. Although "IQ is what IQ tests measure," IQ does give a *rough* estimate of a person's overall intellectual capacity. In *DSM-III*:

Subtypes of Mental Retardation	IQ Levels	Percent of Mentally Retarded	Functional Levels
Mild	50–70	80	"educable"
Moderate	35–49	12	"trainable"
Severe	20–34	7	simple tasks
Profound	Below 20	1	very limited self-care

Other specified family circumstances refer to problems happening within the family which are not categorized elsewhere, such as intense sibling rivalry and mother/father-in-law difficulties.

Parent-child problem refers to problems, such as child abuse, as long as they are not caused by a mental disorder.

Phase of life problem or other life circumstance problem refers to difficulties which primarily arise from major developmental turning points (i.e., crises, "passages"), such as discovering puberty, separating from parents, starting a career, "midlife crises," and retirement.

Uncomplicated bereavement refers to a normal reaction to the death of a loved one. Chapter 11 (p. 192) describes uncomplicated bereavement and how it differs from depression.

References

Abroms, E. M. (1983). Beyond eclecticism. *American Journal of Psychiatry, 140*, 740–745.

Alexander, F. (1950). *Psychosomatic medicine: Its principles and applications.* New York: Norton.

Allgulander, C., Borg, S., & Vikander, B. (1984). A 4–6 year follow-up of 50 patients with primary dependence on sedative and hypnotic drugs. *American Journal of Psychiatry, 141*, 1580–1582.

Amdur, M. J., Tucker, G. J., Detre, T. D., & Markhus, K. (1969). Anorexia nervosa: An interactional study. *The Journal of Nervous and Mental Disease, 148*, 559–566.

American Psychiatric Association. (1952). *Diagnostic and statistical manual of mental disorders* (1st ed.). Washington, DC: Author.

American Psychiatric Association. (1968). *Diagnostic and statistical manual of mental disorders* (2nd ed.). Washington, DC: Author.

American Psychiatric Association. (1973). Task Force Report 7: Megavitamin and Orthomolecular Therapy in Psychiatry. Washington, DC: Author.

American Psychiatric Association. (1980). *Diagnostic and statistical manual of mental disorders* (3rd ed.). Washington, DC: American Psychiatric Press.

American Psychiatric Association. (1985) *DSM-III-R In Development*, (10/5/85). Washington, D.C.: Work Group to Revise *DSM-III*.

Anderson, C. M., Hogarty, G., & Reiss, D. J. (1980). Family treatment of adult schizophrenic patients: A psycho-educational approach. *Schizophrenia Bulletin, 6*, 490–505.

Andreasen, N. C., & Hoenk, P. R. (1982). The predictive value of adjustment disorders: A follow-up study. *American Journal of Psychiatry, 139*, 584–590.

Andreasen, N. C., & Wasek, P. (1980). Adjustment disorders in adolescents and adults. *Archives of General Psychiatry, 37*, 1166–1170.

Asher, R. (1951). Munchausen's syndrome. *Lancet, 1*, 339–341.

Barlow, D. H., Blanchard, E. B., Vermilyea, J. A., Vermilyea, B. B., & DiNardo, P. A. (1986). Generalized anxiety and generalized anxiety disorder: Description and reconceptualization. *American Journal of Psychiatry, 143*, 40–44.

Baron, M., Guren, R., Asnis, L., & Lord, S. (1985). Familial transmission of schizotypal and borderline personality disorders. *American Journal of Psychiatry, 142*, 927–934.

Beck, A. T., Rush, A. J., Shaw, B. F., & Emery, G. (1979). *Cognitive therapy of depression: A treatment manual.* New York: Guilford.

Berglund, M. (1984). Suicide in alcoholism: A prospective study of 88 suicides. *Archives of General Psychiatry, 41*, 888–891.

Blazer, D., George, L. K., Landerman, R., Pennybacker, M., Melville, M. L., Woodbury, M., Manton, K. G., Jordan, K., & Locke, B. (1985). Psychiatric disorders: A rural/urban comparison. *Archives of General Psychiatry, 42*, 651–656.

Bleuler, E. (1911/1950). *Dementia praecox or the group of schizophrenias.* New York: International Universities Press.

Bloch, S., Bond, G., Qualls, B., Yalom, I., & Zimmerman, E. (1976). Patients' expectations of therapeutic improvement and their outcomes. *American Journal of Psychiatry, 133*, 1457–1459.

Blumer, D., & Heilbronn, M. (1984). Antidepressant treatment for chronic pain: Treatment outcome of 1000 patients with the pain-prone disorder. *Psychiatric Annals, 14*, 796–800.

Bowen, M. (1978). *Family therapy in clinical practice*. New York: Jason Aronson.

Breier, A., & Strauss, J. S. (1984). The role of social relationships in the recovery from psychotic disorders. *American Journal of Psychiatry, 141*, 949-955.

Brown, F. (1961). Depression and childhood bereavement. *Journal of Mental Science, 107*, 754-777.

Cannon, W. B. (1932). *The wisdom of the body*. New York: Norton.

Caplan, G. (1964). *Principles of preventive psychiatry*. New York: Basic Books.

Cassileth, B. R., Lusk, E. J., Miller, D. S., Brown, L. L., & Miller, C. (1985). Psychosocial correlates of survival in advanced malignant disease? *New England Journal of Medicine, 312*, 1551-1555.

Caton, C. L. M. (1984). *Management of chronic schizophrenia*. New York: Oxford University Press.

Charatan, F. B. (1985). Depression and the elderly: Diagnosis and treatment. *Psychiatric Annals, 15*, 313-316.

Cleckley, H. (1950). *The mask of sanity*. St. Louis: C. V. Mosby.

Cohen, M. E., Robins, E., Purtell, J. J., Altmann, M. W., & Reid, D. W. (1953). Excessive surgery in hysteria. *Journal of the American Medical Association, 151*, 977-986.

Coles, R., Brenner, J. H., & Meagher, D. (1970). *Drugs and youth: Medical, psychiatric, and legal facts*. New York: Liveright.

Connors, M. E., Johnson, C. L., & Stuckey, M. K. (1984). Treatment of bulimia with brief psychoeducational group therapy. *American Journal of Psychiatry, 141*, 1512-1516.

Coombs, G., & Ludwig, A. M. (1982). Dissociative disorders. In J. H. Greist, J. W. Jefferson, & R. L. Spitzer (Eds.) *Treatment of mental disorders* (pp. 309-319). New York: Oxford University Press.

Cooper, J. E., Kendell, R. E., Gurland, B. J., Sharpe, L., Copeland, J. R. M., & Simon, R. (1972). *Psychiatric diagnosis in New York and London*. New York: Oxford University Press.

Coryell, W., Endicott, J., Andreasen, N., & Keller, M. (1985). Bipolar I, bipolar II, and non-bipolar major depression among the relatives of affectively ill probands. *American Journal of Psychiatry, 142*, 817-821.

Custer, R. L. (1979). An overview of compulsive gambling. Presented at South Oaks Hospital, Amityville, NY.

Datlof, S., Coleman, P. D., Forbes, G. B., & Kreipe, R. E. (1986). Ventricular dilation on CAT scans of patients with anorexia nervosa. *American Journal of Psychiatry, 143*, 96-98.

Davis, J. M. (1975). Overview: Maintenance therapy in psychiatry: I. Schizophrenia. *American Journal of Psychiatry, 132*, 1237-1245.

DeSouza, C., & Othmer, E. (1984). Somatization disorder and Briquet's syndrome: An assessment of their diagnostic concordance. *Archives of General Psychiatry, 41*, 334-336.

Detre, T. D., & Jarecki, H. G. (1971). *Modern psychiatric treatment*. Philadelphia: Lippincott.

Donnelly, J. (1978). The incidence of psychosurgery in the United States, 1971-1973. *American Journal of Psychiatry, 135*, 1476-1480.

Drake, R. E., Gates, C., Whitaker, A., & Cotton, P. G. (1985). Suicide among schizophrenics: A review. *Comprehensive Psychiatry, 26*, 90-100.

Dunbar, H. F. (1946). *Emotions and bodily changes: A survey of literature on psychosomatic relationships* (3rd ed.). New York: Columbia University Press.

Engel, G. L. (1977). The need for a new medical model: A challenge for biomedicine. *Science, 196*(4286), 129-136.

Erikson, E. H. (1968). *Identity: Youth and crisis*. New York: Norton.

Feighner, J. P., Robins, E., Guze, S. B., Woodruff, R. A., Winokur, G., & Munoz, R. (1972). Diagnostic criteria for use in psychiatric research. *Archives General Psychiatry, 26*, 57-63.

Fenichel, O. (1945). *The psychoanalytic theory of neurosis*. New York: Norton.

Fordyce, W. E., Fowler, R. S. Jr., Lehmann, J. F., DeLateur, B. J., Sand, P. L., & Trieschmann, R. B. (1973). Operant conditioning in the treatment of chronic pain. *Archives of Physical Medicine and Rehabilitation, 54*, 399-408.

Freedman, R., & Schwab, P. J. (1978). Paranoid symptoms in patients on a general hospital psychiatric unit: Implication for diagnosis and treatment. *Archives of General Psychiatry, 35*, 387–390.

Freud, S. (1894/1959). Aetiology of the neuroses (Draft B). In J. Strachey (Ed. and Trans.) *The complete psychological works, the standard edition* (Vol. 1, pp. 179–184). New York: Norton.

Freud, S. (1917). Mourning and melancholia. In E. Jones (Ed.) *Collected papers.* New York: Basic Books.

Freud, S. (1919). Lines of advance in psycho-analytic therapy. In J. Strachey (Ed. and Trans.) *Complete psychological works, the standard edition.* (Vol. 17, pp. 157–168). New York: Norton.

Freud, S. (1935/1951). Historical notes: A letter from Freud. *American Journal of Psychiatry, 107*, 786–787.

Ginsberg, G. L. (1985). Adjustment and impulse control disorders. In H. I. Kaplan & B. J. Sadock (Eds.) *Comprehensive textbook of psychiatry* (4th ed.) (pp. 1097–1105). Baltimore: Williams & Wilkins.

Glassman, A. H., Jackson, W. K., Walsh, B. T., & Roose, S. P. (1984). Cigarette craving, smoking withdrawal, and clonidine. *Science, 226*(4676), 864–866.

Glueck, S., & Glueck, E. (1959). *Predicting delinquency and crime.* Cambridge, Mass: Harvard University Press.

Gold, M. S. (1984). *800-Cocaine.* New York: Bantam.

Goodwin, D. W. (1985). Alcoholism and genetics: The sins of the fathers. *Archives of General Psychiatry, 42*, 171–174.

Goodwin, D. W., & Guze, S. B. (1984). *Psychiatric diagnosis.* (3rd ed.) New York: Oxford University Press.

Grinspoon, L., & Bakalar, J. (1985). What is MDMA? *Harvard Medical School Mental Health Letter, 2*(2), 8.

Gruenberg, E., Burke, J. D., & Regier, D. A. (1984). Lifetime prevalence of specific psychiatric disorders in three sites. *Archives of General Psychiatry, 41*, 949–958.

Halmi, K. A., Falk, J. R., & Schwartz, E. (1981). Binge-eating and vomiting: A survey of a college population. *Psychological Medicine, 11*, 697–706.

Hart, K. J., & Ollendick, T. H. (1985). Prevalence of bulimia in working and university women. *American Journal of Psychiatry, 142*, 851–854.

Harvard Medical School Mental Health Letter (1985). Multiple personality. *1*(10), 1–6. April.

Hesselbrock, M. N., Meyer, R. E., & Keener, J. J. (1985). Psychopathology in hospitalized alcoholics. *Archives of General Psychiatry, 42*, 1050–1055.

Hirschfeld, R. M. A., Klerman, G. L., Andreasen, N. C., Clayton, P. J., & Keller, M. B. (1985). Situational major depressive disorder. *Archives of General Psychiatry, 42*, 1109–1114.

Hoffman, R. S., & Koran, L. M. (1984). Detecting physical illness in patients with mental disorders. *Psychosomatics, 25*, 654–660.

Hoffman, S. P., Rosenfeld, R., Wenger, D., & Shimono, J. (1984). The homeless mentally ill: What went wrong? Paper presented at annual meeting of the American Orthospsychiatry Association, Toronto, April.

Hogarty, G. E., Goldberg, S. C., Schooler, N. R., & Ulrich, R. P. (1974). Drugs and sociotherapy in the aftercare of schizophrenic patients: II. Two-year relapse rates. *Archives of General Psychiatry, 31*, 603–608.

Holmes, T. H., & Rahe, R. H. (1967). The Social Readjustment Scale. *Journal of Psychosomatic Research, 11*, 213–218.

Horowitz, M. J. (1985). Disasters and psychological responses to stress. *Psychiatric Annals, 15*, 161–167.

Hsu, L. K. G. (1980). Outcome of anorexia nervosa: A review of the literature (1954 to 1978). *Archives of General Psychiatry, 37*, 1041–1046.

James, W. (1893). *The principles of psychology.* New York: H. Hold and Co.

Janicak, P. G., & Andriukaitis, S. N. (1980). *DSM-III:* Seeing the forest through the trees. *Psychiatric Annals, 10*, 284–297.

Jaspers, K. (1923/1972). *General psychopathology.* Chicago: University of Chicago Press.

Jefferson, J. W., & Ochitill, H. (1982). Factitious disorders. In J. H. Greist, J. W. Jefferson, & R. L. Spitzer (Eds.) *Treatment of mental disorders* (pp. 387–397). New York: Oxford University Press.

Johnson, C., & Flach, A. (1985). Family characteristics of 105 patients with bulimia. *American Journal of Psychiatry, 142*, 1321–1324.

Johnston, L. D., Bachman, J. G., & O'Malley, P. M. (1981). Drugs and the nation's high school students. In G. G. Nahas & H. C. Frick II *Drug abuse in the modern world: A perspective for the eighties* (pp. 87–98). New York, Pergamon Press.

Kahana, R. J., & Bibring, G. L. (1964). Personality types in medical management. In N. E. Zinberg (Ed.) *Psychiatry and medical practice in a general hospital* (pp. 108–123). New York: International Universities Press.

Kandel, E. R. (1983). From metapsychology to molecular biology: Explorations into the nature of anxiety. *American Journal of Psychiatry, 140*, 1277–1293.

Kaplan, H. S. (1974). *The new sex therapy.* New York: Brunner/Mazel.

Katon, W., Egan, K., & Miller, D. (1985). Chronic pain: Lifetime psychiatric diagnoses and family history *American Journal of Psychiatry, 142*, 1156–1160.

Kardiner, A. (1977). *My analysis with Freud.* New York: Norton, p. 69.

Keller, M. B., Lavori, P. W., Rice, J., Coryell, W., & Hirschfeld, R. M. A. (1986). The persistent risk of chronicity in recurrent episodes of nonbipolar major depressive disorder: A prospective follow-up. *American Journal of Psychiatry, 143*, 24–28.

Kellner, R. (1982a). Hypochondriasis and atypical somatoform disorder. In J. H. Greist, J. W. Jefferson, & R. L. Spitzer (Eds.) *Treatment of mental disorders* (pp. 286–303). New York: Oxford University Press.

Kellner, R. (1982b). Disorders of impulse control (not elsewhere classified). In J. H. Greist, J. W. Jefferson, & R. L. Spitzer (Eds.) *Treatment of mental disorders* (pp. 398–418). New York: Oxford University Press.

Kernberg, O. (1975). *Borderline conditions and pathological narcissism.* New York: Jason Aronson.

Kiersch, T. A. (1962). Amnesia: A clinical study of ninety-eight cases. *American Journal of Psychiatry, 119*, 57–60.

Kinsey, A. C., Pomeroy, W. B., & Martin, C. E. (1948). *Sexual behavior in the human male.* Philadelphia: W. B. Saunders.

Kinsey, A. C., Pomeroy, W. B., Martin, C. E., & Gebhard, P. H. (1953). *Sexual behavior in the human female.* Philadelphia: W. B. Saunders.

Klein, D. F. (1964). Delineation of two drug-responsive anxiety syndromes. *Psychopharmacologia, 5*, 397–408.

Klein, D. F., Gittelman, R., Quitkin, F., & Rifkin, A. (1980). *Diagnosis and drug treatment of mental disorders: Adults and children* (2nd ed.). Baltimore: Williams & Wilkins.

Klerman, G. L., Lavori, P. W., Rice, J., Reich, T., Endicott, J., Andreasen, N. C., et al. (1985) Birth-cohort trends in rates of major depressive disorder among relatives of patients with affective disorder. *Archives of General Psychiatry, 42*, 689–693.

Klerman, G. L., Rounsaville, B., Chevron, E., Neu, C., & Weissman, M. M. (1979). *Manual for short-term interpersonal psychotherapy (IPT) of depression.* New Haven: Boston Collaborative Depression Project.

Koenigsberg, H. W., Kaplan, R. D., Gilmore, M. M., & Cooper, A. M. (1985). The relationship between syndrome and personality disorder in *DSM-III*: experience with 2,462 patients. *American Journal of Psychiatry, 142*, 207–212.

Kohut, H. (1971). *The analysis of the self.* New York: International Universities Press.

Koos, E. L. (1954). *The health of Regionville: What the people thought and did about it.* New York: Columbia University Press.

Kovacs, M., & Beck, A. T. (1976). The communication of suicidal intent: A reexamination. *Archives of General Psychiatry, 33*, 198–201.

Kraepelin, E. (1915/1921). *Clinical psychiatry: A text-book for students and physicians,* translated and adapted from the 7th German Edition by A. Ross Deifendorf, New York: Macmillan.

Lacey, J. H. (1983). Bulimia nervosa, binge eating, and psychogenic vomiting: A controlled treatment study and long term outcome. *British Medical Journal, 286*, 1609–1613.

Lewine, R., Burbach, D., & Meltzer, H. Y. (1984). Effect of diagnostic criteria on the ratio of male to female schizophrenic patients. *American Journal of Psychiatry, 141*, 84–87.

Lidz, T., & Fleck, S. (1986). *Schizophrenia and the family* (Revised ed.) New York: International Universities Press.

Lieberman, P. B., & Strauss, J. S. (1984). The recurrence of mania; Environmental factors and medical treatment. *American Journal of Psychiatry, 141*, 77–80.

Liebowitz, M. R., Gorman, J. M., Fyer, A. J., & Klein, D. F. (1985). Social phobia: Review of a neglected anxiety disorder. *Archives of General Psychiatry, 42*, 729–736.

Lief, H. I. (1979). Why sex education for health practitioners? In R. Green (Ed.) *Human sexuality: A health practitioner's text* (2nd ed.) (pp. 3–10). Baltimore: Williams & Wilkins.

Lifton, R. J. (1963). *Thought reform and the psychology of totalism: A study of "brainwashing" in China.* New York: Norton.

Looney, J. G., & Gunderson, E. K. E. (1978). Transient situational disturbances: Course and outcome. *American Journal of Psychiatry, 135*, 660–663.

Ludwig, A. M. (1985). *Principles of clinical psychiatry* (2nd ed.). New York: Free Press.

Mahler, M., Pine F., & Bergman, A. (1975). *The psychological birth of the human infant.* New York: Basic Books.

Malan, D. H. (1979). *Individual psychotherapy and the science of psychodynamics.* Boston: Butterworth.

Marks, I. M. (1981). Review of behavioral psychotherapy, I: Obsessive-compulsive disorders. *American Journal of Psychiatry, 138*, 584–592.

Marks, I. M., Gray, S., Cohen, D., Hill, R., Mawson, D., Ramm, E., & Stern, R. S. (1983). Imipramine and brief therapist-aided exposure in agoraphobics having self-exposure homework. *Archives of General Psychiatry, 40*, 153–162.

Marks, R. M., & Sachar, E. J. (1973). Undertreatment of medical inpatients with narcotic analgesics. *Annals of Internal Medicine, 78*, 173–181.

Marmor, J. (1971). Homosexuality in males. *Psychiatric Annals, 1*(4), 44–59.

Masters, W. H., & Johnson, V. E. (1970). *Human sexual inadequacy.* Boston: Little, Brown.

Masterson, J. F. (1976). *Psychotherapy of the borderline adult: A developmental approach.* New York: Brunner/Mazel.

Maxmen, J. S. (1984). Hospital treatment. In C. L. M. Caton *Management of chronic schizophrenia* (pp. 55–74). New York: Oxford University Press.

Maxmen, J. S. (1986a). *A good night's sleep: A step-by-step program for overcoming insomnia and other sleep problems.* New York: Warner.

Maxmen, J. S. (1986b). *The new psychiatry: How modern psychiatrists think about their patients, theories, diagnoses, drugs, psychotherapies, power, training, families, and private lives.* New York: Mentor.

McGlashan, T. H. (1984). The Chestnut Lodge follow-up study, II: long-term outcome of schizophrenia and the affective disorders. *Archives of General Psychiatry, 41*, 586–601.

McKenna, P. J., Kane, J. M., & Parrish, K. (1985). Psychotic syndromes in epilepsy. *American Journal of Psychiatry, 142*, 895–904.

Menninger, K. (1938). *Man against himself.* New York: Harcourt, Brace & World.

Merikangas, K. R. (1984). Divorce and assortative mating among depressed patients. *American Journal of Psychiatry, 141*, 74–76.

Messer, H. D. (1979). The homosexual as physician. In R. Green (Ed.) *Human sexuality: A health practitioner's text* (2nd ed.) (pp. 117–122). Baltimore: Williams & Wilkins.

Meyers, N. (1974). *The seven-percent solution,* New York: Dutton.

Mitchell, J. E., Hatsukami, D., Eckert E. D., & Pyle R. L. (1985). Characteristics of 275 patients with bulimia. *American Journal of Psychiatry, 142*, 482–488.

Motto, J. A., Heilbron, D. C., & Juster, R. P. (1985). Development of a clinical instrument to estimate suicide risk. *American Journal of Psychiatry, 142*, 680–686.

Mowbray, C. T. (1985). Homelessness in America: Myths and realities. *American Journal of*

Orthopsychiatry, 55, 4–8.

Myers, J. K., Weissman, M. M., Tischler, G. L., Holzer, C. E. III, Leaf, P. J., Orvaschel, H., Anthony, J. C., Boyd, J. H., Burke, J. D., Kramer, M., & Stoltzman, R. (1984). Six-month prevalence of psychiatric disorders in three communities: 1980 to 1982. *Archives of General Psychiatry, 41*, 959–967.

National Academy of Sciences' Institute of Medicine (1984). Research on mental illness and addictive disorders: Progress and Prospects. Washington, DC.

New York State Office of Mental Hygiene (1982). "Who are the homeless?" May.

Norman, K. (1984). Eating disorders. In H. H. Goldman (Ed.) *Review of general psychiatry* (pp. 464–480). Los Altos, CA: Lange.

North, C., & Cadoret, R. (1981). Diagnostic discrepancy in personal accounts of patients with 'schizophrenia.' *Archives of General Psychiatry, 38*, 133–137.

Ochitill, H. (1982). Somatoform disorders. In J. H. Greist, J. W. Jefferson, & R. L. Spitzer (Eds.) *Treatment of mental disorders* (pp. 266–286). New York: Oxford University Press.

Othmer, E., & DeSouza, C. (1985). A screening test for somatization disorder (hysteria). *American Journal of Psychiatry, 142*, 1146–1149.

Oxman, T. E., Rosenberg, S. D., Schnurr, P. P., & Tucker, G. J. (1985). Linguistic dimensions of affect and thought in somatization disorder. *American Journal of Psychiatry, 142*, 1150–1155.

Perley, M., & Guze, S. B. (1962). Hysteria—the stability and usefulness of clinical criteria. *New England Journal of Medicine, 266*, 421–426.

Perry, S. W. (1984). The undermedication for pain. *Psychiatric Annals, 14*(11), 808–811.

Pope, H. G., Jonas J. M., & Jones, B. (1982). Factitious psychosis: Phenomenology, family history, and long-term outcome of nine patients. *American Journal of Psychiatry, 139*, 1480–1483.

Pope, H. G., Hudson, J. I., Jonas, J. M., & Yurgelum-Todd, D (1983). Bulimia treated with imipramine: A placebo-controlled, double-blind study. *American Journal of Psychiatry, 140*, 554–558.

Prien, R. F., & Kupfer, D. J. (1986). Continuation drug therapy for major depressive episodes: How long should it be maintained? *American Journal of Psychiatry, 143*, 18–23.

Redmond, D. E., Jr. (1979). New and old evidence for the involvement of a brain norepinephrine system in anxiety. In W. E. Fann, I. Karacan, A. D. Porkorney, & R. L. Williams (Eds.) *Phenomenology and treatment of anxiety* (pp. 153–203). New York: Spectrum.

Rees, W. D., & Lutkins, S. G. (1967). Mortality or bereavement. *British Medical Journal, 4*(5570), 13–16.

Reich, W. (1949/1968). *Character analysis* (3rd ed.). New York: Noonday Press.

Ries, R. K. (1985). *DSM-III* implications of the diagnoses of catatonia and bipolar disorder. *American Journal of Psychiatry, 142*, 1471–1474.

Riley, V. (1975). Mouse mammary tumors: Alteration of incidence as apparent function of stress. *Science, 189*, 465–467.

Rittenhouse, J. D. (1982). Drugs in the school: The shape of drug abuse among American youth in the seventies. In G. G. Nahas & H. C. Frick II (Eds.) *Drug abuse in the modern world: A perspective for the eighties* (pp. 99–105). New York: Pergamon Press.

Robins, L. N. (1966). *Deviant children grown up.* Baltimore: Williams & Wilkins.

Robins, L. N., Helzer, J. E., Weissman, M. M., Orvaschel, H., Gruenberg, E., Burke, J. D., & Regier, D. A. (1984). Lifetime prevalence of specific psychiatric disorders in three sites. *Archives of General Psychiatry, 41*, 949–958.

Rosenthal, N. E., Sack, D. A., Gillin, J. C., Lewy, A. J., Goodwin, F. K., Davenport, Y., Mueller, P. S., Newsome, D. A., & Wehr, T. A. (1984). Seasonal affective disorder. *Archives of General Psychiatry, 41*, 72–80.

Roy, A. (1985). Early parental separation and adult depression. *Archives of General Psychiatry, 42I*, 987–991.

Rutter, M. (1981). *Maternal deprivation reassessed* (2nd ed.). London: Penguin Books.

Salzman, C. (1985). Benzodiazepine dependence. *The Harvard Medical School Mental Health Letter, 1*(10), 8.

Sederer, L. I. (1986). Depression. In L. I. Sederer (Ed.), *Inpatient psychiatry: Diagnosis and treatment* (2nd ed.). (pp. 3–35). Baltimore: Williams & Wilkins.

Shapiro, D. (1965). *Neurotic styles.* New York: Basic Books.

Shull, H. J., Wilkinson, G. R., Johnson, R., & Schenker, S. (1976). Normal disposition of oxazepam in acute viral hepatitis and cirrhosis. *Annals of Internal Medicine, 84*, 420–425.

Sifneos, P. (1979). *Short-term dynamic psychotherapy, evaluation, and technique.* New York: Plenum.

Skolnick, P., & Paul, S. M. (1983). New concepts in the neurobiology of anxiety. *Journal of Clinical Psychiatry, 44*, 12–19.

Snyder, S. (1981). Dopamine receptors, neuroleptics, and schizophrenia. *American Journal of Psychiatry, 138*, 460–464.

Spitzer, R. L. (1976). More on pseudoscience in science and the case for psychiatric diagnosis: A critique of D. L. Rosenhan's "On being sane in insane places" and "The contextual nature of psychiatric diagnosis." *Archives of General Psychiatry, 33*, 459–470.

Spitzer, R. L., Willlams, J. B. W., & Skodal, A. E. (1980). *DSM-III*: The major achievements and an overview. *American Journal of Psychiatry, 137*, 151–164.

Squire, S. (1983). Is the binge-purge cycle catching? *Ms*, October, pp. 41–46.

Strangler, R. S., & Printz, A. M. (1980). *DSM-III*: Psychiatric diagnosis in a university population. *American Journal of Psychiatry, 137*, 937–940.

Sussman, N., & Hyler, S. E. (1985). Factitious disorders. In H. I. Kaplan & B. J. Sadock (Eds.) *Comprehensive textbook of psychiatry* (4th ed.). (pp. 1242–1247). Baltimore: Williams & Wilkins.

Targum, S. D., Dibble, E. D., Davenport, Y. B., & Gershon, E. S. (1981). The family attitudes questionnaire: Patients' and spouses' views of bipolar illness. *Archives of General Psychiatry, 38*, 562–568.

Vaillant, G. E. (1971). Theoretical hierarchy of adaptive ego mechanisms. *Archives of General Psychiatry, 24*, 107–118.

Vaughn, C. E., & Leff, J. P. (1976). The influence of family and social factors on the course of psychiatric illness: A comparison of schizophrenic with depressed neurotic patients. *British Journal of Psychiatry, 129*, 125–137.

Walsh, F. (1982). *Normal family process.* New York: Guilford.

Walsh, B. T., Stewart, J. W., Roose, S. P., Gladis, M., & Glassman, A. H. (1984). Treatment of bulimia with phenelzine: A double-blind, placebo-controlled study. *Archives of General Psychiatry, 41*, 1105–1109.

Watt, J. A. G. (1985). Hearing and premorbid personality in paranoid states. *American Journal of Psychiatry, 142*, 1453–1455.

Weber, J. J., Elinson, J., & Moss, L. M. (1967). Psychoanalysis and change. *Archives of General Psychiatry, 17*, 687–709.

Weiner, H. (1985). Schizophrenia: Etiology. In H. I. Kaplan & B. J. Sadock (Eds.) *Comprehensive textbook of psychiatry* (4th ed.) (pp. 651–680). Baltimore: Williams & Wilkins.

Weissman, M. M., Leckman, J. F., Merikangas, K. R., Gammon, G. D., & Prusoff, B. A. (1985). Depression and anxiety disorders in parents and children: Results from the Yale family study. *Archives of General Psychiatry, 41*, 845–852.

Wells, C. E., & McEvoy, J. P. (1982). Organic mental disorders. In J. H., Greist, J. W. Jefferson, & R. L. Spitzer (Eds.) *Treatment of mental disorders* (pp. 3–43). New York: Oxford University Press.

Wender, P. H., & Klein, D. F. (1981). *Mind, mood, and medicine: A guide to the new biopsychiatry.* New York: Meridan.

Wilkins, W. (1973a). Expectancy of therapeutic gain: An empirical and conceptual critique. *Journal of Consulting Psychology, 40*, 69–77.

Wilkins, W. (1973b). Client's expectancy of therapeutic gain: Evidence for the active role of the therapist. *Psychiatry, 36*, 184–190.

Williams, J. B. W. (1985). The multiaxial system of *DSM-III*: Where did it come from and where should it go? I. Its origins and critiques. *Archives of General Psychiatry, 42*, 175–180.

Winokur, A., March, V., & Mendels, J. (1980). Primary affective disorder in relatives of patients with anorexia nervosa. *American Journal of Psychiatry, 137,* 695–698.

Winokur, G. (1979). Unipolar depression: Is it divisible into autonomous subtypes? *Archives of General Psychiatry, 36,* 47–52.

Wittgenstein, L. (1958). *Philosophical investigations* (2nd ed.). Trans. G. E. M. Anscomb. New York: Macmillan.

Wynne, L. C., Ryckoff, I. M., Day, J., & Hirsch, S. I. (1958). Pseudo-mutuality in the family relations of schizophrenics. *Psychiatry, 21,* 205–220.

Zborowski, M. (1952). Cultural components in responses to pain. *Journal of Social Issues, 8,* 16–30.

Zimmerman, M. Z., Pfohl, B., Stangl, D., & Coryell, W. (1985). The validity of *DSM-III* Axis IV (Severity of psychosocial stressors). *American Journal of Psychiatry, 142,* 1437–1441.

Index